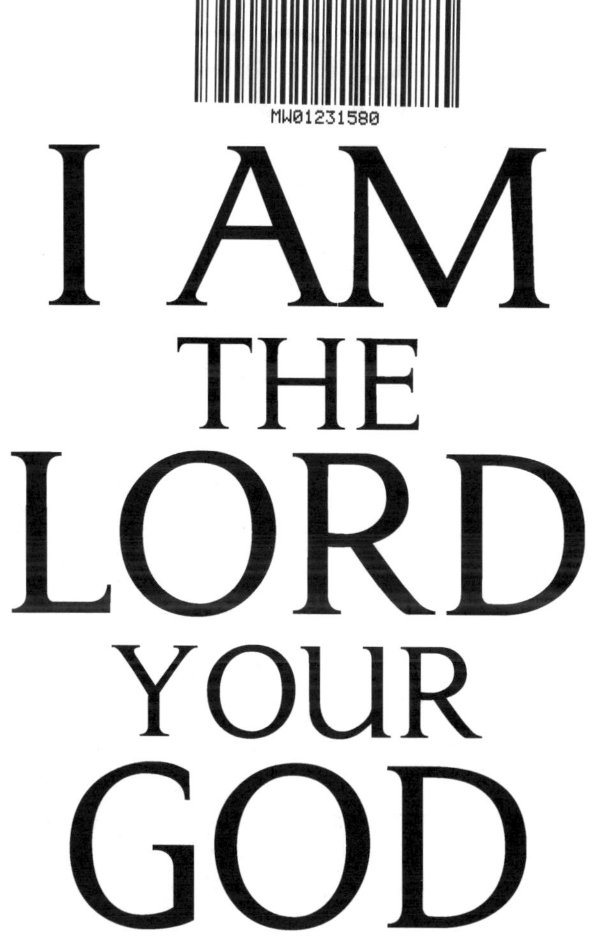

I AM THE LORD YOUR GOD

A thoroughly Biblical View of God

DR. KENNETH O. FRIDAY

Foreword by Dr. Frank M. Barker, Jr.

ISBN: 1492116130
ISBN 13: 9781492116134
Library of Congress Control Number: 2013915418
CreateSpace Independent Publishing Platform
North Charleston, South Carolina

FOREWORD

"Man's chief end is to glorify God and enjoy Him forever." (Shorter Catechism) This book will really help the serious reader to fulfill that challenge and blessing. Ken's focus on God's attributes is so comprehensive, impactful, and insightful! The analysis and elaboration of those attributes is absolutely overwhelming. Applying that knowledge is transformational and God's goal for us is to be conformed to the image of Christ.

The goal of the book is to help you know God personally and intimately. May that be your goal as you read it!

Dr. Frank M. Barker, Jr.
October 7, 2013

Acknowledgements

A book is never produced in a vacuum. My parents, Belon and Ann Friday, were instrumental in forming my worldview. My sweet wife, Carolyn, is the best wife any husband has ever shared life with. My super children, Ben, Daniel, and Mary Ann, are wonderful blessings from the Lord and could not have been more supportive.

Phillip Beckloff and Nathan Gray helped with research and typing. Dr. Jim Fisk, Dr. Jeff Lowman, Dr. Frank Barker, Mr. Vern Betsch, Reverend Benny Parks, and Dr. Rosemary Fisk all helped by reading portions of the manuscript and offering great insights and content analysis. Others provided editing and proofreading assistance. The staff at Create Space were excellent to work with.

To each of these I offer my greatest appreciation. To God alone be all the glory for what He has done through so many willing servants.

CONTENTS

Introduction: The Greatest Thing in Life ix

1. The Exceptional Worth of Knowing God 1
2. God's Necessary Revelation of Himself 19
3. God's Extraordinary and Infinite Attributes 39
4. Is God Beyond Knowing? Yes 57
5. Is God Beyond Knowing? No 71
6. Can God be any Better? Impossible 85
7. Could God be any More Real? Never 99
8. God is Always Above Us! We Live Under His Rule 119
9. God Is Always With Us! We Live in His Presence 141
10. The Names God Chose for Himself 161
11. God's Glory Is Compelling 175

Author Biography 191

Selected Bibliography and Reading List 193

Appendix 1 Reformed Confessional Statements About the Being and Attributes of God 203

Appendix 2 Incomplete List of God's Names, Titles, Attributes, Metaphors, Actions, Dispositions, and Images 211

Appendix 3 Scriptural Survey of the Character of God: Actions, Names, Images, and Attributes of God 221

Appendix 4 The 19 Significant Attributes of God with Related Attributes 405

Introduction: The Greatest Thing in Life

I am a dentist by profession. I am a Christian believer and have a great love of God. I have experienced a growing assurance of my relationship with God as my heavenly Father for over thirty-five years. I sense a strong passion to increase my knowledge of God and deepen my relationship with Him. This writing is a direct result of these motivations. It is a personal tool toward that end.

I desire more than just knowledge or facts about God. My heart is to know Him personally and intimately. It is important for each of us to work to do this intentionally throughout our lives. There is no greater thing in life than to know your Creator. We were all born for this. Our limited and fallen nature makes it essential that God is the source of all knowledge about Himself.

Even though this book has been written to crystallize my personal growth toward God, it might be used by God in your own life. I hope, through the discipline and process of writing, to strengthen my personal relationship with God. Learning about God is an exciting process. I want to drink in as much of His revelation and majesty as I am capable.

I am also writing to be an encouragement to my children and my extended family. I feel a great obligation to share with them the best of what I understand to be the great truths about God. I hope my children and their children will benefit from this material. I hope they too will seek God *"as a deer pants for flowing streams."*[1] This is a notably important quest for each of us. My prayer is that this book would begin a spiritual legacy for generations in my family and the lives of many. It will be a tremendous success if that vision is brought to reality by God's sovereign hand.

Often while researching for writing, I have encountered great books. Some were sources from earlier centuries. Some were rather obscure. Organizations or individuals might have republished them to keep them in print. Other resources I found to be enduring and well-known classics. All these resources revealed how long-lasting the influence of writing can be. It is possible this book might be used by God, long after my death, in the spiritual formation of someone I could never meet personally. This is my prayer. If this writing encourages you, all glory is to God alone for His kind providence.

You will notice the use of capitalization to highlight nineteen of God's attributes. That is, after all, a primary purpose of this book. I have also chosen to italicize all references from the Bible. This is to remind us of their unique and singular authority. I trust these features are more helpful than distracting.

The Jordan River flows through the Sea of Galilee and terminates in the Dead Sea. Minerals that come into and leave the Sea of Galilee by that river allow it to be teeming with life. I have eaten fish from those waters. The flowing in of those same minerals with no outflow makes the Dead Sea a sterile, virtually

---

1 Psalm 42:1.

lifeless environment. God has placed so many rich resources in my Christian life. These pages that follow are an outflow for my own well-being.

There is a great need for each of us to understand God more deeply and intimately than we do. A. W. Tozer surmised, "The Church has surrendered her once lofty concept of God and has substituted for it one so low, so ignoble, as to be utterly unworthy of thinking, worshiping men."[2] This sentiment was expressed in virtually every resource I read on the topic of knowing God. Knowing God faintly or incorrectly has been a chronic problem of each generation of man. "We know of nothing which is more calculated to infuse spiritual vigor into our frames than a scriptural apprehension of the full character of God."[3]

Many of us are simpletons concerning God and who He really is. We may be distracted and preoccupied with the immediate things of life. We might think it is simplifying to limit our concerns to our physical plane of existence and ignore the invisible spiritual realities of life. We intuitively know that our relationship with God will carry obligations. We choose to avoid these obligations. Distance from God is preferred by us as a safer place.

It is true that God is not who we naturally desire Him to be. We would prefer Him to allow us to live our lives without placing any demands on us. We would choose a God who would align with all our affections. We convince ourselves He must be this way. We imagine Him in our minds, but God is so much more than just a mental concept. He is real. When we realize that He is not who we want Him to be, we often question His existence or avoid growing close to Him.

---

2 A. W. Tozer, *The Knowledge of the Holy*, VII.

3 A. W. Pink, *The Sovereignty of God*, 14.

We want to get on with our lives according to our own plans. We will never seek to know the one true God from our own initiative. We are not inclined to see Him as He really is. Our wrong ideas about God render Him unworthy of appropriate adoration and worship. We cannot adore or worship a little god we have made up. The accurate knowledge of God causes us to love Him and live for Him. As we see Him correctly, we will be irresistibly drawn to Him and experience His life-giving presence in our lives.

There are some common wrong ideas concerning God. Some limit God to the role of a celestial grandfather. We are hoping He will serve us and give us what we want. Another error is to fear Him as harsh and heartless. Is God in fact some cosmic killjoy? Would He always want us to do things that would bring us dull and pointless lives? God states, *"For I know the plans I have for you, declares the Lord, plans for welfare and not for evil, to give you a future and a hope."*[4] We find it hard to believe that God actually loves us more than we love ourselves. God knows our genuine needs more than we ever can. This is hard to fathom. All His giving or withholding is because of His loving care. He wisely knows what is best at all times. His timing is perfect.

By choosing not to know Him, we have rendered ourselves incapable of responding to Him in worship. Our faulty reasoning in this area has grave consequences. My use of the word "grave" is intentional. Our misunderstanding is costly unto death. Like throwing the baby out with the bathwater, we ruin our opportunities for happiness and purpose by not knowing the one true God. We do not realize that we are destroying ourselves. God ever remains exactly who He is, no matter what we reason or profess. If millions believe a foolish thing, it still remains a foolish thing.

---

4 Jeremiah 29:11.

Imagine a grandfather who hosts his grandson for a visit. To guide his young charge, the grandfather moves them to the garage. Here, many wonderful tools and materials are available. The grandfather gives license to his grandson's creative efforts. As he lovingly watches, his grandson begins with zeal to make something the grandfather finds confusing. Since he will be required to praise his grandson for his effort, the grandfather studies it closely. He hopes to figure out what this object could possibly be. The results are a crude multi-legged monstrosity with many eyes and a misshapen mouth. The grandfather must finally ask reluctantly, "What is it?" His grandson proudly exclaims, "Why, it's you, Granddad!" The grandfather is startled. Even with his limited skills, how could his grandson possess such a distorted view?

I believe that this story reveals in some limited fashion how we fall short in seeing God as He really is. Our inability to see Him clearly reveals our earthly bondage. We have all been disappointed with events in our lives. We might be jealous of others. God may not have rescued us from some hardship or pain. These things have caused us to retreat and to ignore Him. We flee from intimate fellowship with Him. We try to forget the notion of living for Him. Seeing no real advantage in a relationship with Him, we play it safe by keeping Him at arm's length from ourselves.

You may have heard it said that "God is God, and we are not." This is a truth we are reluctant to acknowledge. We live refusing to consider this. That the one and only true God of the universe would even give us the time of day is beyond our full understanding. It is unimaginable that God's delight is to know us personally and that He rejoices concerning us. But this is exactly what God declares. "*Behold my servant, whom I uphold, my chosen, in whom my soul delights."*[5] *"The Lord your God is in your midst, a mighty one who will save; he will rejoice over you with gladness; he will quiet you by his love; he will exult over you with loud singing."*[6]

Our limited and selfishly designed concept of God is based on what we have decided is best. Our perception has been altered by our desires, and God has become some monstrosity that has little resemblance to His true being. We trust our own determination of who we think God should be. We are not seeking the true God as He has revealed Himself.

A great truth in life is that God holds us to be of value. He is so much more for us than we could ever hope. As Creator of everything and the preserver of the universe, it seems unreasonable that God would love and be concerned for us. It would appear He would have bigger things on His mind than us. Yet God declares His Love and Goodness toward us.

Our misconceptions of who God really is cause us to live our lives consumed with trivial concerns and mindless amusements. It is a blessed thing in life to have times of solitude. We quickly realize these are not times of being alone. These are times to be spent with God. When Satan fails in tempting us to sin, he may be just as happy by keeping us busily occupied with purely earthly things.

I was involved in a lot of wilderness hiking with both my sons. We were taught a strategy in the event we ever discovered ourselves lost in the woods. It was important not to get more lost. We were instructed to S.T.O.P. This meant we were to sit down, think, observe, and plan. We needed to figure out what to do to put ourselves on the right track. Periodically, we all need times to sit and reflect.

---

5 Isaiah 42:1.

6 Zephaniah 3:17.

What are you doing? Are you scurrying around and doing things, which upon further reflection, are unimportant? Are you ignoring God unintentionally or even intentionally? Are you limiting your knowledge of Him for foolish reasons? Are you picking out only the aspects of His character that you find comfortable? Are there some clearly stated attributes of God that you are willfully denying? Are you making up your own version of a nonexistent god?

Let us each sit at God's feet and look at Him and His overwhelming beauty. Listen to what He says about Himself. Pursue the discovery of who He really is. This is, in fact, the greatest discovery anyone can make. He tells us about Himself. There is no other way to learn about Him. He has made Himself knowable. It is exciting to know we can be restored to a right relationship with Him. We can be reconciled to God in spite of His holiness and our sinfulness. God has promised to meet us where we are. His promises are unchanging.

An essential of this book is that it strives to be based on God's reliable Word, the Bible. Scripture alone has an eternal shelf life. During my formal education, I utilized many current academic books. Those books today would best serve as doorstops. The information in them has become outdated. God's Word will never become obsolete. I desire that all this ink and paper remains subservient to the eternal and foundational truths found in holy Scripture. To the degree to which I have achieved this aim, my words will have some lasting value.

We are beginning with two presuppositions. First, only one true God exists, and He is very real. Next, God has made and is actively making Himself known. His greatest vehicle for this is His inspired holy Word, the Bible.

Our own hearts are inclined to mislead us. We must intentionally cling to His Word during this endeavor. Let us strive to seek the real God as He has faithfully and accurately revealed Himself. Let us be honest in our effort. May we know Him as He really is. "*I love those who love me, and those who seek me diligently find me.*[7] May all the contents of this book bring honor and glory to God. May our hearts resound with truth about God as He really is. May our fellowship with our great and awesome God grow deeper and deeper.

---

7 Proverbs 8:17.

Chapter 1
The Exceptional Worth of Knowing God

Thus says the Lord*: "Let not the wise man boast in his wisdom, let not the mighty man boast in his might, let not the rich man boast in his riches, but let him who boasts boast in this, that he understands and knows me, that I am the* Lord *who practices steadfast love, justice, and righteousness in the earth. For in these things I delight, declares the* Lord*."*

Jeremiah 9:23–24

But whatever gain I had, I counted as loss for the sake of Christ. Indeed, I count everything as loss because of the surpassing worth of knowing Christ Jesus my Lord*. For his sake I have suffered the loss of all things and count them as rubbish, in order that I may gain Christ and be found in him, not having a righteousness of my own that comes from the law, but that which comes through faith in Christ, the righteousness from God that depends on faith—that I may know him and the power of his resurrection, and may share his sufferings, becoming like him in his death, that by any means* *possible I may attain the resurrection from the dead. Not that I have already obtained this or am already perfect, but I press on to make it my own, because Christ Jesus has made me his own.*

Philippians 3:7–12

And this is eternal life, that they know you the only true God, and Jesus Christ whom you have sent.

John 17:3

For although there may be so-called gods in heaven or on earth—as indeed there are many "gods" and many "lords"—yet for us there is one God, the Father, from whom are all things and for whom we exist, and one Lord, *Jesus Christ, through whom are all things and through whom we exist. However, not all possess this knowledge.*

1 Corinthians 8:5–7

Formerly, when you did not know God, you were enslaved to those that by nature are not gods. But now that you have come to know God, or rather to be known by God, how can you turn back again to the weak and worthless elementary principles of the world, whose slaves you want to be once more?

Galatians 4:8–9

What if you listed all of the events you imagined would be wonderful to have happen in your life? These are the very best things you could dream up. The sky is the limit. You might include being healed of a painfully progressing terminal illness. You might choose to be reconciled to a family member or a close friend with whom you had suffered a broken relationship. You could wish for extraordinary success in business yielding great monetary gain or a position of high prestige. How about just skipping all the time and effort and being the recipient of great wealth by winning a lottery or discovering buried treasure? Would any of these things make you happy?

You can be sure they would! At least they would for a while. They would generally enhance and bless your life for a time. Yet, for many, the money might fly through their fingers and leave a destructive wake in their lives. This is a common story of those who have received wealth quickly. Often people with wealth eventually realize the real blessing of excess is found in giving to others. Even giving includes hard work and difficult decisions.

You might lose your elevated position due to lack of experience or understanding. We all discover fame is fleeting. Other health issues might arise in one healed, or their mended relationships could again become strained. While good things have the ability to bless you in real ways, they only bring good into some small part of our lives. Life often returns to other struggles and heartaches.

What if you were able to discover one thing that would bless you more than any of the items mentioned? This would bless you now, tomorrow, and even bless you forever and ever. This blessing would continue after your earthly life had ended. It is a blessing beyond anything you could ever imagine. That is the extraordinary goal of this book; to point you to the amazing blessing that awaits all who honestly seek the one true God.

Delivering on such an amazing promise is certainly not based on my wisdom or insight. It is not from any human source. This kind of blessing must come from a supernatural source. You have probably thought about it before. It is the quintessential elephant in the room. It is so obvious that you have had to ignore it, either unconsciously or intentionally. I figure by now, you already know what it is.

The greatest thing of all is meeting God as He really is. We can spend time with Him and grow to enjoy deep fellowship with Him.

The greatest thing of all is meeting God as He really is. We can spend time with Him and grow to enjoy deep fellowship with Him. Now, hold it. You may be thinking this is no big news. You may believe you have your idea of God right where it should be. You probably have envisioned or positioned God right where you feel Him the most comfortable for you. Almost everyone does this. This attitude may be keeping you from knowing God as He really is.

The idea of knowing God may have seemed anticlimactic to you. A response of that type would actually reveal you do not know enough about the one true God to realize what you are missing. Our greatest ignorance is being ignorant of our ignorance.

Which would you say is of greater value, a diamond or air? Which would you think is of more necessity? God is like air in that He is both essential and always surrounds us, yet we tend to undervalue Him because we take Him for granted. When I said knowing Him was the greatest thing of all, there was not one jot of exaggeration. As you grow in real understanding of God, you recognize the great and inestimable value of knowing Him in all His majesty and Glory.

Virtually everyone has a unique mental construct of who God is. This is partly because of the different faiths and religions in our world. Yet, even among Christians, a great diversity exists concerning insights into the nature and character of God. How can this be? What an indictment of our arrogance and lack of intentional reflection. We do a lot of living without thinking. God promises that we will find Him if we honestly seek after Him.

The one real God is so much more than any creation of our imagination. We offend Him as we casually use the phrase, "Well, my God would never do that." You and I may have a god of our imagination, but it is not the God who really is. Our imaginations can create no real god. These gods are only idle speculations and a waste of our time.

We must pursue the one true God who actually is. That is the goal and purpose we must all embrace. Supernatural as He is, there is much we will never know comprehensively of the one true God. We do trust that God has adequately and accurately revealed Himself as He really is.

Nothing is of greater value than intimately knowing God. We have fellowship with Him and are compelled to worship Him. This is the most valuable quest of our lives. In this we give Him the most honor and glory. As we put knowing Him and enjoying Him first, we show God the greatest reverence and adoration. In this attitude, we live a life of praise and worship to the almighty and Sovereign God. He is more than worthy of all our praise and pursuit. How offensive to Him must be our flippant and casual interest in His beauty and being. May we never take God lightly. May we never be distracted by this world to look away from Him. God is the all in all. May He ever be so.

Broughton Knox, the Sydney evangelist of the late twentieth century, said, "The doctrine of God is of utmost importance, for it controls the whole of life."[1] We all have a doctrine or belief about

---

1 Broughton Knox, *The Everlasting God*, 7.

who God really is. This deeply influences how we go about our daily lives. Here we establish our hopes for the future. Here our emotions are set. Our belief about God is the basis for all of our significant decisions. Life contains a series of decisions that have significant impact on our lives.

My father is a Methodist minister. He has served for over sixty years in various churches. I have heard him deliver many sermons. God continues to use many of them to influence me greatly. Some of his favorite illustrations are very memorable.

Dad loved to tell one story I often reflect upon. Passengers were happily riding on a plane. Well into the flight, a voice came over the intercom and said, "This is your captain speaking. I have good news and bad news. The bad news is that the plane's navigational system has completely failed, and we have no idea in which direction we are flying. The good news is that we are experiencing a fifteen-mile-per-hour tailwind, and we are making great time."

Are you focusing on making the best life for yourself or your loved ones, but sense somehow that you are striving after the wrong things?

Do you feel like you are zipping along at breakneck speed with no assurance of where you are heading? Are you focusing on making the best life for yourself or your loved ones, but sense somehow that you are striving after the wrong things? Do you sometimes question your priorities? Do you wonder if you will look up at the end of life and find you have wasted it or ended up at a wrong destination? Every one of us has to consider the direction in which we are traveling. It is important. How do we know if we are heading down the right path?

The great news of knowing about God and personally knowing Him is that here, we also discern where we are going. This is the key to a life of purpose and meaning. Jesus prayed for believers, "*And this is eternal life, that they should know you, the only true God, and Jesus Christ whom you have sent.*"[2] Jesus also said, "*I am the light of the world. Whoever follows me will not walk in darkness, but will have the light of life.*"[3] At the end of the day, I know we all want to discover that we've had a life well spent, involved in doing things that really do matter. "Knowing about God is crucially important for the living of our lives. The world becomes a strange, mad, painful place, and life in it a disappointing and unpleasant business for those who do not know about God. Disregard the study of God, and you sentence yourself to stumble and blunder through life blindfolded, as it were, with no sense of direction and no understanding of what surrounds you. This way you can waste your life and lose your soul."[4] Your ever-deepening relationship with the one true God will give you that assurance of right living. It is all that and much more. Words cannot carry the weight of this life-changing truth.

This is the relationship this book invites you to explore and reach for. And let me tell you, you have never met anyone like the one true God. He is so wonderful and attractive. You will be overwhelmed and changed by this relationship. C. S. Lewis, in *The Chronicles of Narnia*, develops a main character named Aslan, a lion representing Christ. Aslan, responding to the young girl Lucy's exclamation that He is bigger, says, "Every year you grow, you will find Me bigger."[5] God never changes. In fact, He is "*the same yesterday and today and forever.*"[6] We will sense that He

---

2 John 17:3.

3 John 8:12.

4 J. I. Packer, *Knowing God*, 19.

5 C. S. Lewis, *Prince Caspian*, 141.

6 Hebrews 13:8.

appears to enlarge as we increase our understanding of Him and our fellowship with Him. This will make us grow in our faith and relationship more and more. God will always seem to us to grow bigger and bigger. There will always be more of Him to enjoy into eternity! So, let us get started on this exciting journey that will never end.

We are going to pursue knowing God, the one and only true God who really does exist. We are going to agree that He does exist. This book will contain about as much apologetics for the existence of God as God Himself offered in the very first words of His Bible; *"In the beginning, God created the heavens and the earth."*[7] The Bible does not defend the existence of God. It begins with the real God eternally and always present. Intellectual honesty demands this starting point.

We will also accept that He can be known only as He reveals Himself. We are going to pursue knowing Him by His means of revelation. There are many. The primary way we will be viewing Him is through His own inspired and reliably sound message to us, the Bible. Here we will find God as *Logos*, the living Word.

So we're on our way to knowing the one true God. Sir Isaac Newton, in a letter to Robert Hook, wrote of being able to see further than others by standing on the shoulders of giants. His thought was most certainly derived from the writing of the twelfth-century theologian John of Salisbury, "We are like dwarfs sitting on the shoulders of giants. We see more, and things that are more distant, than they did, not because our sight is superior or because we are taller than they, but because they raise us up, and by their great stature, add to ours."[8]

---

7 Genesis 1:1.

8 John Salisbury, *The Metalogicon of John Salisbury*, 167.

We will inform ourselves with valuable quotes from those who have diligently studied God and His attributes. Those who sought God before us have so much to offer. They were very smart. This is an important and humbling realization for modern man. We have exciting access to volumes of information from rich sources in the past. Many resources are readily available from godly writers. We would be foolish not to use their deep insights to aid us in our journey. While we are going to depend primarily on God's Word, the Bible, we are also going to look to those people who have gone before us. They can help us boil down and understand the great truths about God. Many true attributes of God like His Triunity, Infiniteness, immutability, and omnipresence are not terms found in the text of Scripture. Yet, these and many other truths of God are clearly taught in the consistent testimony of the Bible.

If your view of God is wrong, then you are engaging in idolatry, and the consequences will be deadly. This error will ruin you. Even if your intention is sincere, it is possible to be sincerely wrong. You may think you are worshipping the one true God, but if you are not, the results will be startling. They will be your eternal death and separation from God forever.

You may think this seems unreasonable, but God holds us each individually responsible to seek and know Him. "*On that day many will say to me, 'Lord, Lord, did we not prophesy in your name, and cast out demons in your name, and do many mighty works in your name?' And then I will declare to them, 'I never knew you; depart from me, you workers of lawlessness.'*"[9]

Eternal life is found only in knowing the one true God intimately in a reconciled state of adoption through faith in Jesus Christ alone. Before your earthly death, which the Bible routinely

9 Matthew 7:22–23.

calls "sleep" for believers, you can enjoy eternal life. Now, these are bold words, but I am just relating to you what God says in His Word about the critical importance of accurately and actually knowing Him.

A. W. Tozer said, "What comes into our minds when we think about God is the most important thing about us."[10] There is, simply put, nothing more important than knowing God accurately and being in a reconciled relationship with Him. To know Him as He truly is establishes all of life in proper order and perspective. God is much more than the number one priority in our life. He is the very source of establishing every priority of life. To really know Him is our ultimate goal. "Knowing God. Is there any greater theme to study? Is there any nobler goal to aim at? Is there any greater good to enjoy? Is there any deeper longing in the human heart than the desire to know God? Surely, there is not. Christianity's good news is that this knowledge can happen."[11]

To live without this knowledge allows a great deal of deception and misunderstanding in our lives. Often, by the time we have realized this, it is too late. The consequences of our sinful choices and the ways we have failed to yield to God's plan for our lives have already borne destructive results. Let us seek to live great lives by knowing the great and awesome Sovereign Lord.

The transforming reality of being in a reconciled relationship with the God of the universe hinges on you being righteous. You are required to have no sin in your life to fellowship with God. Sin separates you from God. You cannot attain righteousness by your own effort. Each of us is unable to do this. We simply cannot. We don't have the ability. As a matter of fact, we do not in ourselves

---

10 A. W. Tozer, *The Knowledge of the Holy*, 1.

11 J. I. Packer, *Knowing Christianity*, 11.

even have the desire to try. Our default disposition from birth is animosity toward God.

A hygienist in my office, Debbie, shared a story with me concerning her three-year-old daughter, Hannah. As a loving mother, Debbie had instructed Hannah that she must eat her green beans before she would be allowed to leave the supper table. Returning shortly, she found Hannah weeping at the table. Upon asking why she had not instead simply eaten her green beans, Hannah tearfully replied, "Because I can't want to." Now that is real-world theology. This is true for all of us. It is the position in which we all naturally find ourselves. We do have free will, but we only will to do what we want to do. In all of our free moral choices, our willfulness is determined by our desires. Arguably the greatest American theologian, Jonathan Edwards, explained that our will is always enslaved to our desire. Our desire is determined by what we believe to be in our best interest. It is our will that makes the decisions that determine our actions, but it is our desire—or "want to"—that compels our will to choose as it does.

Our will is the intention to take action, and it always follows our desire. Our ability to make any decision against our desire is nonexistent. We "freely" only do what pleases us and what we determine is best for us. In the garden, our perfect representative, Adam, was deceived by temptation and false promises. In Adam, we chose our own wills over the expressed will of God. Ever since this original sin, our "wanters" have been broken, our judgment clouded, and our hearts bent toward rebellion against God.

> *Unless God in the person of the Holy Spirit gives you the desire, you will never overcome your rebellious heart. You will stubbornly refuse to come to God on His terms.*

Unless God in the person of the Holy Spirit gives you the desire, you will never overcome your rebellious heart. You will stubbornly refuse to come to God on His terms. Many will try to repair their broken relationship with God through religious works. These efforts are woefully inadequate to cover our sins and restore fellowship with God due to His incalculable holiness. Such efforts grossly overestimate their ability to help us reach the level of righteousness required to restore any right standing before a holy and righteous God.

We all instinctively refuse to seek a right relationship with God based upon faith in Jesus Christ alone. We are inclined to want to do for ourselves what only God can do. As God reveals Himself to us through His Spirit, He opens our eyes and enables us to do something we could not otherwise do—we must trust in Him alone for our restoration and reconciliation. There is no other provision for our redemption than His finished work in Jesus.

If you are at this moment drawn to Christ and enabled to take this step of faith, acknowledging your sin and trusting in Christ alone for your right standing before God, do that now. Do not put it off. *"See, I have set before you today life and good, death and evil."*[12] *"For he says, 'In a favorable time I listened to you, and in a day of salvation I have helped you.' Behold, now is the favorable time; behold, now is the day of salvation."*[13]

I hope that you have settled your right relationship with God through faith in Jesus Christ alone. He is the only way. *"Jesus said to him, 'I am the way, and the truth, and the life. No one comes to the Father except through me. If you had known me, you would have known my Father also. From now on you do know him and have seen him.'"*[14]

---

12 Deuteronomy 30:15

13 2 Corinthians 6:2.

14 John 14:6–7.

I am not going to fail now to urge you to do this. It is absolutely the most important step you will ever take in your life. Do it now, with and through the enabling regeneration of God's Spirit.

If you have not been adopted into God's family through faith, you will not be able to see God. "*Behold, the* L*ORD's hand is not shortened, that it cannot save, or his ear dull, that it cannot hear; but your iniquities have made a separation between you and your God, and your sins have hidden his face from you so that he does not hear.*"[15] Sin will keep you from fellowship with God. That loss is terrible and greater than you can fathom. "*But to all who did receive him, who believed in his name, he gave the right to become children of God, who were born, not of blood nor of the will of the flesh nor of the will of man, but of God.*"[16] Only God's adopted family members receive the means and power to really know Him.

Theology is a big word, but it should not scare you. It means to study God and His Word to us. When we do this, we often try to gaze upon Him with the same effort that we would if we were learning about any other person. We must remember that God simply cannot be found by us if we study Him purely as an academic subject. This is because in our humanity, we cannot understand Him. This approach only leads to pride and error. Without His Spirit's revelation, we are helplessly unable to learn deep truths about Him that we need to know.

Our hearts are deceptive before and even after conversion. We were all slavishly *possessed* by sin before conversion. After conversion, as God's children, we are only capable of being *oppressed* by sin. We do still sin but we are no longer in bondage to sin. This reality keeps us repentantly at the feet of Jesus and in continual

15 Isaiah 59:1–2.

16 John 1:12–13.

dependence on Him for our right standing before God. We often misinterpret simple truths straight from Scripture.

God is essential for our knowing of Him. His Spirit alone must reveal Himself to us. That is really the only way. As we gain accurate knowledge from God about who He is, through His self-revelation and His illumination of Scripture, we actually begin to see everything else as it really is. All of life comes more into focus. John Calvin said, "Man never attains a true self-knowledge until he has previously contemplated the face of God and come down after such contemplation to look at himself."[17] We will grow the most in knowing about ourselves as we grow in knowing God.

God is faithful. He is always honest and truthful in His Word. The Bible reveals to us that man is made up of both physical and nonphysical parts. Our physical bodies will be with us for all eternity and are presently affected by the Fall, resulting in the curse of death. We are to care for our bodies as stewards and remember they are to be used in the service of God. *"Or do you not know that your body is a temple of the Holy Spirit within you, whom you have from God? You are not your own, for you were bought with a price. So glorify God in your body."*[18] We will one day see our bodies in either a state of eternal glorification or used essentially as vehicles for eternal torment. Our bodies are not inherently evil and are an important component of our full redemption or eternal suffering. We will live eternally, either in God's wonderful presence or cast into utter darkness and anguish. The extremes are polar opposites and beyond our earthly comprehension.

Our spiritual inner man is noncorporeal; it is often called the soul. Also referred to as the heart, here we find our thoughts,

---

17 John Calvin, *Institutes of the Christian Religion*, 37.

18 1 Corinthians 6:19–20.

desires, will, and emotions. Here is the essence of each individual person. We discover ourselves most created in God's image in this area. The heart contains what we know, what we love, and what we choose. Unfortunately, in our fallen state, we cannot trust our own heart for sound knowledge, affection, or decisions. *"The heart is deceitful above all things, and desperately sick; who can understand it? I the LORD search the heart and test the mind, to give every man according to his ways, according to the fruit of his deeds."*[19] We are unable to trust our own judgment and evaluation of our situation. Without God, we are blind, deluded, lost, and spiritually dead. We have no hope outside of God's work of redemption and reconciliation.

Truth is, in essence, reality. Sound logic tells us there is only one truth among many nontruths. Therefore it follows that there is only one reality. We are prone to misinterpret that one reality. Today, many have gone so far as to propose multiple realities. This speculation is considered modern and reinforces the postmodern view called relativism. God helps us to see and understand the world and all that it is from His perspective, the one true perspective. Here and only here is perfect harmony between reality and truth found. All truths come ultimately from God. He alone is the singular source of truth and reality. In every area where any truth is found it is always from and consistent with God.

Seeing things from God's perspective and learning what He thinks about this world gives us the best view of how to live our lives. The greatest improvements in our thinking and how we view and live life flow from an accurate knowledge of God's character. You want to let your knowledge of Him inform and define all of your life. Here is where we find true joy, peace, and strength. By

---

19 Jeremiah 17:9–10.

understanding God's actual nature, we avoid living life poorly, or destructively. God has revealed Himself amply and perfectly in order to give us a sufficient and balanced view of Himself. Please remember that this book you hold in your hand has tremendous limitations. As it contains any distortions or omissions in its presentation of God, this book is wrong and hurtful.

Seek the God of the Word...in His Word... for yourself. Here alone, let His Holy Spirit illuminate you to His true being.

Seek the God of the Word...in His Word...for yourself. Here alone, let His Holy Spirit illuminate you to His true being. This is really the only hope of any accuracy that we have in our knowledge of God. Only by being completely subservient to and accurately reflecting the truths of God's Word does this book have any possibility of containing truth. That is why you will see a lot here referring back to God's Word. "It is from the Word of Truth, and that alone, that we can learn what is God's relation to this world. It is only to be expected that much of the contents of the Bible conflicts with the sentiments of the carnal mind, which is enmity against God."[20] Writing that intentionally connects itself closely to the revelation of God in the Bible has the greatest value in our lives. That kind of book is one that is worthy of being written and read.

You have probably noticed by now that we are avoiding big theological words. They can be helpful, but they can create a hurdle to understanding. They can even cause you to believe you are a little smarter than you really are. Since we want to make this book both conversational and understandable, we will avoid those words as much as possible. We will purpose to speak only

20 A. W. Pink, *The Sovereignty of God*, 13, 18.

about God as He has revealed Himself and to do it in very common words. The majority of us can grow greatly in a deeper and more intentional understanding of who God really is. God is very attractive. The real God is amazingly and overwhelmingly glorious. Often in our lives, His extraordinary beauty may have been clouded or completely lost.

So how do we find out about the God who really is? We have to accept a few simple facts. For God to be really God, He must be infinite. Everything else must be finite. This is a given. We know we are finite, so we must acknowledge that we can never fully comprehend all that He is. There will always be some mystery to God, even after all of our best efforts to understand all that we can about Him. For our own protection and for God's purposes, He has chosen to limit His revelation of Himself to be less than comprehensive. We literally could not be exposed to all of Him. We could not handle His full revelation. That is the way it has to be.

At the same time, we need to be amazed about how much God is personal and relational. He really wants to be known by us. He has made Himself known to us in two primary ways. God has done this in His act of creating everything from absolutely nothing. This includes His planned involvement in the lives of all men before He began time itself. So we all have a real and universal knowledge about God through the testimony of everything that is. In addition to the reality of the way things have been and presently are, God miraculously provided the Bible. Within history, He moved many men to write down the very words that He would have us hear from Him. In a reality that we cannot grasp, His Word is Himself. He came in His Word and in the flesh as His incarnate person of Jesus Christ. Here is our purest way of learning of God: seeing Him in His Son.

We know we could study God forever, and we would never fully grasp all that He is. He has shown us by His actions and His Scripture as much of Him as we need to know. God is so much bigger than what He has revealed of Himself in the Bible. God has spoken of Himself in ways that we can understand, which make Him appear a little less than He really is. He may state in Scripture that He "rises up" or "stretches out His arm." God is a Spirit. He is not corporeal. He exists beyond matter. He does not actually sit or have appendages. These "anthropomorphisms" are God stooping down and speaking of Himself in ways that allow us to better understand Him. As we know more of God and who He really is, we will come to love Him more and more. As we love Him, we will worship Him.

This book is about learning who God really is. The Latin phrase *errare humanum est* means "to err is human." Realizing this, we can avoid man's speculation about God's nature by proof-texting everything to God's Word. We will find out what He says in His Scripture about Himself and not what men think He should be like.

Our working assumptions are that God really is, and that He has adequately and accurately shown Himself to us. Albeit not a complete revelation, God has shown Himself to us. He has done this primarily through His created world, His holy Bible, His incarnation in Jesus, and the inner witness of the Holy Spirit. My ideas, your ideas, and pretty much everyone else's ideas are just going have to sit on the shelf.

We will let God do the deciding of who He is. Only as any idea aligns in perfect accord with God's Word and God's actions will it be accepted. My sincere hope and intention is to keep error to a minimum. Only God's Word is God's Word. This book is not even close to it in truth or authority. What a marvelous journey awaits us as we sit at God's feet and hear from Him alone. Upon reflection, it had to be this way. Only He can do it, for only He is able.

Chapter 2
God's Necessary Revelation of Himself

And God spoke all these words, saying, "I am the Lord *your God, who brought you out of the land of Egypt, out of the house of slavery. You shall have no other gods before me."*

Exodus 20:1–3

"Be still and know that I am God. I will be exalted among the nations, I will be exalted in the earth!"

Psalm 46:10

All Scripture is breathed out by God and profitable for teaching, for reproof, for correction, and for training in righteousness, that the man of God may be complete, equipped for every good work.

2 Timothy 3:16–17

> *"All flesh is like grass and all its glory like the flower of grass. The grass withers, and the flower falls, but the word of the* Lord *remains forever." And this word is the good news that was preached to you.*
>
> 1 Peter 1:24–25

We are completely dependent upon God to enable us to know Him. While we instinctively know this, we persist in fooling ourselves, believing we are able to know God through our own efforts. We continually overestimate our ability in this area. We think we can learn about God through the same process we have gained understanding about everything else. We will simply separate God's being into His various attributes. Then we will study them individually in order to comprehend the whole.

This technique may have served us well in other areas of acquiring knowledge, but with God it will fail us significantly. We must have His enabling help. We must face the truth that we are unable to reach accurate knowledge of God outside of that which He provides. We are that limited. He is that far above and beyond us.

Fortunately, by His own gracious action, God has chosen to reveal Himself. He had no need to do this. God has always possessed a perfect relational fellowship within His own being from all eternity. His greatest gift to us is the gift of Himself. It is the gift of knowing Him intimately. Through knowledge about God comes our ability to know Him personally. In this, the Bible says, we actually find eternal life.

Through knowledge about God comes our ability to know Him personally. In this, the Bible says, we actually find eternal life.

God began revealing Himself to man from the beginning of time, space, and matter through creation. Man originally experienced God's intimate presence in the garden of Eden. When man was expelled from the garden because of his sin, he found himself in a broken world. Man's relationship with God also became estranged at that point. Still, this cursed and fallen world was chock-full of information about God and His character. Other fuller revelations of God would come as time progressed. Despite the devastating results of sin on mankind, God has been and still is undeniable in His existence.

God trumps His unveiling in creation in His revelation provided in His holy Word, the Bible, and through His earthly life as Jesus, the Son. God chose many to become His own graciously adopted children. His Spirit draws—or more like drags—some to reconciliation with Him. This miracle is fully part of God's perfect plan from before created time. "*Even as he chose us in him before the foundation of the world, that we should be holy and blameless before him.*"[1]

There are also other miraculous appearances and special visitations of God mentioned in Scripture. Events in history often reflect various degrees of God's character seen in His undeniable hand of superintending providence. Special insights delivered by prophets or nations like Israel have been used by God to reveal Himself to men.

God has left His fingerprints all over His created universe in so many ways. All that is around us speaks of who God is. We

1 Ephesians 1:4.

must remember that Mother Nature is a fictional idea. Nature should be appreciated as a revealing reflection of God's character. "The Scripture directs us to nature to view God. Nature is not contrary to Scripture, who is the author of both."[2] Herman Bavink suggested, "Men, because of their very nature, having knowledge of the visible and temporal, are also aware of things that are invisible and eternal."[3] God's creativity is seen in His designing the intricate and beautiful details that we see throughout the universe. The scope and scale of our natural world speaks volumes of His even greater power and knowledge.

His wisdom is particularly seen in not only what is but also in what is not. The consistency of cause and effect in nature has been cataloged by science as the "laws of nature." These serve to reflect His Faithfulness and Unchangeableness. "Any science, philosophy, or knowledge which supposes that it can stand on its own pretentions, and can leave God out of its assumptions, becomes its own opposite, and disillusions every one who builds his expectations on it."[4] The order and consistency of our physical world demands God's ordering superintendence.

God has so designed our world that through it we can know a great deal about Him. The details of what we see give evidence of an undeniable Creator.

God has so designed our world that through it we can know a great deal about Him. The details of what we see give evidence of an undeniable Creator. They also reveal a current brokenness. The mind of man speculates about alternative realities and parallel

---

2 Stephen Charnock, *The Existence and Attributes of God*, 86.

3 Herman Bavinck, *Our Reasonable Faith*, 18.

4 Ibid., 20.

universes. These concepts make men appear smart and on the cutting edge of discovering new truths. God did give us a mind able to consider possibilities outside of reality. There may be dimensions of reality of which we are presently unaware. Still, the truth mentioned previously must guide us. There is only one reality we live within. It contains both physical and spiritual dimensions.

This is what we actually experience. We understand the one true perspective from the Bible. Reality is accurately seen only from the flawless perspective of God. The more we see things from God's point of view, the more we align with real truth. All other possibilities are the constructs of our creative imaginations. That is all they are.

Our faith is a reasonable faith. It flows from sound rational thought and principles of logic. Some truths taught in God's Word do seem above logic. These serve to reveal the limits of our logic. Faith is reliable when it is founded on a real thing. It gains its validity not by its intensity or amount, but from its object. If you have great faith based on erroneous facts, the consequences can be devastating. Conversely, if you have small faith in that which is real, things will go much better for you. Sound faith is based on solid reality and truth. There is no truth more solid than the undeniable reality of God.

We must agree with Anselm of Canterbury when he asserts our faith to be "a faith seeking understanding." He said, "I do not seek to understand that I may believe, but I believe that I may understand: This I also believe, that unless I believe I will not understand."[5] Similar to belief in the existence of atoms, which is the logical and reasonable conclusion reached by repeated experiments, belief in God is based on solid and extensive, sound

5 Anselm of Canterbury, *Proslogion*, Chapt. 1, 1077 A. D.

evidence. Even though both God and atoms will not be visible in routine life, their reality is a sound and reasonable conclusion based on confirming evidence. Mankind accepts atoms with far less information than the overwhelming evidence of design, which drives us to conclude a designer.

Past United States President Ronald Reagan said that if he ever met an atheist, he would make sure to take them out to a fine restaurant. Somewhere near the end of their meal, he would ask the atheist if they believed there was a chef who had prepared the meal. Order and design safely presume a hand and mind of origin.

God is not originated from wishful thinking or flights of mental fantasy. He is undeniably obvious. God evidences Himself by activities that allow conclusions to be drawn from sound, reasonable thinking. To deny God's existence requires a great and unfounded faith in man's faulty reasoning and silly speculations.

It is safe to say that professing atheists have at least made the decision to be unreasonable. In courts of law, the proceedings conclude when a preponderance of the evidence instructs a reasonable conclusion. The verdict that follows is said to be beyond a reasonable doubt. But would it be possible to ever obtain evidence so overwhelming that a doubting juror must acquiesce? Not if that juror harbors an unreasonable doubt due to some unrevealed prejudice. A doubting juror can always simply refuse to believe even in the face of overwhelming evidence. More times than not, atheists have hidden motives behind their unbelief. They unconsciously or even consciously have no desire to find God. There are things they are not willing to give up in their lives that keep them from honestly considering the substantial and compelling evidence for God. J. I. Packer has noted that an atheist cannot find God for the same reasons a thief cannot find a policeman. Neither has any real desire to make those discoveries.

The Bible is blunt when it states, *"The fool says in his heart, 'There is no God.'"*[6] We have mentioned before that everyone is a practical theologian. Each and every one of us thinks about God and reaches conclusions about Him. Everybody has his or her own opinion about God. All too often man defaults to unwittingly make God after his own image.

In the famous German fairy tale, "Sneewittchen" or "Snow White," the evil queen sought to answer her incessant question, "Who is the fairest of them all?" by peering into a magic mirror. Often overlooked was her focus while she sought her answer. She was looking at a reflection of herself. The ultimate issue is whether your conclusions are accurate. Do they square up with who God really is? What is your source and method of discovery? Do you want truth, or do you only hope to find some limited or distorted idea of God?

Maybe you are like those who try to reason their way to an adequate comprehension of God. This is often seen in those who have attained theological degrees and credentials. An academic robe is a wonderful accomplishment, but we all must remain cautious. Wisdom is always humble. We must never fool ourselves concerning the value or reach of our own musings. We are held responsible by God to acknowledge His existence, implicitly demanded by His created world. Nevertheless, we must acknowledge that we cannot think our way to an insightful knowledge of who God really is.

> *It is a fool's errand to try to reason our way to deep knowledge about God. We are unable by our reasoning to do this. Here is why in a nutshell: God is infinite and we are finite.*

6 Psalm 14:1.

It is a fool's errand to try to reason our way to deep knowledge about God. We are unable by our reasoning to do this. Here is why in a nutshell: God is infinite and we are finite. In the introduction we highlighted the fact that God is God, and you are not. Our limitations and God's endlessness create a great chasm. Both demand our unconditional surrender in any attempts to know Him through our own efforts.

Consider this helpful analogy. Suppose a man wants to learn about an inanimate object, like a rock. All the initiative lies with the man. Every bit of information about the rock will come from the man's efforts. The rock will just sit there and do nothing. Next, the man wants to study something that is animate, like a dog. The initiative predominately still lies with the man, though he now requires some willingness from the dog. As long as the dog is alive, the dog's participation will facilitate the research.

Now our man begins to study another man. Here, there must be some level of mutual participation. This is particularly true for research in areas that are internal or personal to man. Each man must share in the effort and cooperate toward accurate discovery. Finally, our man comes to study the God of the universe. All the initiative must shift to God alone. All revelation is from Him. Even man's desire to learn about God comes from God alone. When you think about it, man has less of a chance of figuring out God than a rock would have of figuring out a man. I think it is no stretch to state that the gulf between rock and man is significantly less than the one that exists between man and God. Here we see the immense gulf between finite and infinite. This is actually a much greater degree of separation than that which exists between nonlife and life.

Classically, God's revelation of Himself has been grouped into two broad categories. The first category is general revelation, referring to the universal insight that all men have had at all times. "*For what can be known about God is plain to them, because God has shown it to them. For his invisible attributes, namely, his eternal power and divine nature, have been clearly perceived, ever since the creation of the world, in the things that have been made. So they are without excuse.*"[7] From the beginning, man has been fully overburdened with undeniable evidences of God's actual existence.

It is irrational to deny the necessity of a designer when creativeness and incredible design are witnessed all throughout the known universe. The stability and continuance of the world demand a constancy of supervision. There are even aspects within man's own nature that testify to the reality God. Common experiences like shame, trust, duty, and forgiveness all give evidence to our innate moral nature. These elements of the inner self come directly from being created in the image of God. "*They* [those without Scripture] *show that the work of the law is written on their hearts, while their conscience also bears witness, and their conflicting thoughts accuse or even excuse them.*"[8] God has given so much to men through general revelation that everyone is without excuse for rejecting His absolutely essential existence.

Men continually find within themselves an innate awareness of God. "There is no surer evidence in nature that there is a God, than that every man hath a natural principle in him, which continually cites him before God, and puts him in mind of Him, and makes him one way or the other fear Him, and reflects upon Him whether he will or not."[9] No one can honestly deny God's existence. In spite of this, it is still very possible to miss completely who God is in His being and person when left to

---

7 Romans 1:19–20.

8 Romans 2:15.

9 Stephen Charnock, *The Existence and Attributes of God*, 73.

general revelation alone. We require more help in knowing about God. "The inadequacy of general revelation demonstrates the necessity of special revelation."[10] "The knowledge of God derived from nature is insufficient unto salvation."[11]

Special revelation can only be grasped and applied by those whom God chooses to know Him intimately as Father. The incarnate earthly life of God Himself is found in the real man, Jesus. His life among us as completely God and completely man is beyond our full comprehension. We must accept this miracle. We can only ponder it with wonder. In Jesus, we see the highest perfection of special revelation. So much of God was revealed in Jesus's life of thirty-plus years. Jesus declared, "*Whoever has seen me has seen the Father.*"[12] Jesus, distinct from the Father and Holy Spirit, was clearly God's greatest manifestation of Himself to enable our knowing Him. His earthly visitation changed everything. Scripture says, "*Everyone to whom much was given, of him much will be required.*"[13] Since Jesus's earthly life, relationship with God has only been possible through Him. That was a significant watershed change!

> *Jesus, distinct from the Father and Holy Spirit, was clearly God's greatest manifestation of Himself to enable our knowing Him.*

Before Christ, we know that people of faith were reconciled to God. We have a number of them listed in a "hall of faith" found in the eleventh chapter of Hebrews. These include Abel, Enoch,

---

10 Herman Bavinck, *Our Reasonable Faith*, 61.

11 Wilhelmus à Brakel, *The Christian's Reasonable Service*, 23.

12 John 14:9.

13 Luke 12:48.

Noah, Abraham, and Moses, to name just a few. They all lived and died before Jesus paid the price on Calvary for the redemption of God's elect. So what was their path to righteousness before a Holy and pure God? Scripture points us to their faith in that revelation of God that they had received. Genesis states that Abraham *"believed the Lord, and he counted it to him as righteousness."*[14] As we will consider in our discussion of God's eternality, the finished work of Christ was the basis for the righteousness of all who have ever been declared righteous by God. It matters not their location in history relative to the earthly work of Christ.

The next two elements of special revelation are uniquely related. The Bible and the Holy Spirit work in harmony in the life of God's chosen or elect. Granted, nonbelievers have access to the Bible, but to them God's Word seems unintelligible or nonsensical. For them it has the appearance of contradictions and mysteries beyond human understanding. It is much like reading someone else's mail and not being able to understand what is written. God's Word does not correspond to this world's wisdom and understanding. The world deems the Bible inadequate for twenty-first-century man. With all his learning and vast stores of scientific and technological information, man finds Scripture wanting. The Bible is rejected as being archaic and out of touch with modern conclusions. Every analysis of it, through man's perspective, finds it to appear foolish and seemingly filled with error. The Word and the Spirit are God's enabling provisions from Him to allow believers to think correctly about Him.

As God's Spirit resides in His children, this same Spirit opens God's Word to them. The author Himself provides the needed understanding. This process is called illumination. Like a

---

14 Genesis 15:6.

museum light shining on a fine painting, things formerly unseen are quickly brought to light. God's Word becomes a unique and precious revelation to believers as it is made clear by the indwelling presence of the Holy Spirit in their minds and hearts. Here, the very author of Scripture stands with us as we read the Bible. God enlivens Scripture and thereby whispers the very intent of His heart into our spirits. The Holy Spirit also opens every believer's mind to grasp God's perspective on history and see clearly His providential and miraculous activities.

We will spend a lot of our time discussing the attributes and roles of God. To establish the Bible as a reliable source of revealed truth, we will consider the claims of the Bible concerning itself. There are primarily five. God's holy Word is inspired, authoritative, infallible, sufficient, and clear.

To establish the Bible as a reliable source of revealed truth, we will consider the claims of the Bible concerning itself. There are primarily five. God's holy Word is inspired, authoritative, infallible, sufficient, and clear.

Our premise is to know God through His revelation of Himself. Scripture is our foundational resource for this purpose. The Bible is from God Himself, and much of it is about who He is. Almost everything we know about His ultimate revelation, Jesus Christ, is found in Scripture.

Inspiration of Scripture means it was "breathed-out" by God. *"All Scripture is breathed out by God and profitable for teaching, for reproof, for correction, and for training in righteousness."*[15] You could rightly say that Scripture was both inspired and expired.

---

15 2 Timothy 3:16.

"Expired" from God and "breathed in" to men. The Bible clearly and profoundly claims itself to be God speaking. We know in the factual history of Scripture's origin that over forty different men wrote portions of the Old and New Testaments during a period of time spanning over 1,500 years. No other book has ever had this type of origin. If the Bible were from any source other than the hand of God, it could never have fit together into such a consistent and unified message. It clearly is from the supernatural authorship and hand of God. We stand in awe that God's Word and Spirit work together to reveal to us the very "mind of Christ."[16]

Every writer of the Bible was moved by God during diverse eras of history to write down the very words that would become what we know today as the Bible. Did I mention it was written in three different languages? God sovereignly and intentionally moved these men to write what they wrote. He also providentially worked to bring the Bible together. The assembling of the books included in the Old and New Testaments are the result of God's special providence. God's superintending hand alone established the complete and perfect canon of the Bible.

Scripture says of itself, *"For no prophecy was ever produced by the will of man, but men spoke from God as they were carried along by the Holy Spirit."*[17] This means that those who wrote Scripture were compelled to write. They persisted in using their own style and their personalities were not negated. The human authors were not commandeered as though they were robots. Every word that they wrote down was superintended by God and was what He chose, within the natural abilities and tendencies of each writer. This is the meaning of the inspiration of Scripture. God positions

---

16 1 Corinthians 2:12–16.

17 2 Peter 1:21.

Himself as both the speaking and constructing author of the Bible. The fact that we have a true and Faithful word from God about Himself and about the way we should live is a phenomenal reality. God's provision of His Word as His very voice is more than we could have hoped for. He must really want His children to know Him. This is the conclusion of a reasonable faith based on the very testimony of Scripture concerning itself.

The second claim of Scripture is one of authority. God ultimately is the one who gives Scripture its authority. Authority is intrinsic to Scripture as a consequence of its author being God Himself. This spectacular revelation of God is indeed His unexpected grace to us. The authority of Scripture causes it to have an extraordinary level of importance in the life of the Christian. It is a key source in God's revealing of Himself to us. We hold it higher than any earthly, uninspired source of information. This book is, of course, distinctly in the uninspired category of writing.

The Bible is its own best defender and its own best interpreter.

When questioned to defend the authority of Scripture, Charles Spurgeon was reported to have said he would as soon defend a lion. The Bible is its own best defender and its own best interpreter. We understand the meaning of Scripture by its immediate context, but even more so by the content and context of the entirety of Scripture. All facts of history and archaeology completely support Scripture. As we place our trust in the Bible and what it says, we enjoy the blessing of living on an unshakable foundation, given to us by our loving Father.

Truth is either determined by man, or by a Sovereign and omniscient God. Often times what Scripture tells us about God is not what we would have anticipated. It sometimes seems to say exactly the opposite of what we would expect. Here is where we are confronted with a revealing truth about ourselves. Will we trust Scripture to be from God and carry the kind of authority that overrides our limited understanding? Will we try to live as those who hold challenging statements in the Bible hostage to their own final judgment? Taking God "at His Word in His Word" is a matter of faith, obedience, and commitment to God.

Will we trust Scripture to be from God and carry the kind of authority that overrides our limited understanding?

The Bible is also infallible. Once you get inspiration in place, confirming God as author of the Bible, you necessarily get authority. Infallibility immediately follows. It would be impossible to say that God erred in the message of the Bible because of His great power and Righteousness. "Infallibility" means that Scripture will not lead us astray. It is both reliable and trustworthy and it cannot err. "Inerrancy" means only that Scripture contains no false information. These terms may sound the same, but they are not. Infallibility says Scripture could not err, while inerrancy only says Scripture did not err because of its origin from God. Of the two words, infallibility is much stronger.

The Bible itself can never err. It is a true Word from God. It is that much under God's Sovereign hand. Loraine Boettner said the determination of Christianity itself "depends quite largely on the view we take of Scripture. If we believe that the Bible is the very Word of God and infallible, we will develop one conception of Christianity. If we believe that it is only a collection of human writings, perhaps considerably above the average in its spiritual and moral teachings but nevertheless containing many errors, we will develop a radically different conception of Christianity—if, indeed, what we then have can legitimately be called Christianity. Hence we can hardly overestimate the importance of a correct doctrine concerning the inspiration of Scriptures."[18]

It would be difficult to express this better than in the following excerpt from the Chicago Statement on Biblical Inerrancy:

1. God, who is Himself Truth and speaks truth only, has inspired Holy Scripture in order thereby to reveal Himself to lost mankind through Jesus Christ as Creator and Lord, Redeemer and Judge. Holy Scripture is God's witness to Himself.
2. Holy Scripture, being God's own Word, written by men prepared and superintended by His Spirit, is of infallible divine authority in all matters upon which it touches: It is to be believed, as God's instruction, in all that it affirms; obeyed, as God's command, in all that it requires; embraced, as God's pledge, in all that it promises.
3. The Holy Spirit, Scripture's divine Author, both authenticates it to us by His inward witness and opens our minds to understand its meaning.
4. Being wholly and verbally God-given, Scripture is without error or fault in all its teaching, no less in what it states about God's acts in creation, about the events of world history, and about its own literary origins under God, than in its witness to God's saving grace in individual lives.
5. The authority of Scripture is inescapably impaired if this total divine inerrancy is in any way limited or disregarded, or made relative to a view of truth contrary to the

18 Loraine Boettner, *Studies in Theology*, 9.

> Bible's own; and such lapses bring serious loss to both the individual and the Church.[19]

The final two attributes of the Bible are sufficiency and clarity. What we mean when we say the Bible is sufficient is that it is fully adequate and able to equip us completely for all the work God would have us perform. There is absolutely nothing else needed. It is God's full revelation to us of what He knew we would need to live godly lives.

Clarity means that we are enabled by God's Spirit to fully understand its message. Scripture does not require special education to glean from it all God would have it to say to us. Yes, some passages are challenging, but with the help of the Holy Spirit, the simplest and most uneducated of men are able to understand exactly what is needed. With the illuminating presence of the Holy Spirit, all believers are enabled to get the message. The Bible is basically God's self-revelation or unveiling of Himself to all men. "The task of the student of revealed theology is therefore in the first place mainly exegetical."[20] God has provided Himself to give insight to our study, which we require. It is true that God's illuminating Spirit unveils the text and this is exclusively provided to the adopted members of His own family.

God is best revealed in the Bible and in the life of His Son, Jesus Christ. Scripture is God's extremely well-designed message of revelation.

We must never forget a simple and essential truth. God is best revealed in the Bible and in the life of His Son, Jesus Christ. Scripture is God's extremely well-designed message of revelation.

19 Wayne Grudem, *Systematic Theology*, 1204.

20 Robert Lewis Dabney, *Systematic Theology*, 144.

Mark Twain commented, "The difference between the right word and the almost right word is the difference between lightning and a lightning bug." God's Word is His perfect word and is so much more powerful than any amount of lightning. It contains truths that are from God and He alone is the source of all truth. These truths could have come to us from no other source. We could never have deduced them from experiment or observation. God's ways are so much higher than ours. We stand in awe of His work and His person in His Word.

As we come to know Him more and more we also realize how much of God we actually have yet to learn. We will never stop learning many new truths at His hand and some of those will continually amaze us. Scripture is a great window of understanding into the nature, character, and plan of God. Be reminded often that God is vastly much more than all of His combined self-revelations. The very words of Scripture, which are beyond our complete comprehension, are less than the great God to whom they testify. Scripture is an essential and accurate yet limited revelation of God. "The words of Scripture are only part of God's self-revelation."[21] His Word brings to us what He would have us to know about Himself. He does not tell us all that there is about Him. He is vastly greater than even our highest conceptions of Him. Of Jesus we read, *"Now there are also many other things that Jesus did. Were every one of them to be written, I suppose that the world itself could not contain the books that would be written."*[22]

His Word is one of the greatest gifts God has ever given to man. It will continue into eternity.

---

21 Herman Bavinck, *Our Reasonable Faith*, 95.

22 John 21:25.

The orthodox creeds and confessions of the church have consistently been based on a Biblical understanding of who God is. His Word is one of the greatest gifts God has ever given to man. It will continue into eternity. Jesus said, *"Heaven and earth will pass away, but my words will not pass away."*[23] *"Long have I known from your testimonies that you have founded them for ever.... The sum of your word is truth, and every one of your righteous rules endures for ever."*[24]

Billy Graham relates a story of his concerns about apparent contradictions in the Bible. In August 1949, he dueled with these doubts and finally knelt before the open Bible and said, "'Lord, many things in this Book I do not understand. Here and now, by faith, I accept the Bible as Thy Word. I take it all. I take it without reservations. Where there are things I cannot understand, I will reserve judgment until I receive more light.' I discovered the secret that changed my ministry. I stopped trying to prove the Bible was true. I had settled in my own mind that it was, and this faith led to my using the phrase, 'The Bible says.' I found people were desperately hungry to hear what God's Holy Spirit had to say through His Holy Word."[25]

Reading and memorizing Scripture is as essential as it is rewarding. It is as though we are placing vocabulary in our hearts that allows the Holy Spirit to speak to our inner man.

May you and I share that faith that allows us to experience God's Word as His voice directly to us individually. Reading and memorizing Scripture is as essential as it is rewarding. It is as though we

---

23 Matthew 24:35.

24 Psalm 119:152, 160.

25 Billy Graham, *Faith 101: What is the Bible?*, 1.

are placing vocabulary in our hearts that allows the Holy Spirit to speak to our inner man. The revelation of God through His Word is complete. The illumination of the Holy Spirit is required for receiving the true meaning of each verse. May the one true meaning of each passage of Scripture find multiple applications in our lives as we seek to be those in the Word and of the Word.

Chapter 3

God's Extraordinary and Infinite Attributes

He who is the blessed and only Sovereign, the King of kings and LORD *of lords, who alone has immortality, who dwells in unapproachable light, whom no one has ever seen or can see. To him be honor and eternal dominion. Amen.*

1 TIMOTHY 6:15–16

For my thoughts are not your thoughts, neither are your ways my ways, declares the LORD*. For as the heavens are higher than the earth, so are my ways higher than your ways and my thoughts than your thoughts.*

ISAIAH 55:8–9

O LORD GOD*, you have only begun to show your servant your greatness and your mighty hand. For what god is there in heaven or on earth who can do such works and mighty acts as yours?*

DEUTERONOMY 3:24

Who is like you, O Lord, among the gods? Who is like you, majestic in holiness, awesome in glorious deeds, doing wonders?

Exodus 15:11

Let all the earth fear the Lord; let all the inhabitants of the world stand in awe of him! For he spoke, and it came to be; He commanded, and it stood firm.

Psalm 33:8–9

Oh, the depth of the riches and wisdom and knowledge of God! How unsearchable are his judgments and how inscrutable his ways! "For who has known the mind of the Lord, or who has been his counselor? Or who has given a gift to him that he might be repaid?" For from him and through him and to him are all things. To him be glory forever. Amen.

Romans 11:33–36

Blessed are the people to whom such blessings fall! Blessed are the people whose God is the Lord!

Psalm 144:15

Let the heavens praise your wonders, O Lord, your faithfulness in the assembly of the holy ones! For who in the skies can be compared to the Lord? Who among the heavenly beings is like the Lord, a God greatly to be feared in the council of the holy ones, and awesome above all who are around him? O Lord God of hosts, who is mighty as you are, O Lord, with your faithfulness all around you?

... You have a mighty arm; strong is your hand, high your right hand. Righteousness and justice are the foundation of your throne; steadfast love and faithfulness go before you.

Psalm 89:5–8, 13–14

Seek the Lord while he may be found; call upon him while he is near.

Isaiah 55:6

You will seek me and find me, when you seek me with all your heart.

Jeremiah 29:13

There is none like You, O Lord; You are great, and your name is great in might.

Jeremiah 10:6

The house that I am to build will be great, for our God is greater than all gods. But who is able to build him a house, since heaven, even the highest heaven, cannot contain him?

2 Chronicles 2:5–6

How are we to know about God? How can we hope to know God intimately and be in a relationship with Him? These are challenging and perplexing questions. The reward for our efforts is astounding. We need to get some initial truths in place first.

God is personal. There is so much more to knowing Him than the simple accumulation of information. In any personal relationship, communication is essential. Language is the best and highest form of communication between persons. We cannot even speak God's language, which must be so much higher than any human language. God must stoop down to communicate to us by using many human languages. Our task is daunting. It is much more than a stretch for finite man to understand anything of an infinite God. It is really quite impossible. It is all of Him.

The fact is, all our hopes of knowing God hang on one indispensible truth. It is the phenomenal reality that God has declared His desire for our fellowship.

We are trying to know and relate to the one and only true God who has no limits. The fact is, all our hopes of knowing God hang on one indispensible truth. It is the phenomenal reality that God has declared His desire for our fellowship. "*I will give them a heart to know that I am the Lord, and they shall be my people and I will be their God, for they shall return to me with their whole heart.*"[26] "*And you shall love the Lord your God with all your heart and with all your soul and with all your mind and with all your strength.*"[27] "*And this is eternal life, that they know you the only true God, and Jesus Christ whom you have sent.*"[28]

God has clearly expressed His desire that we know Him well. He promises to put this desire into our hearts. Without this affinity being given to us by Him, our natural inclination is to avoid His fellowship. Christianity is truly a relationship and

---

26 Jeremiah 24:7.

27 Mark 12:30.

28 John 17:3.

not a religion. Religions are man's attempt to reach concepts of God. Christianity is the one true God's unfailing reaching out to man. It is more than the establishment of initial relationship. It is the restoration of a presently broken and lost relationship.

On our own, we prefer the darkness to the light of His presence. "*And this is the judgment: the light has come into the world, and people loved the darkness rather than the light because their works were evil.*"[1] This is because of our inherent awareness of our sin. "*God is light, and in him is no darkness at all. If we say we have fellowship with him while we walk in darkness, we lie and do not practice the truth. But if we walk in the light, as he is in the light, we have fellowship with one another, and the blood of Jesus his Son cleanses us from all sin.*"[2]

As we grow in knowing about God, we are drawn to know Him personally. Here we find eternal life. God has taken the initiative to reveal Himself to us in many ways. Even more extraordinary, He desires to know us. That God would even give us the time of day is remarkable. "*We love because he first loved us.*"[3] "*But God shows his love for us in that while we were still sinners, Christ died for us.*"[4] "*I love those who love me, and those who seek me diligently find me.*"[5] God rewards those who seek Him with the overwhelming gift of His intimate fellowship.

Only as God cares about us and recognizes us do we have any real worth or dignity. In creating us in His image, God bestowed us with great worth. In our world today, man's effort to rid himself of God and any obligation to Him has done so much more

---

1 John 3:19.

2 I John 1:5–7.

3 I John 4:19.

4 Romans 5:8.

5 Proverbs 8:17.

damage to man than to God. God is God, whether we do or do not acknowledge or worship Him. When we declare, "there is no God," we do no damage to God. We only destroy all dignity and worth of man. The worldviews of naturalism and evolution, by their exclusion of God, have given rise to the abortions and massive human genocides seen in recent centuries.

> *When we declare, "there is no God," we do no damage to God. We only destroy all dignity and worth of man.*

The Biblical worldview contains explicit supernaturalism. "There is an uncompromised supernaturalism at the heart of the Christian worldview, and we must not let the world's skepticism with regard to these things affect our belief systems. We must trust and affirm that there is much more to reality than meets the eye."[6] There is a real, spiritual realm where myriads of created spiritual beings are active. One of these spiritual beings, Satan, rebelled against God and leads a legion of fellow rebellious demonic minions, called fallen angels or demons. They torment humanity as God allows. They are powerful, but God continues as Sovereign over their every effort. The majority of God's created spiritual beings remain obedient to God and now serve as His heavenly host. These angelic beings serve God as warriors, messengers, and ministering agents.

The Bible is replete with the visitations and effects of angelic and demonic activities in the physical realm of earthly existence. *"For we do not wrestle against flesh and blood, but against the rulers, against the authorities, against the cosmic powers over this present darkness, against the spiritual forces of evil in the heavenly places."*[7] Our lives will include encounters with both sides of this celestial aisle. We

6 R. C. Sproul, *Unseen Realities*, 9.

7 Ephesians 6:12.

need to be aware of this reality. We must avail ourselves of God's provisions for spiritual victory in our very real spiritual battles. In Christ we are always more than conquerors. We only lose spiritual conflicts when we fight in our own efforts and strength.

God has made Himself known to us in many ways. He has also provided, at great cost, an extraordinary means of our reconciliation. This is the sacrificial payment for sin made by Jesus Christ. The very pinnacle of God's revelation of Himself is the life of Jesus, His Son. *"In the beginning was the Word, and the Word was with God, and the Word was God. He was in the beginning with God. All things were made through him, and without him was not any thing made that was made."*[8] *"Long ago, at many times and in many ways, God spoke to our fathers by the prophets, but in these last days he has spoken to us by his Son, whom he appointed the heir of all things, through whom also he created the world. He is the radiance of the glory of God and the exact imprint of his nature, and he upholds the universe by the word of his power. After making purification for sins, he sat down at the right hand of the Majesty on high, having become as much superior to angels as the name he has inherited is more excellent than theirs."*[9]

We do not know everything there is to know about the universe. We do know it is immense. Its edges have proven to be beyond our sounding. Nevertheless, the universe is finite. Only God is infinite. The often-asked conundrum, "Can God create a stone so big He cannot pick it up?" has a simple answer. No. God is so much higher than all His created works. He would never create anything that exists outside of His sovereignty. As Creator of everything, God alone possesses the attribute of Infiniteness. God could easily create a rock so big that no other created thing

8 John 1:1–3.

9 Hebrews 1:1–4.

could pick it up. The reality is that the sum of everything in the universe is infinitesimally smaller than God.

The reality is that the sum of everything in the universe is infinitesimally smaller than God.

It does not appear that God is going to allow us to reach the edge of creation. It seems God knows that if we reached any edge of creation, mankind would fixate there and expend inordinate time and energy trying to discover what was beyond it. In our measurements of matter and light in deepest space, we discern an outward movement. The edge boundary thereby continues to outpace our puny exploration. "*Thus says God, the Lord, who created the heavens and stretched them out.*"[10] God appears to still be stretching out the heavens even in the present.

Philosophers have stated for years that our minds cannot grasp infinity. They are right. Without God's help, we are lost. Walter Kaiser said, "One of the greatest achievements in preaching would be a whole new appreciation for the majesty and greatness of our God as presented in the Scriptures."[11] We must acquiesce in humility and admit our limited ability.

Our terms are inadequate to capture God. The vocabulary of any language has some limit to its capacity for expressing concepts. As new things come into our world, languages expand. In theology, we try to create terms to express certain aspects of God. Terms like *infinite, omnipotent, omnipresent, omniscient, aseity,* and *Trinity* apply only to God. These can be both helpful and confusing. If we speak of "veritology," we dive for a dictionary, only to find it is not listed. The Latin word for truth, *veritas,* has been

10 Isaiah 42:5.

11 Walter C. Kaiser, *The Majesty of God in the Old Testament*, 9.

combined with "ology" to come up with the intentional study of truth. Many words are found only in systematic theologies. They are our futile efforts to create a language of understanding to grasp at our incomprehensible God.

My oldest son, Ben, exhibited this creativity when he was a little over two years of age. He was assimilating a number of words per day into his vocabulary. It was intriguing to hear the things he would come up with to express himself. Once he remarked about something he had done "yesterday night." We knew there was no such word in the English language. But its meaning was clear. We are driven to awe concerning our feeble comprehension of God and who He really is. We can only grasp at the fringes of His inexhaustible being.

Our hope for knowing God actually comes from only one source. It is God alone, and He wants to be known. He desires our fellowship. This exciting truth should blow your socks off. When we mess up in sin and ruin our intimate fellowship with Him, God Himself works to restore it. How could this be? It is overwhelmingly wonderful. This is the clear and consistent message of Scripture. God seeks us out like a shepherd finding His lost sheep. He celebrates the restoration of our relationship with Him. This is really too much to grasp.

In the book of Exodus, Moses encountered God in a burning bush. Moses reluctantly obeyed and trusted God. Following God's command, he appeared before the great Pharaoh of Egypt to demand the release of Israel from slavery. Moses already had a strained history with Pharaoh. The Egyptian empire was built upon the backs of the Jewish slaves. How could this work out? After numerous plagues, prophesied and occurring, the slaves of Israel were released. It was a marvel for all to behold.

Later, Moses made a very ambitious request. He asked God to reveal Himself in His Glory. It proved to be more dangerous than he realized. If God had granted his initial request, Moses would have died! *"Moses said to the* Lord, *'See, you say to me, "Bring up this people," but you have not let me know whom you will send with me. Yet you have said, "I know you by name, and you have also found favor in my sight." Now therefore, if I have found favor in your sight, please show me now your ways, that I may know you in order to find favor in your sight.... Please show me your glory.' ... 'But,'* [God] *said, 'you cannot see my face, for man shall not see me and live.' And the* Lord *said, 'Behold, there is a place by me where you shall stand on the rock, and while my glory passes by I will put you in a cleft of the rock, and I will cover you with my hand until I have passed by. Then I will take away my hand, and you shall see my back, but my face shall not be seen.'"*[12] God provided Moses with an exposure to His partial and survivable Glory.

God has always made a way throughout history for men to be reconciled to Him. Well before God's creation and man's short period of innocence in the garden, God had plans and decrees in place to restore our broken relationship with Him.

God has always made a way throughout history for men to be reconciled to Him. Well before God's creation and man's short period of innocence in the garden, God had plans and decrees in place to restore our broken relationship with Him. Our sins separate us from fellowship with God. Restoration has always been grounded upon Jesus's sinless life, unmerited death, and Spirit-empowered resurrection. God took an apparent great defeat and

12 Exodus 33:12–13, 18, 20–23.

used it for the greatest good. To Him alone be all glory, for this great thing He has done.

God can righteously provide complete reconciliation to Himself without an individual's actual knowledge of Jesus. Old Testament saints are proof of this. Nevertheless, God's redemption of man to Himself is always founded on the finished work of Jesus Christ. Before Jesus came to earth, Abraham believed God. This was counted unto him as righteousness. But when God sent Jesus to live among us, we beheld God as never before. Man was also given a greater insight into God's plan of reconciliation. Before and after the finished work of Jesus, upon which our reconciliation with God depends, God is able to come through his Spirit and grant new life.

The gospel is the message of new life through redemption. This redemption is not based on any work of our own doing. The sacrificial death of Jesus was the payment made and received for our sins. This alone is the essential foundation of our reconciliation with God. C. S. Lewis noted that the gospel is not what we would expect.[13] We would naturally expect our restoration with God to be the result of our own efforts. It would not be based on some representative payment that we had nothing to do with. We do not prefer this because there is zero credit to us.

We want to do something for our salvation. We desire to pat ourselves on the back. But our way could not work because our need is too great. God's economy is vastly different. We are counted unrighteous because of our federal representative, Adam. Similarly, we are also freely gifted and imputed with righteousness because of the finished work of Jesus. How amazing that we would hesitate to embrace this unique transaction. It

---

13 C. S. Lewis, *Mere Christianity*, 66–67.

works so much to our benefit. Human pride clouds our ability to admire this gracious blessing like we should.

Salvation through Jesus Christ was put in place by God. God is not in any way constrained by this. God can draw men unto Himself both through or outside of their hearing the gospel.

Without the gospel, His Spirit draws with a more limited revelation. The gospel message of Christ is very important, but we must never forget an important truth. Without God, information will not save you. Jesus told the men of his day, "*You search the Scriptures because you think that in them you have eternal life; and it is they that bear witness about me, yet you refuse to come to me that you may have life.*"[14] We have all benefited from things of which we were totally unaware. God applies the Righteousness of Christ to the standing of all those whom He chooses to make His adopted children.

With the gospel, we receive clarity. With the gospel, we also receive increased accountability. God has said in his Word, "*Everyone to whom much was given, of him much will be required.*"[15] After hearing the gospel, God will draw you to Himself through Jesus as the now clear path to God. Instead of seeing this as limiting, it is a well-defined and more understandable way. Jesus told his disciples that He alone was the only way to the Father. "*Jesus said to him, 'I am the way, and the truth, and the life. No one comes to the Father except through me.'*"[16] No one can come to God except through the merit and person of Jesus Christ. The very best manifestation of God is found in the earthly life of Jesus. Jesus said, "*Have I been with you so long, and you still do not know me, Phillip? Whoever has seen me has seen the Father. How can you*

---

14 John 5:39-40

15 Luke 12:48

16 John 14:6.

say, 'Show us the Father?' Do you not believe that I am in the Father and the Father is in me?"[17] It is not possible to reject Jesus and be reconciled to God at the same time. Once our spiritual eyes are opened, we accept them together as one.

The Unity of God makes knowing Him challenging. God is unique in that He is always completely present. He has no parts. He reveals Himself to be three persons in one being. You never get one person of God without the others. You might intend to eat an elephant "one bite at a time," but this procedure is not possible with God. God should not be dissected into component attributes that we then consider individually to reach a knowledge of Him. Like a fine diamond, we may study its facets, but we cannot appreciate the diamond by gazing at the facets separately.

God is unique in that He is always completely present. He has no parts. He reveals Himself to be three persons in one being. You never get one person of God without the others.

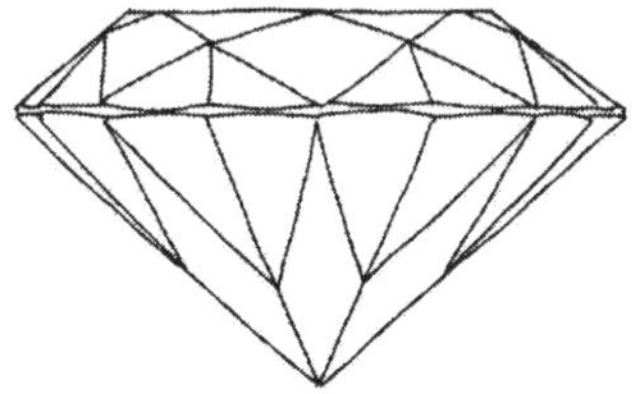

The blueprint used to cut a diamond is intricate. You really do not have anything until the final facet is complete. Each facet has its beauty only as it remains intact and is related to the others.

17 John 14:9–10.

All the facets reflect concurrently and have an ever-present influence on one another.

Knowing about God is more than listing his attributes in some checklist. There is not one single aspect of God that we can ever fully comprehend. Each attribute of God is best understood in its relation with all His other attributes. Every attribute shares in God's attribute of Infiniteness and many are clear and beyond debate. I have chosen nineteen attributes of God to consider in this book. We know these are attributes of God because of His testimony of Himself in Scripture.

When I began seeking to know God intentionally, I purposed to locate all the most extensive lists of God's attributes from great theologians. I knew that their lists would vary slightly. Next, I planned to simply coalesce them into a complete and exhaustive list. Then—voilà!—I would have the most definitive list of God's attributes in the history of theology. Boy, was I wrong!

This idea did not work for many reasons. First, each theologian admitted his list was incomplete. They all realized it is not possible to have an exhaustive list. Next, the kicker arrived. They all concurred that each attribute of God was infinite. At least the various lists were helpful and insightful. The definitive list just did not work out. God's attributes were grouped in many different arrangements. A sampling of these are listed in second part of Appendix 1.

Most categories or groupings of God's attributes overlap. They are only constructs, like the diamond analogy, used to aid us in our limited comprehension of God. None of them should be viewed as final or exclusive. Each includes the major attributes of God mentioned most often in the Bible. Appendix 2 also has a partial list of the actions, names, images, attributes, titles and dispositions of God found in Scripture. Although nonexhaustive, it can still serve as a helpful tool. Use it as a springboard to jump into the inexhaustible ocean of God and His unlimited being. Appendix 3 is a survey of every reference to God found in all of Scripture.

One of the most common methods of grouping God's attributes has been to divide them into those considered shared or not shared by man. Those that were not shared were designated as incommunicable and those that were shared were called communicable. The incommunicable attributes—those held by God alone—were His attributes including omnipresence, unity, immutability, eternity, and self-existence. Attributes that were shared with man were God's perfections like glory, jealousy, truthfulness, righteousness, wisdom, freedom, invisibility, omnipotence, spirituality, and wrath.

These were a little confusing to me. I have never figured out how to be invisible. I certainly hope I have some aspect of unity or integrity in my life. Lists within just the reformed tradition of Christian theology varied concerning the incommunicable and communicable attributes of God. When I see diversity even within segments of the broader Christian faith, I realize the challenge of finding any definitive categorized list of the attributes of God.

One succinct and simple listing of the attributes of God comes from the Shorter Catechism: "God is a spirit, infinite, eternal, and unchangeable, in His being, wisdom, power, holiness, justice, goodness, and truth."[18] A fuller explanation of God's nature comes from the Westminster Confession of Faith. Chapter II, articles I & II state:

> There is but one only living and true God, who is infinite in being and perfection, a most pure spirit, invisible, without body, parts, or passions, immutable,

---

18 G. I. Williamson, *The Shorter Catechism*, 15.

> immense, eternal, incomprehensible, almighty, most wise, most holy, most free, most absolute, working all things to the counsel of His own immutable and most righteous will, for His own glory; most loving, gracious, merciful, long-suffering, abundant in goodness and truth, forgiving iniquity, transgression, and sin; the rewarder of them that diligently seek Him; and withal most just and terrible in His judgments; hating all sin, and who will by no means clear the guilty.
>
> God hath all life, glory, goodness, blessedness, in and of Himself; and is alone in and unto Himself all-sufficient, not standing in need of any creatures which He hath made, nor deriving any glory from them, but only manifesting His own glory in, by, unto, and upon them: He is the alone fountain of all being, of whom, through whom, and to whom, are all things; and hath most sovereign dominion over them, to do by them, for them, and upon them, whatsoever Himself pleaseth. In His sight all things are open and manifest; His knowledge is infinite, infallible, and independent upon the creature, so as nothing is to Him contingent, or uncertain. He is most holy in all His counsels, in all His works, and in all His commands. To Him is due from angels and men, and every other creature, whatsoever worship, service, or obedience, He is pleased to require of them.[19]

These two statements can guide us both in sentiment and comprehensiveness of attributes to consider investigating.

---

19 G. I. Williamson, *The Westminster Confession of Faith for Study Classes*, 23.

Appendix 1 also includes other historic creedal statements about the nature of God. Here we find the result of a special collaboration among sound biblical scholars. God's providence in church history caused these two statements to contain rich insight and fervent reverence.

The categories we will use are the ones I find to be the most helpful. They are flawed. They are not any final word. We will use them only as a helpful tool, which we acknowledge is arbitrary and limited. We group the Bible's most often expressed attributes of God into three broad categories:

1. **His constitutional attributes.** These are the ones we associate with God's unique make-up. They serve to give insight into God's essential nature. They are Infiniteness, Spirit, Triunity, Unchangeableness, Self-Existence, and Personal.
2. **His moral attributes.** These reflect God's character. They also are often referred to as His perfections or excellencies. They are Truth, Goodness, Holiness, Love, Wrath, and Faithfulness.
3. **His positional attributes.** These highlight how God relates to all of His creation. These represent God's most prominent roles of affiliation with us. Here we find God as Sovereign, Creator, Master, Judge, Redeemer, and Father.

All of these taken together point to the Glory of God. God's Glory is not technically an attribute per se. It is the sum radiant brilliance of His presence. His presence is His Glory. God dwells in unapproachable light. To be in His nearer presence causes a recognizable change in the beholder. "*When Moses came down from*

Mount Sinai, with the two tablets of the testimony in his hand as he came down from the mountain, Moses did not know that the skin of his face shone because he had been talking with God."[20]

> *God's Glory is not technically an attribute per se. It is the sum radiant brilliance of His presence. His presence is His Glory.*

These categories of God's attributes will be considered over the next six chapters. They are also further considered in Appendix 4. Within each category, many other scripturally confirmed characteristics of God will be seen. These groups are intended to present God in His complete being. I hope to view God in His integral Unity. I have sought to avoid the more routine style of simply listing His individual attributes. Let us approach the king of kings and the lord of lords with great reverence and humility. We may be assured that He calls us to this endeavor. With hearts of awe and wonder, our Spirit-enabled efforts will be richly rewarded. These rewards are staggering and life-changing. We are looking upon the overwhelming incomprehensible being of God. We are unworthy and unable without the enabling of His Spirit.

20 Exodus 34:29.

Chapter 4

Is God Beyond Knowing? Yes

Have you not known? Have you not heard? The Lord *is the everlasting God, the Creator of the ends of the earth. He does not faint or grow weary; his understanding is unsearchable.*

Isaiah 40:28

Behold, God is great, and we know him not; the number of his years is unsearchable.

Job 36:26

O the depth of the riches and wisdom and knowledge of God! How unsearchable are his judgments and how inscrutable his ways!

Romans 11:33

Great is the Lord, *and greatly to be praised, and his greatness is unsearchable.*

Psalm 145:3

And the Spirit of the Lord *shall rest upon him, the Spirit of wisdom and understanding, the Spirit of counsel and might, the Spirit of knowledge and the fear of the* Lord.

Isaiah 11:2

That their hearts may be encouraged, being knit together in love, to reach all the riches of full assurance of understanding and the knowledge of God's mystery, which is Christ, in whom are hidden all the treasures of wisdom and knowledge.

Colossians 2:2–3

God is spirit, and those who worship him must worship in spirit and truth.

John 4:24

Where shall I go from your Spirit? Or where shall I flee from your presence? If I ascend to heaven, you are there! If I make my bed in Sheol, you are there! If I take the wings of the morning and dwell in the uttermost parts of the sea, even there your hand shall lead me, and your right hand shall hold me.

Psalm 139:7–10

Go therefore and make disciples of all nations, baptizing them in the name of the Father and of the Son and of the Holy Spirit, teaching them to observe all that I have commanded you. And behold, I am with you always, to the end of the age.

MATTHEW 28:19–20

The grace of the LORD *Jesus Christ and the love of God and the fellowship of the Holy Spirit be with you all.*

2 CORINTHIANS 13:14

Maintain the unity of the Spirit in the bond of peace. There is one body and one Spirit—just as you were called to the one hope that belongs to your call—one LORD, *one faith, one baptism, one God and Father of all, who is over all and through all and in all.*

EPHESIANS 4:3–6

We will begin looking at our first grouping of God's perfections to focus on what we are calling His "constitutional" attributes. Attributes are the essentials of what God has revealed about Himself. They are the aspects of God that, if removed, would make Him no longer God. Remembering that our effort is cautioned by His Infiniteness and Unity—there are many challenges to our knowing about Him. All our categories are limited in their truth. God, by His Infiniteness, must have attributes we can never know, and they are of an unlimited number. In this sense, it is true that God will ever be incomprehensible.

> *As we acknowledge the unsearchableness of God, we are just as confident that God has given us a revelation of Himself that makes Him knowable to us.*

As we acknowledge the unsearchableness of God, we are just as confident that God has given us a revelation of Himself that makes Him knowable to us. His is not a deceptive revelation. It is one that we can utilize to know accurately His divine person. Through this, we have real fellowship with Him. We quickly realize that to know Him leads directly knowing Him personally and loving Him.

The First Three Constitutional Attributes of God

- **Infiniteness:** Unfathomable, Unsearchable, Unimaginable, Unknowable, Unique, Boundless, Incomprehensible, Immeasurable, Mysterious, Omnipresent, Ubiquitous
- **Spirit:** Distinct in Being, Immaterial or Noncorporeal, Invisible, Supernatural, Transcendent
- **Triunity:** Trinity, Unity, Simplicity or Uncompoundedness, Persons, Offices and Internal Fellowship

Infiniteness

The Infiniteness of God makes Him unimaginable, unfathomable, unsearchable, incomprehensible, and a perpetual mystery. Many times, when discussing the attributes of God, theologians have chosen to describe God by using negation. It is actually easier to tell you what God is *not*. We readily admit that positively stated attributes can only hope to capture some of all that God is. From God's Infiniteness proceeds His omnipresence. Boundless in His very nature, God is always both here and everywhere. "*Am I a God at hand, declares the* LORD, *and not a God far away? Can a man hide himself in secret places so that I cannot see him? declares the* LORD. *Do I not fill heaven and earth? declares the* LORD."[1] "*Great is the* LORD, *and greatly to be praised, and his greatness is unsearchable.... The* LORD *is near to all who call on him, to all who call on him in truth.*"[2] God also exists beyond or above time. He is always and ever in the past, present, and future. A better way to say this might be that everything that has happened or will happen is always in the present to God.

With new discoveries concerning deep space, we continue to learn of the immensity of the universe. There is so much more than a lot of stars and nothingness. Amazing structures of astounding complexity and scale—beautiful wonders of color and light—fill the universe. The Glory of God through His creation is being seen in fresh new ways as the Hubble telescope and other methods extend our understanding into deeper space.

The scale of space requires extraordinary measures of distance. The light-year (LY) is now so small, at a mere 5.8 trillion miles, that it has lost its place as the standard of measuring long distances. The parsec (pc), at a measly 19 trillion miles or 3.26 light-years, merely moved us usefully outside our own galaxy of the Milky Way. We quickly needed the megaparsec (Mpc), a measurement of one million parsecs or 3.2 million light-years, and the gigaparsec (Gpc) representing 3.262 billion light-years. This brought us to one-fourteenth of our still limited view of the observable universe! Our best present map of the universe, the 2MASS Redshift Survey, reaches out a mere 380 million miles. That is under one-tenth of a light-year! "*Thus says the* LORD, *your*

---

1 Jeremiah 23:23–24.

2 Psalm 145:3, 18.

Redeemer, who formed you from the womb: 'I am the L*ORD*, *who made all things, who alone stretched out the heavens, who spread out the earth by myself.'"*[3] God is infinitely larger than the finite universe. We have presently detected only a portion of the universe. And yet, there is no place in space and beyond where God is not present all the time. God's Infiniteness is a statement of endlessness. It is the basis of His omnipresence.

> *God is beyond measuring. He has no limits. He is beyond all comparison. He alone is unique.*

God is beyond measuring. He has no limits. He is beyond all comparison. He alone is unique. Infiniteness is a significant game-changing attribute of God. We struggle to relate to Him in this. We must accept the awesome incomprehensibility of God. His transcendence and omnipresence force us to a posture of awe and wonder. God's attribute of Infiniteness influences all of His other attributes. It catapults God to be incalculably higher than man. Our best source of knowledge about God is found in His holy Word. Here is the great value to our lifelong study of God's Word. We must have God's revelation. We are fallen and easily deceived. We depend on Him completely to know Him. His Infiniteness always outpaces our understanding.

Spirit

"God is spirit, and those who worship him must worship in spirit and truth."[4] God as Spirit means His essential being is nonphysical, nonmaterial, and noncorporeal. God exists as a being distinct from the physical world. He does possess flesh in the person of

---

3 Isaiah 44:24.

4 John 4:24.

Jesus Christ and in some few timely manifestations. This means no aspect of God can routinely be perceived by our five physical senses. God being Spirit renders Him beyond our natural discovery. In answering the question, "What is God like?" Tozer responds, "God is not like anything; that is, He is not exactly like anything or anybody."[5] Only as God chooses to become manifested materially is He discernable to us through our physical senses.

Directly related to God as Spirit we understand the invisibility of God. "*To the King of ages, immortal, invisible, the only God, be honor and glory forever and ever. Amen.*"[6] As a four-year-old boy, I loved the color comics in the Sunday newspaper. Also at this time of life, my constant response to every declarative statement was "why?" One Sunday morning, as I lay on the comics spread out on the den floor, my father directed me to come get ready to go to church. I asked, "Why?" and his response, as it had been many times before was, "So we can go learn about Jesus." Then he added that I needed to go wash my hands before coming to breakfast. To this oft-repeated instruction, "why?" was met with the common answer, "Because of germs." As I walked to the bathroom to wash my hands, my parents report that I was overheard to say to myself, "Germs and Jesus, germs and Jesus, that's all I ever hear around this house, and I ain't never seen neither one of 'em!"

God is essentially absent from any material presence. In this we acknowledge His transcendence. Yet, we do still perceive His ever-present spiritual nearness. This we experience through the spiritual inner man called our soul.

Our spirits are either alive to God's Spirit through new birth in Christ Jesus or they are clouded by our sinful natures. "*The*

---

5 A. W. Tozer, *The Knowledge of the Holy*, 161–162.

6 1 Timothy 1:17.

Spirit himself bears witness with our spirit that we are children of God."[7] *"These things God has revealed to us through the Spirit. For the Spirit searches everything, even the depths of God. For who knows a person's thoughts except the spirit of that person, which is in him? So also no one comprehends the thoughts of God except the Spirit of God. Now we have received not the spirit of the world, but the Spirit who is from God, that we might understand the things freely given us by God. And we impart this in words not taught by human wisdom but taught by the Spirit, interpreting spiritual truths to those who are spiritual. The natural person does not accept the things of the Spirit of God, for they are folly to him, and he is not able to understand them because they are spiritually discerned."*[8]

It is a part of all men, believers and nonbelievers, to have within us an innate spiritual inner awareness that God really is. *"For what can be known about God is plain to them, because God has shown it to them. For his invisible attributes, namely, his eternal power and divine nature, have been clearly perceived, ever since the creation of the world, in the things that have been made. So they are without excuse."*[9] Stephen Charnock said, "For though God be so inaccessible that we cannot know Him perfectly, yet He is so much in the light that we cannot be totally ignorant of Him; as He cannot be comprehended in His essence, He cannot be unknown in His existence."[10] God's spiritual being is the most excellent form of existence. Since God has chosen to exist in this way, it is safe to assume it is the best and highest form of being.

---

7 Romans 8:16.

8 1 Corinthians 2:10–14.

9 Romans 1:19–20.

10 Stephen Charnock, *The Existence and Attributes of God*, 25–26.

> *God's spiritual being is the most excellent form of existence. Since God has chosen to exist in this way, it is safe to assume it is the best and highest form of being.*

God does not have a body, but He has chosen at limited times to reveal Himself in physical manifestations. God appeared to Abraham as a smoking fire pot and a flaming torch. Moses witnessed God as a burning bush, and he even beheld the back of God's Glory. To all Israel, God appeared as a pillar of cloud and fire. There were manifestations of supernatural thunder, lightning, earthquakes, whirlwinds, and fire from heaven. God also has chosen to have anthropomorphic-type manifestations. These include a writing finger and, ultimately, His incarnation among us in the person of the Son, Jesus Christ.

No greater manifestation of God than Jesus has or ever will be seen in this present age. The messiah had been promised for generations in the Old Testament. When Jesus arrived in the form of a baby, He provided to man his highest opportunity to behold God. Here all the fullness of man and God met to direct us to a deeper understanding of God. Being reconciled to God became clearer than at any other point in previous time. The finished work of Christ, though not applied to all, was capable of reconciling all men to God.

In Him, we behold the greatness of God, the lord of all and the king of the universe. We have a glimpse of God. It is more than we can take in. To God be the glory, this marvelous thing He has done. Jesus was the gift of God Himself, in the flesh, actually handled by men. What an astounding revelation of the Infinite, Spiritual God.

Triunity

"Triunity" is one of those creative words not commonly found in the dictionary. It is meant to express both the unity and t rinity of

God. Unity means God is simple and noncompounded. He is without parts. God is always all wherever He is, which is everywhere. You never get part of God or one attribute more than the other. All attributes, without number, are present at all times. God is one and there are no divisions in His essence and being. "God is not composite and is not susceptible of division in any sense of the word."[11]

That there is only one true God was the main distinctive of the Hebrew faith. "*Hear, O Israel: The LORD our God, the LORD is one.*"[12] This is the Jewish Shema, highlighting the profound concept of the oneness of God. Virtually all early nations tended toward belief in a plethora of deities. Israel alone held belief in monotheism. Today, among major faiths, only Judaism, Christianity, and Islam hold belief in one deity. Three persons in the one being of God has been stated in Scripture from its very first verses.

In Christianity, the teaching of the Shema was reiterated by Paul in the New Testament. "*Therefore, as to the eating of food offered to idols, we know that 'an idol has no real existence,' and that 'there is no God but one.' For although there may be so-called gods in heaven or on earth—as indeed there are many 'gods' and many 'lords'—yet for us there is one God, the Father, from whom are all things and for whom we exist, and one LORD, Jesus Christ, through whom are all things and through whom we exist.*"[13]

God is clearly taught in Scripture to be three in person while He is one in being. Concerning the persons of the Godhead, more than sixty verses mention the presence of the three persons of Father, Son, and Holy Spirit. "*And I* [Jesus] *will ask the*

---

11 Louis Berkoff, *Systematic Theology*, 62.

12 Deuteronomy 6:4.

13 1 Corinthians 8:4–6.

Father, and he will give you another Helper, to be with you forever."[14] "*The grace of the* Lord *Jesus Christ and the love of God and the fellowship of the Holy Spirit be with you all.*"[15] "*For through him* [Jesus] *we both have access in one Spirit to the Father.*"[16] "*There is one body and one Spirit—just as you were called to the one hope that belongs to your call—one* Lord, *one faith, one baptism, one God and Father of all, who is over all and through all and in all.*"[17] "*According to the foreknowledge of God the Father, in the sanctification of the Spirit, for obedience to Jesus Christ and for sprinkling with his blood.*"[18]

Orthodox Christianity has always held to the basic tenet that there is one unchanging God carrying out one eternal and unaltered plan of redemption. Many efforts to understand the mystery of "three in one" have all come up short. Here is proof that God's revelation of Himself was not purely a construct of man's imagination. Would man conceive of a God whom he cannot understand enough to explain to others? It has been said that if we deny the trinity we will lose our soul; and if we try to comprehend the trinity, we will lose our mind. Perhaps the best way to reconcile the apparent paradox is to say God is one in essence or being and three in persons.

Many efforts to understand the mystery of "three in one" have all come up short. Here is proof that God's revelation of Himself was not purely a construct of man's imagination.

14 John 14:16.

15 2 Corinthians 13:14.

16 Ephesians 2:18.

17 Ephesians 4:4–6.

18 1 Peter 1:2.

The trinitarian doctrine of God is taught also in the Old Testament. "*Then God said, 'Let us make man in our image, after our likeness.'*"[19] "*Then the LORD God said, 'Behold, the man has become like one of us in knowing good and evil.'*"[20] "*And I heard the voice of the LORD saying, 'Whom shall I send, and who will go for us?'*"[21] The distinctions within the Godhead always refer to person, never being or essence. Each of the three persons is distinct, yet each of them subsists with constant union in the single oneness of God's being. This is who God proclaims Himself to be.

Each person of the Godhead appears to have different offices or distinctions in activity. The Father initiates creation and the plan of redemption. The Son carries out creation and redeems fallen creation. The Holy Spirit illuminates, regenerates, and sanctifies, giving a necessary inward witness to our spirits of our true faith. The multiple persons within the one true God are each beyond our full comprehension.

C. S. Lewis had helpful insight.[22] He proposed it would be like beings who only lived in two dimensions trying to grasp a three-dimensional entity. How could they? A point single would struggle mightily to comprehend a line or any flat two-dimensional shape. The fictional book *Flatland* creatively explores this conundrum.[23]

I have always been fascinated with two-dimensional drawings of three-dimensional objects. Who could have guessed my interest would help in being accepted to dental school? The aptitude test for

19 Genesis 1:26.

20 Genesis 3:22.

21 Isaiah 6:8.

22 C. S. Lewis, *Mere Christianity*, 161–162.

23 Edwin A. Abbott, *Flatland*, 3–5.

application includes many perception questions. Consider the cubes below. How many cubes have exactly three sides exposed?

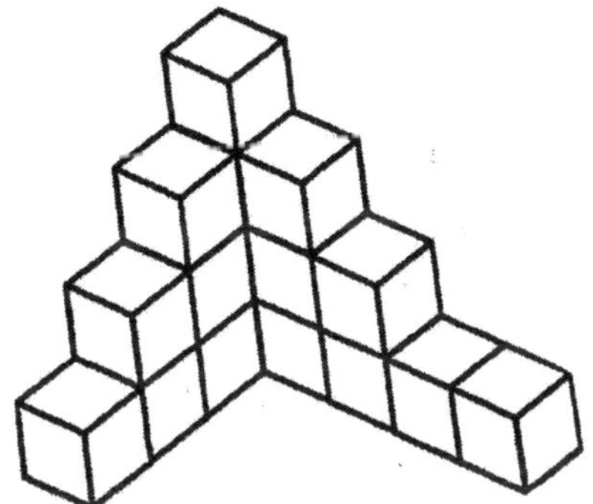

The answer is five. The four internal bottom cubes and the tricky hidden back corner. There are rules of convention in these drawings like vanishing points and two-point perspective. Sometimes, the rules are violated. Try to figure out this simple line drawing that violates the conventions. There is an impossible transition in the middle.

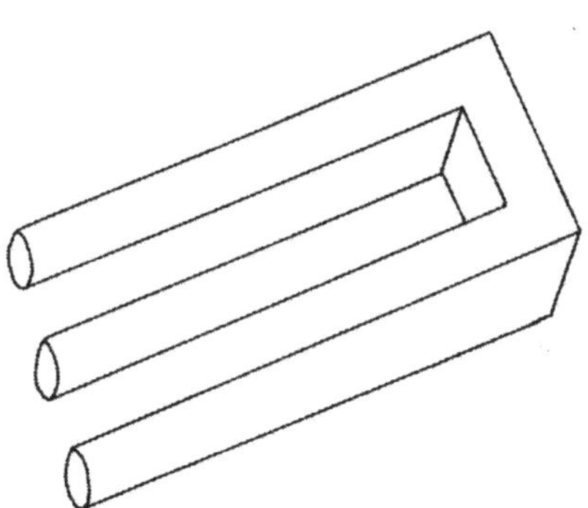

With your hand covering the right of the drawing you see three tubes. Covering the left half reveals a squared pipe turned on itself. I have digressed by using these simple drawings in order to remind us how much God, particularly in His trinitarian being, is beyond our mental conceptualization. God exists beyond our paths of thought and understanding. He overwhelms our imagination by the reality of His "otherness." The uniqueness of God is absolute. The trinitarian nature of God is beyond our grasping.

The apparent paradox of God's Triunity is undeniability affirmed in the Word of God. Many things concerning God reveal the limits of our finite understanding. Mystery concerning God can be profound in our present state. As we move beyond our earthly life, we will see more clearly. *"For now we see in a mirror dimly, but then face to face. Now I know in part; then I shall know fully, even as I have been fully known."*[24] The mystery of God's Triunity as revealed in Scripture is explained as far as we should carry it in our speculation. We must wait to understand this reality ever clearer in our eternity with Him.

---

24 1 Corinthians 13:12.

Chapter 5

Is God Beyond Knowing? No

If we are faithless, he remains faithful—for he cannot deny himself.

2 Timothy 2:13

That which we have seen and heard we proclaim also to you, so that you too may have fellowship with us; and indeed our fellowship is with the Father and with his Son Jesus Christ. And we are writing these things so that our joy may be complete.

1 John 1:3–4

For I the Lord *do not change; therefore you, O children of Jacob, are not consumed.*

Malachi 3:6

Jesus Christ is the same yesterday and today and forever.

Hebrews 13:8

God is not a man, that he should lie, or a son of man, that he should change his mind. Has he said, and will he not do it? Or has he spoken, and will he not fulfill it?

Numbers 23:19

And now, Father, glorify me in your own presence with the glory that I had with you before the world existed.

John 17:5

Every good gift and every perfect gift is from above, coming down from the Father of lights with whom there is no variation or shadow due to change.

James 1:17

For those whom he foreknew he also predestined to be conformed to the image of his Son, in order that he might be the firstborn among many brothers. And those whom he predestined he also called, and those whom he called he also justified, and those whom he justified he also glorified.

Romans 8:29–30

For by him all things were created, in heaven and on earth, visible and invisible, whether thrones or dominions or rulers or authorities—all things were created through him and for him. And he is before all things, and in him all things hold together.

Colossians 1:16–17

God has provided many ways for us to know Him. We can know about Him accurately. We can know Him personally and intimately. This reality is amazing and beyond our full appreciation. To contemplate the vastness of God is staggering. God is always a firm rock. He remains the same outside of time itself. His Self-Existence means He is unaffected by anything outside of Himself. Our singular and completely autonomous God is ever the same and always with us. We will now consider the remaining three constitutional attributes of God.

> *To be enabled to experience His intimate presence in our lives is beyond comprehension.*

Remaining Constitutional Attributes of God

- **Unchangeableness:** Immutable, Everlasting, Firm, Rock, Consistent, Unrepentant
- **Self-Existence:** Absolute, Immortal, Eternal, Omniscience, Being, Essence, Self-Sufficient, Free, Alone, Only
- **Personal:** Near, Intimate, Accessible, Knowable, Immanent, Relational, Revealer

Unchangeableness

God possesses the essential attribute of Unchangeableness or immutability. This is clearly revealed in Scripture. "*Of old you laid the foundation of the earth, and the heavens are the work of your hands. They will perish, but you will remain; they will all wear out like a garment. You will change them like a robe, and they will pass away, but you are the same, and your years have no end. The children of your servants shall dwell secure; their offspring shall be established before you.*"[1] We are reminded that the stability and unchanging nature of God gives great security to our lives. Our present lives and all our hopes for the future depend on God being consistent and dependable. God will not change the rules. What we learn of Him never needs to be updated because He has changed. Still, there will always be more of Him of which to learn.

A mentor in my Christian life is Dr. Byrle Kynerd. Often I have heard him recite the lyrics, "Jesus loves me, this I know, for the Bible tells me so." It is such a beautiful statement of faith. The words remind us of the tremendous comfort in the enduring firmness and everlasting truth of God's Unchangeableness. We find it comforting when God says in His Word, "*For I the* LORD *do not change,*"[2] God is the rock solid foundation of our lives. He is always consistent, and we can count His everlasting stability.

In God's Word, we find many instances where God is said to repent or relent of His intended action.[3] Has God changed? Other passages speak of God stating He was sorry He had made man or made Saul king.[4] In what sense did God change or not change? The fact is that, while God does always respond rightly to new and different situations, His purposes and plans never change. His intended actions have changed to fit the new situation. His response has become different, but He is the still the same. It appears God gives us evidence of His ever-present care by this manner of revelation.

---

1 Psalm 102:25–28.

2 Malachi 3:6.

3 Exodus 32:9–14; Isaiah 38:1–6, Jonah 3:4, 10.

4 Genesis 6:6, 1 Samuel 15:11.

The fact is that, while God does always respond rightly to new and different situations, His purposes and plans never change.

God's attributes of Self-Existence and omniscience allow for His unchanging decrees and plans. Here we see an example of God's use of anthropomorphisms. He has stated His action to accommodate our limited comprehension. His sorrows about the way things exist are really His displeasures of man's sinfulness and its results. His repenting actions are consistently based in His ever-constant nature and His always-solid judgments and intentions. "*The counsel of the Lord stands forever, the plans of his heart to all generations.*"[5]

The great immediate result of God's Unchangeableness is our comfort. God is eternal. He is beyond all that is created. His plans and nature are unaffected by anything other than Himself. His perfection of being renders Him unchangeable. We can depend on Him and be secure in Him. In this aspect of God's person, we find our refuge, our shield, and our security. We are safe in Him. Resting in the truth that God is always and ever on the throne is one of our greatest comforts and encouragements during our times of disappointment and struggles.

Self-Existence

The Self-Existence of God renders Him completely independent. He is the source of all that is. He is uncreated and eternal. God's immortality provides Him absolute knowledge and foreknowledge. God's omniscience allows Him to have all knowledge in the now. He never learns any new information. Nothing is ever hidden from God.

---

5 Psalm 33:11.

He is incapable of making mistakes. You can see how this attribute of God is stunning and broad in its significance.

No apologetic for God's existence is offered in the Bible. *"In the beginning, God created the heavens and the earth."*[6] The Bible introduces God as always having been. He is always present, always before, and always after. In one sense God is "always," but in another He is "beyond always." He is above time and dwells outside of time. That's hard to wrap your brain around.

The Bible introduces God as always having been. He is always present, always before, and always after. He is above time and dwells outside of time.

God alone is the source of all being. Everything is upheld in its very existence by Him alone. The term "aseity" means that God is absolutely freestanding and depends on nothing else for His existence. He is devoid of any need. His being is autonomous and independent to everything except Himself. "*Worthy are you, our* L*ORD* *and God, to receive glory and honor and power, for you created all things, and by your will they existed and were created.*"[7] We see Scripture over and over speak to the essential, absolute, and foundational independence of God.

The world's proposition that everything came from nothingness or some eternal raw material with no directing or causative agent is absurd. Intellectual honesty requires we relegate this to pure fantasy. When I was in college, some lectures were built purely on speculation or fanciful ideas. Walking from one of these more liberal presentations, a classmate of mine commented, "You know,

---

6 Genesis 1:1.

7 Revelation 4:11.

being open-minded is a great thing, but you can be so open-minded that your brains fall out." Proposing that everything came from chance, even if matter is assumed to just already exist, flies in the face of sound logic. To say everything erupted from nothing is even more ridiculous.

God's revelation does not set forth the eternality of matter. From the very beginning Scripture clearly teaches God is the ultimate source of all that is. "*Where were you when I laid the foundation of the earth? Tell me, if you have understanding. Who determined its measurements—surely you know! Or who stretched the line upon it? On what were its bases sunk, or who laid its cornerstone.*"[8] This is an expression of God's role as the ground and source of everything.

A reality of being outside of time is that, from God's perspective, every event is always in the present. God knows everything in His omniscience, and all that God knows is known only in His now. God observes all events in time as if they were happening in the same instant. This astounding reality does not make events confusing to Him. God even sees our thoughts before we think them. He knows all things that do happen and all things that could have happened. He even knows everything that all men might have ever thought. He does not just know all things that ever have been, are, or will be. He also knows all contingencies of everything that could have been but were not.

God's great knowledge gives rise to His perfect wisdom in all His actions. His acts display His power. How and when He acts displays His wisdom. Wisdom refers to timing and extent. God's wise actions are always perfectly timed. God's actions are always informed by complete knowledge and understanding. His boundless omniscience perfectly supplies His infinite wisdom. Here we

---

8 Job 38:4–6.

find the harmony of God's mind and will. All He does, He does perfectly with full knowledge and flawless insight and understanding. God is never surprised by any development or event. His foreknowledge precludes that possibility.

How God answers prayers occurring at the same time is exacerbated but also resolved by this fact. He does not hear them all bunched up in time. He is always hearing all prayers throughout all time. When you exist outside of time, now is the same as eternity. *"O Lord, you have searched me and known me! You know when I sit down and when I rise up; you discern my thoughts from afar. You search out my path and my lying down and are acquainted with all my ways. Even before a word is on my tongue, behold, O Lord, you know it altogether."*[9]

God is independent of everything else and completely self-sufficient. Jesus said, *"For as the Father has life in himself, so he has granted the Son also to have life in himself."*[10] This truth brings great amazement at God's care and provision for creation. How astonishing is His Love for His chosen redeemed. His interest arises not from need. God's interest is exclusively His good pleasure. All of God's actions and plans emanate from His person. His plans are never thwarted or limited. All God purposes, He does. Everything that comes to pass, God has ordained. He works all that is for His Glory.

Personal

God is Personal and is therefore relational. He is near and intimate. He is accessible and ever-present. God has chosen to reveal Himself in various ways to cause us to know of Him and to know Him intimately. It is utterly fantastic to discover who God really is. His greatness and goodness are overwhelming. It is phenomenal

9 Psalm 139:1–4.

10 John 5:26.

to learn that the God of the universe, the one true God, desires fellowship with us. He has chosen to share Himself with us.

God is a Spirit with mind, will, and emotions. Our bodies are essential to our life, but our real person is our inner man. It is our spiritual and noncorporeal self. It is who we are inside that counts. God is not limited by any physical aspect as we are. We do live here in earthly tents of flesh. We read in Scripture, *"For we know that if the tent that is our earthly home is destroyed, we have a building from God, a house not made with hands, eternal in the heavens."*[11]

In the incarnate Son, flesh is part of God's being. This allows Him to fully share in all our experiences and in this God relates to us completely. *"For we do not have a high priest who is unable to sympathize with our weaknesses, but one who in every respect has been tempted as we are, yet without sin."*[12] God exists primarily as Spirit. Through Jesus we can experience actual friendship with God. *"Greater love has no one than this, that someone lay down his life for his friends. You are my friends if you do what I command you. No longer do I call you servants, for the servant does not know what his master is doing; but I have called you friends, for all that I have heard from my Father I have made known to you."*[13]

God's attributes of nearness and immediacy provide for our constant communion with Him. He hears our thoughts before we speak to Him. His own are never away from His presence and loving care.

God's attributes of nearness and immediacy provide for our constant communion with Him. He hears our thoughts before

11 2 Corinthians 5:1.

12 Hebrews 4:15.

13 John 15:13–15.

we speak to Him. His own are never away from His presence and loving care. "*Who shall separate us from the love of Christ? Shall tribulation, or distress, or persecution, or famine, or nakedness, or danger, or sword?... No, in all these things we are more than conquerors through him who loved us. For I am sure that neither death nor life, nor angels nor rulers, nor things present nor things to come, nor powers, nor height nor depth, nor anything else in all creation, will be able to separate us from the love of God in Christ Jesus our Lord.*"[14]

When Jesus was speaking to His disciples about His coming death, they responded with great concern that He should not leave them. They even offered to go with Jesus in order to keep Him nearby. His reassurance was that it was good that He go. This would allow the Holy Spirit to come. The Spirit could be more immediately with them at all times and places. "*And I will ask the Father, and he will give you another Helper, to be with you forever, even the Spirit of truth, whom the world cannot receive, because it neither sees him nor knows him. You know him, for he dwells with you and will be in you. I will not leave you as orphans; I will come to you.*"[15]

Many times, in our fellowship with God, we long for His presence with us to be more like our experience with our loved ones here on earth. The story is told of a young child whose fear of being alone made sleep difficult. After multiple parental responses to calls in the night, the child was reassured, "You're not alone, God is right here with you." To this reasoning, the child responded, "But I want somebody with skin on."

As we mature in the Christian faith, we realize an ever-increasing awareness of God's presence. This communion is experienced as an

14 Romans 8:35, 37–39.

15 John 14:16–18.

> *ongoing holy conversation. This is one our best assurances of the truth of our salvation.*

As we mature in the Christian faith, we realize an ever-increasing awareness of God's presence. This communion is experienced as an ongoing holy conversation. This is one our best assurances of the truth of our salvation. If you have a real relationship with God, you will know it. The converse is true. It is common among men to deny their estrangement from God before others. They may fool others, but they seldom fool themselves. We all know the current status of our relationship with our wonderfully personal God.

God has emotions. He expresses them only in Righteous ways. There is no inherent sinfulness in the emotions of anger or jealousy. "*For they have rejected the law of the LORD of hosts, and have despised the word of the Holy One of Israel. Therefore the anger of the LORD was kindled against his people, and he stretched out his hand against them and struck them.*"[16] God is without sin in all His actions.

In God's jealousy, He is completely justified in a way that no human can be. As the one and only true God, He is rendered the right of demanding to be feared and honored by men. The first of the Ten Commandments says, "*You shall have no other gods before me. You shall not make for yourself a carved image, or any likeness of anything that is in heaven above, or that is in the earth beneath, or that is in the water under the earth.... For I the LORD your God am a jealous God, visiting the iniquity of the fathers on the children to the third and fourth generation of those who hate me, but showing steadfast love to thousands of those who love me and keep my commandments.*"[17]

---

16 Isaiah 5:24–25.

17 Exodus 20:3–6.

God is clearly revealed in the Bible to express emotions. He rejoices,[18] is pleased,[19] and moved to pity.[20] He hates idolatry, injustice, violence, and divorce. He is grieved,[21] and weeps.[22] There are those who think that God being emotional threatens His Unchangeableness or Sovereignty. They propose God to be impassible or necessarily without emotion.

God's emotions might be viewed as further anthropomorphisms of God. The Bible is again revealing Him in ways we can comprehend. It is true that God's ways are often beyond our total grasping. "*Oh, the depth of the riches and wisdom and knowledge of God! How unsearchable are his judgments and how inscrutable his ways! For who has known the mind of the Lord, or who has been his counselor?*"[23]

It would seem a great loss to the personal and relational nature of God if we removed His emotions. Proposing God to be impassible in His nature may be motivated by a desire to exclude God from the changeableness or sin often associated with human emotional outbursts. The emotions of God are not at all like human passions, which often reveal human frailty. God uses His emotions to show the reality of His real feelings. They never effect any change in His Being or Sovereign position. We must look to Scripture to form our view of God's passions. They are on a much higher plane than our fallible human emotions.

God is never moved by His feelings to do anything that alters or changes any aspect of His total being. He is at all times fully

---

18 Zephaniah 3:17.

19 1 Kings 3:10.

20 Judges 2:18.

21 Psalm 78:40.

22 John 11:35.

23 Romans 11:33–34.

who the Bible reveals Him to be. Our limited minds are not able to reconcile some of the truths in Scripture concerning God. He is able to be emotional without any change in His being. All His attributes remain ever-present.

Who would desire a God removed from all feeling and emotion? I don't even know if it's possible to have an authentic relationship with someone who is void of passion. Love itself is both a volitional decision and an emotional expression. We are not only glad that God's Love is unwavering and eternal, but we are equally happy that His Love is emotional and passionate. God's emotions never violate His steadfastness and unchangeable nature.

God as He has revealed Himself to us is better than our reasoning or logic. He is one in being, first and foremost, yet is also of internal fellowship and offices of three persons, Father, Son, and Holy Spirit. God is pure Spirit, with no corporeal limits. He is totally unique and above our own experiences.

He is both Infinite and omnipresent. Our heavenly Lord is unchangeable and is thereby our source of great comfort and security. He is the only Self-Existent being and the source of everything that is. God is omniscient in all understanding and knowledge. His completely informed and perfect actions are tempered and timed by His unerring wisdom.

Being Personal, God is imminent and relational in our daily lives at all times. We have the incomparable opportunity to know Him intimately and in a personal and individual manner. God reminds us of both His immensity and His closeness. "*When I look at your heavens, the work of your fingers, the moon and the stars, which you have set in place, what is man that you are mindful of him, and the son of man that you care for him? Yet you have made him a little lower that the heavenly beings and crowned him with glory and honor. You have given him dominion over the works of your hands; you have put all things under his feet, all sheep and oxen, and also the beasts of the field, the birds of the heavens, and the fish of the sea, whatever passes along the paths of the seas. O LORD, our LORD, how majestic is your name in all the earth!"*[24] God really is good, and great, and perfect. He is so much better than any god we could imagine or reason out. We are always called to believe and honor God's revelation of Himself provided in the Bible. May we only serve and adore the one true God. We never expected Him to be only what we constructed. We always knew deep down that He was really better than we imagined Him to be. What a joy to glimpse some of the wonder and beauty of God.

---

24 Psalm 8:3–9.

Chapter 6

Can God be Any Better? Impossible

The sum of your word is truth, and every one of your righteous rules endures forever.

Psalm 119:160

Righteousness and justice are the foundation of your throne; steadfast love and faithfulness go before you.

Psalm 89:14

The Rock, his work is perfect, for all his ways are justice. A God of faithfulness and without iniquity, just and upright is he.

Deuteronomy 32:4

Sanctify them in the truth; your word is truth.

John 17:17

For you, O Lord, are good and forgiving, abounding in steadfast love to all who call upon you. Give ear, O Lord, to my prayer; listen to my plea for grace. In the day of my trouble I call upon you, for you answer me. There is none like you among the gods, O Lord, nor are there any works like yours. All the nations you have made shall come and worship before you, O Lord, and shall glorify your name. For you are great and do wondrous things; you alone are God.

Psalm 86:5–10

So that in the coming ages he might show the immeasurable riches of his grace in kindness toward us in Christ Jesus.

Ephesians 2:7

The Lord is good, a stronghold in the day of trouble; He knows those who take refuge in him.

Nahum 1:7

Who will not fear, O Lord, and glorify your name? For you alone are holy. All nations will come and worship you.

Revelation 15:4

Oh, how abundant is your goodness, which you have stored up for those who fear you.

Psalm 31:19

"Ascribe to the Lord the glory due his name; bring an offering and come before him! Worship the Lord in the splendor of holiness.

I Chronicles 16:29

The answer to our questioning chapter title is "No!" God could not be better. He is beyond our most superlative language and expressions. This book is an offer to consider the only one true God who is beyond comprehension. "We do not and cannot know the number of God's attributes. Being infinite as He is, God must possess countless attributes about which we know nothing beyond the fact that they will all be consistent with the ones about which we know."[1]

How can we even hope to consider adequately the moral attributes of God? In the area of morality, God's attributes are often referred to as His perfections or excellencies. Saying God is Holy is focusing on His perfection of separation and purity from all unrighteousness, sin, and evil.

God, who is perfectly Good, is extraordinarily worthy of our worship and praise. He is above all. He sets Himself apart from all else. Let us be filled with wonder and awe at who He is. God's attributes distinguish Him. They elevate Him above all others in value and virtue. God is fantastically worthy in His moral being in ways beyond our understanding.

---

1 Robert Reymond, *What is God?*, 7.

God's Moral Attributes

- **Truth:** Righteous, Illuminating, Honest, Zealous, Virtuous, Upright
- **Goodness:** For us, Favor, Hope, Benevolent, Giver, Kind, Encourager, Helper
- **Holiness:** Perfect, Unapproachable, Light, Incomparable, Blameless, Incorruptible, Pure, Blessedness, Sinlessness

Truth

Also called the veracity of God, in His Truth we find that God will never deceive us or mislead us. His intentions are always pure and righteous. God's motives are ever virtuous and upright. We can count on what He says and live by His instructions as correct and dependable. God's Word, as His inspired revelation, contains no error and is of the greatest value in our lives. God's rules in the physical world are so consistent they are called "laws." In the spiritual realm, His rules are just as dependable. Past United States President Theodore Roosevelt said, "A thorough understanding of the Bible is better than a college education." I could not agree more. A working knowledge of God's Word fits us for life better than any other academic studies or achievements.

God and His Truth are revealed more in His Word than in any other place. Even the best knowledge pertaining to the life and death of Jesus Christ is contained in its pages. "*Thomas said to him, 'Lord, we do not know where you are going. How can we know the way?' Jesus said to him, 'I am the way, and the truth, and the life. No one comes to the Father except through me.'*"[2] All we know of God's Son are bits and pieces outside of the Bible. In Scripture, considered to be "the mind of Christ," we are introduced to Jesus

---

2 John 14:5–6.

as the way of salvation. The Bible also introduces us to a perfect worldview and passion for God. *"But as for you, continue in what you have learned and have firmly believed, knowing from whom you learned it and how from childhood you have been acquainted with the sacred writings, which are able to make you wise for salvation through faith in Christ Jesus."*[3] *"In him you also, when you heard the word of truth, the gospel of your salvation, and believed in him, were sealed with the promised Holy Spirit, who is the guarantee of our inheritance until we acquire possession of it, to the praise of his glory."*[4]

When we have received the witness of the Holy Spirit in our spirits, we are confident of our salvation. John Wesley, the founder of Methodism, questioned his own salvation early in his ministry. His father, knowing of his uncertainty, gave counsel to John by directing him to the "inward witness" of the Spirit of God. Our hearts and minds know where we are in relation to God. God honestly declares all situations to us and we are in error whenever we think reality is different than His Truth.

God is not some cosmic prankster who treats us with actions and decisions full of intentional deception. It is because of whom He reveals Himself to be in the area of truthfulness that our confidence is rock solid. We can trust Him. He is honest and all His dealings are filled with integrity and uprightness. There is no misinformation in His revelation to us. His will for us is very clear. We are to be obedient and faithful in all our ways. Often our confusions are the results of our willfulness and sin.

> *We can trust Him. He is honest and all His dealings are filled with integrity and uprightness.*

3 2 Timothy 3:14–15.

4 Ephesians 1:13–14.

> *There is no misinformation in His revelation to us. His will for us is very clear.*

In His Truth, there is freedom and the best of life. In glorifying God through our lives we grow to enjoy Him now and forever. "*So Jesus said to the Jews who had believed him, 'If you abide in my word, you are truly my disciples, and you will know the truth, and the truth will set you free.'*"[5] "*There is therefore now no condemnation for those who are in Christ Jesus. For the law of the Spirit of life has set you free in Christ Jesus from the law of sin and death.*"[6] "*But now that you have been set free from sin and have become slaves of God, the fruit you get leads to sanctification and its end, eternal life. For the wages of sin is death, but the free gift of God is eternal life in Christ Jesus our Lord.*"[7] In His truthful plan, each of us has before us the path to freedom from the bondage of sin. Proper response to that plan leads to a marvelous and fulfilling life. Jesus said, "*The thief comes only to steal and kill and destroy. I came that they may have life and have it abundantly.*"[8] Our lives will be either in service to God or to sin. We must decide and act by God's grace to trust in Christ alone for our salvation. Our default condition is sinful independence and pride. This is common among all men. Sin will render us fit only for eternal punishment.

Let us always trust and act on God's Truth concerning reality. All truth is God's Truth. He indwells all honest and accurate facts with His presence. When you find any truth in any subject of life, God is there. May we all come to honor the reality of God's virtue of His Truth and righteousness in our lives and faith. God is always and ever true. We all believe in something. What do you

---

5 John 8:31–32.

6 Romans 8:1–2.

7 Romans 6:22–23.

8 John 10:10.

believe in? You can always believe in our safe and trustworthy relationship with God. He is Truth.

Goodness

The Goodness of God is my favorite attribute. All attributes of God are important. They are essential to His perfect and inexhaustible being. But I must confess, the attribute of His Goodness continually astounds and encourages me. Elemental to this excellence of God is that He is declared "for us." "*What then shall we say to these things? If God is for us, who can be against us? He who did not spare his own Son but gave him up for us all, how will he not also with him graciously give us all things?*"[9]

The Goodness of God gives us hope as we trust in our helper, encourager, and kind friend. "*For I know the plans I have for you, declares the LORD, plans for welfare and not for evil, to give you a future and a hope. Then you will call upon me and come and pray to me, and I will hear you. You will seek me and find me, when you seek me with all your heart.*"[10] God gives us so much hope as He covenants to be both with us and for us.

His benevolence and favor affect our outlook on life. As we wonder about God's intentions, we entertain concerns about life and its purpose. To have God Himself state that He has us on His heart, with a favorable disposition toward us, is better than any itemized list of assurances. This intention of God, "for our good," results in a life of joy, peace, and hope. With this assurance we can persevere and be steadfast in hardships and trials which assuredly will come. "*The LORD is good to all, and his mercy is over all that he has made.*"[11]

---

9 Romans 8:31–32.

10 Jeremiah 29:11–13.

11 Psalm 145:9.

> *This intention of God, "for our good," results in a life of joy, peace, and hope. With this assurance we can persevere and be steadfast in hardships and trials which assuredly will come.*

As we think and live in His newness of life, God's promise to us is dynamically transforming. "*Do not be conformed to this world, but be transformed by the renewal of your mind, that by testing you may discern what is the will of God, what is good and acceptable and perfect.*"[12] "*They shall speak of the might of your awesome deeds, and I will declare your greatness. They shall pour forth the fame of your abundant goodness and shall sing aloud of your righteousness.*"[13] Is not your heart and soul moved to excitement by this declaration of God's intentional Goodness toward you?

I hope you and I never move away from an ever-present awareness of God's Goodness toward us. This confidence causes us to trust God even when we find His ways scary or challenging. Toward the end of C. S. Lewis's *The Lion, the Witch, and the Wardrobe*, two characters were discussing Aslan, the lion representing Christ. Lucy asked Mr. Beaver, "Is He safe?" to which the beaver responded, "No, He is not safe, but He is good."[14] We realize that God's plans and demands on our lives may contain challenges and struggles. We can know for sure they are for our good and our best. This is all because of God's declaration that He is "for us" in His great Goodness.

---

12 Romans 12:2.

13 Psalm 145:6–7.

14 C. S. Lewis, *The Lion, the Witch, and the Wardrobe*, 86.

Holiness

The perfection of God's Holiness reminds us of His being set apart, pure, and perfect. We are immediately driven to awe and reverence by God's Holiness. We possess an innate sense of our broken and fallen condition. In awareness of our sinfulness, we address God with, "hallowed be thy name." We declare how wonderful it is to dwell above sin and this evil world. We know we frequently yield to our sinful and evil desires. Our imaginations seem to track toward compromised morality. "*The Lord saw that the wickedness of man was great in the earth, and that every intention of the thoughts of his heart was only evil continually.*"[15] We are consistently able to recognize right from wrong, even in our fallen state. This is because of our God-given moral compass, the conscience. However, through violations over time, even our innate moral awareness can become severely compromised and even appear lost.

My conversion to Christianity was not heroic or exciting. It was, however, unique. I had considered myself to be a true Christian for six years, until God used a special relationship to bring real saving grace to my heart. A true Christian was brought into my life who was, nevertheless, entertaining some unsound doctrine. I recognized these ideas as containing error even while a non-Christian myself. I found myself defending the integrity of Christianity, a faith I had not truly experienced in my own life. God used my defense of truth as the vehicle to bring into my head and heart the regenerating work of His Holy Spirit. When I had my spiritual eyes opened, I realized my need to place all my hope for salvation in the person and work of Jesus Christ alone. I had been defending a faith I did not actually have myself. God used a

---

15 Genesis 6:5.

true believer's error to bring a nonbeliever like me into His kingdom. God really can draw a straight line with a crooked stick. He graciously works to begin straightening the stick also.

What is impossible for God to do? In one sense, nothing. Yet because of God's integrity to His nature, there are many things He will never do. He cannot lie, or sin, or be unjust, or be deceptive. Ambrose, an early church Father remarked, "What is impossible to God? Not that which is difficult to His power, but that which is contrary to His nature." God never breaks the law of His own self. He always keeps His promises. He is completely guided by His consistent Holiness. God is absolutely untainted by sin. God's actions are always guided by His Holiness and will.

Our calling relative to God's Holiness is clear. *"It is written, 'You shall be holy, for I am holy.'"*[16] We only grow in holiness by the enabling work of God's Holy Spirit. He alone empowers us to separate from sinful patterns and actions. This ever-progressing process is called our sanctification. We will never be completely holy until we reach the finish line of our earthly life and are glorified with Him in heaven. Until then, we are called to allow God to strengthen us to do His will and overcome sin with an ever-increasing consistency. An illustration of the path of sanctification is found in Appendix 3. You might find it helpful in conceptualizing your own progress in conversion and sanctification. Where would you say you are on the path to personal holiness?

In the writing of Reverend Henry Scougal, his zeal in pursuing holiness led him to conclude; "There is no slavery so base as that whereby a man becomes a drudge to his own lusts, or any victory as that which is obtained over them. Never can that person be capable of anything that is noble and worthy, who is sunk

---

16 1 Peter 1:16.

in the gross and feculent pleasures of sense, or bewitched with the light and airy gratifications of fancy; but the religious soul is of a more sublime and divine temper; it knows it was made for higher things, and scorns to step aside one foot out of the ways of holiness for the obtaining of any of these."[17] Let us seek to stay clear of sin in this world and not to live carelessly close to it. Never allow yourself to take sin lightly. God does not. He hates sin to the extreme. Sin's consequences are terrible and costly. We should seek to be in the very center of God's intentions for our lives. In this way, we serve and honor Him alone.

Let us seek to stay clear of sin in this world and not to live carelessly close to it. Never allow yourself to take sin lightly. God does not. He hates sin to the extreme.

God's Holiness is one of His most worshipped and honored attributes. It is a key or foundational attribute around which His other attributes seem oriented. In our analogy of a diamond, the diamond-cutter marks and strikes the raw diamond to establish the initial surface. This becomes the face or table of the diamond. All the other polished facets are oriented to this first cut. God's Holiness is central to His being, somewhat like the face of a round-cut diamond.

17 Henry Scougal, *The Life of God in the Soul of Man*, 77.

The radiant light of God's Glory flows out of His Holiness. Maybe this is why Holiness is central to Isaiah's vision of God seated on His throne. Those surrounding the throne said, "*Holy, holy, holy is the* L*ORD* *of hosts; the whole earth is full of his glory!*"[18] In the book of Revelation, John relates a similar vision. As God is seated on His throne, angels continually declare, "*Holy, holy, holy, is the* L*ORD* *God Almighty, who was and is and is to come!*"[19]

The Bible reveals God in His crystal-clear perfection of Holiness. "*Who is like you, O* L*ORD*, *among the gods? Who is like you, majestic in holiness, awesome in glorious deeds, doing wonders?*"[20] God's Holiness makes Him both great and Good. His being is our standard of Righteousness. He has no shadow in His being, He dwells in unapproachable light.

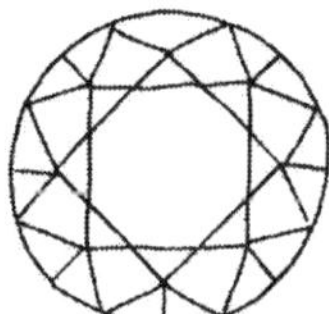 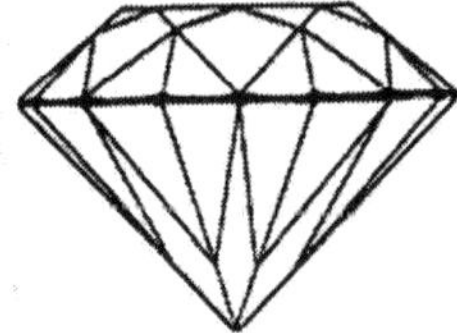 

There are many perspectives from which we may view a diamond. All diamonds are meant to be viewed by gazing upon their faces. Our best vision of God is probably one focused on His perfect Holiness.

God's Unchangeableness makes His Holiness incorruptible. May you and I always strive to be like Jesus in His example of a sinless earthly life. Our standard is set high. We are called forward to personal obedience and holiness. We walk by faith, aware

---

18 Isaiah 6:3.

19 Revelation 4:8.

20 Exodus 15:11.

we will never attain any righteousness on our own. We give glory to God by our Spirit-enabled successes in obedience to do His will and in personal piety. We must be intentional in being like God in His attribute of Holiness. He has called us to this. "*You shall be holy to me, for I the Lord am holy and have separated you from the peoples, that you should be mine.*"[21]

21 Leviticus 20:26.

Chapter 7

Could God Be Any More Real? Never

Beloved, let us love one another, for love is from God, and whoever loves has been born of God and knows God. Anyone who does not love does not know God, because God is love.

1 John 4:7–8

The reward for humility and fear of the Lord *is riches and honor and life.*

Proverbs 22:4

If we confess our sins, he is faithful and just to forgive us our sins and to cleanse us from all unrighteousness.

1 John 1:9

Say to them, As I live, declares the Lord God, *I have no pleasure in the death of the wicked, but that the wicked turn from his way and live; turn back, turn back from your evil ways, for why will you die, O house of Israel?*

Ezekiel 33:11

Whoever believes in the Son has eternal life; whoever does not obey the Son shall not see life, but the wrath of God remains on him.

John 3:36

And do not fear those who kill the body but cannot kill the soul. Rather fear him who can destroy both soul and body in hell.

Matthew 10:28

It is good to give thanks to the Lord, *to sing praises to your name, O Most High; to declare your steadfast love in the morning, and your faithfulness by night.*

Psalm 92:1–2

The steadfast love of the Lord *never ceases; his mercies never come to an end; they are new every morning; great is your faithfulness. "The* Lord *is my portion," says my soul, "therefore I will hope in him."*

Lamentations 3:22–24

But who are you, O man, to answer back to God? Will what is molded say to its molder, 'Why have you made me like this?' Has the potter no right over the clay, to make out of the same lump one vessel for honorable use and another for dishonorable use? What if God, desiring to show his wrath and to make known his power, has endured with much patience vessels of wrath prepared for destruction, in order to make known the riches of his glory for vessels of mercy, which he has prepared beforehand for his glory?

Romans 9:20–23

"I have loved you," says the Lord. But you say, "How have you loved us?" "Is not Esau Jacob's brother?" declares the Lord. "Yet I have loved Jacob, but Esau I have hated. I have laid waste his hill country and left his heritage to jackals of the desert."

Malachi 1:2–3

Behold, the storm of the Lord! Wrath has gone forth, a whirling tempest; it will burst upon the head of the wicked.

Jeremiah 23:19

In the remaining groupings of God's moral attributes, we will consider His Love, Wrath, and Faithfulness. God's Love, we commonly overemphasize. His Wrath, we routinely tend to ignore. God's Love may be our favorite attribute of God and His Wrath we find to be His most offensive. Nevertheless, in order to remain faithful to our determined commitment to rely distinctly on His witness of Himself in Scripture, we cannot choose from the perfections of God. They are wholly His testimony of Himself and do not come from the logic or wishes of man. God is completely Faithful to His revelation of Himself found in the Bible.

The Remaining Categories of God's Moral Attributes

- **Love:** Generous, Long-suffering, Patient, Merciful, Gracious, Sympathetic, Caring, Gentle, Grieving
- **Wrath:** Anger, Revenging, Unforgiving, Remembering, Fiery, Self-Control
- **Faithfulness:** Unfailing, Trustworthy, Dependable, Reliable, Steadfast, Loyal, Persistent

Love

We all rally to this attribute. Man finds great comfort in the fact of God's Love. It is absolutely and truly an essential and glorious attribute of God. Yet, we must issue a caveat. We are often guilty of overemphasizing the Love of God, and thereby trample the Holiness and Justness of God. D. A. Carson says, "Today we've sentimentalized God, turning Him into a Being controlled by the emotion of love."[1] We like a God whose Love renders Him incapable of judging sins. It is a false hope that God will overlook or forget our sin. This is simply not the clear testimony found in Scripture.

We like a God whose Love renders Him incapable of judging sins. It is a false hope that God will overlook or forget our sin. This is simply not the clear testimony found in Scripture.

As we consider sins we do not think we have committed, we are fine with God being Holy and just. But for those sins which we cannot deny our willful transgressions of, we foolishly hope that the Love of God will override His Holiness.

1 D. A. Carson, *The Difficult Doctrine of the Love of God*, 13.

We have already acknowledged that all of God's attributes are active at all times. We dare not fool ourselves and ignore those attributes of God that we hope to avoid. We fool ourselves if we think God's Love trumps or somehow negates His Holiness and justice.

Can you imagine a diamond with one or more facets just missing? It is impossible for an integral and revealed attribute of God to simply be absent. If it were, the whole of God would be denied and what we would have is not God at all. We are all guilty of this gross distortion of God's true being.

We are reminded of this truth in the modern parable of the blind men. Each man was allowed to touch an elephant, but only allowed to touch a different part of the elephant. One who touched the ear concluded an elephant was like a large leaf. Another who touched the trunk deduced an elephant was like a rope. Yet a third, who handled the leg, assumed the elephant to be like a tree. Man's orchestrated concepts of God routinely distort the truth about the one true God. We are prejudiced by our own self-interest and thereby misled to faulty conclusions concerning who God really is.

The very real attribute of God's Love must be viewed in light of His other attributes. What we seek is the best and most accurate understanding of God. This comes from His full revelation. God shows His highest Love for us when He grants us the opportunity to see His glorious person. To know Him is eternal life. Our goal must be to see God in proper balance. Only a diamond in its proper dimensions can be seen at its fullest beauty. A shallow or deep cutting allows the light to break out randomly. Perfect proportions are required for the light to react properly and reflect back on itself and emerge from the top of the diamond.

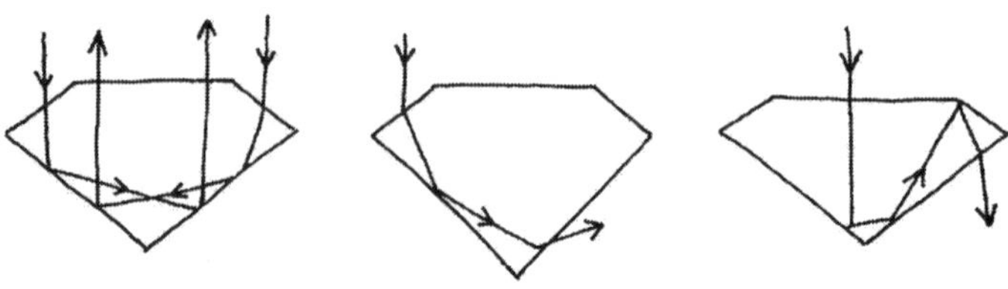

God's patience is a great blessing to us. If His patience did not exist, none would be reconciled to Him.

God's Love causes Him to be long-suffering and patient. In this way He gives us a chance for reconciliation with Him. God's patience is a great blessing to us. If His patience did not exist, none would be reconciled to Him. Reconciliation takes place in time. If His final judgment of our sins instantaneously followed their occurances, our hope would be lost. We would all perish. God's moral attribute of Love provides for the patience of God. We must praise God for His patience. "Long-suffering" is an oft-used term that can remind us of the pain our sin causes God.

Our sinfulness is an affront to God. God shows His great Love for us when He grieves for our state of sin-slavery and our separation from Him. He is affronted by our sin, but "we need not concern ourselves about God! He can take care of Himself."[2] Our sin actually hurts only us. It offends God, but it does Him no harm. The great mercy and grace of God are the double-barreled expression of God's Love.

Most of us have heard the hip-pocket definitions of mercy and grace. Mercy is not getting what you do deserve, while grace is getting what you don't deserve. These definitions are way too simple, really. God's mercy is sometimes called His "loyal love."

---

2 Bruce Ward, *God's Greater Glory*, 13.

God's people confessed, "*But they and our fathers acted presumptuously and stiffened their neck and did not obey your commandments. They refused to obey and were not mindful of the wonders that you performed among them, but they stiffened their neck and appointed a leader to return to their slavery in Egypt. But you are a God ready to forgive, gracious and merciful, slow to anger and abounding in steadfast love, and did not forsake them. Even when they had made for themselves a golden calf and said, 'This is your God who brought you up out of Egypt,' and had committed great blasphemies, you in your great mercies did not forsake them in the wilderness.*"[3] How overwhelming to remember God's merciful Love. In our very instant of stubborn rebellion and rebuffing of Him as the one true God, He shows Himself to be full of amazing mercy.

God's Grace is even more unexpected and undeserved. As we see God as He really is, we begin to see ourselves more clearly. "Man is an enigma whose solution can be found only in God."[4] Worldviews should answer three questions: how did things begin, why are they are presently imperfect, and how can things be made right? Notice that every worldview, no matter how diverse, admits things are messed up. God's grace and mercy are His answers to our broken world.

The Bible reveals that man is born into bondage. Man lives a completely sin-crushed life. The consequences of our state are debilitating. "*Jesus answered them, 'Most assuredly, I say to you, whoever commits sin is a slave of sin.*'"[5] "*For you say, I am rich, I have prospered, and I need nothing, not realizing that you are wretched, pitiable,*

3 Nehemiah 9:16–19.

4 Herman Bavinck, *The Doctrine of God*, 23.

5 John 8:34. NKJV

poor, blind, and naked."[6] *"And you were dead in the trespasses and sins in which you once walked, following the course of this world, following the prince of the power of the air, the spirit that is now at work in the sons of disobedience—among whom we all once lived in the passions of our flesh, carrying out the desires of the body and the mind, and were by nature children of wrath, like the rest of mankind."*[7]

The revelation of God through Scripture is that we are each shackled and crushed by sin. We are blinded, pitiable, and even spiritually dead. We are unable to improve our condition. Man has no hope of a meaningful future through his own efforts. Our brokenness and sin even ruin our communication and appeal to God. *"But your iniquities have made a separation between you and your God, and your sins have hidden his face from you so that he does not hear."*[8] We are choked by our flesh and rendered helpless and hopeless.

Now enters the loving grace of God! My senior pastor, Harry Reeder, always says his favorite phrase in the Bible is "But God." Continuing in the previous passage noted from the book of Ephesians, *"But God, being rich in mercy, because of the great love with which he loved us, even when we were dead in our trespasses, made us alive together with Christ—by grace you have been saved—and raised us up with him and seated us with him in the heavenly places in Christ Jesus, so that in the coming ages he might show the immeasurable riches of his grace in kindness toward us in Christ Jesus. For by grace you have been saved through faith. And this is not your own doing; it is the gift of God, not a result of works, so that no one may boast."*[9] This is big-time, great news. These verses encapsulate the essential message

---

6 Revelation 3:17.

7 Ephesians 2:1–3.

8 Isaiah 59:2.

9 Ephesians 2:4–9.

in the Bible concerning our reconciliation to God by God. This is called the gospel, and that means the good news.

> *God's loving grace and mercy are wonderful beyond description. In this great gospel, God has healed man's totally undone condition. He alone is able to provide the gift of reconciliation to Himself.*

We might ask why is this great gospel only called the good news. It is the greatest of all declarations. God's loving grace and mercy are wonderful beyond description. In this great gospel, God has healed man's totally undone condition. He alone is able to provide the gift of reconciliation to Himself. To God be all the Glory for this great thing He has done. Paul later reminds us, "*So that no human being might boast in the presence of God. And because of him you are in Christ Jesus, who became to us wisdom from God, righteousness and sanctification and redemption, so that, as it is written, 'Let the one who boasts, boast in the LORD.*'"[10]

As we see God's Sovereign good pleasure and will, we stand in awe of the generous, gentle, long-suffering, caring, merciful, and gracious Love of God. God is much better than we could ever imagine. His works are beyond our most elaborate hope. God alone is worthy of all praise. None others even compare.

Wrath

I am now compelled to follow meditating on the amazing Love of God with an equal consideration of His awful Wrath. This is God's clear revelation of Himself. His Wrath is an attribute we would prefer to ignore but cannot. The Wrath of God, along with His fiery anger, are taught in Scripture much more than are His

---

10 1 Corinthians 1:29–31.

Love, grace, and mercy combined. I make no apology for soberly considering the Wrath of God. A concordance will render literally hundreds of references to God's Wrath and anger. These are found throughout the Bible. God reveals Himself as one who remembers and is unforgiving of sin. God is greatly offended by sin. Because of His very being, He can have no fellowship with sin. "*Do not be unequally yoked with unbelievers. For what partnership has righteousness with lawlessness? Or what fellowship has light with darkness?*"[11]

God holds us thoroughly accountable for our sin. He only is the righteous revenger. He executes all judgment with complete self-control. God condemns to destruction with no passion and in perfect harmony with all His other attributes. His incorruptible Holiness and righteousness never dwell in union with sin. God can have no fellowship with many things, but they are all covered by the one word: "sin."

Sin is always and only rebellion against God. Scripture requires that true knowledge of God has the fear of God as its essential foundation. "*The fear of the Lord is the beginning of knowledge; fools despise wisdom and instruction.*"[12] "*The way of a fool is right in his own eyes, but a wise man listens to advice.*"[13] "*Fear God and give him glory, because the hour of his judgment has come, and worship him who made heaven and earth, the sea and the springs of water.*"[14]

Even with God's great Love, He has not chosen to reconcile every individual to Himself. It appears that those He chooses to redeem are less than half of all men. This is a hard but true saying. It can give false security to say that God loves sinners while hating

11 2 Corinthians 6:14.

12 Proverbs1:7.

13 Proverbs 12:15.

14 Revelation 14:7.

their sin. Any statement that causes the conscience to feel better about itself than it should is dangerous, as it provides a false sense of peace in sin. Outside of a restored relationship with God through His Son, you are in a state of rank rebellion.

Sinners need to hear of the true Holiness and exacting righteousness of God. Sin is enabled by our ignorance of God's greatness. God must be firmly established in His Holy justice and terrible Wrath. God has chosen some whom He will bring to Himself. He has not chosen others. We must accept His right and prerogative to do as He wills. We know He does all for His Glory. His actions are according to His perfect plan and His good pleasure. God is perfectly just and Righteous in these actions. Our lack of full understanding is expected. His ways are higher than our comprehension. The wisdom and plan of God is inscrutable by man. It is amazing that the one true God reconciled many to a restored fellowship as His adopted children.

The fear of God is an extreme reverence and respect for God. It is the proper acknowledging of who He is. He is God, after all. The first sin of man found in the Bible was man's usurpation of God's authority and his doubting of God's truthfulness and motives. Adam and Eve both reasoned they could do better than to trust God. God will not tolerate sinful rebellion. He is an unforgiving rememberer. This is consistent with His separation from all sin. "A lot of us want God. But on our terms. And God won't play."[15] Once again, God is God, and we are not. His ways are regularly beyond our understanding.

God's divine attributes are those things essential to God. To remove any of them would distort and destroy an accurate understanding of God. "The perfections of God, therefore, are

---

15 Peter Lewis, *The Message of the Living God*, 83.

attributes without which He would cease to be God."[16] God's hatred of sin mirrors His Holiness, which stirs Him to action. We must acknowledge His detestation of sin. Sin's consequences are devastatingly severe. God has declared, *"See now that I, even I, am he, and there is no god beside me; I kill and I make alive; I wound and I heal; and there is none that can deliver out of my hand. For I lift up my hand to heaven and swear, As I live forever, if I sharpen my flashing sword and my hand takes hold on judgment, I will take vengeance on my adversaries and will repay those who hate me."*[17] Make no mistake; sin is hatred toward God.

God's hatred of sin mirrors His Holiness, which stirs Him to action. We must acknowledge His detestation of sin. Sin's consequences are devastatingly severe.

God is just and will render reward for both righteousness and sinfulness. We all were insurrectionists against God's righteous rule. As judge and governor, He has a right to Wrath. His Wrath is not a vindictive emotion but a vindication of His Sovereign role and His Holy being. What God does defines righteousness.

God's justice is witnessed as He condemns to hell those who die impenitent in their sin. "The 'eternal bifurcation' of the saved and the unsaved is found in more than fifty passages of Scripture."[18] Hell is discussed using vivid images that are scary and paradoxical. Burning fire and total darkness seem irreconcilable. Hell is a real place of eternal torment and anguish. It is an extreme penalty eternally paid for an extreme wrong done against the extreme Holiness

16 Charles Hodge, *Systematic Theology*, Vol. 1, 369.

17 Deuteronomy 32:39–41.

18 Robert Reymond, *What is God?*, 208.

of the God of the universe. God is completely Righteous in executing this just and severe penalty for sin.

When my cousin and I were young boys, we had nothing to play with one hot summer day. We asked our Grandpa Friday if he would "forward" our Christmas presents and buy us inexpensive inflated balls. We thought we had nothing to lose. He would surely forget our agreement by next Christmas. Even if he remembered, certainly he would still choose to bless us with Christmas presents anyway. We were very cute boys.

After the deal was struck, we burst the balls in hours. Next Christmas, when presents were opened, we asked Grandpa about our presents from him. He reminded us of our summer agreement. We got nothing. It was a great lesson in the integrity he lived by. God is never forgetful of our sin. He is not mocked by our shrewdness and conniving ways. We will be held accountable for our sin. We must have a righteous savior. We have no other hope. God is just at all times. The wages for our sins will be paid when the record books are balanced in the end.

God's demand for His full acknowledgement as the one and only true God is reasonable and right. Our desire to make God who we would have Him to be, for our own selfish interests, offends Him more than we can imagine. There is no blemish on the character of God. "How could He who is infinitely holy disregard sin and refuse to manifest His 'severity' toward it? The very nature of God makes hell as real a necessity, as imperatively and eternally requisite, as heaven is."[19] Even our present broken world reveals God's Glory. The payment for sin should remind us of its hideousness. We must see God in His full splendor and might. In this we realize the wonder of salvation and its great victory.

---

19 A. W. Pink, *The Attributes of God*, 83.

God is mysterious in His ways. They are beyond our explanation. He requires our reconciliation to come through the atoning payment made by Jesus's death. God holds those who reject Jesus accountable for their sins, and they suffer great loss. We should be silent when God is silent. Why He has perfectly and wisely ordered things to be this way we cannot comprehend in our present state. It is a reality hard for us to accept. Jesus said, "*But I will warn you whom to fear: fear him who, after he has killed, has authority to cast into hell. Yes, I tell you, fear him!*"[20] Jesus is speaking of God.

Are we to live in constant dread and despair? This is absolutely not God's intention. He desires that we respond to His Holiness and our sinfulness by being reconciled to Him through the blood of Jesus. We require a righteousness we cannot attain by our own efforts. We are in a very tight spot. We are called by God to acknowledge our condemning sin. We must turn to Him alone for His free gift of salvation. I might add: free to us, but supremely costly to God. "*All we like sheep have gone astray; we have turned—every one—to his own way; and the Lord has laid on him the iniquity of us all.*"[21] Simply put, God is fair when He looks upon us in the sin of Adam, our truly accurate representative. But God is extremely gracious when He looks upon us in the Righteousness of Christ.

The Bible presents us with a gospel that is so much better than anything we could have conceived. We have the gift of right standing and reconciliation with God, provided by the unbelievable sacrifice of Jesus, God Himself. "*Greater love has no one than this, that someone lay down his life for his friends.*"[22] Even beyond our great redemption, we now live as God's beloved. He is known to

---

20 Luke 12:5.

21 Isaiah 53:6.

22 John 15:13.

us like never before. "*For our sake he made him to be sin who knew no sin, so that in him we might become the righteousness of God.*"[23]

> *God has done all the required work for us.*
> *All of our reconciliation with Him is of Him.*
> *His Love has caused His real Wrath to be satisfied.*

God has done all the required work for us. He alone is to be praised for our salvation. All of our reconciliation with Him is of Him. Here is the basis of our assurance of salvation. Here is our removal of fear and condemnation. His Love has caused His real Wrath to be satisfied "*But God shows his love for us in that while we were still sinners, Christ died for us. Since, therefore, we have now been justified by his blood, much more shall we be saved by him from the wrath of God. For if while we were enemies we were reconciled to God by the death of his Son, much more, now that we are reconciled, shall we be saved by his life. More than that, we also rejoice in God through our* Lord *Jesus Christ, through whom we have now received reconciliation.*"[24]

Perfect Love casts out all our fears. "*So we have come to know and to believe the love that God has for us. God is love, and whoever abides in love abides in God, and God abides in him. By this is love perfected with us, so that we may have confidence for the day of judgment, because as he is so also are we in this world. There is no fear in love, but perfect love casts out fear. For fear has to do with punishment, and whoever fears has not been perfected in love.*"[25] God's great Love removes dread from the lives of those who believe. To those in

---

23 2 Corinthians 5:21.

24 Romans 5:8–11.

25 I John 4:16–18.

their sin, dread of judgment may well be used by God to drive them to Himself. In this way, there is actually mercy and compassion in proclaiming the Wrath of God. Messages including fire and brimstone can be preached in love and from a heart of concern. The fear of God has always been for His Glory and for our good. Let us never forget that God is God. He alone established the way things are. Man's opinions are biased and have no power to change the way things really are.

Faithfulness

God's Faithfulness means God has integrity and is influenced by nothing outside of Himself. When God determines something, nothing will change His intentions. You are guaranteed that He will never do anything inconsistent with Himself. This attribute of God confirms that His promises are trustworthy. Our faith could not be placed in anything more dependable than the character of God. There is a great comfort and confidence in knowing He will never disappoint us.

When our lives have unexplainable hardships and terrible things occur, we find great solace in the Faithfulness of God. He is always consistent. He is never unreliable. "*But this I call to mind, and therefore I have hope: The steadfast love of the Lord never ceases; his mercies never come to an end; they are new every morning; great is your faithfulness.*"[26] God is always and completely trustworthy. He is ever-persistent and dependable. This knowledge of God does many things for us.

In the Faithfulness of God, we find hope.
We look to God instinctively.

26 Lamentations 3:21–23.

In the Faithfulness of God, we find hope. When things get tough, consequences and events become magnified in their importance. We look to God instinctively. When God proves Himself to be Faithful and able, we are affected profoundly. Our hearts are inclined to follow Him in a new way. He puts hardships in our lives for our good. They are also for His Glory. He proves Himself Faithful in provisions and protections we therein experience.

As God is Faithful, we realize He is always truthful. When He says something, we can depend on it. A profound trust in Him grows. This we could find in no other way. God's attribute of Faithfulness is key to our relationship with Him. We have faith to live as He directs. We know it is for our good. He will make good on all of His promises.

God is always consistent with all of His attributes. He is always Faithful to His revelation of Himself in the Bible. All of His acts and words are in perfect harmony with who He is. God has perfect integrity. God is dependable all of the time. *"God is not a man, that he should lie, or a son of man, that he should change his mind. Has he said, and will he not do it? Or has he spoken, and will he not fulfill it?"*[27] When God says anything, you can count on it with your life.

God is completely Trustworthy. We know His Word never fails. *"For as the rain and the snow come down from heaven and do not return there but water the earth, making it bring forth and sprout, giving seed to the sower and bread to the eater, so shall my word be that goes out from my mouth; it shall not return to me empty, but it shall accomplish that which I purpose, and shall succeed in the thing for which I sent it."*[28] God never breaks His covenants or promises.

---

27 Numbers 23:19.

28 Isaiah 55:10–11.

A critical area in which God's Faithfulness is important is His promise to help us when we are tempted. We read in His Word a great promise, "*No temptation has overtaken you that is not common to man. God is faithful, and he will not let you be tempted beyond your ability, but with the temptation he will also provide the way of escape, that you may be able to endure it.*"[29] Even when we are not faithful to God in our actions or words, He is always Faithful to Himself, never being anything toward us but loyal and steadfast. "*The saying is trustworthy, for: If we have died with him, we will also live with him; if we endure, we will also reign with him; if we deny him, he also will deny us; if we are faithless, he remains faithful—for he cannot deny himself.*"[30]

Why would we ever place our trust for the future in anything other than God and the promises of His Word? "*He who calls you is faithful; he will surely do it.*"[31] "*He remembers his covenant forever, the word that he commanded, for a thousand generations.*"[32] God is never distracted by anything other than Himself. He is always all Himself at all times. There is no single part of God you will ever see in action alone. He only acts in His whole being. He is always totally consistent and Faithful to Himself. A. W. Pink said, "How refreshing, then, how unspeakably blessed, to lift our eyes above this scene of ruin, and behold One who is faithful, faithful in all things, faithful at all times."[33] It is to the great honor and praise of God's character that we can trust Him through times of difficulty.

---

29 I Corinthians 10:13.

30 II Timothy 2:11–13.

31 I Thessalonians 5:24.

32 Psalm 105:8.

33 A. W. Pink, *The Attributes of God*, 52.

> *There is no single part of God you will ever see in action alone. He only acts in His whole being. He is always totally consistent and Faithful to Himself.*

These moral attributes of God have placed before our eyes His wonderful and awe-inspiring person. God is Holy. In this attribute, we realize more than ever that He is distinct and excellent. God is morally above all, and He is the standard of purity and Righteousness. His Goodness causes us to live with the realization that we are the apple His eye. God's great Love toward us is seen in the combination of His grace and mercy. In these we experience God as the Son and are amazed at His sacrifice to reconcile us to Himself. God's Wrath is an important and meaningful perfection in His great character. We must soberly respond to the reality of His extreme hatred of all sin. His costly provision for our reconciliation is ever before us.

God's Faithfulness to us is eternal and everlasting. He will always be true to His Word and Himself. Let us seek to be like God. May we always respect Him for who He is. We must remember that He alone is God, often in ways we can only partially grasp. We live by a reassured faith because our confidence is in the very real God. We know God is worthy. He has proven Himself beyond any and all doubt.

Chapter 8

God is Always Above Us! We Live Under His Rule.

Whatever the Lord *pleases, he does, in heaven and on earth, in the seas and all deeps.... Your name, O* Lord*, endures forever, your renown, O* Lord*, throughout all ages.*

Psalm 135:6, 13

For I am God, and there is no other; I am God, and there is none like me, declaring the end from the beginning and from ancient times things not yet done, saying, "My counsel shall stand, and I will accomplish all my purpose."

Isaiah 46:9–10

Many are the plans in the mind of a man, but it is the purpose of the Lord *that will stand.*

Proverbs 19:21

"See now that I, even I, am he, and there is no god beside me; I kill and I make alive; I wound and I heal; and there is none that can deliver out of my hand."

DEUTERONOMY 32:39

For his dominion is an everlasting dominion, and his kingdom endures from generation to generation; all the inhabitants of the earth are accounted as nothing, and he does according to his will among the host of heaven and among the inhabitants of the earth; and none can stay his hand or say to him, "What have you done?"

DANIEL 4:34–35

For my thoughts are not your thoughts, neither are your ways my ways, declares the LORD. *For as the heavens are higher than the earth, so are my ways higher than your ways and my thoughts than your thoughts.*

ISAIAH 55:8–9

He who is the blessed and only Sovereign, the King of kings and LORD *of lords, who alone has immortality, who dwells in unapproachable light, whom no one has ever seen or can see. To him be honor and eternal dominion. Amen.*

1 TIMOTHY 6:15-16

Masters, do the same to them, and stop your threatening, knowing that he who is both their Master and yours is in heaven, and that there is no partiality with him.

EPHESIANS 6:9

Have you not known? Have you not heard? The Lord *is the everlasting God, the Creator of the ends of the earth.*

Isaiah 40:28

Thus says the Lord, *the King of Israel and his Redeemer, the* Lord *of hosts: "I am the first and I am the last; besides me there is no god. Who is like me? Let him proclaim it. Let him declare and set it before me, since I appointed an ancient people. Let them declare what is to come, and what will happen. Fear not, nor be afraid; have I not told you from of old and declared it? And you are my witnesses! Is there a God besides me? There is no Rock; I know not any."*

Isaiah 44:6–8

The many ways that God relates to us give us insight into our proper response to Him. I have grouped the predominant relationships into a broad arbitrary category, called God's positional attributes. These six are the ones most portrayed in Scripture, and they give definition to God's role or station in association with mankind. There are many others. We are called buildings, and He is the builder. We are referred to as soldiers, with Him as our commander. We are also considered athletes, and He determines the outcome of our participation and our awards. The major positional ways in which God relates to us are Sovereign, Master, Creator, Judge, Redeemer, and Father. In these six relational attributes, we find our most prominent associations to the one and only true God of the Bible.

God's Positional Attributes

- **Sovereign:** Almighty, Mighty, Divine, King, Omnipotent, Great, Supreme, Ruler, Dominion, Purposeful, Providence, Lofty, Exalted, Strong Tower, Fortress, Rock
- **Creator:** Word, Life, Physician, Healer, Organizer, Orderer
- **Master:** Lord, Owner, Manager, Teacher, Guide, Counselor, Instructor

Sovereign

The Sovereignty of God is an important and encompassing attribute. It is a core positional distinctive in any balanced vision of God. In this role we see God's almighty divinity and great dominion. His infinite power is called His omnipotence. Although God can do all things, He is ever consistent with His own nature. God's integrity determines that which He will do and that which He will not do. God will never cause anything to come to pass that violates His own being. God, although all-powerful, cannot—rather *will* not—do anything to compromise His perfect self. The only thing that limits God is Himself. God always acts with integrity and simplicity. All He does emanates from who He is and is always consistent with all He is.

> *Although God can do all things, He is ever consistent with His own nature. God's integrity determines that which He will do and that which He will not do.*

God is the only lofty king and exalted ruler. He consistently executes His purpose, plan, and providential authority. God is fixed as a strong tower and rock. God is portrayed in His exalted position as king of kings and lord of lords. "*The Lord is king forever and ever."*[1] *"But the* Lord *is the true God; he is the living God and the everlasting King. At his wrath the earth quakes, and the nations cannot endure his Indignation."*[2] *"To the King of the ages, immortal, invisible, the only God, be honor and glory forever and ever."*[3] *"He who is the blessed and only Sovereign, the King of kings and* Lord *of lords, who alone has immortality, who dwells in unapproachable light, whom no one has ever seen or can see. To him be honor and eternal dominion. Amen."*[4]

God is always over all things. He rules with an arm that is never shortened. A.W. Pink felt Sovereignty most completely captured the position of the whole being of God best. Each of us will be greatly served in our relationship to God if we never lose constant awareness of His Sovereignty. *"Our God is in the heavens; he does all that he pleases."*[5] As the powerful King Nebuchadnezzar finally came to his senses, Scripture records his declaration, *"I blessed the Most High, and praised and honored him who lives forever, for his dominion is an everlasting dominion, and his kingdom endures from generation to generation; all the inhabitants of the earth are accounted as nothing, and he does according to his will among the host of heaven and among the inhabitants of the earth; and none can stay his hand or say to him, 'What have you done?'"*[6]

God is the supreme ruler of all. He does what He pleases and is never influenced by anything outside of Himself. His divine will is the most free will. By alone serving as the fountain of His own being, God is alone independent. *"For I know that the* Lord *is*

---

1 Psalm 10:16.

2 Jeremiah 10:10.

3 1 Timothy 1:17.

4 1 Timothy 6:15–16.

5 Psalm 115:3.

6 Daniel 4:34–35.

great, and that our Lord is above all gods. Whatever the Lord pleases, he does, in heaven and on earth, in the seas and all deeps.... Your name, O Lord, endures forever, your renown, O Lord, throughout all ages."[7]

In our world today, too much credit is given to chance or luck. Chance and luck are not actual entities. Both of them are ideas or concepts with no physical presence. Chance is therefore not a causative agent. It cannot produce any effect. This error has distorted our accurate understanding of reality. The hope of evolutionary theory rests on the faulty premise that chance plus an enormous amount of time caused everything that is to come to be. Evolution is an impossible premise and exists only in the unchallenged imagination of man.

Modern man has fulfilled the Scripture, which says, *"For what can be known about God is plain to them, because God has shown it to them. For his invisible attributes, namely, his eternal power and divine nature, have been clearly perceived, ever since the creation of the world, in the things that have been made. So they are without excuse. For although they knew God, they did not honor him as God or give thanks to him, but they became futile in their thinking, and their foolish hearts were darkened. Claiming to be wise, they became fools."*[8] In math we learned that nothing multiplied by a whole lot was still nothing. Many today have been duped by false reasoning in this deceptive shell game. There is no pea under the cup, no matter how many cups there are. Chance is nothing beyond an idea. It has never caused anything to come to be.

Paying my way through college caused me to work with multiple surveying crews. Here I learned of the elusive "fozziduece" as the smallest thing in the universe. I was a college student.

---

7 Psalm 135:5–6, 13.

8 Romans 1:19–22.

I was not going to fall for some whimsy from a bunch of older men. When I questioned them about recent discoveries in quantum physics, they further explained to me that the fozziduece always dynamically maintains its position as the smallest particle. It does this by becoming smaller when any new theoretically smaller particle is proposed. Whatever the smallest thing is, we can rest assured God already directs its every movement. The theory of evolution and the concept of the fozziduece are both squarely in category of absurd chimera.

Nothing, no matter how infinitesimally small or insignificant, has ever occurred outside of God's rule and reign. No event has ever occurred without first being initiated by God's Sovereign hand. It should comfort us to know that all things, even the seemingly worst of things, occur within God's supervision.

> *God clearly states in His self-revelation that he is working his perfect plan, which has been in place from all eternity past.*

It has been said that we may not know what the future holds, but we do know who holds the future. God clearly states in His self-revelation that he is working his perfect plan, which has been in place from all eternity past. "*In him we have redemption through his blood, the forgiveness of our trespasses, according to the riches of his grace, which he lavished upon us, in all wisdom and insight making known to us the mystery of his will, according to his purpose, which he set forth in Christ as a plan for the fullness of time, to unite all things in him, things in heaven and things on earth. In him we have obtained an inheritance, having been predestined according to the purpose of him who works all things according to the counsel of his will.*"[9]

---

9 Ephesians 1:7–11.

All of God's actions are true to His character and being. He only does that which is consistent with His wisdom, will, and good pleasure. Yet, this does not allow us to conclusively predict all of His actions. His decrees and plans are generally beyond our comprehension or basic understanding. *"For my thoughts are not your thoughts, neither are your ways my ways, declares the LORD. For as the heavens are higher than the earth, so are my ways higher than your ways and my thoughts than your thoughts. For as the rain and the snow come down from heaven and do not return there but water the earth, making it bring forth and sprout, giving seed to the sower and bread to the eater, so shall my word be that goes out from my mouth; it shall not return to me empty, but it shall accomplish that which I purpose, and shall succeed in the thing for which I sent it."*[10] All of life is under the Sovereign plan and control of God.

He alone rules over all eternity. Those things that we could never expect or comprehend are all in His inclusive reign and rule. God has a big plan. It is only seen by Him. It is understandably beyond our understanding. We will grow less ignorant of His plan as we progressively learn of Him both now and into all eternity. Instead of doubting God's total control when we experience devastating events, we can be comforted knowing we can trust those events are within God's perfect plan and permission. *"And we know that for those who love God all things work together for good, for those who are called according to his purpose."*[11]

All things are not good in this life. Yet, in God's overarching plan, all things believers experience are knit together for their good. God superintends the laws of life to bless His own with consequences for their benefit. Much of this we cannot

---

10 Isaiah 55:8–11.

11 Romans 8:28.

understand. God is Infinite in His knowledge, and we are so limited. One of my favorite truisms is often credited to the actor and Hollywood cowboy, John Wayne. He states, "Life is hard. It's harder when you're stupid." We must realize the devastating consequences of our costly free will. God has allowed our real moral choices to mess up things terribly. Man denies responsibility for his sin and its consequences. We always default to shift blame for the results of our sinful action onto others.

Within God's overarching Sovereignty, He has granted us real freedom. Our actions have real consequences. They are all within the ever-active control of God. Man regularly over- or understates the concept of free will. We should not get too excited about our free will. One of our earliest free acts was sinful and resulted in the devastating consequences of the curse and fall. God gave only one prohibition in the garden. Within a short time, Adam entertained temptation and that resulted in sin. Adam was our perfect representative. He distrusted God. His disobedience was rebellion and a dethroning hatred of God as Sovereign.

Notice Adam's response when questioned by God concerning his sin. Even in Adam's admission of sin, he tries to shift causal responsibility to his wife and even back to God Himself. In the area of freedom, we hope to avoid all responsibility or consequences. This is simply not the way things are. We must we never doubt God, even when we don't understand Him. The consequences of our distrust are real and hurtful.

We will ultimately find ourselves in a better place when we go where God directs. The short-term may be very tough. Sometimes things may seem unreasonable. God will be with us as we endure these hardships. God puts us in hard spots for reasons He alone knows. He never leaves our side. He always surrounds His children with His presence and protection.

The founder of the Navigators, Dawson Trotman, often said, "God gave you a lot of leading when He gave you a brain." We should be wise and prudent in the way we live. Events proceed often by the predictable patterns of cause and effect. We correctly plan and act in ways purposing to have good results. We view this natural order of things as God's hand embedded in the known laws of nature. When God tips His Sovereign hand, through some obviously orchestrated or amazingly unique series of events, we say this was God's providence. When the laws of nature are physically altered, we call this a miracle of God. God is intimately and always involved in every aspect of His creation, whether routine, providential, or miraculous. He never sleeps at the switch, and His arm is never shortened. He is perfectly attentive and able.

It is very helpful to properly understand God's will. His will is unique and complex, as we would expect. God clearly has a decretive Sovereign will distinctly revealed in the Bible. This is His will alone, and it is fully understood only by Himself. It is beyond our understanding. The Bible calls this the decrees or oracles of God. We are incapable of comprehending how or why God ordains everything to be the way it is. He controls every single thing. This is His predetermined will, which causes all things to happen just as He intended from all eternity.

We are incapable of comprehending how or why God ordains everything to be the way it is.

There is also a preceptive or prescribed aspect of God's will. This is His will known to man in different degrees. It is written on the conscience of all men of all times. It is also revealed in much greater detail in God's inspired words of Scripture. This is His moral law, the will of God that man routinely violates. This will of God is thwarted within limits and with consequences that God alone prescribes. God also blesses man's obedience to His prescribed will. This is the will of God, which we routinely know but sinfully violate.

Finally, God also has a will of disposition. In His will are things both pleasing and displeasing to Him. God delights in His Holiness and righteousness. He emphatically states that He dislikes the death of the wicked.[12] God expresses Himself in this way to make clear that He is not gleeful or vindictive toward those who bear the aweful consequences of His intentional and perfect judgment. God is consistent in His integrity of character to do things He says He finds no joy in. We must never forget that in these things, God is internally upright and undivided.

When seeking to know God's will, we should remember our obligation to faithful and obedient action. God's decretive will contains a mystery. His secret counsel is concealed. As we walk by faith, obedient to His known, perceptive will, we glorify Him best. We need to be feasting on God's Word with the highest regard and intention of obedience. God guides us as we seek to do the revealed will of God found in His Word. Let us be obedient and proceed by faith to do the next right thing. In this attitude and action, God's will is an exciting adventure and a confirmation in our lives. God's way of living is the best way, and the rewards are unbelievable.

Let us be obedient and proceed by faith to do the next right thing. In this attitude and action, God's will is an exciting adventure and a confirmation in our lives.

It is impossible to discuss the far-reaching and deeper ramifications of God's Sovereignty in such a limited space. A.W. Pink's

12 Ezekiel 18:23; 33:11.

book, *The Sovereignty of God* is a wonderful start toward further considerations in this area. God's Sovereignty outpaces our intellectual limits, and we can only wonder at the way things are. Why does evil and sin exist? Why is God sometimes silent or seem to be absent? We know God is always present. We are to live by faith and obedience. Obedience requires our right response to things that are revealed. They tend to make some sense. Faith requires our right response to things that are more hidden. These are often harder to understand. Will you obey without understanding? Our best response is always to trust in God. It is the ultimate nonsensical contradiction to ever say "No, Lord."

He alone is worthy of our uninterrupted and completely faithful obedience. We can trust our Sovereign God who causes and upholds all things. As is proclaimed in the childhood song, He does really "have the whole world in His hands." Our hope and peace in this world are bolstered by this great truth. In our anxiety and fretfulness we deny God's Sovereignty and impugn His great character. There are only two paths before us: faith or fear.

Things occur exactly as God wills them in their extent and timing. Wisdom is manifested in things done in His perfect way and in His proper time. Time does not limit God's perspective. *"I am God, and there is no other; I am God, and there is none like me, declaring the end from the beginning and from ancient times things not yet done, saying, 'My counsel shall stand, and I will accomplish all my purpose,' calling a bird of prey from the east, the man of my counsel from a far country. I have spoken, and I will bring it to pass; I have purposed, and I will do it."*[13]

God allows this fallen world to exist for purposes beyond our full understanding. We find life challenging when faith is

---

13 Isaiah 46:9–11.

required. Here is where we say with Job, "*I know that you can do all things, and that no purpose of yours can be thwarted. 'Who is this that hides counsel without knowledge?' Therefore I have uttered what I did not understand, things too wonderful for me, which I did not know.*"[14] The Sovereignty of God causes both our faithful obedience and our security. All things are in His plan and purpose, and that is very comforting news. God is worthy of our unconditional trust because He has proven Himself to be so.

Creator

Nothing so establishes God's position and power as His relational attribute of being the Creator of everything. Everything came into being exclusively because of His mighty hand. The Bible tells us this from the very first verse: "*In the beginning, God created the heavens and the earth.*"[15] God did not labor in creating the entire universe. He spoke things into existence from nothing. Eight times in the first chapter of the creation account we read, "and God said," followed by an immediate presence of new material reality. Life itself was initiated by His breath, which is His word of power.

The first thirty-four verses of the Bible tell us of God's creation of everything from nothing. He spoke into existence all space, all matter and even time. No verses in Scripture establish God's power so significantly. How should we interpret these creation verses? Should we determine them to be history, poetry, or symbolic mythology? Many in our modern world today choose an accommodation to the evolutionary perspective of origins, willfully misinterpreting God's clear revelation. The skepticism of man gives genesis to man's faulty interpretation of the past.

---

14 Job 42:2–3.

15 Genesis 1:1.

Everything we know from before approximately 2,500 BC, is based on man's presumptive speculation or the testimony of Scripture. Not a single secular written record is available. Archeological artifacts require interpretation. None come with dates on them. So who are we going to trust concerning our view of the past and the issue of when time began? If Scripture is interpreted to conform to the ideas of man, a distortion of God's clear revelation is required. Is the Bible sufficient to yield a correct view of the past? Is the Bible too primitive to reveal truth? To what limited degree is insight from the scientific method able inform our understanding concerning the past? Should we ignore God's eyewitness account of how everything began?

So who are we going to trust concerning our view of the past and the issue of when time began? If Scripture is interpreted to conform to the ideas of man, a distortion of God's clear revelation is required.

This choice is not between science or faith, nor is it between fact or belief. It is between two interpretations of the same information. Should the consensus of "historical science," dealing with results not repeatedly observable or testable, be taken as authoritative over God's testimony in Scripture? John MacArthur says it best. "I am convinced the correct interpretation of Genesis chapter 1 through 3 is the one that comes naturally from a straightforward reading of the text. It teaches us that the universe is relatively young, albeit with an appearance of age and maturity—and that all of creation was accomplished in the span of six literal days."[16] This is the understanding shared by St. Augustine, Martin Luther, John Calvin, and Charles Spurgeon, among many others.

16 John MacArthur, *Think Biblically!*, 61.

Do we take God to be clear in the way He inspired Scripture to be written? "*By faith we understand that the universe was created by the word of God, so that what is seen was not made out of things that are visible.*"[17] In 2005, Dr. Steve Boyd, a Hebrew scholar, performed a significant statistical analysis on the first thirty-four verses of the Bible. His study randomly selected fifty texts from a pool of two hundred and ninety-seven distinctly historical narratives from the Bible. Also chosen randomly were fifty texts from two hundred and fifty clearly poetical narratives from Scripture. After rigorous study, distinctive verb forms were found characteristic to both literary types. The Hebrew preterit verb was only found to be used in historical narratives. Upon evaluation, using these mathematically established distinctives, the Creation account in Genesis was found to be clearly written as history. This finding carried a statistical accuracy of 99.9973 percent![18]

> *Yes—God could have created the universe in any manner He chose. But what does He clearly state He did in the text of Scripture?*

Six literal days of creation is important. Here God's role as supernatural and all-powerful Creator is confirmed. God is not relegated to a virtually unnecessary role. Could He bring about our supernatural redemption if He couldn't create supernaturally? Yes—God could have created the universe in any manner He chose. But what does He clearly state He did in the text of Scripture? If we decide God used billions of years to bring about this present world, how long might He choose to take to create

17 Hebrews 11:3.

18 Stephen Boyd, *Thousands, Not Millions*, extra features.

the new heavens and new earth spoken of in Revelation?[19] Peter states, "*But the day of the Lord will come like a thief, and then the heavens will pass away with a roar, and the heavenly bodies will be burned up and dissolved, and the earth and the works that are done on it will be exposed. Since all these things are thus to be dissolved, what sort of people ought you to be in lives of holiness and godliness, waiting for and hastening the coming of the day of God, because of which the heavens will be set on fire and dissolved and the heavenly bodies will melt as they burn! But according to his promise we are waiting for new heavens and a new earth in which righteousness dwells.*"[20]

The gospel of reconciliation through God's gracious gift of His Son is supernatural. God is supernatural. Every statement of Jesus and Scripture concerning first things supports a literal interpretation of the Genesis creation account. The concept of a Sabbath rest is based on the first seven days of God's work of creation. Failing to accept the Bible's clear narrative concerning the events of the Creation week calls into question our trust in the rest of God's revelation.

So what does God's positional attribute as Creator mean in my relationship with Him? He is able to cause all things to come to pass. There is nothing too big for Him to do. The omnipotence of God, which we looked at under His Sovereignty, is on display for all to see. One of the most amazing statements in Holy Scripture is found in the Genesis account of creation. Consider this statement: "*And God made the two great lights—the greater light to rule the day and the lesser light to rule the night—and the stars.*"[21] Here, mentioned in three words as almost an afterthought, is God's creation of the stars, which fill a yet unfathomable universe.

---

19 Revelation 21:1–5.

20 2 Peter3:10–13.

21 Genesis 1:16.

All the stars are known by God in His omniscience. "*To whom then will you compare me, that I should be like him? says the Holy One. Lift up your eyes on high and see: who created these? He who brings out their host by number, calling them all by name, by the greatness of his might, and because he is strong in power not one is missing.*"[22] "*He determines the number of the stars; he gives to all of them their names. Great is our Lord, and abundant in power; his understanding is beyond measure.*"[23] Who has not stopped on a clear night and marveled at the wonder of the innumerable stars?

God's creation continually provides an undeniable testimony of His power and reality in an undeniable universal language. "*The heavens declare the glory of God, and the sky above proclaims his handiwork. Day to day pours out speech, and night to night reveals knowledge. There is no speech, nor are there words, whose voice is not heard. Their voice goes out through all the earth, and their words to the end of the world.*"[24] "*For his invisible attributes, namely, his eternal power and divine nature, have been clearly perceived, ever since the creation of the world, in things that have been made. So they are without excuse.*"[25] Man must willfully ignore and deny God's revelation clearly seen in His Creation.

Our mighty Creator God is the author of all life and death. He sustains and superintends over all of His awesome creation with His ever-present hand of order. All laws of nature are in fact His organizing and intentional design. All health and healing is from our eternal physician. We stand in awe of God, who not only caused all things to miraculously come into being but also currently holds them in existence. God is both transcendent

---

22 Isaiah 40:25–26.

23 Psalm 147:4–5.

24 Psalm 19:1–4.

25 Romans 1:20.

and imminent in His role as Creator and sustainer. His power and Glory are displayed by His unfathomable universe.

Master

As Master, we recognize God as owner of all. Our role is one of servant and steward. We will serve someone. It may be God, some faulty idol, our own selves, or even Satan himself. But we must serve someone or something. It is the way we are wired. It has been said that no man lives without a god. We all serve a god. That god can even be ourselves. Here we see the self-deception and irony of atheism. Denying the self-evident reality of God in the face of overwhelming evidence is intellectual suicide. Proclaiming that there is no God, nonbelievers seek to free themselves from the obligations of the true Master. They are unwittingly enslaving themselves to false gods. Scripture states emphatically that the awareness of God as Master resides in all men. "*Knowing that you also have a Master in heaven*."[26]

> *Proclaiming that there is no God, nonbelievers seek to free themselves from the obligations of the true Master. They are unwittingly enslaving themselves to false gods.*

In many cultures, when an indentured slave was set free, he might choose to willingly become a bond servant. This was his free choice to continue to serve his previous Master even though his legal debt had been paid in full. Often the slave would even take the name of the family he had chosen to continue to serve. Scripture cautions us against being slaves to anything other than Christ. "*For he who is called in the Lord while a slave is the Lord's freedman. Likewise he who is called while*

26 Colossians 4:1.

free is Christ's slave."[27] As God's adopted heirs, we are relationally closer than this type of slave and master relationship. God is in every sense our heavenly Father, and we are His children.

However, we are to relate to God as owner and Master of all we possess. He alone directs us to use all of our worldly possessions intentionally for His purposes. Never forget to honor God by how you use your gifts and blessings. Everything is from Him and unto Him. Spiritual arthritis occurs when the open hand of stewardship, full of God's blessings, possessively closes. These gifts are now held fast in the clutch of false personal ownership. In this we sin and are greatly deceived.

Our main response to God as Lord and Master is to be an obedient servant. All our life and efforts should be to give God glory and honor. This allows our Master to bless us. *"And whatever you do, in word or deed, do everything in the name of the Lord Jesus, giving thanks to God the Father through him.... Whatever you do, work heartily, as for the Lord and not for men, knowing that from the Lord you will receive the inheritance as your reward. You are serving the Lord Christ."*[28] *"For even when we were with you, we would give you this command: If anyone is not willing to work, let him not eat. For we hear that some among you walk in idleness, not busy at work, but busybodies. Now such persons we command and encourage in the Lord Jesus Christ to do their work quietly and to earn their own living."*[29]

Here is our proper understanding of work. All work is to God's Glory. Only when we are providentially placed in debilitating conditions mentally or physically are we free from the command to work. God has put great joy and fulfillment in work. It

---

27 1 Corinthians 7:22 NKJV.

28 Colossians 3:17, 23–24.

29 2 Thessalonians 3:10–12.

is His means for our own provision and the provision of those under our care.

Work and stewardship are always to honor God alone and to see His blessings for our earthly needs. Work has a proper place in life and is balanced by our obedient observance of a Sabbath rest. Many other obligations of life are fulfilled in work. Our role as parents and good citizens in any culture is enabled by being productive workers. May we always honor God as Master and owner by the excellence of our labor.

We are taught caution about overvaluing earthly possessions. The Bible contrasts this wrong attitude with the act of sacrificial giving.

In the Bible, many teachings and parables of Jesus concerned money and stewardship. We are taught caution about overvaluing earthly possessions. The Bible contrasts this wrong attitude with the act of sacrificial giving: "*For the love of money is a root of all kinds of evils. It is through this craving that some have wandered away from the faith and pierced themselves with many pangs.*"[30] "*No one can serve two masters, for either he will hate the one and love the other, or he will be devoted to the one and despise the other. You cannot serve God and money.*"[31] "*Jesus looked up and saw the rich putting their gifts into the offering box, and he saw a poor widow put in two small copper coins. And he said, 'Truly, I tell you, this poor widow has put in more than all of them. For they all contributed out of their abundance, but she out of her poverty put in all she had to live on.*"[32] Nothing so reveals our allegiance and

30 1 Timothy 6:10.

31 Matthew 6:24.

32 Luke 21:1–4.

heart's desire quite like our pattern of giving to God and to others. *"Honor the Lord with your wealth and with the first fruits of all your produce; then your barns will be filled with plenty, and your vats will be bursting with wine."*[33] *"And let us not grow weary of doing good, for in due season we will reap, if we do not give up. So then, as we have opportunity, let us do good to everyone, and especially to those who are of the household of faith."*[34]

Jesus's teaching about the rich man who put all his confidence in his earthly wealth concludes with Him designating this man as a fool. Jesus encourages us to lay up all our treasures in heaven and not on earth.[35] During Jesus's earthly ministry, a rich young ruler asked Him what he must do to gain eternal life. After some discourse, Jesus perceived his wealth was his life. As the young man would not give up his love of possessions, he chose the earthly security of temporal things over obedience to Jesus.[36]

Ownership is the primary issue in stewardship before God. Others key elements are wisdom and endeavor. We honor God by our intentional use and increase of those things entrusted to us. *"Everyone to whom much was given, of him much will be required, and from him to whom they entrusted much, they will demand the more."*[37] In one of the longer parables of Jesus, servants who were squandering their master's wealth were severely condemned. They were stripped of that which they were managing and called His enemies. Their punishment was death—*"But as for these enemies*

---

33 Proverbs 3:9–10.

34 Galatians 6:9–10.

35 Luke 12:16–20.

36 Matthew 19:16–22.

37 Luke 12:48.

of mine, who did not want me to reign over them, bring them here and slaughter them before me."[38]

God takes seriously how we view and handle His earthly blessings. In an astounding parable, Jesus told of tenants who sought to usurp the possessions of an owner. They hoped to claim his property as their own. The consequences were staggering. *"What will the owner of the vineyard do? He will come and destroy the tenants and give the vineyard to others."*[39]

Another parable concerning nonproductivity gives us hope. An owner commanded his vinedresser to destroy a barren fig tree. The vinedresser's appeal for another year of opportunity was granted.[40] Sometimes when we fail to honor God in our prompt stewardship, He is mercifully longsuffering and provides a life-giving second chance. God may delay the consequences of our actions so that we might have the opportunity to again honor Him as the Master who owns everything.

---

38 Luke 19:12–27.

39 Mark 12:1–11.

40 Luke 13:6–9.

Chapter 9

God Is Always With Us! We Live in His Presence.

"Do not be deceived, my beloved brothers. Every good gift and every perfect gift is from above, coming down from the Father of lights with whom there is no variation or shadow due to change. Of his own will he brought us forth by the word of truth, that we should be a kind of firstfruits of his creatures.

James 1:16–18

"And when you pray, do not heap up empty phrases as the Gentiles do, for they think that they will be heard for their many words. Do not be like them, for your Father knows what you need before you ask him. Pray then like this: Our Father in heaven, hallowed be your name. Your kingdom come, your will be done, on earth as it is in heaven. Give us this day our daily bread, and forgive us our debts, as we also have forgiven our debtors. And lead us not into temptation, but deliver us from evil."

Matthew 6:7–13

But now thus says the LORD, he who created you, O Jacob, he who formed you, O Israel: "Fear not, for I have redeemed you; I have called you by name, you are mine."

ISAIAH 43:1

There is only one lawgiver and judge, he who is able to save and to destroy. But who are you to judge your neighbor?

JAMES 4:12

I am the LORD. I have spoken; it shall come to pass; I will do it. I will not go back; I will not spare; I will not relent; according to your ways and your deeds you will be judged, declares the LORD GOD.

EZEKIEL 24:14

God is a righteous judge, and a God who feels indignation every day.

PSALM 7:11

For the LORD is our judge; the LORD is our lawgiver; the LORD is our king; he will save us.

ISAIAH 33:22

"I the LORD search the heart and test the mind, to give every man according to his ways, according to the fruit of his deeds."

JEREMIAH 17:10

Rise up; come to our help! Redeem us for the sake of your steadfast love!

Psalm 44:26

He has delivered us from the domain of darkness and transferred us to the kingdom of his beloved Son, in whom we have redemption, the forgiveness of sins.

Colossians 1:13–14

And call no man your father on earth, for you have one Father, who is in heaven.

Matthew 23:9

One God and Father of all, who is over all and through all and in all.

Ephesians 4:6

The last of God's positional attributes include those in the grouped headings of Judge, Redeemer, and Father. We will again find a balance between attributes of God we find very comforting and those we realize to be very sobering. He is our heavenly Father. This may be our best overarching conception of Him as His redeemed, which brings us great joy. With that blessed revelation, we must balance the sobering truth that He is the just Judge of all men. He will righteously render payment due for sins of thought and behavior. Our view of God must always be true to His revelation of Himself in His Word and through the life of

Jesus Christ. In Jesus the pinnacle of God's redemption is accomplished. God as Redeemer is our only hope of glory and eternity.

The Remaining Positional Attributes of God

- **Judge:** Just, Impartial, Purifying, Evaluating, Rewarder
- **Redeemer:** Reconciler, Justifier, Sanctifier, Savior, Searching, Rescuer, Shepherd, Forgiving, Peace, Precious
- **Father:** Provider, Protector, Responsive, Nurturer, Counselor, Singer, Tester, Chastener

Judge

As Judge, God executes all the justice required by His impartial Righteous Holy being. God is not mocked. All required penalty or reward for dishonoring or honoring His rule and reign will be exacted. God's Holiness demands His just Wrath on the onerous stench of sin. He never falters in His role as a just Judge. He alone declares pure those whom He chooses and casts into outer darkness those outside of His adoptive plan. The rewards for righteousness only come as a result of the finished work of Christ. Without His enabling Spirit, all our thoughts and actions are sinful, every single one. All sins are paid for. Many sins are paid for by the Righteousness of Christ. Many others are paid for by those committing those sins by their eternal punishment. The payment is either extremely gracious through the sacrifice of Jesus or extraordinarily severe upon man. There is no in-between or grading on a curve.

> *All sins are paid for. Many sins are paid for by the Righteousness of Christ. Many others are paid for by those committing those sins by their eternal punishment.*

The Bible clearly states that God is not the author of sin. This means that God does not create sin. Yet sin does exist, and God caused all that is. How can this be? God *permitted* sin through temptation to occur in the realm of actual moral freedom. God's Sovereignty was and is ever present. The freedom of Satan and man allowed for sin. Man can choose to obey or disobey God. The Bible says sin entered through temptation and deception. We want to blame God for sin, but we cannot. God made us to be free, but we would like to deny our responsibility. God's design in this area is beyond our full grasp.

Although His sacrifice is sufficient to pay for all of the sins of all men, His blood is only applied to the sins of those whom He has chosen. God is both just and mercifully gracious in the same instant. At no time or place is one attribute of God found more than any other. He has the right and authority to determine who will receive justice and punishment based on their own record and who will receive justice paid for them by His only Son.

The free gift of righteousness before an exacting Judge came at a dear cost to our loving Father. His Son was our sacrificial lamb. An illustration to help our understanding begins with a guilty young man appearing before a just and righteous judge. After the appropriate sentence is determined, the judge is now revealed to be the young man's father. He removes his robe and comes down off the bench. As the loving father, he offers to pay the penalty for his guilty son. As judge, he was just. As father, he is sacrificially willing to suffer to pay the debt of justice. The cost is borne by a substitute.

The Bible clearly teaches that God punishes sin and rewards good. Our conscience confirms the rightness of this. Some limited aspects of punishment are visited upon us during this earthly life. The more significant effects of sin are settled after death. "*The righteousness of the blameless keeps his way straight, but the wicked falls by his own wickedness."*[1] The consequences for sin and righteousness in this world are not yet fully exacted. Wicked sinners have even taken the long-suffering of God as an opportunity of importunity. "*You have wearied the* LORD *with your words. But you say, 'How have we wearied him?' By saying, 'Everyone who does evil is good in the sight of the* LORD*, and he delights in them.' Or by asking, 'Where is the God of justice?'*"[2]

God is clear in His Word concerning His Wrath and fiery Justice. "*It is appointed for man to die once, and after that comes judgment.*"[3] In Psalm 73, Asaph was wrestling with the apparent violation of God's Righteousness. He concluded that all would be made right. "*For I was envious of the arrogant when I saw the prosperity of the wicked.... Behold, these are the wicked; always at ease, they increase in riches.... Until I went into the sanctuary of God; then I discerned their end.... For behold, those who are far from you shall perish; you put an end to everyone who is unfaithful to you.*"[4] The final accounting for our motives and actions will be much more detailed and consequential than we can even conceive. The consequences of sin are not only a part of life but a devastating final reckoning at the end of this present age.

> *The final accounting for our motives and actions will be much more detailed and consequential than we can even conceive.*

---

1 Proverbs 11:5.

2 Malachi 2:17.

3 Hebrews 9:27.

4 Psalm 73:3, 12, 17, 27.

Jesus's teaching reveals a glorious throne where He will separate all people of all time finally into "sheep and goats." The sheep will hear, "*Come, you who are blessed by my Father, inherit the kingdom prepared for you from the foundation of the world.*"[5] The goats will be condemned as they hear, "'*Depart from me, you cursed, into the eternal fire.'... These will go away into eternal punishment, but the righteous into eternal life.*"[6] "*Do you suppose, O man—you who judge those who practice such things and yet do them yourself—that you will escape the judgment of God? Or do you presume on the riches of his kindness and forbearance and patience, not knowing that God's kindness is meant to lead you to repentance? But because of your hard and impenitent heart you are storing up wrath for yourself on the day of wrath when God's righteous judgment will be revealed. He will render to each one according to his works:... for those who are self-seeking and do not obey the truth, but obey unrighteousness, there will be wrath and fury.*"[7]

God is Holy and serious about the separation from His fellowship caused by sin. "*For if we go on sinning deliberately after receiving the knowledge of the truth, there no longer remains a sacrifice for sins, but a fearful expectation of judgment, and a fury of fire that will consume the adversaries.... For we know him who said, 'Vengeance is mine; I will repay.' ...It is a fearful thing to fall into the hands of the living God.*"[8] What we must never forget is that our decisions in life have eternal consequences. They really do matter. Life is much more than a dress rehearsal. This is the very real drama and we had better perform in light of eternity. "*For all have sinned and fall short of the glory of God, and are justified by his grace as a gift, through redemption that is*

---

5 Matthew 25:34.

6 Matthew 25:41, 46.

7 Romans 2:3–6, 8.

8 Hebrews 10:26–27, 30–31.

in Christ Jesus, whom God put forward as a propitiation by his blood, to be received by faith. This was to show God's righteousness, because in his divine forbearance he had passed over former sins. It was to show his righteousness at the present time, so that he might be just and the justifier of the one who has faith in Jesus."[9] Could God have made it any clearer?

At a time that you can be certain will occur, God will review our lives and pronounce judgment that will have eternal ramifications. "*Then I saw a great white throne and him who was seated on it. From his presence earth and sky fled away, and no place was found for them. And I saw the dead, great and small, standing before the throne, and books were opened. Then another book was opened, which is the book of life. And the dead were judged by what was written in the books, according to what they had done. And the sea gave up the dead who were in it, Death and Hades gave up the dead who were in them, and they were judged, each one of them, according to what they had done. Then Death and Hades were thrown into the lake of fire. This is the second death, the lake of fire. And if anyone's name was not found written in the book of life, he was thrown into the lake of fire.*"[10]

At no more important time in this text must I reiterate that these are not my thoughts and ideas. We are remaining true to the Word of God, and these are His promises. These things will come to pass just as He has decreed. If you don't feel fear and dread for yourself or for others outside of God's redemptive family, you are not wrestling soberly with God's declared intentions. We sometimes hear that the preaching of hellfire and brimstone is cruel. Nothing could be further from the truth. A compassionate and passionate appeal, warning of impending judgment, is needed. Failing to call out to those in harm's way is the greatest indifference and lack of love.

---

9 Romans 3:23–26.

10 Revelation 20:11–15.

> *If you don't feel fear and dread for yourself or for others outside of God's redemptive family, you are not wrestling soberly with God's declared intentions.*

Again we read in Scripture, "*See that you do not refuse him who is speaking. For if they did not escape when they refused him who warned them on earth, much less will we escape if we reject him who warns from heaven.... He has promised, 'Yet once more I will shake not only the earth but also the heavens.' This phrase, 'Yet once more,' indicates the removal of things that are shaken—that is, things that have been made—in order that the things that cannot be shaken may remain. Therefore let us be grateful for receiving a kingdom that cannot be shaken, and thus let us offer to God acceptable worship, with reverence and awe, for our God is a consuming fire.*"[11]

God as Judge is one of the most sobering relationships we have with Him. We dare not be cavalier about this very real positional attribute of God. We must never ignore any of God's revelation concerning Himself. Our goal is to know our wonderful God whose Holiness and hatred of sin and injustice demands an accounting. All sin is rebelliousness and treason against His perfect being. We must fearfully revere God. He Faithfully upholds and defends His Holiness and righteousness.

Redeemer

God relates to us as our Redeemer. This is an amazing truth about His character. Almost the entire Bible tells of man's plight in a fallen state. Like bookends, only the first two and last two chapters in the Bible speak of man outside of his fallen condition. With a design beyond our understanding, God planned from the very

11 Hebrews 12:25–29.

beginning that He would redeem some fallen men and women to Himself. God set things up just like they are. He alone chooses those whom He redeems. He does not choose all. This is called God's election. There is no part of His plan of reconciliation to Himself that He determined after anything was created. "*Blessed be the God and Father of our* L*ORD* *Jesus Christ, who has blessed us in Christ with every spiritual blessing in the heavenly places, even as he chose us in him before the foundation of the world, that we should be holy and blameless before him. In love he predestined us for adoption as sons through Jesus Christ, according to the purpose of his will.*"[12] This is the undeserved clear testimony found in the Holy Bible.

> *God set things up just like they are. He alone chooses those whom He redeems. He does not choose all.*

To God alone be all glory and honor for His plan of salvation. As reconciler, all three persons of the Godhead are involved. He completely justifies, sanctifies, and glorifies His chosen. We are given a role in our ongoing sanctification progress. As our savior He is both our searching rescuer and shepherd. "*For thus says the* L*ORD* *God: Behold, I, I myself will search for my sheep and will seek them out. As a shepherd seeks out his flock when he is among his sheep that have been scattered, so will I seek out my sheep, and I will rescue them from all places where they have been scattered.*"[13]

God is ever ready to celebrate His joyous reunion with each of His lost sheep. "*What man of you, having a hundred sheep, if he has lost one of them, does not leave the ninety-nine in the open country, and go after the one that is lost, until he finds it? And when he has found it, he lays it on his shoulders, rejoicing. And when he comes home, he calls*

12 Ephesians 1:3–5.

13 Ezekiel 34:11–12.

together his friends and his neighbors, saying to them, 'Rejoice with me, for I have found my sheep that was lost.' Just so, I tell you, there will be more joy in heaven over one sinner who repents than over ninety-nine righteous persons who need no repentance."[14] All of God's chosen cause a grand celebration in the heavenly realm at the point of their second birth into the kingdom of God.

God is full of forgiveness and peace. He chose some because of His pleasure to save certain individuals. Our question must not be, "Why did He only chose some and not all?" We should never ask, "Why did He make Jesus the only way to Himself?" The only question that should be asked is, "Why did God make a way for any?" God created the universe. He placed many souls in ongoing generations to inhabit His creation. We have all sinned. Why does anything good happen to bad people? He lets us all have it so much better than we deserve. This is His grace common to all.

We sometimes say Adam's sin was the original sin. There were actually a lot of earlier sins than Adam's sin. Satan had already sinfully rebelled while in heaven before his appearance in the garden. Scripture alludes to the fall of possibly one-third of the heavenly host following Satan in his sin. They were all cast to earth. We don't know how many sins that represents, but it was a multitude.[15]

Even Eve sinned before Adam sinned. Adam's sin was really "the sin" in terms of its devastating consequences for all of us. Adam served as our true representative or federal head. Serving in this position, Adam's sin was counted by God against all of mankind. This resulted in the fall. It is stated in Scripture that all humanity was afterward born in sin as his offspring. "*Therefore,*

---

14 Luke 15:4–7.

15 Revelation 12:4.

just as sin came into the world through one man, and death through sin, and so death spread to all men because all sinned."[16]

A Hungarian proverb states, "Adam ate the apple, and our teeth still ache." I don't know about you, but I did not really like the fact that Adam's sin was credited to me. I have realized though, like many things in God's plan, His ideas are so much better than I could ever imagine or hope. By setting forth God's economy in this manner of representation, God now is justified in allowing Christ's perfect record to be accepted as payment for my debt of sin. His grace is most highly manifested in our receiving the righteousness of Christ, which we do not deserve.

The gospel is the unexpected cure for our broken relationship with God. We are stunned that this is the way things work. Consider the story of a mother who learns she has cancer and it is incurable. She decides to live her last days as normally as possible. She continues to decline. One evening, while the family is enjoying dinner, a dish is passed and a piece of broccoli falls into the mashed potatoes. The kids are never going to eat that, so mom eats it. At her next doctor's appointment, she is found to be cancer free. Further research finds that broccoli covered in mashed potatoes cures cancer. This is astounding. Now it becomes very challenging to convince people who know they have cancer that this will heal them. It is further impossible to get those people who are in denial about their cancer to accept and partake of this healing remedy. Unless God opens your eyes, the good news of the gospel sounds a lot like mashed potatoes on broccoli.

Adam is my perfect representative. If anything, I would not have made it as far as the tree before my first sin. "*For if many died through one man's trespass, much more have the grace of God and the free gift by the grace of that one man Jesus Christ abounded for many.*

16 Romans 5:12.

And the free gift is not like the result of that one man's sin. For the judgment following one trespass brought condemnation, but the free gift following many trespasses brought justification. For if, because of one man's trespass, death reigned through that one man, much more will those who receive the abundance of grace and the free gift of righteousness reign in life through the one man Jesus Christ. Therefore, as one trespass led to condemnation for all men, so one act of righteousness leads to justification and life for all men."[17]

God has given to those He chooses the free gift of declared righteousness. This bestows right standing before Him and overcomes the law of sin and death. Those not chosen are shown justice. Those chosen enjoy unimaginable mercy and grace. To some He is fair. To others He is far beyond fair. It's not equal, but it is fair or better than fair. This is God's revelation of Himself and His plan in the Bible. You will either see hope in these facts or resist them. Your embracing of these truths reveals God's work of effectual calling and regeneration in your heart. He calls all but makes the calling effectual in the lives of only His chosen.

As you realize your opportunity to have a right relationship with God through trusting alone in the name and work of Jesus Christ, your eyes have been opened. God's Holy Spirit enlivens your heart, and in this you receive eternal life. Your trust is not to be in God's plan or even God's Word, but in His Son Jesus Christ alone. *"He himself bore our sins in his body on the tree, that we might die to sin and live to righteousness. By his wounds you have been healed. For you were straying like sheep, but have now returned to the Shepherd and Overseer of your souls."*[18] *"You do not have his word*

---

17 Romans 5:15–18. The word "all" refers to all kinds, not each and every one.

18 1 Peter 2:24–25.

abiding in you, for you do not believe the one whom he has sent. You search the Scriptures because you think that in them you have eternal life, and it is they that bear witness about me, yet you refuse to come to me that you may have life."[19] You must trust in Christ alone for your salvation. There is no other way. These are not my thoughts, but God declaring His ways, speaking through His revelation found in the Bible.

> *You must trust in Christ alone for your salvation. There is no other way. These are not my thoughts, but God declaring His ways, speaking through His revelation found in the Bible.*

Your trust must be in Christ alone. This means you die to yourself and your own merit. You come to own your own sin and acknowledge your guilt before a Holy God. Conversion includes both repentance and faith. Here we experience salvation with all of its vital elements of justification and adoption. Here true converts begin to consistently experience the inward witness. The Holy Spirit dwells in your heart, speaking to your inner nature. Here is true assurance of salvation, as we become aware of the indwelling of God's spiritual presence. "*All who are led by the Spirit of God are sons of God.... The Spirit himself bears witness with our spirit that we are children of God.*"[20] "*But when the fullness of time had come, God sent forth his Son, born of woman, born under the law, to redeem those who were under the law, so that we might receive adoption as sons. And because you are sons, God has sent the Spirit of his Son into our hearts, crying, 'Abba! Father!' So you are no longer a slave, but a son, and if a son, then an heir through*

19 John 5:38–40.

20 Romans 8:14, 16.

God."[21] We are promised that we will persevere in our obedient walk of faith with God's enabling help. His Spirit colabors in our sanctification as we become more like Christ. This process of sanctification continues until believers sleep at their earthly departure. We will awaken in glory with Christ for the fullness of eternity.

God has chosen from all eternity past to be the Redeemer of His chosen elect. This is an essential and glorious relational attribute. We are overcome with gratitude and love for Him because He first showed His great Love for us. "*This is my commandment, that you love one another as I have loved you. Greater love has no one than this, that someone lay down his life for his friends.*[22] "*We love because he first loved us.... Whoever loves God must also love his brother.*"[23] Our immediate and continued response to God's Love toward us as Redeemer is to love Him and others. Have you followed this path of faith to our victorious savior and prince of peace? Prayerfully consider the call of God's Spirit in your life unless you would die in your sin. Right now is the best time for your redemption and adoption as a child of God.

Father

The positional attribute of the God of the universe being our heavenly Father is truly extraordinary. This is the positional attribute most mentioned by Jesus. God is our responsive and nurturing counselor. He continually provides for us and protects us. He is always singing over us and comforting us. These actions are amazing. We wonder at having such a personal and intimate

---

21 Galatians 4:4–7.

22 John 15:12–13.

23 1 John 4:19, 21.

relationship with God as our Father. What a fantastic inheritance we have been given as the adopted children of our heavenly Father.

> *We wonder at having such a personal and intimate relationship with God as our Father. What a fantastic inheritance we have been given as the adopted children of our heavenly Father.*

God is clearly revealed in Scripture to be a singular being made up of three Persons. These persons are the Father, the Son, and the Holy Spirit. Why would one of these three persons be viewed as a specially highlighted positional attribute? It is really because we need to have an overarching idea with which to grasp how we relate to God. God is much more complex and infinitely outstretches all our ideas of Him. We know the way we live our lives is greatly influenced by our conception of God. Stephen Charnock, Dan DeHaan, and many other authors feel this is our best relational conception of God. Our best association with God is as our loving Father.

As believers we all have one heavenly Father. "*Have we not all one Father? Has not one God created us?*"[24] "*But now, O Lord, you are our Father; we are the clay, and you are our potter; we are all the work of your hand.*"[25] From the beginning of time and God's unfolding revelation of Himself, the Fatherhood of God has been at the forefront of His relating to His own chosen people. "*For all who are led by the Spirit of God are sons of God. For you did not receive the spirit of slavery to fall back into fear, but you have received the Spirit of adoption as sons, by whom we cry, 'Abba! Father!' The Spirit himself bears witness with our spirit that we are children of God, and if children, then heirs—heirs of God and fellow heirs with Christ, provided we suffer with him in order that we may also be*

---

24 Malachi 2:10.

25 Isaiah 64:8.

glorified with him."[26] "*See what kind of the love the Father has given to us, that we should be called children of God; and so we are. The reason why the world does not know us is that it did not know him. Beloved, we are God's children now, and what we will be has not yet appeared; but we know that when he appears we shall be like him, because we shall see him as he is. And everyone who thus hopes in him purifies himself as he is pure.*"[27]

Jesus referred to God as both His and our Father well over a hundred times in the gospel of John alone. In the four Gospels (Matthew, Mark, Luke, and John), we find reference to God as our heavenly Father one hundred and eighty-nine times. In Jesus's high priestly prayer of John 17, the role of God as our heavenly Father was a major theme. Jesus asked His Holy Father to glorify Him, to keep the believers in the Father's name. He also asked our Father to sanctify us in the truth and make all believers one.

As our Father, God comforts us in times of trouble as a caring parent. "*Blessed be the God and Father of our Lord Jesus Christ, the Father of mercies and God of all comfort, who comforts us in all our affliction, so that we may be able to comfort those who are in any affliction, with the comfort with which we ourselves are comforted by God.*"[28] God nurtures us by His loving care and tender affection. God's Grace strengthens us to be His ministers and bring His loving-kindness to others.

God as Father is our protector. He will never allow His own to find themselves outside of His powerful care and protection. "*The Lord is your keeper; the Lord is your shade on your right hand.... The Lord will keep you from all evil; he will keep your life.*"[29] "*For God*

26 Romans 8:14–17.

27 I John 3:1–3.

28 2 Corinthians 1:3–4.

29 Psalm 121:5, 7.

alone, O my soul, wait in silence, for my hope is from him. He only is my rock and my salvation, my fortress; I shall not be shaken. On God rests my salvation and my glory; my mighty rock, my refuge is God."[30]

As our provider, God is always gracious. He gives His own good gifts and gives abundantly beyond what we deserve. I am glad He is so wise in what He gives. I would suffer untoward consequences if He gave me everything I wanted or childishly thought I needed. His fathering skills are perfect and should never be questioned. *"If any of you lacks wisdom, let him ask God, who gives generously to all without reproach, and it will be given him."*[31] *"And my God will supply every need of yours according to his riches in glory in Christ Jesus."*[32] *"Bring the full tithe into the storehouse, that there may be food in my house. And thereby put me to the test, says the* Lord *of hosts, if I will not open the windows of heaven for you and pour down for you a blessing until there is no more need."*[33] Most of God's provision extends beyond our awareness and full comprehension.

Each of the Ten Commandments have elements of God's protection and provision. God relates to His people at all times as their loving and gracious Father. God's children are in His family. They relate to Him not simply as creatures or even servants, but as the children of a caring Father. *"Or which one of you, if his son asks him for bread, will give him a stone? Or if he asks for a fish, will give him a serpent? If you then, who are evil, know how to give good gifts to your children, how much more will your Father who is in heaven give good things to those who ask him!"*[34]

---

30 Psalm 62:5–7.

31 James 1:5.

32 Philippians 4:19

33 Malachi 3:10

34 Matthew 7:9–11.

Let us never forget our privileged relationship with God as Father. This is our best conception of our standing with Him. He has declared His Love and care for each of His children. Let us never fear because we feel alone. His watchful eyes never fail to see all things real and possible. The comfort and peace found in His parental arms are always ours. "*For I am sure that neither death nor life, nor angels nor rulers, nor things present nor things to come, nor powers, nor height nor depth, nor anything else in all creation, will be able to separate us from the love of God in Christ Jesus our LORD.*"[35]

> *Let us never fear because we feel alone. His watchful eyes never fail to see all things real and possible. The comfort and peace found in His parental arms are always ours.*

God's positional attributes are broad and far-reaching. They are beyond our arbitrary grouping. They are always present equally in the simple and indivisible being of God. His Sovereignty demonstrates His dominion, providential plan, and unchanging will. All that happens is always under His omnipotent hand. As Master, He owns everything, and we never possess anything. Everything under our care is as His stewards and servants. God's role as Creator establishes more than anything else His almighty power and unique being. He is an unerring Judge and His Righteous penalty for sin is severe. As our reconciler, we see His role as Redeemer through His person Jesus Christ. Our salvation through Christ brings us into the blessed relationship with God as our heavenly Father. We enjoy this life-fulfilling role as God's children forever.

---

35 Romans 8:38–39.

Chapter 10
The Names God Chose for Himself

"That you may know and believe me and understand that I am he. Before me no god was formed, nor shall there be any after me. I, I am the Lord, *and besides me there is no savior. I declared and saved and proclaimed, when there was no strange god among you; and you are my witnesses,"* declares the Lord, *"and I am God. Also henceforth I am he; there is none who can deliver from my hand; I work, and who can turn it back?"*

Isaiah 43:10–13

As your name, O God, so your praise reaches to the ends of the earth.

Psalm 48:10

Those who know your name put their trust in you.

Psalm 9:10

The L*ORD* *is my shepherd; I shall not want. He makes me lie down in green pastures. He leads me beside still waters. He restores my soul. He leads me in paths of righteousness for his name's sake. Even though I walk through the valley of the shadow of death, I will fear no evil, for you are with me; your rod and your staff, they comfort me. You prepare a table before me in the presence of my enemies; you anoint my head with oil; my cup overflows. Surely goodness and mercy shall follow me all the days of my life, and I shall dwell in the house of the* L*ORD* *forever.*

Psalm 23

For to us a child is born, to us a son is given; and the government shall be upon his shoulder, and his name shall be called Wonderful Counselor, Mighty God, Everlasting Father, Prince of Peace. Of the increase of his government and of peace there will be no end.

Isaiah 9:6–7

I will dwell among the people of Israel and will be their God. And they shall know that I am the L*ORD* *their God, who brought them out of the land of Egypt that I might dwell among them. I am the* L*ORD* *their God.*

Exodus 29:45–46

We give thanks to you, L*ORD* *God Almighty, who is and who was, for you have taken your great power and begun to reign.*

Revelation 11:17

In the beginning was the Word, and the Word was with God, and the Word was God. He was in the beginning with God. All things were made through him, and without him was not any thing made that was made. In him was life, and the life was the light of men.... He was in the world, and the world was made through him, yet the world did not know him. He came to his own, and his own people did not receive him. But to all who did receive him, who believed in his name, he gave the right to become children of God, who were born, not of blood nor or the will of the flesh nor of the will of man, but of God. And the Word became flesh and dwelt among us, and we have seen his glory, glory as of the only Son from the Father, full of grace and truth.

John 1:1–4, 10–14

When I set out to intentionally know the one and only true God, I realized early on that it was a much bigger task than I had envisioned. I immediately discovered that the idea of a definitive and all-inclusive list of attributes was impossible. Next I discovered God was known by more than just His attributes. God's actions, attitudes, and the dispositions of His heart, earthly manifestations including His incarnate Son, and inspired names also help us to know Him. God is manifestly bigger than all things taken together. His persons and being, revealed only in part, are significantly beyond our full grasping. The one true God is awesome. He vastly outstretches our understanding and imagination.

From William Shakespeare's *Romeo and Juliet* comes the oft-quoted phrase, "A rose by any other name would smell as sweet." Juliet was arguing that family names should not separate her and Romeo. In her case, she may have been right. Some names are arbitrary and hold limited meaning. This is not so when we come to God. God's choices of what He calls Himself in the Bible are very important. The words He uses as His names are actually one of His significant ways of revealing Himself to us.

> *God's choices of what He calls Himself in the Bible are very important. The words He uses as His names are actually one of His significant ways of revealing Himself to us.*

Names often yield insight and identity. Every name or title concerning God in the Bible is inspired. It is God telling us who He is and how He is to be known. This information about God is directly from Him. We must work to understand the meaning of each of the names and titles for God, which He chose. Each one yields some insight into His nature. Complicating our task is the fact that the inspired Word of God came to us in the three languages of Hebrew, Aramaic, and Greek. A helpful way to study the various biblical names of God is to group them by their language, frequency, and the relationships they have to one another.

Groupings of the Predominant Names of God

The first grouping of God's names are the Hebrew names. They are found throughout the Bible. These names are listed below and followed by the number of times they appear in Scripture. In our first grouping, multiple conjoined names share the roots of Elohim, El, and Elohei. Many of these may appear only once throughout Scripture.

Elohim and El

Elohim—Deity, over 2,570

El—The Mighty One, Strong One, over 250

Eloah—God, singular form of Elohim, over 70

El Shaddai—The Almighty, All-Sufficient God, over 48
Elohim Chayim—The Living God 30
Elohim HaAv—God the Father 13
El Elyon—God Most High, 3
El Kanno—The Jealous God, 15
El Olam—God of Eternity, 4

Elohim: This first name of God is found in Genesis 1:1, the first verse of the Bible, "*In the beginning, God created the heavens and the earth.*" It is a plural noun form that is almost always used with a singular verb form. The implications of the trinitarian nature of God are obvious. It is the second most used name for God in the Bible's original text. Generally translated in English Bibles as "Lord," "God," or "Jehovah", it carries with it the implicit meaning of the Godhead. Elohim is the name of God as Creator and Judge. There exist many "Elohei" constructs like Elohei Avraham (the God of Abraham),[1] Elohei Chasdi (God of Kindness),[2] Elohei Haelohim (the God of gods),[3] Elohei Ma'uzzi (God of my Strength),[4] Elohei Mikkarov (God who is near), and Elohei Merachok (God who is far).[5] This is only a small sampling of the many "Elohei" constructs.

El: First appearing halfway through Genesis, El appears as "*There he erected an altar and called it El-Elohe-Israel.*"[6] El is often seen as a more pagan term for God. Carrying the meaning of "Supreme God, Father of Mankind," it is almost always

1 Exodus 3:15.

2 Psalm 59:17.

3 Deuteronomy 10:17, Joshua 22:22, Psalm 136:2.

4 2 Samuel 22:33, Psalm 31:5, 43:2.

5 Jeremiah 23:23.

6 Genesis 33:20.

associated with another modifier. Some of these are El Echad (the One God),[7] El Hanne'eman (the Faithful God),[8] El Emet (the God of Truth),[9] El Tsaddik (the Righteous God),[10] El Hakkavod (the God of Glory),[11] and El Hakkadosh (the Holy God).[12] This is only a partial listing of the El constructs.

The second grouping of names includes the most often used and prominent Hebrew name for God found in Scripture. This is the Hebrew "Yud-Hay-Vav-Hay" (YHWH). These four letters called a "tetragrammaton" were considered by the Israelites to be too holy for men to vocalize. This name is found translated in English Bibles as "LORD" in all capitals. YHWH was substituted in spoken readings of the Scripture by the more familiar Adonai, which is rendered "Lord" in English translations. "Adonai" is the plural verbal parallel to YWHW with both titles meaning "Lord or Master." Over time, the vowels from Adonai were combined with the consonants from YHWH to yield the word "Jehovah." Confusingly, Jehovah is used in English translations, but is not found in any early manuscripts of the Bible. Titles in this group include:

YHWH, Yah, and Adonai

YHWH (Yahweh)—I Am, He Exists, He Causes to Be, over 6,800

Adonai—My Lord 439

---

7 Malachi 2:10.

8 Deuteronomy 7:9.

9 Psalm 31:5.

10 Isaiah 45:21.

11 Psalm 29:3.

12 Isaiah 5:16.

Yah—The Independent One over 50
YHWH Elohim—Majestic, Omnipotent Lord 21
YHWH-Jireh—The God Who Provides 1
YHWH-Rophe—The God Who Heals 1
YHWH-Nissi—God my Banner 1
YHWH-M'Kaddesh—God Who Sanctifies 1
YHWH-Shalom—God is Peace 1
YHWH-Tsidkenu—God our Righteousness 2
YHWH-Rohi—God my Shepherd 1
YHWH-Shammah—The Lord is There 1

Adonai Elohim—The Source of All Being, Personal Creator of All 19
Hashem—The Name 2
Ehyeh asher Ehyeh—I Am That I Am 2

YHWH: This unpronounceable name appears first in the Bible in Genesis 2:4 as, "*These are the generations of the heavens and the earth when they were created, in the day that the LORD God made the earth and the heavens.*" Here YHWH is actually introduced by the combination "YHWH-Elohim." Again often rendered as "Jehovah" in English Bibles, it clearly carries the strong pronouncement of God's Being. The pronounceable name "Yahweh" came by transliterations of the unpronounceable YHWH into Greek in early Christian literature. Strictly speaking, Yahweh is the plain name for God. It is not derived from His work, but from His being. When Moses asked for His name, "*God said to Moses, 'I AM Who I AM.' And he said, 'Say this to the people of Israel, I AM has sent me to you.' God also said to Moses, 'Say this to the people of Israel, The LORD, the God of your fathers, the God of Abraham, the God of Isaac, and the God of Jacob, has sent me to you.*

This is my name forever, and thus I am to be remembered throughout all generations. Go and gather the elders of Israel together and say to them, The Lord, the God of your fathers, the God of Abraham, of Isaac, and of Jacob, has appeared to me.'"[13] Often, combinations of YHWH are seen rendered as combinations of Jehovah. Trying to stay nearer the text of Scripture, we kept them as YHWH combinations. There are many YHWH combinations mostly referring to one action of God found in Scripture.

Strictly speaking, Yahweh is the plain name for God. It is not derived from His work, but from His being.

Adonai: Distinctly meaning lord, Master, or owner, Adonai is also often found in Scripture as a plural form with a singular Hebrew verb. This may also speak to the Triunity of God's three persons in His one essential being. "Adonai Adonai" is rendered in English as "Lord YHWH" or "Lord God." There are over thirty-four instances of this repetitive usage.

Yah: Possibly a shortened form of YHWH, Yah first appears in Exodus 15:2, as "*The Lord is my strength and my song, and he has become my salvation; this is my God, and I will praise him, my father's God, and I will exalt him.*" Moses and Israel had just been rescued from the chariots of Pharaoh. Yah combines to form the ending in such words as Hallelu-Yah and within the names Elijah (Eliyahu), Isaiah(Yeshayah), and Jeremiah (Yirmyah). It is also found imbedded in the Hebrew name for Jesus "Yahshua."

The third grouping of God's names is the small Aramaic or Syriac usage of Elah and Abba. These are primarily found in the

13 Exodus 3:14–16.

books of Ezra and Daniel where Aramaic had replaced Hebrew as the common speech of the Jews. Here we see the wonderful harmony of God's authorship in His inspired Word, regardless of its diverse historical and cultural settings of origin.

Elah and Abba

Elah—Awesome, Fearful One 20
Abba—familiar Father, Daddy 3

Elah: Here we find the clear meaning "Awesome and Fearful One." Nowhere in the Aramaic passages of Scripture is YHWH or Elohim used. Elah is found seventeen of its twenty occurrences in the two books of Ezra and Daniel.

Abba: Abba is the transliteration of the Aramaic word for Father. Found in the New Testament only three times, it is an endearing term of intimacy between a child and his or her loving parent. Jesus used it when asking His Father to remove His cup of suffering,[14] and in two instances where it is the cry of the Spirit of God in the believer.[15] To guard against too great of a casual familiarity with God, English translations render it as "Abba, Father," intending to maintain a "respectful intimacy."

The final grouping includes the Greek titles and names of God found exclusively in the New Testament. Of the many terms used in reference to God, these four were used multiple times. All others have virtual singular usage.

---

14 Mark 14:36.

15 Romans 8:15; Galatians 4:6.

Theos, Kurios, Pater, and Logos

Theos—The One Supreme Deity, God 1,172
Kurios—Lord or Master 687
Pater—Father, over 400
Logos—The Word, Spokesman 316

Theos: Theos is the basis of the word "theology," the study of God. It can both speak of the one true God or even false gods. Jesus even used the word to refer to human rulers![16] This means that the context, more than any other factor, determines how we understand this word for God.

Kurios: Often, New Testament references to the one true God as "Lord" are rendered from the Greek word "kurios." Although meaning Supreme Authority, sometimes the word can mean simply "sir, master or owner." Kurios can even be translated "husband" or "idol." Once again, the principle in Greek is context of usage more than intrinsic meaning of a word. Kurios was used often of YHWH or for the divinity of Jesus as Lord.

Pater: Pater means Father or nearest ancestor. It carries the meaning of originator or founder. Moving away from the more flexible meanings of "theos" and "kurios" we find more specificity here. Almost one third of pater's usage in the New Testament is seen in the one book of John. Pater seems to specifically link us as adopted children of our heavenly Father.

Logos Logos means "of speech" and embodies a word uttered by a living voice. It may also contain elements of a decree or mandate.

---

16 John 10:34–36.

It is used in John as the essential Word of God, Jesus Christ. Here is the divine reason and plan that coordinates and stabilizes a dynamic ever-changing universe.

> *Logos means "of speech" and embodies a word uttered by a living voice.*
>
> *It is used in John as the essential Word of God, Jesus Christ.*

The vast majority of times that the word "LORD" (with capital letters) is found in our English translations, it designates the original Hebrew YHWH. "Lord" (where only the first letter is capitalized) denotes the use of the Hebrew word Adonai. Yahweh and Jehovah have emerged to us from sources outside of the original autograph of Scripture. These have been useful to the Church universal in theological discourse. Be reminded, however, that those words are not biblical in origin.

"El" and "Elohim" are translated almost three thousand times in English Old Testament translations as "God." The names refer to God as Creator, Sovereign, and Judge in particular. Notably, this is the name of God seen exclusively in the first chapter of Genesis. A very important name of God—Elohim—by being in the plural form, may be our first true insight to God's thrice Holy nature.

The remaining groups helped us to understand the names of God as found in the Aramaic and Greek portions of God's Word. In Aramaic, "Elah" revealed God's awesome fearfulness, yet "Abba" reminded us of His nurturing Fatherhood. There are various Greek names found in God's inspired Word. The most used names of "Theos," "Kurios," and "Pater" revealed God's place as the one true God, Lord, and Father. The fourth name, "Logos," referred us to the mystical relationship between the mind of Christ and holy Scripture.

Continuing to study the biblical names of God, we move to Jesus and His many revealing names and titles. There are easily over five hundred of these identified in Scripture. His earthly parents, Joseph and Mary, may have called Jesus by the Hebrew name "Joshua" or "Yeshua." "Jesus" was our Lord's Greek name. The name Jesus was a rather common name during the period of Jesus's earthly life. Joshua is a shortened form of "Jehoshua" meaning "Jehovah our Savior." Jesus/Joshua is from the Hebrew verb "yasha" meaning "saved." So Jesus's very common given name carried with it the promise that He was the "Jehovah Savior."

His earthly parents, Joseph and Mary, may have called Jesus by the Hebrew name "Joshua" or "Yeshua." "Jesus" was our LORD's Greek name.

"Lord" and "Christ" were associated with Jesus from His very birth. "Lord," from "kurios" denotes acknowledgment of highest respect due to the Master and owner of all. "Christ," from the Greek "Christos" means "Anointed One." It is related to "Messiah" from the Old Testament, representing a completed work of a promised hope. There are other Old Testament prophetic names of Jesus including Shiloh, the Desire of All Nations, the Branch, and the Ensign of the Peoples.

At birth, Jesus was given the names Immanuel, the Dayspring From On High, Wonderful Counselor, the Mighty One, the Everlasting Father, and the Prince of Peace.[17] Jesus fulfilled the prophecy of being "Immanuel," meaning "God With Us." We read from the Bible, *"And the Word became flesh and dwelt among us, and*

17 Isaiah 9:6

we have seen his glory, glory as of the only Son from the Father, full of grace and truth.... No one has ever seen God; the only God, who is at the Father's side, he has made him known."[18]

Two unique and often confusing titles of Jesus were Son of Man and Son of God. "Son of Man" was a name Jesus used to refer to Himself over eighty times. This name highlighted His role as Messiah coming as a king. His actual human nature was real and cojoined to His fully complete divine nature. "Son of God" reminds us of His co-eternal and co-equal nature with the Father. Jesus asked, "'*Who do people say that the Son of Man is?'... Simon Peter replied, 'You are the Christ, the Son of the living God.' And Jesus answered him, 'Blessed are you, Simon Bar-Jonah! For flesh and blood has not revealed this to you, but my Father who is in heaven.*'"[19]

How are we to understand Jesus being the Word or "Logos"? John gives us insight, found in Revelation, where we see Jesus distinctly named "The Word of God."[20] God seems to be stating that Jesus communicates the Godhead just as the Word is a revelation of God Himself. Jesus is the ultimate communication of God to man concerning Himself. Jesus is the Word of God incarnate. Scripture refers to itself as the mind of Christ.[21]

Many times Jesus directly claimed for Himself the title of YHWH. He said, "I am the bread of life; I am the light of the world; I am the door; I am the good shepherd; I am the resurrection and the life; I am the way, the truth, and the life; I am the true vine; and before Abraham was, I am."[22] These are

18 John 1:14, 18.

19 Matthew 16:13, 16–17.

20 Revelation 19:13.

21 1 Corinthians 2:16.

22 John 6:35; 8:12; 10:9; 10:11; 11:25; 14:6; 15:1, 5; 8:58.

astounding self-revelations of Jesus's deity. Many of His other names are included in the incomplete list found in Appendix 2. Just like the incomprehensible attributes of God, Jesus's names actually elude our comprehensive listing. "*Then I saw heaven opened, and behold, a white horse! The one sitting on it is called Faithful and True, and in righteousness he judges and makes war. His eyes are like a flame of fire, and on his head are many diadems, and he has a name written that no one knows but himself.*"[23]

God has certainly ordained and inspired each of His many names included in Scripture. These were given to us for insight into His being and character. Let us honor and reverence God in our every use of His many names. "*You shall not take the name of the* Lord *your God in vain, for the* Lord *will not hold him guiltless who takes his name in vain.*"[24] Each time we utter any of His names, we must remember He is the one great God we worship. We should never forget the admonition in Jesus's teaching on prayer, "*Pray then like this: 'Our Father in heaven, hallowed be your name.'*"[25] May He be praised and held in highest esteem by our every breath. May we glorify Him, our one and only true God. To His name alone be all glory forever and ever.

> *Just like the incomprehensible attributes of God, Jesus's names actually elude our comprehensive listing.*

23 Revelation 19:11.

24 Exodus 20:7.

25 Matthew 6:9.

Chapter 11
God's Glory Is Compelling

O Lord, our Lord, how majestic is your name in all the earth! You have set your glory above the heavens.... When I look at your heavens, the work of your fingers, the moon and the stars, which you have set in place, what is man that you are mindful of him, and the son of man that you care for him?

Psalm 8:1, 3–4

The heavens declare the glory of God, and the sky above proclaims his handiwork. Day to day pours out speech, and night to night reveals knowledge. There is no speech, nor are there words, whose voice is not heard.... The fear of the Lord is clean, enduring forever; the rules of the Lord are true, and righteous altogether. More to be desired are they than gold, even much fine gold; sweeter also than honey and drippings of the honeycomb. Moreover, by them is your servant warned; in keeping them there is great reward.

Psalm 19:1–3, 9–11

Even before a word is on my tongue, behold, O L*ORD*, *you know it altogether. You hem me in, behind and before, and lay your hand upon me. Such knowledge is too wonderful for me; it is high; I cannot attain it. Where shall I go from your Spirit? Or where shall I flee from your presence?... For you formed my inward parts; you knitted me together in my mother's womb. I praise you, for I am fearfully and wonderfully made. Wonderful are your works; my soul knows it very well. My frame was not hidden from you, when I was being made in secret, intricately woven in the depths of the earth. Your eyes saw my unformed substance; in your book were written, every one of them, the days that were formed for me, when as yet there was none of them. How precious to me are your thoughts, O God! How vast is the sum of them! If I would count them, they are more than the sand. I awake, and I am still with you.*

Psalm 139:4–7, 13–18

I will extol you, my God and King, and bless your name forever and ever. Every day I will bless you and praise your name forever and ever. Great is the L*ORD*, *and greatly to be praised, and his greatness is unsearchable. One generation shall commend your works to another, and shall declare your mighty acts. On the glorious splendor of your majesty, and on your wondrous works, I will meditate. They shall speak of the might of your awesome deeds, and I will declare your greatness. They shall pour forth the fame of your abundant goodness and shall sing aloud of your righteousness.*

Psalm 145:1–7

Now the appearance of the glory of the L*ORD* *was like a devouring fire on the top of the mountain in the sight of the people of Israel.*

Exodus 24:17

For in him the whole fullness of deity dwells bodily.

Colossians 2:9

I glorified you on earth, having accomplished the work that you gave me to do. And now, Father, glorify me in your own presence with the glory that I had with you before the world existed.

John 17:4–5

Turns out the Glory of God is not really an attribute of God, per se. God's Glory is the radiance of the full and complete majesty of all His attributes in concert together. In our diamond analogy, it is the stunning brilliance of a perfect diamond with an infinite internal light source. "*Praise the Lord, my soul. Lord my God, you are very great; you are clothed with splendor and majesty. The Lord wraps himself in light as with a garment; he stretches out the heavens like a tent.*"[1] "*For with you is the fountain of life; in your light do we see light.*"[2] "*Send out your light and your truth; let them lead me; let them bring me to your holy hill and to your dwelling!*"[3]

I was always told, "Don't look at the sun. You'll go blind." So I have never looked at the sun—well, just a glance or two. I still have my vision. This is not a recommendation I have been willing to challenge. I spent many summers working on large construction projects. One day, I began to feel like I had sand in my eyes when there was nothing there. I was told I had burned

1 Psalm 104:1–2 NIV.

2 Psalm 36:9.

3 Psalm 43:3.

my eyes by watching a welder's arc. I had been a great distance away from the welder, and I had only momentarily watched him at work. I wish somebody had warned me about that! It is no wonder welders wear those big, deeply tinted helmets.

God's radiant Glory will not just burn or blind. It will consume us in an instant. God is just that brilliantly glorious. Man's eternal error is understating the vast gulf that separates who he is and who God is. "*I will give to the Lord the thanks due to his righteousness, and I will sing praise to the name of the Lord, the Most High.*"[4] J. B. Phillips states, "To many people, conscience is almost all that they have by way of knowledge of God. It is extremely unlikely that we shall ever be moved to worship, love, and serve a nagging inner voice that at worst spoils our pleasure and at best keeps us rather negatively on the path of virtue."[5] Even God's partially manifested Glory at the final judgment will be awe-inspiring and overwhelming. As a tender Father, He has limited His accurate revelation of Himself to what we are able to handle. God has provided a perfectly balanced revelation of Himself. His carefully limited revelation is perfect for us and free of distortion.

God is just that brilliantly glorious. Man's eternal error is understating the vast gulf that separates who he is and who God is.

He has not yet revealed all of His attributes to us. God cannot be completely seen in an unfiltered manner by fallen men. Even the eyes of the redeemed here on earth cannot bear gazing on God's unlimited Glory. God is good as He protects us from His overwhelming being. God is light and will be the source of light in

4 Psalm 7:17.

5 J. B. Phillips, *Your God is Too Small*, 15.

the new heaven and the new earth. "*The sun shall be no more your light by day, nor for brightness shall the moon give you light; but the Lord will be your everlasting light, and your God will be your glory.*"[6] We will never lose our awestruck wonder at God's presence and person.

We will spend all of eternity with God as His heavenly children. We will dwell in His ever-immediate presence and the illuminating light of His Glory. Still we will never, in all of eternity, attain a full knowledge of His being. God's majesty is so beyond anything we could ever hope to grasp. Our eternal blessing will be to forever learn more of Him and never complete the task.

During my early education, I read a mythological Norse tale of the proud warrior, Thor. When challenged with the physical test of draining a chalice of liquid, he arrogantly threw himself at the task. He over-confidently knew he would be successful. After a herculean effort, he was forced to finish his draught from the cup. To his surprise, the volume in the cup had been only lowered one inch. Later it was revealed that the cup had been connected to the ocean. This is like our foolish self-confidence in expecting to comprehensively fathom God.

One of my favorite inspirational events is to stand at the edge of the Grand Canyon. Each trip to the Grand Canyon, I consistently hear people say "Wow!" It has actually amused me how common this is. I am confident this kind of wonder and awe will not even touch our amazement when we behold God in His Glory. Many times in Scripture, those who have a direct experience with a manifestation of God immediately fall prostrate before Him.

In our earthly lives, as we grow closer to God, others will noticeably see in us a reflection of the Glory of God.

6 Isaiah 60:19.

In our earthly lives, as we grow closer to God, others will noticeably see in us a reflection of the Glory of God. God said of His Son Jesus, *"I am the Lord; I have called you in righteousness; I will take you by the hand and keep you; I will give you as a covenant for the people, a light for the nations, to open the eyes that are blind, to bring out the prisoners from the dungeon, from the prison those who sit in darkness."*[7] Multiple times, Jesus gave a light-giving illumination to darkened hearts and reflected the Glory of His heavenly Father.

We serve an awesome Father in heaven. He is both Spirit and infinite. He alone is Righteous and Unchanging. Only the Lord exists autonomously outside of time. This is something we struggle to understand. He is the only true and perfect God, the Sovereign Redeemer and Judge who is filled with both Love and Wrathful zeal for His Holiness. These accumulated excellencies are but a slight taste of His immense Glory, which outshines the sun. Our spontaneous response to glimpsing His radiant Glory is to fall before Him. We worship Him because of who He is. John's response to being in the stunning yet tempered presence of God is compelling. *"When I saw him, I fell at his feet as though dead. But he laid his right hand on me, saying, 'Fear not, I am the first and the last, and the living one. I died, and behold I am alive forevermore, and I have the keys of Death and Hades.'"*[8] The only proper position of man before a Holy and Glorious God is prostration of heart and body. We must worship Him always in spirit and truth. "When a person, yielding to God and believing the truth of God, is filled with the Spirit of God, even his faintest whisper will be worship."[9] He must be worshipped in a manner worthy of His excellence and majesty.

---

7 Isaiah 42:6–7.

8 Revelation 1:17–18.

9 A. W. Tozer, *Whatever Happened to Worship?*, 14.

God's Glory has always been in front of man from the very beginning. "*Praise the Lord! Praise the Lord from the heavens; praise him in the heights! Praise him, all his angels; praise him, all his hosts!... Let them praise the name of the Lord! For he commanded and they were created. And he established them forever and ever; he gave a decree, and it shall not pass away.... Let them praise the name of the Lord, for his name alone is exalted; his majesty is above earth and heaven.*"[10] Praises for the Glory of God spontaneously erupted from the moment of creation's beginning. The praises of God's creation continue to this day.

In probably the most audacious request of all time, Moses asked God to show him His Glory. God was gracious. Instead of correcting Moses's impossible desire, God actually fulfilled it enough to reassure Moses for his task at hand. "*Moses said, 'Please show me your glory.' And* [God] *said, 'I will make all my goodness pass before you and will proclaim before you my name "The Lord." And I will be gracious to whom I will be gracious, and will show mercy on whom I will show mercy. But,' he said, 'you cannot see my face, for man shall not see me and live.'*"[11] God then reveals His "back" only to Moses, whom He had placed in the cleft of a rock. Here is a perfect example of God's kind and limited revelation of Himself. We are unable to drink deeply from a cup attached to the ocean.

Ever before us is the important and stunning reality of God's beauty. We read in the Bible, "*One thing have I asked of the Lord, that will I seek after: that I may dwell in the house of the Lord all the days of my life, to gaze upon the beauty of the Lord and to inquire in his temple. For he will hide me in his shelter in the day of trouble; he will conceal me under the cover of his tent; he will lift me high upon a*

---

10 Psalm 148:1–2, 5–6, 13.

11 Exodus 33:18–20.

rock."[12] These verses give us marvelous insight into our joy and blessing in the presence of God for all eternity as His redeemed. His face we shall see then to a much greater degree. "*For we know in part and we prophesy in part, but when the perfect comes, the partial will pass away. When I was a child, I spoke like a child, I thought like a child, I reasoned like a child. When I became a man, I gave up childish ways. For now we see in a mirror dimly, but then face to face. Now I know in part; then I shall know fully, even as I have been fully known.*"[13]

Concerning the new heaven, we read in God's Holy Word, "*No longer will there be anything accursed, but the throne of God and of the Lamb will be in it, and his servants will worship him. They will see his face, and his name will be on their foreheads. And night will be no more. They will need no light of lamp or sun, for the* Lord *God will be their light, and they will reign forever and ever.*"[14] Not only will our heavenly Father shine forth, but we as His family will be radiant also. Both Moses and Jesus returned from extraordinary exposures to God's presence, illuminated and transfigured. Our experience of heaven is to be greater than our puny minds can entertain. Our joy in the Lord's presence will be better than our wildest imagination.

Not only will our heavenly Father shine forth, but we as His family will be radiant also.

God's Glory is before us. His beauty is so attractive and His presence so brilliant. We are consumed by devotion and adoration. Worship follows immediately and constantly. Here and into all eternity we are compelled by His greatness and awesomeness to fall before Him in adoring praise. God is jealous for His honor. He is

12 Psalm 27:4–5.

13 1 Corinthians 13:9–12.

14 Revelation 22:3–5.

Righteous in His desire for our worship and devotion. We are compelled to have times of private and corporate worship. These are the proper patterns of the Christian's life. "I can safely say, on the authority of all that is revealed in the Word of God, that any man or woman on this earth who is bored and turned off by worship is not ready for heaven."[15] We realize all of life is to be a continual worship of God. Augustine of Hippo said man cannot be content unless he praises God. He declared that since we were made for God, our hearts would never find peace or rest except in God.

We were really created to enjoy God and to glorify Him forever. The Westminster Standard's Larger Catechism has as its first question, "What is the chief and highest end of man?" to which it gives this answer, "Man's chief and highest end is to glorify God, and fully to enjoy him forever."[16] This assertion is neither idle nor ill-informed. We find in Scripture, *"For from him and through him and to him are all things. To him be glory forever. Amen."*[17] *"So, whether you eat or drink, or whatever you do, do all to the glory of God."*[18] *"You guide me with your counsel, and afterward you will receive me to glory. Whom have I in heaven but you? And there is nothing on earth that I desire besides you. My flesh and my heart may fail, but God is the strength of my heart and my portion forever. For behold, those who are far from you shall perish; you put an end to everyone who is unfaithful to you. But for me it is good to be near God; I have made the Lord God my refuge, that I may tell of all your works."*[19]

---

15 A. W. Tozer, *Whatever Happened to Worship?*, 14.

16 Morton H. Smith, *Harmony of the Westminster Confession and Catechisms*, 11.

17 Romans 11:36.

18 1 Corinthians 10:31.

19 Psalm 73:24–28.

Jesus prayed for those given to Him, "*that they may all be one, just as you, Father, are in me, and I in you, that they also may be in us, so that the world may believe that you have sent me. The glory that you have given me I have given to them, that they may be one even as we are one,... so that the world may know that you sent me and loved them even as you loved me.*"[20] What an overwhelming encouragement to those adopted into His family.

How do we give God the glory He deserves in this life? Certainly by our continual worship and intimate fellowship with Him.

How do we give God the glory He deserves in this life? Certainly by our continual worship and intimate fellowship with Him. Further, our entire lives are to be lived for Him, under His acknowledged Sovereignty and intentionally unto His Glory. Martin Luther often used the Latin phrase, *Coram Deo*. This means "living before the face of God." Living every moment in the immediate presence of God is really an exhortation to holy living. Everything we do and say is to honor Him. We are constantly to do all things in attitude and excellence to glorify God.

We realize here the meaning of our duty as Christians. Man was created in God's presence and he is blessed to grow in God's presence. Ultimately, we will dwell in God's presence. The very name given to Jesus of Immanuel reminds us that God is "with us." Our faith and lives are built on the foundation of the immediate and ever-present relationship with our very Creator. God's presence, through His Spirit, gives life all of its meaning. We are finally whole when we are in Him, and He is in us.

---

20 John 17:21–23.

In our lives, we glorify God by our continual thanksgiving and loving appreciation for His many undeserved blessings. We continually thank God for who He is. As we do this, we testify with word and action to God's great Glory. We praise God as we find Him with us in suffering. We do good works to His honor alone. We show our great love for God by our obedience to His revealed will in Scripture. We ultimately glorify God by everything we do and think. Our very desires and intentions become His, and we long only for more of Him. We ever-increasingly become conformed to the likeness of Jesus, our highest earthly example of holy living.

The Bible's account of Jesus's visit to the home of Lazarus illustrates this truth. Martha was *"distracted with much serving"* while her sister Mary *"sat at the LORD's feet and listened to his teaching."* Martha asked Jesus to encourage her sister to help her in her busyness—to which Jesus replied, *"Martha, Martha, you are anxious and troubled about many things, but one thing is necessary. Mary has chosen the good portion, which will not be taken away from her."*[21]

God with His finger wrote into stone these admonitions: *"I am the LORD your God.... You shall have no other gods before me.... You shall not make for yourself a carved image...* [to] *bow down to... for I the LORD your God am a jealous God, visiting the iniquity of the fathers on the children to the third and the fourth generation of those who hate me, but showing steadfast love to thousands of those who love me and keep my commandments. You shall not take the name of the LORD your God in vain, for the LORD will not hold him guiltless who takes his name in vain. Remember the Sabbath day, to keep it holy... the seventh day is a Sabbath to the LORD your God."*[22] Clearly, God takes His honor and name to be much more worthy than we normally revere them.

---

21 Luke 10:38–42.

22 Exodus 20:2–10.

Man always tends to revere himself. By this, we limit our appreciation and acknowledgment of God as He really is. What a great irony. In our attempt to establish our own autonomy and to assert our lofty self-worth, our dignity is lost. Without God we exist more than live. We have no ethical base upon which to live. We discover no real purpose and meaning in our actions. No future exists that causes our conduct to matter. We live under an illusion of freedom. We think we are getting away with rebelling against God. God, in the revelation of His Word, states clearly that we are deceiving ourselves. As we choose to ignore and distort who He is, we condemn ourselves to His just and Righteous judgment.

"Often people come to Christ with selfish motives, but we were created and re-created for God's pleasure and Glory."[23] Salvation is more about giving God Glory than saving lost sinners. We must all ask ourselves the important question: Does my life give God Glory? God has a desire for His Glory. He loves and saves His own for His own Glory. *"But the Lord takes pleasure in those who fear him, in those who hope in his steadfast love."*[24] *"The Lord is not slow to fulfill his promise as some count slowness, but is patient toward you, not wishing that any should perish, but that all should reach repentance."*[25] *"For I have no pleasure in the death of anyone, declares the Lord God; so turn, and live."*[26] *"For he says, 'In a favorable time I listened to you, and in a day of salvation I have helped you.' Behold, now is the favorable time;*

23 Dan DeHaan, *The God You Can Know*, 31.

24 Psalm 147:11.

25 2 Peter 3:9.

26 Ezekiel 18:32.

behold, now is the day of salvation. We put no obstacle in anyone's way."[27]

> *Salvation is more about giving God Glory than saving lost sinners.*

Have you made this declaration based on faith and repentance? If not, this very moment, you have before you both the offer of God's saving grace and the hope of eternity. When God calls us, we will respond to His offer of salvation. True conversion yields new birth in God's family as we trust in Jesus Christ alone for our salvation. This is the way of abundant and true life. All lives outside of the Righteousness of Jesus will perish. This continual perishing will be filled with anguish and continue into eternity. Why would you not receive this free gift from God?

You are an offspring of Adam. Like him, you natually doubt God's Word and His motives. In your doubt, you are missing who God is and the relationship you can have with Him. This book is intended to direct each and every person who reads it to encounter the one and only true God. By your own ability, He will remain your Creator only and never become your legally declared Father. Your adoption into the family of God is your only hope for eternity. Right now, make your election sure and go to Him, the author and finisher of your faith. Admit your sinfulness and turn from your will for your life. Agree with God that you need Him. He holds the way to eternal life. Place your trust in Christ alone for your salvation and right standing before God. As God enables you to do this, you have God's Faithful promise of His redemption. You are immediately declared righteous and

---

27 2 Corinthians 6:2–3.

clean. You are now an adopted child of God, walking the new path of sanctification.

> *Place your trust in Christ alone for your salvation and right standing before God. As God enables you to do this, you have God's Faithful promise of His redemption.*

Along this new life, you will never stop growing in your relationship with your heavenly Father, and you will become more like Jesus. This is the exciting adventure you were made for. Real new life can begin now. You will encounter things in this fallen world that will cause struggles. Now the presence of His Holy Spirit will be with you through them. You will endure until your final step here on this present earth and "fall asleep." You will awaken in His presence to a magnitude you've never experienced while on earth. You will share in His Glory by your own glorification! Your wait to see God will be over. You will see Him as He is, with a new capacity to experience His immediate presence forever. This is our hope of glory. It is worth so much more than our foolish and self-confident pride. God is always ready to accept all who are called into His family and kingdom.

This book hopes to be an accurate yet incomplete vision of the one true God. Only as it has stayed consistent with His revelation of Himself in Scripture has it been accurate. I pray that any distortion that has certainly crept in through nuance or fact will be exposed as error. May God negate and diminish in the hearts and minds of all who read this book those errors that must be here. God will always be best revealed in His holy Word. Here we discover Jesus, the very manifestation of God Himself in the flesh. Here is the best place for you to learn of Him and sit at His feet. Be like Mary, who reverently sat at Jesus's feet, listening to Him. Do not be consumed with the trivial concerns of this world.

> *Enjoy fellowship with your loving Lord. Be in His presence through His Word to you. Always seek God in His Word.*

Enjoy fellowship with your loving Lord. Be in His presence through His Word to you. Always seek God in His Word. "*Let the word of Christ dwell in you richly, teaching and admonishing one another in all wisdom, singing psalms and hymns and spiritual songs, with thankfulness in your hearts to God.*"[28] God has made a way for your acceptance before Him. He longs for you to become a member of His family, both now and forever. My dear friend, hear His call. Seek Him while He may yet be found. Don't sit on the railroad track of life and wait for death. Enjoy new life in Him, through Him, and unto Him. "*And this is eternal life, that they know you the only true God, and Jesus Christ whom you have sent.*"[29] My prayer is that this book has in some small way shown you more of God. This knowledge of God will enable your intimate fellowship with Him. To God alone be all Glory. He alone is worthy.

---

28 Colossians 3:16.

29 John 17:3.

Author Biography

Kenneth O. Friday is a practicing dentist with a large practice of over three thousand patients, spanning more than thirty years. He has also been a ruling elder at Briarwood Presbyterian Church, for over twenty years.

Friday's formal education includes a BA in religion from Birmingham Southern College, a DMD from the University of Alabama in Birmingham School of Dentistry, and an FAGD from the Academy of General Dentistry.

Friday created and managed a Walk Thru Nativity that included fourteen scenes. The successful nativity has run for twenty years, with a current annual attendance of 8,500 individuals.

Friday has been the director of youth ministries at several churches, as well as a Sunday school teacher. He considers all his interests and activities critical in furthering his interest and experience in theology and interpersonal communication.

Selected Bibliography and Reading List

Abbott, Edwin A. *Flatland*. New York, NY: Dover Publications, Inc., 1952.

à Brakel, Wilhelmus. *The Christian's Reasonable Service: Volume I*. Ligonier, PA: Soli Deo Gloria Publications, 1992.

Bates, William. *The Harmony of the Divine Attributes in the Contrivance and Accomplishment of Man's Redemption by the Lord Jesus Christ*. London, England: EEBO Editions.

Bavinck, Herman. *Our Reasonable Faith*. Grand Rapids, MI: Eerdmans Publishing Co., 1956.

Bavinck, Herman. *The Doctrine of God*. Carlisle, PA: The Banner of Truth Trust, 1977.

Berkhof, Louis. *Systematic Theology*. Grand Rapids, MI: Eerdmans Publishing Co., 1947.

Boice, James M. *Foundations of the Christian Faith.* Downers Grove, IL: InterVarsity Press, 1986.

Bridges, Jerry. *The Pursuit of Holiness.* Colorado Springs, CO: NavPress, 2006.

Buswell, J. Oliver. *A Systematic Theology of the Christian Religion: Volume I.* Grand Rapids, MI: Zondervan, 1977.

Calvin, John. *Institutes of the Christian Religion: Volume I.* Philadelphia, PA: The Westminster Press, 1973.

Carson, D. A. *The Difficult Doctrine of the Love of God.* Wheaton, IL: Crossway, 2000.

Charnock, Stephen. *The Existence and Attributes of God.* Grand Rapids, MI: Baker Books, 1996.

Chapman, John. *A Sinner's Guide to Holiness.* Sydney, Australia: Matthias Media, 2005.

Dabney, Robert Lewis. *Systematic Theology.* St. Louis, MO: Presbyterian Publishing Company of St. Louis, 1878.

DeHann, Dan. *The God You Can Know.* Chicago, IL: Moody Press, 1982.

Demarest, Bruce and Gordon Lewis. *Integrative Theology: Volume I.* Grand Rapids, MI: Zondervan, 1987.

Edgar, Brian. *The Message of the Trinity.* Downers Grove, IL: InterVarsity Press, 2004.

Erickson, Millard. *God the Father Almighty.* Grand Rapids, MI: Baker House Co., 1988.

Evans, Tony. *Our God is Awesome.* Chicago, IL: Moody Press, 1994.

George, Jim. *A Young Man after God's Own Heart.* Eugene, OR: Harvest House Publishers, 2005.

Graham, Billy. *Faith 101: What is the Bible?* Nashville, TN: Thomas Nelson, 2006.

Grudem, Wayne. *Christian Beliefs: Twenty Basics Every Christian Should Know.* Grand Rapids, MI: Zondervan, 2005.

Grudem, Wayne. *Systematic Theology.* Grand Rapids, MI: Zondervan, 1999.

Gunter, Sylvia. *Prayer Portions.* Hoover, AL: Alphagraphics, 2012.

Ham, Steve. *In God We Trust: Why Biblical Authority Matters for Every Believer.* Green Forest, AR: Master Books, 2010.

Hay, John and David Webb. *Who is God? And How Can I Really Know Him?* Anderson, IN: Apologia Press, 2009.

Hodge, A. A. *Outlines of Theology*. Grand Rapids, MI: Zondervan, 1977.

Hodge, Charles. *Systematic Theology*. Grand Rapids, MI: Eerdmans Printing Co., 1981.

Horton, T. C. and Charles Hurlburt. *Names of Christ*. Chicago, IL: Moody Press, 1994.

Ingram, Chip. *God as He Longs for You to See Him*. Grand Rapids, MI: Baker Books, 2004.

Jensen, Rosemary. *Praying the Attributes of God*. Grand Rapids, MI: Kregel Publications, 2002.

John of Salisbury. *The Metalogicon of John Salisbury*. Berkeley, CA: University of California Press, 1955.

Kaiser, Walter C., Jr. *The Majesty of God in the Old Testament*. Grand Rapids, MI: Baker Publishing Group, 2007.

Kennedy, D. James. *Truths that Transform: Christian Doctrines for Your Life*. Old Tappan, NJ: Power Books, 1974.

Knight, George. *The Names of God*. Uhrichsville, OH: Barbour Publishing, Inc., 2009.

Knox, Broughton. *The Everlasting God*. Sydney, Australia: Matthias Media, 2009.

Lewis, C. S. *Mere Christianity.* New York, NY: Harper Collins Publishers, 1980.

Lewis, C. S. *Prince Caspian.* New York, NY: Harper Collins Publishers, 1951.

Lewis, C. S. *The Lion, the Witch and the Wardrobe.* New York, NY: Harper Collins Publishers, 1950.

Lewis, Peter. *The Message of the Living God.* Downers Grove, IL: InterVarsity Press, 2000.

MacArthur, John. *Right Thinking in a Word Gone Wrong.* Eugene, OR: Harvest House Publishers, 2009.

MacArthur, John. *Think Biblically! Recovering a Christian Worldview.* Wheaton, IL: Crossway, 2003.

Manser, Martin H. *The Westminster Collection of Christian Quotations.* Louisville, KY: Westminster John Knox Press, 2001.

McDowell, Josh and Sean McDowell. *77 Facts About God and the Bible.* Eugene, OR: Harvest House Publishers, 2012.

McDowell, Sean and Stan Jantz. *God Quest: Discover the God Your Heart is Searching For.* Vista, CA: Outreach, Inc., 2011.

Moreland, J. P. *Love Your God with All Your Mind: The Role of Reason in the Life of the Soul.* Colorado Springs, CO: NavPress, 1997.

Murphey, Cecil. *God—More than Just a Name.* Nashville, TN: Broadman and Holman Publishers, 2001.

Myers, Warren and Ruth. *Experiencing God's Attributes.* Colorado Springs, CO: NavPress, 2003.

Nash, Ronald. *The Concept of God.* Grand Rapids, MI: Zondervan, 1983.

Packer, J. I. *Knowing Christianity.* Downers Grove, IL: InterVarsity Press, 1995.

Packer, J. I. *Knowing God.* Downers Grove, IL: InterVarsity Press, 1973.

Packer, J. I. *A Quest for Godliness: The Puritan Vision of the Christian Life.* Wheaton, IL: Crossway, 1990.

Philip, Robert. *The Eternal; or The Attributes of Jehovah.* London, England: James Clarke & Co., 1874.

Phillips, J. B. *Your God Is Too Small.* New York, NY: Macmillan Publishing Co., 1961.

Pink, A. W. *The Attributes of God.* Grand Rapids, MI: Baker Book House, 1975.

Pink, A. W. *The Doctrine of Sanctification: Discerning Real and False Notions of Holiness.* Great Britain: Christian Focus Publications, 1998.

Pink, A.W. *The Sovereignty of God.* Grand Rapids, MI: Baker Books, 1984.

Piper, John. *The Dangerous Duty of Delight: Daring to Make God Your Greatest Desire.* Colorado Springs, CO: Multnomah Books, 2011.

Piper, John. *The Pleasures of God; Meditations on God's Delight in Being God.* Portland, OR: Multnomah Press, 1991.

Pratney, W. A. *The Nature and Character of God; The Magnificent Doctrine of God in Understandable Language.* Minneapolis, MN: Bethany House Publishers, 1988.

Reymond, Robert. *A New Systematic Theology of the Christian Faith.* Nashville, TN: Thomas Nelson Publishers, 1998.

Reymond, Robert. *What is God?* Roos-Shire, Great Britain: Christian Focus Publications, 2007.

Ryken, Philip and Michael LeFebvre. *Our Triune God; Living in the Love of the Three-In-One.* Wheaton, IL: Crossway, 2011.

Scougal, Henry. *The Life of God in the Soul of Man.* Harrisonburg, VA: Sprinkle Publications, 2005.

Shaw, Robert. *The Reformed Faith: An Exposition of the Westminster Confession of Faith.* Scotland, UK: Christian Focus Publications, 2008.

Shedd, William G. T. *Dogmatic Theology.* Phillipsburg, NJ: Presbyterian and Reformed Publishing Co., 2003.

Sherman, Doug. *More Than Ordinary: Enjoying Life with God.* Colorado Springs, CO: NavPress, 2011.

Smallman, Stephen. *Spiritual Birthline: Understanding How We Experience the New Birth.* Wheaton, IL: Crossway, 2006.

Smallman, Stephen. *What is True Conversion?* Phillipsburg, NJ: Presbyterian and Reformed Publishing, 2005.

Smith, Morton. *Harmony of the Westminster Confession and Catechisms.* Taylors, SC: Presbyterian Press, 1990.

Sproul, R. C. *Does God Control Everything?* Orlando, FL: Reformation Trust Publishing, 2012.

Sproul, R. C. *Discovering the God Who Is: His Character and Being, His Power and Personality.* Ventura, CA: Regal, 1995.

Sproul, R. C. *Essential Truths of the Christian Faith.* Carol Stream, IL: Tyndale House Publishers, 1992.

Stevens, Jarrett. *The Deity Formerly Known as God.* Grand Rapids, MI: Zondervan, 2006.

Stone, Nathan. *Names of God.* Chicago, IL: Moody Publishers, 2010.

Stott, John R. W. *Basic Christianity.* Downers Grove, IL: InterVarsity Press, 1971.

Thousands...Not Billions: Questioning an Icon of Evolution; Questioning the Age of the Earth. El Cajon, CA: The Institute for Creation Research, 2005.

Towns, Elmer L. *The Names of Jesus*. Colorado Springs, CO: Accent Publications, 1987.

Tozer, A. W. *God's Pursuit of Man*. Camp Hill, PA: Wing Spread Publishers, 2007.

Tozer, A. W. *The Attributes of God: Volumes I & II*. Camp Hill, PA: Wing Spread Publishers, 2007.

Tozer, A. W. *The Knowledge of the Most Holy*. New York, NY: Harper One, 1961.

Tozer, A. W. *Whatever Happened to Worship?* Camp Hill, PA: Wing Spread Publishers, 2012.

Troxel, A. Craig. *What is Man?* Phillipsburg, NJ: Presbyterian and Reformed Publishing, 2010.

Turretin, Francis. *Institutes of Elenctic Theology*. Phillipsburg, NJ: Presbyterian and Reformed Publishing, 1992.

Ware, Bruce. *God's Greater Glory*. Wheaton, IL: Crossway, 2004.

Wells, David F. *What Is the Trinity*. Phillipsburg, NJ: Presbyterian and Reformed Publishing, 2012.

Williamson, G. I. *The Westminster Confession of Faith for Study Classes*. Philadelphia, PA: Presbyterian and Reformed Publishing, 1964.

Williamson, G. I. *The Shorter Catechism for Study Classes*. Phillipsburg, NJ: Presbyterian and Reformed Publishing, 1970.

Wong, Amy Ng. *The Everyday Guide to God*. Uhrichsville, OH: Barbour Publishing, Inc., 2002.

Appendix 1

REFORMED CONFESSIONAL STATEMENTS ABOUT THE BEING AND ATTRIBUTES OF GOD

Belgic Confession (1561)

There is One Only God. We all believe with the heart, and confess with the mouth, that there is one only simple and spiritual Being, which we call God; and that He is eternal, incomprehensible, invisible, immutable, infinite, almighty, perfectly wise, just, good, and the overflowing fountain of all good.

Heidelberg Catechism (1563)

What doth God enjoin in the first commandment? That I, as sincerely as I desire the salvation of my own soul, avoid and flee from all idolatry, sorcery, soothsaying, superstition, invocation of saints, or any other creatures; and learn rightly to know the only true God; trust in Him alone; with humility and patience submit to Him; expect all good things from Him only; love, fear, and glorify Him with my whole heart; so that I renounce and forsake all creatures, rather than commit even the least thing contrary to His will.

What is idolatry? Idolatry is, instead of, or besides that one true God who has manifested Himself in His Word, to contrive, or have any other object, in which men place their trust.

Which is the first petition? Hallowed be Thy name; that is, grant us, first, rightly to know Thee, and to sanctify, glorify and praise Thee in all Thy works, in which Thy power, wisdom, goodness, justice, mercy and truth, are clearly displayed.

Second Helvitic Confession (1566)

We believe and teach that God is one in essence or nature, subsisting by Himself, all-sufficient in Himself, invisible, without a body, infinite, eternal, the Creator of all things both visible and invisible, the chief good, living, quickening and preserving all things, almighty and supremely wise, gentle or merciful, just and true.

And we detest the multitude of gods, because it is expressly written, "The LORD our God is one LORD" (Deut. 6:4). "I am the LORD thy God,...... thou shalt have no other gods beside Me (Exod. 20:2-3). "I am the LORD, and there is none else, there is no God beside Me...... I am the LORD and there is none else...... a just God and a Saviour; there is none beside Me" (Isa. 45:6,21). "The LORD God, merciful and gracious, long-suffering, and abundant in goodness and truth" (Exod. 34:6).

Westminster Confession of Faith (1647)

There is but one only, living, and true God, who is infinite in being and perfection, a most pure spirit, invisible, without body, part, or passions; immutable, immense, eternal, incomprehensible, almighty, most wise, most holy, most free, most absolute; working all things according to the counsel of His own immutable and most righteous will, for His own glory; most loving, gracious, merciful, long-suffering, abundant in goodness and truth, forgiving iniquity, transgression, and sin; the rewarder of them that diligently seek Him; and withal, most just, and terrible in His judgments, hating all sin, and who will by no means clear the guilty.

God hath all life, glory, goodness, blessedness, in and of Himself; and is alone in and unto Himself all-sufficient, not standing in need of any creatures which He hath made, nor deriving any glory from them, but only manifesting His own glory in, by, unto, and upon them. He is the alone fountain of all being, of whom, through whom, and to whom are all things; and hath most sovereign dominion over them, to do by them, for them, or upon hem whatsoever Himself pleaseth. In His sight all things are open and manifest, His knowledge is infinite, infallible, and independent upon the creature, so as nothing is to Him contingent, or uncertain. He is most holy in all His counsels, in all His works, and in all His commands. To Him is due from angels and men, and every other creature, whatsoever worship, service, or obedience He is pleased to require of them.

Westminster Shorter Catechism (1647)

God is a Spirit, infinite, eternal, and unchangeable, in His being, wisdom, power, holiness, justice, goodness, and truth. There is but One only, the living and true God.

Westminster Larger catechism (1648)

The Scriptures make known what God is, the persons in the Godhead, His decrees, and the execution of His decrees. God is a Spirit, in and of Himself infinite in being, glory, blessedness, and perfection, all-sufficient, eternal, unchangeable, incomprehensible, everywhere present, almighty, knowing all things, most wise, most holy, most just, most merciful and gracious, long-suffering, and abundant in goodness and truth.

Diverse Groupings of the Attributes of God

It can be difficult to separate a characteristic of God's Being from one of His actions. (Nurturing vs. Redeemer, Love vs Supporting, etc.). Below are various groups and listings of His attributes, including up to 25 of the common ones shown here:

Personal	Creator	Spirit
Invisible	Omnipresent	Omnipotent
Omniscient	Being	Self-Existent
Eternal	Infinite	Goodness
Love	Mercy	Gracious
Faithful	Just	Jealous
Wrath	Sovereign	Immutability
Unity	Trinity	Holy
Truth	Righteous	Simplicity
Freedom	Patience	

1.

Incommunicable

Aseity (self-existent, self-sufficient), Eternity, Immutability, Omnipresence, Unity

Communicable

Beauty, Blessedness, Freedom, Glory, Goodness, Holiness, Invisibility, Jealous, Knowledge, Love, Mercy, Omnipotence, Peace, Perfection, Righteousness, Spirituality, Truthfulness, Will, Wisdom, Wrath

2.

Incommunicable

1. Independence (self-sufficiency, aseity)
2. Immutability

3. Infinity, Infinitude
    a. Eternity
    b. Immensity, Omnipresence
4. Oneness
    a. Numerical Oneness, Unity
    b. Qualitative oneness, Simplicity

Communicable

1. Those designating God as Life and Spirit
    a. Spirituality
    b. Invisibility
2. Those describing God as perfect in self-consciousness
    a. Knowledge, Omniscience
    b. Wisdom
    c. Veracity
3. Those indicating God's Ethical Nature
    a. Goodness
    b. Righteousness
    c. Holiness
4. Those designating God as Lord, King, and Sovereign
    a. Will
    b. Freedom
    c. Omnipotence
5. Those summarizing and revealing and complementing these above
    a. Perfection
    b. Blessedness
    c. Glory

3.

Absolute- always present to the same degree

1. Spirituality
2. Infinity
3. Perfection

Relative- shown to man in differing degrees according to God's purpose and wisdom.

1. Time and Space
   Eternity, Immensity
2. Creation
   Omnipresence, Omnipotence, Omniscience
3. Toward Moral Beings
   Grace, Mercy, Goodness, Love, Wrath, Justice, Jealousy, Vengence, Transcendence, Immanence

4.

Passive- modes of existing, essence, (Divine Person)

Self-existent, Simple, Eternal, Immense, One(Unity)

Active- in action, (Divine Attributes)

Omnipotence, Omniscience, Wisdom, Goodness

5.

Natural- belonging to the constitutional nature, as opposed to the Will of God

Self-existence, Infinity, Eternity, Immutability, Omnipotence, Omniscience, Omnipresence

Moral
Truth, Goodness, Holiness, Justice, Mercy, etc.!

(Both natural and moral categories include wisdom)

6.
Immanent (Intransitive)- those not going forth to operate, but remaining internal in the divine essence
Immensity (Omnipresence), Eternity, Simplicity, Self-existence, etc.!

Emmanent (Transitive)- those issuing forth and producing effects external to God
Omnipresence, Benevolence, Justice, etc.!

7.
Positive- belonging in a finite degree to the creature

Negative- those attributes from which all finite imperfection is negated or removed

8.
Absolute- those attributes expressing God's relation to Himself
Simplicity, Self-existence, Unity, Eternity

Relative- those attributes expressing God's relation to the world
Omnipotence, Omnipresence, etc.!

9.

Active- involving action

Omnipresence, Justice, Benevolence

Passive- involving rest

Self-existence, Immensity, Eternity, etc.!

10.

Constitutional Attributes	**Moral Attributes**	**Positional Attributes**
1. Unity/Trinity	1. Holy	1. Sovereign
2. Spirit	2. Good	2. Master
3. Infinite	3. Truth/Righteous	3. Creator
4. Unchangeable	4. Love	4. Judge
5. Self-Existent	5. Wrath	5. Redeemer
6. Personal	6. Faithful	6. Father

Glory

Appendix 2

INCOMPLETE LIST OF GOD'S NAMES, TITLES, ATTRIBUTES, METAPHORS, ACTIONS, DISPOSITIONS, AND IMAGES

A

Abba, Father
Abiding
Abounding
Absolute
Accessible
Adonai, Lord Master
Advocate
All
Alone176
Almighty God
Alpha and Omega
Amazing
Amen
Ancient of Days
Angel of the Lord
Anger
Answer
Architect/Builder
Arm of the Lord
Ascended
Atonement
Author/Finisher of faith and of life
Authority
Avenger
Awesome

B

Balm of Gilead
Banner to the People
Beautiful
Beginning and End
Beloved Son of God
Benevolent
Betrayed (Judas)
Betrothed
Blameless
Blessed Hope
Blesses
Boundless
Bread from Heaven
Bread of Life
Bridegroom
Bright morning star
Brightness of the glory of God
Brother
Burden-bearer

C

Captain of the
Lord's host
Caring
Causes to bear fruit (Spirit)
Chief cornerstone
Chief shepherd
Choice and Precious
Chosen of God
Christ
Christ Jesus our Lord
Christ the power of God
Cleansing
Comforter
Coming again
Commander of the army of the Lord
Compassionate
Complete
Conquering
Consolation
Consistent
Constant
Consuming fire
Cornerstone
Counselor
Conveys God's thoughts (Spirit)
Convicts
Covenant keeping
Cover for sin
Creator
Crucified

D

Dangerous
Defender
Deliverer
Denied (Peter)
Dependable
Desire of nations
Discerner

Discloses what is to come
Divine
Dominion
Door
Dwelling Place

E
El Shaddai (all-sufficient)
El Elyon (most high God)
Elohim (eternal God)
Elroi (God who sees)
Empowers
Encourager
Enduring
Enthroned
Eternal God
Eternal life
Essence/being
Evaluator
Everlasting Father
Everlasting name
Exalted
Excellent
Expected one

F
Faithful
Father of: lights, compassion, Jesus, mercy, Isaac, fatherless
Fills
Fire
Firm
First and last
Firstborn of creation
For us
Forerunner
Forgiving
Foreknowledge
Fortress
Foundation stone
Free
Friend
Friend of slaves

G
Gate for the sheep
Generous
Gentle
Gift of God
Giver of every good gift
Giver of life
Glorifier
Glorious Lord
Glory of Israel
God of: all comfort, Abraham, grace, Daniel, deliverances, gods, glory, heaven, hope, Isaac, Israel, Jacob, Jerusalem, Jeshurun, our fathers, armies of Israel, love and peace, the Lord, one and only, retribution, vengeance, savior, father, who sees

Good
Good Shepherd
Governor
Gracious
Great (God/King)
Great high priest
Guard and Guardian of my soul
Grief
Groans
Guarantor of a better covenant
Guide

H

Has a sword (Spirit)
Hater of Idolatry
Head of the Church
Head of Everyman
Healer
Heavenly
Heir of all things
Help and Helper
Hiding place
High and exalted one
Holy
Holy Spirit
Hope (of Israel)
Honest
Horn of salvation
Humble?
Husband

I

I AM
Illuminating
Impartial
Immaterial
Immortal
Immanuel, always with us
Immense
Immortal
Indispensable
Incarnate
Incomprehensible
Incorruptible
Incomparable
Indwelling
Infinite
Inheritance
Innocent
Intercessor
Inscrutable
Instructor
Invisible

J

Jealous God
Jehovah-Jirah (provider)
Jehovah-M'Kaddesh (sanctification)
Jehovah-Nissi (Banner)
Jehovah-Rohi (Shepherd)
Jehovah-Rophe (Healer)

Jehovah-Shammah (ever-present)
Jehovah-Shalom (peace)
Jehovah-Tsidkenu (righteousness)
Jesus: Christ our Lord, of Nazareth, the Son of God
Joy
Judge of all the earth
Just one and justifier

K

Known—revealer
Keeper
Kind
King: eternal, of glory, of Israel, of the Jews, of Kings

L

Lamb (of God)
Lamp
Lawgiver
Liberty
Life and life-giving Spirit
Light: of the nations, of revelation, of the world
Lily of the valleys
Lion of Judah
Living bread
Living: God, water (unfailing spring)
Long-suffering
Lord: God, the Almighty, Jesus Christ, of all, of glory, of the harvest, of hosts, of Lord of the Sabbath, your God, will provide, who makes you holy, who heals, righteousness, Jehovah, is my banner, is peace, is there, most high, of all the earth, of earth, of harvest, of the whole world, our God, maker
Love and loving
Lover of my soul
Loving kindness
Lowly in heart
Loyal

M

Magnificent
Maker (of all things)
Majesty
Majestic Glory
Man: Jesus Christ, of sorrows, whom God appointed
Manager
Master
Marred, pierced, stricken, rejected
Marvelous
Mediator
Meek
Merciful
Messiah
Mighty: God, One, of Israel, of Jacob

Morning Star
Most High God

N

Name above all names
Near
Never Failing
None other
Nurturing

O

Obedient Son
Offering for sin
Offspring of David
Omnipotent
Omnipresent
Omniscient
On high forever
One of Sinai
<u>Only</u>: begotten Son, God our savior, one, wise God
Opposes the sinful flesh
Over all
Overcome
Overseer
Owner

P

Passover, blood of the Lamb
Patient
Peace
Perseverance
Persistence
Physician
Portion of Jacob
Potter
Power of God
Pours out God's love
Preserver
Precious cornerstone
Presence
Present
Priest
<u>Prince</u>: of peace, of princes
Proceeds from the Father (Spirit)
Promise of the Father
Prophet
Propitiation for our sins
Protector
Provider
Punctual
Purposeful
Pure and Purifier
Providential

Q

Quenchable
Quiet
Quieter of the storm
Quick and powerful Word of God

R

Rabbi

Rabboni

Radiance of His Glory

Ransom

Reality

Reconciliation

Redeemer and redemption

Refiner

Refining fire

Refuge

Reigns

Relational

Reliable

Reminds

Renews

Repentant

Requestable

Rescuer

Responsive

Restorer of my soul

Rests on believers (Spirit)

Resurrection and life

Revelation

Reviving One

Rewards and reward

Rich

Righteous: one, Judge, servant

Rock: of salvation, refuge, and strength

Root and offspring of David and Jesse

Rose of Sharon

Ruler

S

Safety

Salvation

Sanctuary

Sanctification

Sanctuary

Sanctifier

Satisfaction

Savior: of Israel, the world

Scepter

Searching

Seals

Searches all things

Seed of Abraham

Seeker

Self-sustaining

Sent

Servant of God

Sets free

Shade

Shadow of the Almighty

Shelter

Shepherd of Israel

Shield

Sinless

Simple
Sin-bearing sacrifice
Son of: David, God, the Highest, Man, Righteousness, the Most High
Song
Source
Sovereign (Lord)
Speaks to the churches
Spirit of: power, Christ, counsel, glory, His Son, the living God, fear of the Lord, son-ship, sovereign Lord, understanding, wisdom and revelation, your Father, adoption, grace, holiness, truth
Splendid
Spotless (unblemished)
Stay
Steadfast
Stone
Strength
Strong deliverer
Stronghold
Strong tower
Strives with sinners (Spirit)
Suffering servant
Sufficient
Sun and shield
Sun of righteousness
Supernatural
Supreme
Sure and our surety
Sustainer
Sympathetic

T

Teacher (from God)
Tester
Testifies with our spirit
Tortured
Tower of strength
Transcendence
Transforms
Triune
True: God, light, riches
Trustworthy
Truth

U

Ubiquitous
Unchanging
Upholder of all things
Upright one
Unapproachable
Understanding
Unfailing
Unfathomable
Unimaginable
Uniting
Unique
Unsearchable
Unspeakable gift
Untiring

V

Vengeance
Victorious Warrior
Victory
Vindicator
Vine
Vinedresser
Virtuous
Voice of the Lord

W

Wall of fire
Way
Wind
Wise
Witness to the peoples
Wonderful counselor
Word of life
Worthy
Wrath

Y

Yahweh

Z

Zealous
Zion's King

Appendix 3

SCRIPTURAL SURVEY OF THE CHARACTER OF GOD: ACTIONS, NAMES, IMAGES, AND ATTRIBUTES OF GOD

Genesis 1

- Creator v. 1
- Matter from naught v. 1
- Source of existence v. 1
- Spirit of God v. 2
- God said vv. 3, 6, 9, 11, 14, 20, 24, 26, 28, 29
- He sees vv. 4, 10, 12, 18, 21, 25, 31
- Source of light v. 3
- Maker v. 7
- Blesses vv. 22, 28
- Triune v. 26
- Delegates v. 28
- God v. 1

Genesis 2

- LORD vv. 4, 5, 7, 8, 9, 15, 16, 18, 19, 21, 22
- Finishes v. 1
- Rests v. 2
- Institution of the Sabbath v. 3
- LORD God v. 5
- Caretaker v. 9
- Forms v. 7
- Breaths life v. 7
- Commands v. 16
- High regard for relationships vv. 18-25

Genesis 3

- LORD vv. 1, 8, 9, 13, 14, 21, 22, 23
- Punishes disobedience vv. 14-19
- Promises redemption vv. 15, 21

Genesis 4

- LORD vv. 1, 3, 4, 6, 9, 10, 13, 15, 16, 26
- Helps his people v. 1
- Instructs v. 7

Genesis 5

- LORD v. 29
- Intimacy with man v. 24
- Gives rest (Noah) v. 29

Genesis 6

- LORD vv. 3, 5, 6, 7, 8
- Abides in man (Spirit) v. 3
- Limits man v. 3
- Grief v. 6
- Regret v. 7
- Sees the earth v. 11
- Preserves the blameless v. 18

Genesis 7

- LORD (Yahweh) vv. 1, 5, 16
- Sees the righteous v. 1
- Destroys the corrupt v. 4

Genesis 8

- LORD vv. 20, 21, 26
- Remembers the righteous v. 7
- Spirit v. 1
- Gives new opportunities v. 17
- Smells v. 21
- Has a heart v. 21
- Sustains the earth v. 22

Genesis 9

- LORD v. 26
- Blesses v. 1
- Permits animals for food v. 3
- Established covenant v. 11
- Gives a sign of his covenant v. 13
- Consequences for sin v. 25
- Blessings for uprightness vv. 26, 27

Genesis 10

- LORD v. 9

Genesis 11

- LORD vv. 5, 6, 8, 9
- Sees v. 5
- Triune v. 7
- Enforces his commandments vv. 7, 8

Genesis 12

- LORD vv. 1, 4, 7, 8, 17
- God speaks v. 1
- Personal interaction v. 1
- Blesses v. 2
- Looks out for his own v. 3

Genesis 13

- LORD vv. 4, 10, 13, 14, 18
- Reaffirming vv. 14-17

Genesis 14

- LORD v. 22
- God Most High vv. 19, 22
- Deliverer v. 20

Genesis 15

- LORD vv. 1, 2, 4, 6, 7, 13, 18
- Foreknowledge v. 13
- Divine pledge v. 17
- Lord GOD vv. 2, 8
- Shield v. 1
- LORD vv. 1, 2, 4, 6, 7, 8, 13, 18

Genesis 16

- LORD vv. 2, 5, 7, 9, 10, 11, 13
- Angel of the LORD vv. 7, 9, 10
- Living one v. 14
- Sees v. 14
- Hears (Ishmael) v. 11

Genesis 17

- LORD v. 1
- God Almighty v. 1
- Covenant maker and orchestrator vv. 1-2
- Promises
- Upholds His word v. 19
- Hears (Abraham) v. 20

Genesis 18

- LORD vv. 1, 3, 10, 12, 13, 14, 17, 19, 20, 22, 26, 27, 30, 31, 32, 33
- Attention to all detail v.21

Genesis 19

- LORD vv. 2, 13, 14, 16, 18, 24, 27
- Divine mercy v. 16
- Hears pleas vv. 18-21
- Righteous wrath vv. 24-25

<u>Genesis 20</u>

- LORD vv. 4, 18

<u>Genesis 21</u>

- LORD vv. 1, 33
- Keeps his promises v. 1

<u>Genesis 22</u>

- Tests Abraham v. 1
- Provider v. 14
- Rewards obedience v. 18
- LORD vv. 11, 14, 15, 16

<u>Genesis 23</u>

- LORD vv. 11, 15

<u>Genesis 24</u>

- Lord v. 3
- God of heaven v. 3
- God of earth v. 3
- LORD vv. 1, 3, 7, 12, 18, 21, 27, 31, 35, 40, 42, 44, 48, 50, 51, 52, 56
- Blesses v. 1
- Sends angels v. 40

<u>Genesis 25</u>

- Blesses (Isaac) v. 2
- Answers prayer v. 21
- LORD vv. 21, 22, 23

<u>Genesis 26</u>

- Appears (Isaac) v. 2
- Covenant vv. 3-5
- Makes room v. 22
- With His chosen v. 24
- Blesses v. 29
- LORD vv. 2, 12, 22, 24, 25, 28, 29

<u>Genesis 27</u>

- LORD vv. 7, 20, 27, 29, 37

<u>Genesis 28</u>

- God Almighty v. 3
- LORD v. 13
- Dream giver and interpreter vv. 12-16
- LORD vv. 13, 16, 21, 31, 32, 33, 35

<u>Genesis 29</u>

- Sees v. 32
- Hears v. 33
- LORD

<u>Genesis 30</u>

- LORD vv. 24, 27, 30

<u>Genesis 31</u>

- Instructs v. 3
- Blesses His people v. 9
- LORD vv. 3, 35, 49

<u>Genesis 32</u>

- God's camp v. 2
- LORD v. 18

<u>Genesis 33</u>

- El-Elohe-Israel (God, the God of Israel) v. 20
- Unmerited favor v. 10
- LORD vv. 8, 13, 14, 15

<u>Genesis 34</u>

<u>Genesis 35</u>

- God of Isaac, of Israel v. 10
- God Almighty v. 11
- Speaks v. 10

<u>Genesis 36</u>

<u>Genesis 37</u>

- Dream giver vv. 5-11

<u>Genesis 38</u>

- LORD v. 19

<u>Genesis 39</u>

- LORD vv. 2, 3, 5, 21, 23
- With Joseph vv. 2, 3, 21, 23
- Gave favor v. 21

<u>Genesis 40</u>

- Interpreter of dreams v. 8
- LORD v. 1

<u>Genesis 41</u>

- Recognized before Pharaoh v. 38
- Spirit of God v. 38

<u>Genesis 42</u>

- LORD vv. 30, 33

Genesis 43

- LORD v. 20

Genesis 44

- LORD vv. 5, 7, 8, 9, 16, 18, 19, 20, 22, 24, 33

Genesis 45

- LORD vv. 8, 9

Genesis 46

- "I am God" v. 3
- Speaks (to Israel) v. 2
- Vision giver v. 2

Genesis 47

- LORD vv. 18, 25

Genesis 48

- Walks with His chosen v. 15
- Shepherds v. 15
- Redeems from all evil v. 16

Genesis 49

- Shaddai (Almighty) v. 25
- Shepherd v. 24
- Stone of Israel v. 24
- LORD v. 18

Genesis 50

- God will visit and take His people into His promise v. 24

Exodus 1

- Allows persecution vv. 8-14
- God's faithful flourish v. 21

Exodus 2

- Hears v. 24
- Sees v. 25
- Knows v. 25
- Remembers covenant v. 24

Exodus 3

- Angel of the LORD v. 2
- God of... your father, Abraham, Isaac, and Jacob vv. 6, 15
- LORD vv. 2, 4, 7, 15, 16, 18
- Sees vv. 7, 9
- Hears vv. 7, 9
- Knows his people's sufferings vv. 7, 9
- Delivers v. 8
- Sends v. 10
- I AM v. 14
- Remembered throughout all generations v. 15
- God of the Hebrews v. 18

Exodus 4

- God of... your father, Abraham, Isaac, and Jacob v. 5
- Provides signs to cause belief and establish credibility vv. 1-9
- LORD vv. 1, 2, 4, 5, 6, 10, 11, 13, 14, 19, 21, 22, 27, 28, 30, 31
- Accommodates us in our weakness v. 14
- Instructs v. 19

Exodus 5

- LORD vv. 1, 2, 17, 21, 22
- God of Israel, of the Hebrews vv. 1, 3
- LORD vv. 1, 2, 3, 17, 21, 22

Exodus 6

- LORD vv. 1, 2, 3, 6, 7, 8, 10, 12, 13, 26, 28, 30
- God Almighty v. 3
- Remembers covenant v. 5
- Outstretched arm v. 6
- Deliver and redeem. 6
- Judgment v. 6
- LORD vv. 1, 2, 3, 6, 7, 8, 10, 12, 13, 26, 28, 29, 30

Exodus 7

- Commands His chosen to speak v. 2
- Judgment v. 4
- LORD vv. 1, 5, 6, 8, 10, 13, 14, 16, 17, 19, 20, 22, 25

Exodus 8

- LORD vv. 1, 5, 8, 10, 12, 13, 15, 16, 19, 20, 22, 24,26, 27, 28, 29, 30, 31
- Finger of God v. 19
- Answered prayer v. 31

Exodus 9

- LORD vv. 1, 3, 4, 5, 6, 8, 12, 13, 20, 21, 22, 23, 27, 28, 29, 30, 33, 35
- Speaks (Moses) v. 12

Exodus 10

- LORD vv. 1, 2, 3, 7, 8, 9, 10, 11, 12, 13, 16, 17, 18, 19, 20, 21, 24, 25, 26, 27
- LORD your God vv. 8, 16, 17
- LORD our God vv. 25, 26
- Hardened Pharaoh's heart vv. 20, 27

Exodus 11

- LORD vv. 1, 3, 4, 7, 9, 10
- Said vv. 19
- Grants favor v. 3
- Magnifies His name v. 9
- Hardened Pharoah's heart v. 10

Exodus 12

- Hebrew calendar v. 2
- LORD vv. 1, 11, 12, 14, 23, 25, 27, 28, 29, 31, 36, 41, 42, 43, 48, 50, 51
- Passover vv. 11, 27
- Favor v. 36
- Hosts of the LORD v. 41

Exodus 13

- LORD vv. 1, 3, 5, 6, 8, 9, 11, 12, 14, 15, 16, 21
- Said vv. 1, 17
- Law of the LORD v. 9
- Pillar of cloud vv. 21, 22
- Pillar of fire vv. 21, 22

Exodus 14

- LORD vv. 1, 4, 8, 10, 13, 14, 15, 18, 21, 24, 25, 26, 27, 30, 31
- Hardened Pharaoh's heart vv. 4, 8, 17
- Salvation v. 13
- Angel of God v. 9
- Savior (Israel) v. 31
- Great power v. 31

Exodus 15

- LORD vv. 1, 2, 3, 6, 11, 16, 17, 18, 19, 21, 25, 26
- Right hand vv. 6, 12
- Man of war v. 3
- Blast of nostrils v. 8
- Majestic in holiness v. 11
- Awesome in glorious deeds v. 11
- Doing wonders v. 11
- Steadfast love v. 13
- Redeemed v. 13
- Guide v. 13
- Your arm v. 16
- Purchased His people v. 16
- Reigns forever v. 18
- Established His sanctuary v. 17
- Triumphed gloriously v. 21
- Made a statute, rule, commandment v. 28
- Healer v. 28
- Tests v. 25

Exodus 16

- LORD vv. 3, 4, 6, 7, 8, 9, 10, 11, 12, 15, 16, 23, 25, 28, 29, 32, 33, 34
- Tests v. 4

Exodus 17

- LORD vv. 1, 2, 4, 5, 7, 14, 15, 16
- The rock v. 6
- Banner v. 15

Exodus 18

- LORD vv. 1, 8, 9, 10, 11
- Delivered vv. 9, 10

Exodus 19

- LORD vv. 3, 7, 8, 9, 10, 11, 18, 20, 21, 22, 23, 24
- Eagles wings v. 4
- Kingdom of Priests v. 6
- Holy nation v. 6
- Thick cloud v. 9
- Came down on Mt. Sinai v. 11
- Descended in fire v. 18

Exodus 20

- LORD vv. 2, 5, 7, 10, 11, 12, 22
- LORD your God v. 2
- 10 commandments vv. 3-17
- Jealous v. 5
- Visits iniquities v. 5
- Steadfast love v. 6
- Made everything in six days, rested on the Sabbath v. 11
- Tests v. 20

Exodus 21

- Gives rules v. 1

Exodus 22

- LORD v. 20
- Laws vv. 1-31

Exodus 23

- Laws vv. 1-33
- LORD your God v. 19
- Angel (Jesus) v. 20
- Provides and prepares v. 20
- Obedient prosper greatly vv. 20-25
- LORD vv. 17, 19, 25

Exodus 24

- LORD vv. 1, 2, 3, 4, 5, 7, 8, 12, 16, 17
- Covenant v. 8
- Visible v. 10
- God of Israel v. 10
- Reveals Himself vv. 10, 11
- Dwelt v. 16
- Devouring fire v. 17

Exodus 25

- LORD vv. 1
- Sanctuary of dwelling in our midst v. 8
- His testimony vv. 16, 21
- Speaks v. 22
- Bread of the presence v. 30

Exodus 26

- Tabernacle (dwelling place of God) vv. 1-27

Exodus 27

- LORD v. 21

Exodus 28

- Filled with a spirit of skill v. 3
- LORD vv. 12, 29, 30, 35, 36, 38
- Anoints, ordains, and consecrates v. 41

Exodus 29

- LORD vv. 11, 18, 23, 24, 25, 26, 28, 41, 46
- God of Israel v. 45
- Dwells among us v. 45
- LORD and God of Israel v. 46

Exodus 30

- Atonement tax vv. 11-16
- LORD vv. 10, 11, 12, 13, 14, 15, 16, 17, 20, 22, 34, 37

Exodus 31

- Gives people ability v. 3
- Sabbath v. 15
- Spirit of God v. 3
- LORD vv. 1, 12, 13, 15, 17

Exodus 32

- Wrath v. 10
- Relented v. 14
- God wrote v. 16
- LORD God of Israel v. 27
- LORD vv. 5, 7, 9, 11, 14, 22, 26, 27, 29, 30, 31, 33, 35
- Angel v. 34
- Book of life vv. 32-33

Exodus 33

- LORD vv. 1, 5, 7, 9, 11, 12, 17, 19, 21
- Angel v. 2
- Face to face v. 11
- Friend v. 11
- Pillar of cloud v. 10
- Presence (Moses) v. 14
- His Glory vv. 18, 22
- Hand v. 22
- Back v. 22
- Face v. 22

Exodus 34

- LORD vv. 1, 4, 5, 6, 9, 10, 14, 23, 24, 26, 27, 28, 32, 34
- Write v. 1
- Descended v. 5
- Merciful v. 6
- Gracious v. 6
- Slow to anger v. 6
- Abounding in steadfast love and faithfulness v. 6
- Love for thousands v. 7
- Forgiving iniquity and transgression and sin v. 7
- Visits iniquity v. 7
- Awesome v. 10
- Jealous v. 10
- Covenant v. 27
- 10 commandments v. 28

Exodus 35

- Sabbath regulations vv. 2, 3
- LORD vv. 1, 2, 4, 5, 10, 21, 22, 24, 29, 30
- Holy place v. 19
- Moves and stirs v. 21
- Spirit of God v. 31

Exodus 36

- Stirs hearts v. 2
- LORD vv. 1, 2, 5

Exodus 37

- Ark v. 1

Exodus 38

- LORD v. 22

Exodus 39

- LORD vv. 1, 5, 7, 21, 26, 29, 30, 31, 32, 42, 43

Exodus 40

- LORD vv. 1, 16, 19, 21, 23, 25, 27, 29, 32, 34, 35, 38
- Glory v. 34
- Cloud v. 35, 37
- Fire v. 38
- Seen v. 8

Leviticus 1

- LORD vv. 1, 2, 3, 5, 9, 11, 13, 14, 17
- Smells vv. 9, 17

Leviticus 2

- LORD vv. 1, 2, 3, 8, 9, 10, 11, 12, 14, 16
- Food offering v. 16

Leviticus 3

- LORD vv. 1, 3, 5, 6, 7, 9, 11, 14, 16
- Peace offering requirements v. 16

Leviticus 4

- LORD vv. 1, 2, 3, 4, 6, 7, 13, 15, 17, 18, 22, 24, 27, 31, 35
- Sin offering requirements vv. 1-35
- Atonement vv. 31, 35
- Forgiveness v. 35

Leviticus 5

- LORD vv. 6, 7, 12, 14, 15, 17, 19
- Guilt offering requirements vv. 14-19
- Atonement v. 18

Leviticus 6

- LORD vv. 1, 2, 6, 7, 8, 14, 15, 18, 19, 20, 21, 22, 24, 25
- Guilt offering (requires compensation for offenses) vv. 1-7

Leviticus 7

- LORD vv. 7, 11, 14, 20, 21, 22, 25, 28, 29, 30, 35, 36, 38
- Law of offerings (guilt, peace) vv. 1-38

Leviticus 8

- LORD vv. 1, 4, 5, 9, 13, 17, 21, 26, 27, 28, 29, 34, 35, 36
- Smells (pleasing aroma) v. 21
- Total dedication and purification of His priests v. 22

Leviticus 9

- Appears before the purified in His glory vv. 4, 6, 24
- LORD vv. 2, 4, 5, 6, 7, 10, 21, 23, 24
- Consumes v. 24

Leviticus 10

- LORD vv. 1, 2, 3, 6, 7, 8, 11, 12, 13, 15, 17, 19
- Consumes (Nadab and Abihu die) v. 2
- Speaks to Aaron v. 12
- Bears the iniquity of the congregation through His priests v. 17
- Desires fear from His people v. 19

Leviticus 11

- LORD vv. 1, 44, 45
- Holy v. 45
- Unclean is the antithesis of holy vv. 1-47
- LORD your God v. 44

Leviticus 12

- LORD vv. 1, 7
- Purification after childbirth vv. 1-8

Leviticus 13

- LORD v. 1
- Laws about leprosy vv. 1-59

Leviticus 14

- LORD vv. 1, 11, 12, 16, 18, 23, 24, 27, 29, 31, 33
- Law for cleansing lepers vv. 1-57

Leviticus 15

- LORD vv. 1, 14, 15, 30
- Laws about bodily discharges vv. 1-33
- Speaks v. 1

Leviticus 16

- LORD vv. 1, 2, 7, 8, 9, 10, 12, 13, 18, 30, 34
- Day of Atonement vv. 1-34
- Speaks v. 1

Leviticus 17

- LORD vv. 1, 2, 4, 5, 6, 9
- Place of sacrifice vv. 1-9
- Speaks v. 1

Leviticus 18

- LORD vv. 1, 2, 4, 5, 6, 21, 30
- Speaks v. 1
- Unlawful sexual relations vv. 1-30
- Separate from other peoples v. 3
- LORD your God v. 4
- Abomination of homosexual acts v. 22
- LORD your God v. 30

Leviticus 19

- LORD vv. 1, 2, 3, 4, 5, 8, 10, 12, 14, 16, 18, 21, 22, 24, 26, 28, 30, 31, 32, 34, 36, 37
- Speaks v. 1
- LORD your God v. 2
- Love your neighbor as yourself v. 18
- Prostitution makes a land depraved v. 29
- Honor old men v. 32

Leviticus 20

- LORD vv. 1, 7, 8, 24, 26
- Speaks v. 1
- Face vv. 5, 6
- Abomination of homosexuality v. 13
- Commands holiness v. 22
- LORD your God v. 24
- Condemns necromancy v. 27

Leviticus 21

- LORD vv. 1, 6, 8, 12, 15, 16, 21, 23
- Only the sanctified may enter His presence v. 23
- Speaks v. 1

Leviticus 22

- LORD vv. 1, 2, 3, 8, 9, 15, 16, 17, 18, 21, 22, 24, 26, 27, 29, 30, 31, 32, 33
- I am the LORD vv. 30, 33
- Speaks v. 1

Leviticus 23

- LORD vv. 1, 2, 3, 4, 5, 6, 8, 9, 11, 12, 13, 16, 17, 18, 20, 22, 23, 25, 26, 27, 28, 33, 34, 36, 37, 38, 39, 40, 41, 43, 44
- Speaks v. 1

Leviticus 24

- LORD vv. 1, 3, 4, 6, 7, 8, 9, 12, 13, 16, 22, 23
- Speaks v. 1
- Blaspheming the Name warrants death v. 16

Leviticus 25

- LORD vv. 1, 2, 4, 17, 38, 55
- Speaks v. 1
- The Hebrews may not take one another as a slave v. 46
- LORD your God v. 55

Leviticus 26

- LORD vv. 1, 2, 13, 44, 45, 46
- Speaks v. 1
- Broken the bar of His people's yoke and made them walk erect so that they will prosper and have increase and victory v. 13
- Sevenfold fury against those who do not listen to Him and walk contrary to Him vv. 26, 27
- Remembers His covenant with Abraham, Jacob, and Isaac for those who humble themselves and confess their sin vv. 40-45

Leviticus 27

- LORD vv. 1, 2, 9, 11, 14, 16, 21, 22, 23, 26, 28, 30, 32, 34
- Speaks v. 1
- Commandments v. 34

Numbers 1

- LORD vv. 1, 19, 48, 54
- Spoke to Moses after two years into the wilderness v. 1
- Ordered consensus of Israel's warriors: 603,550 v. 46
- Levites separate from the warriors to care for the tabernacle vv. 47-54
- Invasion of Canaan imminent v. 3

Numbers 2

- LORD vv. 1, 33, 34

Numbers 3

- LORD vv. 1, 4, 5, 11, 13, 14, 16, 39, 40, 41, 42, 44, 45, 51

Numbers 4

- LORD vv. 1, 17, 21, 37, 41, 45, 49

Numbers 5

- LORD vv. 1, 4, 5, 6, 8, 11, 16, 18, 21, 25, 30

Numbers 6

- LORD vv. 1, 2, 5, 6, 8, 12, 14, 16, 17, 20, 21, 22, 24, 25, 26
- Aaron's blessing: The Lord bless you and keep you; the Lord make his face to shine upon you and be gracious to you; the Lord lift up his countenance upon you and give you peace. vv. 24-26

Numbers 7

- LORD vv. 3, 4, 11, 89

Numbers 8

- LORD vv. 1, 3, 4, 5, 10, 11, 12, 13, 20, 21, 22, 23

Numbers 9

- LORD vv. 1, 5, 7, 8, 9, 10, 13, 14, 18, 19, 20, 23

Numbers 10

- LORD vv. 1, 9, 10, 13, 29, 32, 33, 34, 35, 36

Numbers 11

- LORD vv. 1, 2, 3, 10, 11, 16, 18, 20, 23, 24, 25, 28, 29, 31, 33
- Hand v. 23
- Anger v. 33
- Fire of the LORD consumed some of the people when they complained about food v. 1

Numbers 12

- LORD vv. 2, 4, 5, 6, 8, 9, 11, 13, 14
- Came down in a pillar of cloud v. 5

- Anger (Miriam and Aaron for opposing Moses and challenging His authority) v. 9
- Vision and dream v. 6
- Intimacy with the meek v. 3

Numbers 13

- LORD vv. 1, 3

Numbers 14

- LORD vv. 3, 8, 9, 10, 11, 13, 14, 16, 17, 18, 20, 21, 26, 28, 35, 37, 40, 41, 42, 43, 44
- Glory v. 10
- Face to face v. 14
- Pillar of cloud and fire v. 15
- Slow to anger v. 19
- Abounding in steadfast love v. 19
- Forgiving iniquity and transgression v. 19
- Visits iniquity v. 19
- Pardons v. 20
- Glory v. 20
- Hears v. 28

Numbers 15

- LORD vv. 1, 3, 4, 7, 8, 10, 13, 14, 15, 17, 19, 21, 22, 23, 24, 25, 28, 30, 31, 35, 36, 39, 41
- Smells vv. 3, 7, 10, 24

Numbers 16

- LORD vv. 3, 5, 7, 9, 11, 15, 16, 17, 19, 20, 23, 28, 29, 30, 35, 36, 38, 40, 41, 42, 45, 46
- Glory v. 19
- Consume v. 20
- Had the earth swallowed up whole families and dwellings v. 32
- Killed 14,700 in a plague v. 49

Numbers 17

- LORD vv. 1, 7, 9, 10, 11, 13

Numbers 18

- LORD vv. 1, 6, 8, 12, 13, 15, 17, 19, 20, 24, 25, 26, 28, 29

Numbers 19

- LORD vv. 1, 2, 13, 20
- Laws for purification vv. 1-22
- Holiness, God, and life versus uncleanness, sin, and death. vv. 1-22

Numbers 20

- LORD vv. 3, 4, 6, 7, 9, 12, 13, 16, 23, 27
- Glory v. 8
- Punishes rebellion v. 27

Numbers 21

- LORD vv. 2, 3, 6, 7, 8, 14, 16, 34
- Hears v. 3
- Sent fiery serpents among the impatient people v. 6
- Bronze serpent v. 9
- Gave Og into the hand of the Israelites v. 34

Numbers 22

- LORD vv. 8, 13, 18, 19, 22, 23, 24, 25, 26, 27, 28, 31, 32, 34, 35
- Blesses people v. 12
- Angel of the LORD vv. 22, 23, 24, 26, 31, 34, 35

Numbers 23

- LORD vv. 3, 5, 8, 12, 15, 16, 17, 21, 26
- Put a word in Balaam's mouth v. 5
- Does not lie or change His mind v. 19

Numbers 24

- LORD vv. 1, 6, 11, 13
- Spirit of God (came upon Balaam) v. 2

Numbers 25

- LORD vv. 3, 4, 10, 16
- Anger (against Israel) vv. 3, 4
- Wrath v. 11
- Jealous v. 11

Numbers 26

- LORD vv. 1, 4, 9, 52, 61, 65

Numbers 27

- LORD vv. 3, 5, 6, 11, 12, 15, 16, 17, 18, 21, 22, 23

Numbers 28

- LORD vv. 1, 3, 6, 7, 8, 11, 13, 15, 16, 19, 24, 26, 27

Numbers 29

- LORD vv. 2, 6, 8, 12, 13, 36, 39, 40

Numbers 30

- LORD vv. 1, 2, 3, 5, 8, 12, 16

Numbers 31

- LORD vv. 1, 3, 7, 16, 21, 25, 28, 29, 30, 31, 37, 38, 39, 40, 41, 47, 50, 52, 54

Numbers 32

- LORD vv. 4, 7, 9, 10, 12, 13, 14, 20, 21, 22, 23, 25, 27, 29, 31, 32

Numbers 33

- LORD vv. 2, 4, 38, 50

Numbers 34

- LORD vv. 1, 13, 16, 29

Numbers 35

- LORD vv. 1, 9, 34

Numbers 36

- LORD vv. 2, 5, 6, 10, 13

Deuteronomy 1

- LORD vv. 3, 6, 8, 10, 11, 19, 20, 21, 25, 26, 27, 30, 31, 32, 34, 36, 37, 41, 42, 43, 45

Deuteronomy 2

- LORD vv. 1, 2, 7, 9, 12, 14, 15, 17, 21, 29, 30, 31, 33, 36, 37

Deuteronomy 3

- LORD vv. 2, 3, 18, 20, 21, 22, 23, 24, 26
- LORD your God vv. 21, 22

Deuteronomy 4

- LORD vv. 1, 2, 3, 4, 5, 7, 10, 12, 14, 19, 20, 21, 22, 23, 24, 25, 27, 29, 30, 31, 34, 35, 39
- Obedience commanded for success in taking the promise land vv. 1-14
- Near to His people v. 7
- Jealous v. 24
- Merciful v. 31
- Voice v. 26
- Presence and power v. 37
- Unique v. 39

Deuteronomy 5

- LORD vv. 2, 3, 4, 5, 6, 9, 11, 12, 14, 15, 16, 22, 24, 25, 27, 28, 32, 33
- Jealous v. 9
- Steadfast v. 10
- Love v. 10

Deuteronomy 6

- LORD vv. 1, 2, 3, 4, 5, 10, 12, 13, 15, 16, 17, 18, 19, 20, 21, 22, 24, 25
- LORD our God v. 4
- One v. 4
- Commands v. 2
- Greatest commandment v. 5
- LORD your God vv. 13, 15, 17
- Jealous v. 15
- Anger v. 15

Deuteronomy 7

- LORD vv. 1, 2, 4, 6, 7, 8, 9, 12, 15, 16, 18, 19, 20, 21, 22, 23, 25
- Anger v. 4
- His chosen are a treasured people out of all others v. 6
- LORD your God v. 6
- Love v. 7
- Oath v. 8
- Love v. 8
- Destroys v. 10
- Commands v. 11
- Steadfast love v. 12
- Outstretched arm v. 19

Deuteronomy 8

- LORD vv. 1, 2, 3, 5, 6, 7, 10, 11, 14, 18, 19, 20

- Commands v. 8
- Tests v. 2
- Humbles v. 3
- Disciplines v. 5
- Warns v. 19

Deuteronomy 9

- LORD vv. 3, 4, 5, 6, 7, 8, 9, 10, 11, 12, 13, 16, 18, 19, 20, 22, 23, 24, 25, 26, 28
- Anger v. 8
- Sees v. 13
- Outstretched arm v. 29

Deuteronomy 10

- LORD vv. 1, 4, 5, 8, 9, 10, 11, 12, 13, 14, 15, 17, 20, 22
- Owns heaven, heaven's heaven, and earth and all that is in it v. 14

Deuteronomy 11

- LORD vv. 1, 2, 4, 7, 9, 12, 13, 17, 21, 22, 23, 25, 27, 28, 29, 31

Deuteronomy 12

- LORD vv. 1, 4, 5, 7, 9, 10, 11, 12, 14, 15, 18, 20, 21, 25, 26, 27, 28, 29, 31

Deuteronomy 13

- LORD vv. 3, 4, 5, 10, 12, 16, 17, 18

Deuteronomy 14

- LORD vv. 1, 2, 21, 23, 24, 25, 26, 29

Deuteronomy 15

- LORD vv. 4, 5, 6, 7, 9, 10, 14, 15, 18, 19, 20, 21
- Blesses vv. 4, 6, 14

Deuteronomy 16

- LORD vv. 1, 2, 5, 6, 7, 8, 10, 11, 15, 16, 17, 18, 20, 21, 22
- Passover instructions vv. 1-8

Deuteronomy 17

- LORD vv. 1, 2, 8, 10, 12, 14, 15, 16, 19

Deuteronomy 18

- LORD vv. 2, 5, 6, 7, 9, 12, 13, 14, 15, 16, 17, 21, 22
- Prophet v. 15

Deuteronomy 19

- LORD vv. 1, 2, 3, 8, 9, 10, 14, 17

Deuteronomy 20

- LORD vv. 1, 4, 13, 14, 16, 17, 18

Deuteronomy 21

- LORD vv. 1, 5, 8, 9, 10, 23
- Atonement v. 8
- Redeemed v. 8

Deuteronomy 22

- LORD vv. 5

Deuteronomy 23

- LORD vv. 1, 2, 3, 5, 8, 14, 18, 20, 21, 23
- Walks among the camp v. 14
- Blesses v. 20
- LORD your God v. 21

Deuteronomy 24

- LORD vv. 4, 9, 13, 15, 18, 19

Deuteronomy 25

- LORD vv. 15, 16, 19
- LORD your God vv. 1, 2, 3, 4

Deuteronomy 26

- LORD vv. 1, 2, 3, 4, 5, 7, 8, 10, 11, 13, 14, 16, 17, 18, 19
- LORD your God v. 19

Deuteronomy 27

- LORD vv. 2, 3, 5, 6, 7, 9, 10, 15
- Promised v. 3

Deuteronomy 28

- LORD vv. 1, 2, 7, 8, 9, 10, 11, 12, 13, 15, 20, 21, 22, 24, 25, 27, 28, 35, 36, 37, 45, 47, 48, 49, 52, 53, 58, 59, 61, 62, 63, 64, 65, 68
- Voice v. 1
- Blesses vv. 2, 3, 4, 5, 6, 8
- Curses vv. 15-20

Deuteronomy 29

- LORD vv. 1, 2, 4, 6, 10, 12, 15, 18, 20, 21, 22, 23, 24, 25, 27, 28, 29
- Gives hearts to understand, eyes to see, and ears to hear v. 4

- Warning against idolatry
- Anger vv. 20, 23, 27
- Jealousy v. 20
- Wrath v. 28
- Fury v. 28

Deuteronomy 30

- LORD vv. 1, 2, 3, 4, 5, 6, 7, 8, 9, 10, 16, 20
- Restores fortunes v. 3
- Blesses v. 1
- Curses v. 1
- Commands obedience with His voice v. 2
- Circumcises hearts v. 6
- Curses enemies and makes abundantly prosperous vv. 7, 9
- Enables obedience v. 6
- Takes delight in prospering His people v. 9
- His will is not too hard or unknown v. 11
- Gives responsibility to Israel to "choose life" v. 19
- Our life and length of days v. 20
- Gives life to those who hold fast to Him v. 20

Deuteronomy 31

- LORD vv. 2, 3, 4, 5, 6, 7, 8, 9, 11, 12, 13, 14, 15, 16, 23, 25, 26, 27, 29
- Destroys nations v. 3
- Commands strength and courage v. 6
- Will not leave or forsake you v. 6
- Pillar of could v. 15
- Anger v. 29
- Omniscient v. 16

Deuteronomy 32

- LORD vv. 3, 6, 12, 19, 27, 30, 36, 48
- Speaks v. 1
- Rock vv. 4, 18
- Faithful v. 4
- Without iniquity v. 4
- Just v. 4
- Upright v. 4
- Creates, makes, and establishes v. 6
- Most High v. 8
- Rock of salvation v. 15
- Rock vv. 30, 31
- Jealous v. 16
- Anger v. 16, 22
- Sees v. 19
- Spurns and hides His face from the unfaithful vv. 19, 20
- Vengeance and recompense is His v. 35
- Compassion for His servants v. 36
- Kills and gives life; wounds and heals v. 39
- Repays those who hate Him v. 41
- Makes drunk His arrows with blood and his sword to devour flesh v. 42
- Repays v. 43
- His word is our very life v. 47
- Makes His people jealous v. 21

Deuteronomy 33

- LORD vv. 2, 5, 7, 11, 12, 13, 21, 23, 29
- Came from ten thousands of holy ones and with flaming fire at His right hand v. 2
- None like Him v. 26
- Rides through the heavens to your help and through the skies in His majesty v. 26
- Eternal v. 27
- Dwelling place v. 27
- Everlasting arms v. 27
- Saves v. 29
- Shield of help v. 29
- Sword of triumph v. 29

Deuteronomy 34

- LORD vv. 1, 4, 5, 9, 10, 11
- Buried Moses v. 6
- Knew Moses face to face v. 10

Joshua 1

- LORD vv. 1, 9, 11, 13, 15, 17
- Will not leave nor forsake v. 5
- Commands strength and courage vv. 6, 7, 9, 18
- Book of the Law v. 8
- With you wherever you go (Joshua) v. 9
- LORD your God v. 9, 11, 17

Joshua 2

- LORD vv. 9, 10, 11, 12, 14, 24
- God in the heavens above and the earth beneath v. 11
- LORD your God v. 11

Joshua 3

- LORD vv. 3, 5, 7, 9, 11, 13, 17
- Performs wonders v. 5

Joshua 4

- LORD vv. 1, 5, 7, 8, 10, 11, 13, 15, 18, 23, 24
- Mighty v. 24
- Feared forever v. 24

Joshua 5

- LORD vv. 1, 2, 6, 9, 14, 15
- Circumcised the sons of Israel v. 2
- Rolled away the reproach from Egypt v. 9
- Ceased to provide manna as soon as Israel could eat the fruit of the Promised Land v. 12
- Commander of the LORD's army (pre-incarnate Christ) v. 14

Joshua 6

- LORD vv. 2, 6, 7, 8, 12, 13, 16, 17, 19, 24, 26, 27

Joshua 7

- LORD vv. 1, 6, 7, 8, 10, 13, 14, 15, 19, 20, 23, 25, 26
- Anger v. 1
- Commands consecration v. 13
- Turned from His burning anger v. 26

Joshua 8

- LORD vv. 1, 7, 8, 18, 27, 30, 31, 33

Joshua 9

- LORD vv. 9, 14, 18, 19, 24, 27

Joshua 10

- LORD vv. 8, 10, 11, 12, 14, 19, 25, 30, 32, 40, 42
- The LORD fought for Israel vv. 14, 42

Joshua 11

- LORD vv. 6, 8, 9, 12, 15, 20, 23
- Gives enemies into His people's hands v. 8
- Promised land given to Israel as Joshua faithfully took it v. 23

Joshua 12

- LORD v. 6

Joshua 13

- LORD vv. 1, 8, 14, 33
- Inheritance (tribe of Levi) v. 33

Joshua 14

- LORD vv. 2, 5, 6, 7, 8, 9, 10, 12, 14

Joshua 15

- LORD v. 13

Joshua 16

Joshua 17

- LORD vv. 4, 14

Joshua 18

- LORD vv. 3, 6, 7, 8, 10

Joshua 19

- LORD vv. 50, 51

Joshua 20

- LORD v. 1

Joshua 21

- LORD vv. 2, 3, 8, 44, 45
- Promises are unfailing v. 45
- Enemies cannot withstand the LORD's deliverance v. 44

Joshua 22

- LORD vv. 2, 3, 4, 5, 9, 16, 17, 18, 19, 22, 23, 24, 25, 27, 28, 29, 31, 34

- Greatest commandment v. 5

Joshua 23

- LORD vv. 1, 3, 5, 8, 9, 10, 11, 13, 14, 15, 16
- Not one word of the LORD's promises has failed v. 14
- Anger against idolatry v. 16

Joshua 24

- LORD vv. 2, 7, 14, 15, 16
- Jealous v. 19

Judges 1

- LORD vv. 1, 2, 4, 19, 22
- Repays v. 7

Judges 2

- LORD vv. 1, 4, 5, 7, 8, 10, 11, 12, 13, 14, 15, 16, 17, 18, 20, 22, 23
- Angel of the LORD vv. 1, 4
- Never breaks covenants v. 1
- Anger vv. 12, 20
- Gave them over v. 14
- Hand v. 15
- Sworn v. 15
- Raised up judges v. 16
- Moved to pity v. 18
- Voice v. 20
- Tests v. 22

Judges 3

- LORD vv. 1, 4, 7, 8, 9, 10, 12, 15, 25, 28
- Tests v. 1
- Taught Israel war v. 2
- Anger v. 8
- Sold His people into the hand of the enemy v. 8
- Raised up a deliverer (Othniel, Ehud, Shamgar) v. 9, 15, 31
- Spirit of the LORD v. 10

Judges 4

- LORD vv. 1, 2, 3, 6, 9, 14, 15
- Sold His people into the hand of the enemy v. 2
- Raised up a judge/deliverer (Deborah) v. 4

Judges 5

- LORD vv. 2, 3, 4, 5, 9, 11, 13, 23, 31
- God of Israel v. 5
- Angel of the LORD v. 23

Judges 6

- LORD vv. 1, 6, 7, 8, 10, 11, 12, 13, 14, 15, 16, 21, 22, 23, 24, 25, 26, 27, 34
- Angel of the LORD vv. 11, 12, 20, 21, 22
- Spirit of the LORD v. 27

Judges 7

- LORD vv. 2, 4, 5, 7, 9, 15, 18, 20, 22

Judges 8

- LORD vv. 7, 19, 23

Judges 9

Judges 10

- LORD vv. 6, 7, 10, 11, 15, 16
- Raised up judges (Tola and Jair) vv. 1, 3
- Sold Israel into the hands of the enemy v. 7
- Anger v. 7
- Impatient v. 16

Judges 11

- LORD vv. 9, 10, 11, 21, 23, 24, 27, 29, 30, 31, 32, 35, 36
- God of Israel v. 21
- The LORD our God v. 25
- Delivers enemies into His people's hands vv. 21, 32
- Spirit of the LORD was upon Jephthah v. 29

Judges 12

- LORD v. 3
- Raised up judges (Ibzan, Elon, and Abdon) vv. 8-15

Judges 13

- LORD vv. 1, 3, 8, 13, 15, 16, 17, 18, 19, 20, 21, 23, 24, 25
- Angel of the LORD vv. 3, 6, 9, 15, 16, 18, 20
- Gave Israel into the hands of the Philistines for forty years v. 1
- Blesses Samson v. 24
- Spirit of the LORD stirred Samson v. 25

Judges 14

- LORD vv. 4, 6, 19
- Sought an opportunity against the Philistines v. 4
- Spirit of the LORD rushed upon Samson vv. 5, 19

Judges 15

- LORD vv. 14, 18
- Spirit of the LORD v. 14
- Granted great salvation through Samson v. 18

Judges 16

- LORD vv. 20, 28

Judges 17

- LORD vv. 2, 3, 13

Judges 18

- LORD v. 6

Judges 19

- LORD v. 18

Judges 20

- LORD vv. 1, 18, 23, 26, 27, 28, 35
- Gave Gibeah into the hand of Israel on the third day v. 28
- Defeated Benjamin before Israel v. 35

Judges 21

- LORD vv. 3, 5, 7, 8, 15, 19

Ruth 1

- LORD vv. 6, 8, 9, 13, 17, 21
- Hand of the LORD v. 13

Ruth 2

- LORD vv. 4, 12, 13, 20
- God of Israel v. 12
- Repay and reward v. 12
- Providence v. 3
- Wings of refuge v. 12

Ruth 3

- LORD vv. 10, 13

Ruth 4

- LORD vv. 11, 12, 13, 14

1 Samuel 1

- LORD vv. 3, 5, 6, 7, 9, 10, 11, 12, 15, 19, 20, 21, 22, 23, 24, 26, 27, 28
- LORD of hosts v. 3
- Closed and opened Hannah's womb vv. 5, 20

1 Samuel 2

- LORD vv. 1, 2, 3, 6, 7, 8, 10, 11, 12, 17, 18, 20, 21, 24, 25, 26, 27, 30
- Exults hearts v. 1
- Exalts strength v. 1
- Salvation v. 1
- Holy v. 2
- Knowledge v. 3
- Weighs actions v. 3
- Kills and brings to life v. 6
- Makes poor and makes rich, brings low and exalts v. 7
- Protects the faithful v. 9
- Cuts off the wicked in darkness v. 9
- Judge v. 10
- Exalts the power of his anointed v.10
- Reveals Himself v. 27

1 Samuel 3

- LORD vv. 1, 3, 4, 6, 7

1 Samuel 4

- LORD vv. 3, 4, 5, 6

1 Samuel 5

- LORD vv. 3, 4, 6, 9
- His hand was very heavy on the Philistines during the seven months they had the ark vv. 6, 7, 11

<u>1 Samuel 6</u>
- LORD vv. 1, 2, 8, 11, 14, 15, 17, 18, 19, 20, 21
- God of Israel v. 5
- Struck down seventy of His people for looking at the ark v. 19

<u>1 Samuel 7</u>
- LORD vv. 1, 2, 3, 4, 5, 6, 8, 9, 10, 12, 13, 17
- Delivers those who serve Him only v. 3

<u>1 Samuel 8</u>
- LORD vv. 6, 10, 18, 21, 22
- Rejected by His people v. 7

<u>1 Samuel 9</u>
- LORD vv. 15, 17
- Reveals v. 15

<u>1 Samuel 10</u>
- LORD vv. 1, 6, 17, 18, 19, 22, 24, 25
- Spirit of the LORD v. 6
- Gave Saul a new heart v. 9
- God of Israel v. 18
- Rejected v. 19
- Touched the hearts of men of valor v. 26

<u>1 Samuel 11</u>
- LORD vv. 7, 13, 15
- Spirit of God (Saul) v. 6
- Dread of the LORD v. 7
- Salvation vv. 9, 13

<u>1 Samuel 12</u>
- LORD vv. 3, 5, 6, 7, 8, 9, 10, 11, 12, 13, 14, 15, 16, 17, 18, 19, 20, 22, 23, 24
- Commands obedience to His voice v. 15
- Protects His name v. 22
- Demands full service with one's whole heart v. 20
- Pleased in making a people for Himself v. 22
- Warns against empty things v. 21
- Sweeps away the wicked v. 25
- Calls for fear and service v. 24

<u>1 Samuel 13</u>
- LORD vv. 12, 13, 14

<u>1 Samuel 14</u>
- LORD vv. 3, 6, 10, 12, 23, 33, 34, 35, 39, 41, 45

<u>1 Samuel 15</u>
- LORD vv. 1, 2, 10, 11, 13, 15, 16, 17, 18, 19, 20, 21, 22, 23, 24, 25, 26. 28, 30, 31, 33, 35
- LORD of hosts v. 2
- Regrets (Saul) v. 10
- The Glory of Israel will not regret v. 29
- Not a man v. 29
- Rejected Saul v. 23
- LORD your God v. 30

<u>1 Samuel 16</u>
- LORD vv. 1, 2, 4, 5, 6, 7, 8, 9, 10, 2, 13, 14, 16
- Looks on the heart (versus appearance) v. 7
- Spirit of the LORD (David) v. 13
- Sent a harmful spirit to torment Saul v. 14
- Gave David favor in Saul's eyes v. 22

<u>1 Samuel 17</u>
- LORD vv. 37, 45, 46, 47
- Living vv. 26, 36
- LORD of hosts v. 45
- Saves not with sword and spear v. 47
- The battle is the LORD's v. 47

<u>1 Samuel 18</u>
- LORD vv. 8, 12, 15, 17, 28
- Set David over the men of war v. 5
- Tormented Saul with a harmful spirit v. 10
- Gave David great success in all his undertakings v. 14

- Gave David more success than all of Saul's servants v. 30

1 Samuel 19

- LORD vv. 5, 6
- Salvation v. 5
- Spirit of God vv. 20, 23

1 Samuel 20

- LORD vv. 3, 8, 12, 13, 14, 15, 16, 21, 22, 23, 42
- God of Israel v. 12
- Steadfast love v. 14

1 Samuel 21

- LORD vv. 6, 7

1 Samuel 22

- LORD vv. 10, 12, 17, 22

1 Samuel 23

- LORD vv. 2, 4, 10, 11, 12, 18, 21
- God of Israel v. 10

1 Samuel 24

- LORD vv. 4, 6, 8, 10, 12, 15, 18, 19, 21

1 Samuel 25

- LORD vv. 24, 25, 26, 27, 28, 29, 30, 31, 32, 34, 38, 39, 41
- Blessed v. 32
- God of Israel vv. 32, 39
- Avenger (Nabal) v. 39

1 Samuel 26

- LORD vv. 9, 10, 11, 12, 15, 16, 17, 18, 19, 20, 21, 23, 24
- Gave a deep sleep to Saul and his men v. 12
- Rewards every man for his righteousness and his faithfulness v. 23

1 Samuel 27

1 Samuel 28

- LORD vv. 6, 10, 16, 17, 18, 19

1 Samuel 29

- LORD vv. 4, 6, 8, 10

1 Samuel 30

- LORD vv. 6, 8, 23, 26
- Supplied David with strength as he sought it v. 6

1 Samuel 31

2 Samuel 1

- LORD vv. 10, 12, 14, 16
- Allows His anointed to be slain vv. 14-16

2 Samuel 2

- LORD vv. 1, 5, 6, 7
- Steadfast love and faithfulness v. 6

Samuel 3

- LORD vv. 9, 18, 21, 28, 39
- Repays the evildoer according to his wickedness v. 39

2 Samuel 4

- LORD vv. 8, 9
- Redeems from every adversary v. 9
- Blood is required for wickedness v. 11

2 Samuel 5

- LORD vv. 2, 3, 10, 12, 19, 20, 23, 24, 25
- God of hosts (with David v. 10
- Established David v. 12
- Strikes down the enemy v. 24

2 Samuel 6

- LORD vv. 2, 5, 7, 8, 9, 10, 11, 12, 13, 14, 15, 16, 17, 18, 21
- LORD of hosts vv. 2, 18
- Anger (struck down Uzzah) v. 8
- Blesses (Obed-edom) v. 11

2 Samuel 7

- LORD vv. 1, 3, 4, 5, 8, 11, 18, 19, 20, 22, 24, 25, 26, 27, 28, 29
- Word of the LORD v. 4
- Moved with the people of Israel and shepherded them v. 7
- Steadfast love v. 15
- LORD God v. 18
- Unique v. 22
- Redeemer v. 23

- Worker of awesome things v. 23
- Establishes His people forever v. 24
- God over Israel v. 27
- LORD of hosts v. 26
- Words are truth v. 28
- Spoken v. 29
- House of His servant shall be blessed forever v. 16

<u>2 Samuel 8</u>

- LORD vv. 6, 11, 14
- Gave victory to David wherever he went v. 14

<u>2 Samuel 9</u>

- LORD v. 11
- Kindness v. 3

<u>2 Samuel 10</u>

- LORD vv. 3, 10, 12

<u>2 Samuel 11</u>

- LORD vv. 9, 11, 13, 27
- Displeased by David's adultery and murder over Bathsheba v. 27

<u>2 Samuel 12</u>

- LORD vv. 1, 5, 7, 9, 11, 13, 14, 15, 20, 22, 24, 25
- Sends Nathan to David v. 1
- Despised by David v. 9
- Put away David's sin v. 13
- Disciplines v. 14
- Raised up evil against David's house v. 11
- Loved Solomon v. 24

<u>2 Samuel 13</u>

- LORD vv. 32, 33

<u>2 Samuel 14</u>

- LORD vv. 9, 11, 12, 15, 17, 18, 19, 20, 22

<u>2 Samuel 15</u>

- LORD vv. 7, 8, 15, 20, 21, 25, 31
- Steadfast love and faithfulness v. 20

<u>2 Samuel 16</u>

- LORD vv. 4, 8, 9, 10, 11, 12, 18
- Ordains v. 14

<u>2 Samuel 17</u>

- LORD v. 14

<u>2 Samuel 18</u>

- LORD vv. 19, 28, 31, 32

<u>2 Samuel 19</u>

- LORD vv. 7, 19, 20, 21, 26, 27, 28, 30, 35, 37
- Blessed v. 28
- LORD your God v. 28

<u>2 Samuel 20</u>

- LORD vv. 6, 19

<u>2 Samuel 21</u>

- LORD vv. 1, 3, 6, 7, 9
- Responds to pleas of the faithful v. 14

<u>2 Samuel 22</u>

- LORD vv. 1, 2, 4, 7, 14, 16, 19, 21, 22, 25, 29, 31, 32, 42, 47, 50
- Rock vv. 2, 3, 32, 47
- Fortress v. 2
- Deliverer vv. 2, 44, 49
- Shield vv. 3, 31, 36
- Horn of salvation v. 3
- Stronghold v. 3
- Refuge vv. 3, 33
- Savior v. 3
- Worthy to be praised v. 3
- Hears v. 7
- Anger v. 8
- Smoke from His nostrils v. 9
- Devouring fire from His mouth v. 9
- Bowed the heavens v. 10
- Rode on a cherub v. 11
- Thundered from heaven v. 14
- Uttered His voice v. 14
- Arrows and lightning v. 15
- Rebukes v. 16
- Rescues vv. 18, 20
- Rules and statutes v. 23
- Rewards the righteous and clean v. 25
- Merciful to the merciful v. 26

- Tortures the crooked v. 27
- Saves the humble and brings down the haughty v. 28
- Lamp v. 29
- Perfect v. 31
- True v. 31
- Makes, secures, trains, and gives vv. 34-37
- Shield of salvation v. 36
- Gentleness v. 36
- Equips with strength v. 40
- Lives v. 47
- Exalted v. 47
- Rock of salvation v. 47
- Shows steadfast love to His anointed v. 51

2 Samuel 23

- LORD vv. 2, 10, 12, 16, 17
- God of Jacob v. 1
- Spirit v. 2
- God of Israel v. 3
- Rock of Israel v. 3
- Covenant v. 5

2 Samuel 24

- LORD vv. 1, 3, 10, 11, 12, 14, 15, 16, 17, 18, 19, 21, 22, 23, 24, 25
- Anger (against Israel) v. 1

1 Kings 1

- LORD vv. 2, 11, 13, 17, 18, 20, 21, 24, 27, 29, 30, 31, 33, 36, 37, 43, 47, 48
- Redeemer (David) v. 29
- Blessed v. 48
- God of Israel v. 48

1 Kings 2

- LORD vv. 3, 4, 8, 15, 23, 24, 26, 27, 28, 29, 30, 32, 33, 38, 42, 43, 44, 45

1 Kings 3

- LORD vv. 1, 2, 3, 5, 7, 10, 15, 17, 26
- Gave Solomon a wise and discerning mind v. 12
- Steadfast love v. 6

1 Kings 4

1 Kings 5

- LORD vv. 3, 4, 5, 7, 12

1 Kings 6

- LORD vv. 1, 2, 11, 19, 37

1 Kings 7

- LORD vv. 12, 40, 45, 48, 51

1 Kings 8

- LORD vv. 1, 4, 6, 9, 10, 11, 12, 15, 17, 18, 20, 21, 22, 23, 25, 28, 44, 53, 54, 56, 57, 59, 60, 61, 62, 63, 64, 65, 66
- The glory of God filled the house of the LORD vv. 10, 11
- Fulfilled His promise to David v. 15
- Looks at the heart v. 18
- Unique v. 23
- Steadfast love v. 23
- Faithful v. 24
- God of Israel v. 26
- Heavens cannot contain Him v. 27
- No word has failed v. 56
- Blessed v. 56
- Gave Israel rest v. 56
- One v. 60
- Showed goodness to David and Israel v. 66

1 Kings 9

- LORD vv. 1, 2, 3, 8, 9, 10, 15, 25
- Anger (toward Solomon) v. 9

1 Kings 10

- LORD vv. 1, 5, 9, 12

1 Kings 11

- LORD vv. 2, 4, 6, 9, 10, 11, 14, 31

1 Kings 12

- LORD vv. 15, 24, 27

1 Kings 13

- LORD vv. 1, 2, 3, 5, 6, 9, 17, 18, 20, 21, 26, 32

1 Kings 14

- LORD vv. 5, 7, 11, 13, 14, 18, 21, 22, 24, 26, 28

- Anger vv. 9, 15
- God of Israel v. 13
- Speaks through Ahijah v. 18
- Jealousy v. 22

<u>1 Kings 15</u>
- LORD vv. 3, 4, 5, 11, 14, 15, 18, 26, 29, 30, 34
- Anger v. 30

<u>1 Kings 16</u>
- LORD vv. 1, 7, 12, 13, 19, 25, 26, 30, 33, 34
- Spoke through Jehu v. 7
- Anger vv. 7, 13, 33
- God of Israel vv. 13, 33

<u>1 Kings 17</u>
- LORD vv. 1, 2, 5, 8, 12, 14, 16, 20, 21, 22, 24
- God of Israel v. 1

<u>1 Kings 18</u>
- LORD vv. 1, 3, 4, 7, 8, 10, 11, 12, 13, 14, 15, 18, 21, 22, 24, 30, 31, 32, 36, 37, 38, 39, 46
- God of Abraham, Isaac, and Israel v. 36
- Consumed Elijah's offering with fire v. 38

<u>1 Kings 19</u>
- LORD vv. 4, 7, 9, 10, 11, 12, 14, 15
- God of hosts v. 10, 14
- Passed by in a great and strong wind, an earthquake, a fire, and a low whisper vv. 11, 12

<u>1 Kings 20</u>
- LORD vv. 4, 9, 13, 14, 28, 35, 36, 42

<u>1 Kings 21</u>
- LORD vv. 3, 17, 19, 20, 23, 25, 26, 28
- Regards the humble v. 29

<u>1 Kings 22</u>
- LORD vv. 5, 6, 7, 8, 11, 12, 14, 15, 16, 17, 19, 20, 21, 22, 23, 24, 28, 38, 43, 52, 53
- Anger v. 53

<u>2 Kings 1</u>
- LORD vv. 3, 4, 6, 15, 16, 17

<u>2 Kings 2</u>
- LORD vv. 1, 2, 3, 4, 5, 6, 14, 16, 19, 21, 24

<u>2 Kings 3</u>
- LORD vv. 2, 10, 11, 12, 13, 14, 15, 16, 17, 18

<u>2 Kings 4</u>
- LORD vv. 1, 16, 27, 26, 30, 33, 43, 44

<u>2 Kings 5</u>
- LORD vv. 1, 3, 4, 11, 16, 17, 18, 20

<u>2 Kings 6</u>
- LORD vv. 12, 17, 18, 20, 26, 27, 33
- Took Elijah up to heaven in chariots of fire v. 11

<u>2 Kings 7</u>
- LORD vv. 1, 2, 6, 16, 19
- Made a sounds of a great army v. 6

<u>2 Kings 8</u>
- LORD vv. 1, 5, 8, 10, 12, 13, 18, 19, 27

<u>2 Kings 9</u>
- LORD vv. 3, 6, 7, 12, 25, 26, 36

<u>2 Kings 10</u>
- LORD vv. 10, 16, 17, 23, 30, 31, 32

<u>2 Kings 11</u>
- LORD vv. 3, 4, 7, 10, 13, 15, 17, 18, 19

<u>2 Kings 12</u>
- LORD vv. 2, 4, 9, 10, 11, 12, 13, 14, 16, 18

<u>2 Kings 13</u>
- LORD vv. 2, 3, 4, 5, 11, 17, 23
- Anger v. 3
- Listens (Jehoahaz) v. 4
- Gracious v. 23
- Compassionate v. 23
- Remembers Hid covenant with Abraham, Isaac, and Jacob v. 23

<u>2 Kings 14</u>
- LORD vv. 3, 6, 14, 24, 25, 26, 27

2 Kings 15
- LORD vv. 3, 5, 9, 12, 18, 24, 28, 34, 35, 37

2 Kings 16
- LORD vv. 2, 3, 8, 14, 18

2 Kings 17
- LORD vv. 2, 7, 8, 9, 11, 12, 13, 14, 15, 16, 17, 18, 19, 20, 21, 23, 25, 28, 32, 33, 34, 35, 36, 39, 41
- Anger at secret idolatry v. 11
- Commands fear before offering deliverance v. 39
- Makes a covenant v. 35

2 Kings 18
- LORD vv. 3, 5, 6, 7, 12, 15, 16, 22, 25, 30, 32, 35
- God of Israel v. 5
- With Hezekiah, making his way prosperous v. 7

2 Kings 19
- LORD vv. 1, 4, 6, 14, 15, 16, 17, 19, 20, 21, 23, 31, 32, 33, 35
- God of Israel v. 15
- Enthroned above the cherubim v. 15
- Creator v. 15

2 Kings 20
- LORD vv. 1, 2, 3, 4, 5, 8, 9, 11, 16, 17, 19
- Hears (Hezekiah's prayer) v. 5
- Sees (Hezekiah's tears) v. 5
- Healer (Hezekiah's sickness) v. 5
- Deliverer (Hezekiah and Jerusalem) v. 6
- Defender v. 6

2 Kings 21
- LORD vv. 2, 4, 5, 6, 7, 9, 10, 12, 16, 20, 22
- Anger vv. 6, 15

2 Kings 22
- LORD vv. 2, 3, 4, 5, 8, 9, 13, 15, 16, 18, 19
- Wrath vv. 13, 17
- Anger v. 17
- God of Israel v. 15
- Hears (humbled king of Judah, Josiah) v. 19

2 Kings 23
- LORD vv. 2, 3, 4, 6, 7, 9, 11, 12, 16, 19, 21, 23, 24, 25, 26, 27, 32, 37
- Anger v. 26

2 Kings 24
- LORD vv. 2, 3, 4, 9, 13, 19, 20
- Destroyed Judah v. 3
- Anger v. 20

2 Kings 25
- LORD vv. 9, 13, 16

1 Chronicles 1

1 Chronicles 2
- LORD v. 3

1 Chronicles 3

1 Chronicles 4

1 Chronicles 5
- Destroyed false gods v. 25
- God of Israel v. 26
- Stirs spirits v. 26

1 Chronicles 6
- LORD vv. 15, 31, 32

1 Chronicles 7

1 Chronicles 8

1 Chronicles 9
- LORD vv. 19, 20, 23

1 Chronicles 10
- LORD vv. 13, 14
- Put Saul to death and turned the kingdom over to David v. 14

1 Chronicles 11
- LORD vv. 2, 3, 9, 10, 14, 18

1 Chronicles 12
- LORD v. 23

1 Chronicles 13
- LORD vv. 2, 6, 10, 11, 14

1 Chronicles 14
- LORD vv. 2, 10, 17

1 Chronicles 15

- LORD vv. 2, 3, 12, 13, 14, 15, 25, 26, 28, 29

1 Chronicles 16

- LORD vv. 2, 4, 7, 8, 10, 11, 14, 23, 25, 26, 28, 29, 31, 33, 34, 36, 37, 39, 40, 41
- Wondrous v. 9
- Utters judgments and miracles v. 12
- Rebuked kings on account of His chosen ones v. 21
- Feared among all other gods v. 25
- Splendor and majesty are before Him v. 27
- Reigns v. 31
- God of Israel v. 36
- Blessed v. 36
- Great and greatly to be praised v. 25
- Steadfast love endures forever v. 41

1 Chronicles 17

- LORD vv. 1, 3, 4, 7, 10, 16, 17, 19, 20, 22, 23, 24, 26, 27
- LORD of hosts v. 24
- Pleased to bless forever the house of David v. 27

1 Chronicles 18

- LORD vv. 6, 11, 13
- Gave victory to David wherever he went v. 13

1 Chronicles 19

- LORD v. 13

1 Chronicles 20

1 Chronicles 21

- LORD vv. 3, 9, 10, 11, 12, 13, 14, 15, 16, 17, 18, 19, 22, 23, 24, 26, 27, 28, 29, 30
- Allowed Satan to incite David to number Israel v. 1

1 Chronicles 22

- LORD vv. 1, 5, 6, 7, 8, 11, 12, 13, 14, 16, 18, 19
- God of Israel v. 6
- Made Solomon a man of rest v. 9

1 Chronicles 23

- LORD vv. 4, 5, 13, 24, 25, 28, 30, 31, 32

1 Chronicles 24

- LORD v. 19

1 Chronicles 25

- LORD vv. 3, 6, 7

1 Chronicles 26

- LORD vv. 12, 22, 27, 30

1 Chronicles 27

- LORD v. 23

1 Chronicles 28

- LORD vv. 2, 4, 5, 8, 9, 10, 12, 13, 18, 19, 20
- Searches all hearts and understands every plan and thought v. 9
- Found by those who seek Him v. 9
- Casts off forever those who forsake Him v. 9
- With His chosen until His plans are completed v. 20

1 Chronicles 29

- LORD vv. 1, 5, 8, 9, 10, 11, 16, 18, 20, 21, 22, 23, 25
- Blessed v. 10
- His is the greatness and the power and the glory and the victory and the majesty v. 11
- Power and might are in His hand v. 12
- Head above all v. 12
- Ruler of all v. 12
- Glorious v. 13
- Tests the heart v. 17
- Takes pleasure in uprightness v. 17
- God of Abraham, Isaac, and Israel v. 18
- Grants whole hearts v. 19

2 Chronicles 1

- LORD vv. 1, 3, 5, 6, 9

- Gave Solomon wisdom, knowledge, riches, possession, and honor like none saw before him or have seen since v. 12

2 Chronicles 2

- LORD vv. 1, 4, 11, 12, 14, 15
- Heaven cannot contain Him v. 6

2 Chronicles 3

- LORD v. 1

2 Chronicles 4

- LORD v. 16
- God of Israel v. 4

2 Chronicles 5

- LORD vv. 1, 2, 7, 10, 13, 14
- His glory filled His house v. 14

2 Chronicles 6

- LORD vv. 1, 4, 7, 8, 10, 11, 12, 14, 16, 17, 19, 41, 42
- He alone knows the hearts of the children of mankind v. 30
- Steadfast love vv. 14, 42
- Covenant keeping v. 14

2 Chronicles 7

- LORD vv. 1, 2, 3, 4, 6, 7, 10, 11, 12, 21, 22
- Good v. 3
- Steadfast love endures forever vv. 3, 6
- Forgiving v. 14
- Punishes idolatry v. 22

2 Chronicles 8

- LORD vv. 1, 11, 12, 16

2 Chronicles 9

- LORD vv. 4, 8, 11
- Put wisdom into Solomon's mind v. 23

2 Chronicles 10

- LORD v. 15

2 Chronicles 11

- LORD vv. 2, 4, 14, 16

2 Chronicles 12

- LORD vv. 1, 2, 5, 6, 7, 9, 11, 12, 13, 14
- Turns wrath from the humble v. 12

2 Chronicles 13

- LORD vv. 5, 6, 8, 9, 10, 11, 12, 14, 18, 20
- Gave Jeroboam into Abijah's hand v. 16

2 Chronicles 14

- LORD vv. 2, 4, 6, 7, 11, 12, 13, 14
- Defeated the Ethiopians before Asa and Judah v. 12

2 Chronicles 15

- LORD vv. 2, 4, 8, 9, 11, 12, 13, 14, 15
- Found by those who seek Him v. 2
- Forsakes those who forsake Him v. 2
- Spirit of God v. 1
- God of Israel v. 12
- Gave rest v. 15

2 Chronicles 16

- LORD vv. 2, 7, 8, 9, 12
- "For the eyes of the LORD run to and fro throughout the whole earth, to give strong support to those whose heart is blameless toward Him. You have done foolishly in this, for from now on you will have wars." v. 12
- With His servant Asa vv. 7-9

2 Chronicles 17

- LORD vv. 3, 5, 6, 9, 10, 16
- Inquired of before deciding to go to war v. 4

2 Chronicles 18

- LORD vv. 4, 6, 7, 10, 11, 13, 15, 16, 18, 19, 20, 22, 23, 27, 31
- With Jehoshaphat and established his kingdom v. 5
- Put a lying spirit in the mouth of Ahab's prophets vv. 18-22

- Declares disaster v. 22
- Spirit of the LORD v. 23
- Speaks by prophets v. 27
- Helps v. 31
- Moves troops in battle v. 31
- Providential results in battle v. 33

2 Chronicles 19

- LORD vv. 2, 4, 6, 7, 8, 9, 10, 11
- Wrath vv. 2, 10
- Finds good in spite of wickedness v. 3
- No injustice or partiality, and takes no bribes v. 7
- With the upright v. 11

2 Chronicles 20

- LORD vv. 3, 4, 5, 6, 13, 14, 15, 17, 18, 19, 20, 21, 22, 26, 27, 28, 29, 32, 37
- Sought for help vv. 3, 4
- God in heaven v. 6
- Holds power and might in His hands v. 6
- Cannot be withstood v. 6
- Drove out the inhabitants of Canaan and gave the land to Israel v. 7
- Friend of Abraham v. 7
- Executes judgment v. 11
- Spirit of the LORD v. 14
- Leads a prophet to declare that God owns the battle v. 15
- With us v. 17
- Set an ambush v. 22
- House of the LORD v. 28
- Steadfast love endures forever v. 21
- Salvation v. 17
- Gave rest v. 30
- Sight of the LORD v. 32
- Destroys (those who join themselves with evil doers) v. 37

2 Chronicles 21

- LORD vv. 6, 7, 10, 12, 14, 16, 18
- Keeps His promises (not willing to destroy the house of David) v. 7
- Brings plagues to those enticed by whoredom v. 14
- Stirs up anger of men to accomplish His will v. 16
- Struck Jehoram with a fatal bowel disease v. 18

2 Chronicles 22

- LORD vv. 4, 7, 9
- Sees v. 4
- Ordains downfalls v. 7
- Anoints people to destroy v. 7
- Preserves the line of Judah from the evil queen, Athaliah v. 12

2 Chronicles 23

- LORD vv. 3, 5, 6, 12, 14, 16, 18, 19, 20
- Preserves David's line v. 3
- House of the LORD vv. 5, 12, 18, 19, 20
- People of the LORD v. 16

2 Chronicles 24

- LORD vv. 2, 4, 6, 7, 8, 9, 12, 14, 18, 19, 20, 21, 22, 24
- Eyes v. 2
- House of the LORD vv. 4, 5, 7, 8, 11, 12, 13, 14, 21, 27
- Abandoned by men v. 18
- Served by Moses vv. 6, 9
- Wrath on Judah and Jerusalem v. 18
- Sent prophets v. 19
- Clothed Zechariah with the Spirit of God v. 20
- Delivers to destruction those that forsake Him v. 24

2 Chronicles 25

- LORD vv. 2, 4, 7, 9, 15, 27
- "Each one should die for his own sin" v. 4
- Able to give much more than we can dream v. 9
- Anger v. 15

- Determined to destroy Amaziah after his idolatry vv. 16, 20

2 Chronicles 26

- LORD vv. 4, 5, 16, 17, 18, 19, 20, 21
- Instruct people to fear Him v. 5
- Eyes v. 4
- Helps (marvelously) vv. 7, 15
- Struck King Uzziah v. 20

2 Chronicles 27

- LORD vv. 2, 3, 6
- Eyes v. 2
- Temple of the LORD v. 2
- Makes might those who follow Him v. 6

2 Chronicles 28

- LORD vv. 1, 3, 5, 6, 9, 10, 11, 13, 19, 21, 22, 24, 25
- Eyes v. 1
- Drove out people of abominations v. 3
- Delivered 120,000 mighty men of Judah into the hand of Pekah v. 6
- Wrath vv. 11, 13
- Anger vv. 9, 25

2 Chronicles 29

- LORD vv. 2, 3, 5, 6, 8, 10, 11, 15, 16, 17, 18, 19, 20, 21, 25, 27, 30, 31, 32, 35
- God of Israel v. 10
- Chooses people to stand in His presence v. 11
- Fierce anger v. 10
- House of the LORD vv. 15, 16, 17, 18, 20, 25
- Atonement for Israel's sins v. 24
- Consecrates His people v. 31
- Provided for His people v. 36
- House of the LORD v. 31

2 Chronicles 30

- LORD vv. 1, 5, 6, 7, 8, 9, 12, 15, 17, 18, 19, 20, 21, 22
- House of the LORD vv. 1, 15
- Desolates people v. 7
- Fierce anger v. 8
- Gracious v. 9
- Merciful v. 9
- Will not turn His face from those who return to Him v. 9
- Regards genuine repentance over obedience to the law v. 19
- Hears v. 27
- Holy habitation v. 27

2 Chronicles 31

- LORD vv. 2, 3, 4, 6, 8, 10, 11, 16, 20
- Blessed v. 8
- Blesses v. 10

2 Chronicles 32

- LORD vv. 8, 11, 16, 17, 21, 22, 23, 24, 26
- Allows persecution and lies to be told to His people v. 16
- Sent an angel to cut of Assyria's mighty warrior and commanders v. 21
- Regards humility and stays His wrath v. 26
- Tests (Hezekiah) v. 31

2 Chronicles 33

- LORD vv. 2, 4, 5, 6, 9, 10, 11, 12, 13, 15, 16, 17, 18, 22, 23
- Eyes vv. 2, 6
- Anger v. 6
- "In Jerusalem shall be my name forever." vv. 4, 7
- Is God (Manasseh) v. 13
- God of Israel v. 16
- Sees v. 22

2 Chronicles 34

- LORD vv. 2, 8, 10, 14, 15, 17, 21, 23, 24, 27, 30, 31, 33
- Eyes v. 2
- Wrath v. 21
- Reveals His word v. 14
- God of Israel vv. 26, 33
- Brings disaster v. 24

2 Chronicles 35

- LORD vv. 1, 2, 3, 6, 12, 16, 26

2 Chronicles 36

- LORD vv. 5, 7, 9, 10, 12, 16, 18, 21, 22. 23
- Sees vv. 5, 9, 12
- God of Israel v. 13
- Compassionate v. 15
- Raises wrath on those who mock His messengers, despise His words, and scoff at His prophets v. 16
- No remedy for the unrepentant v. 16

Ezra 1

- LORD vv. 1, 2, 3, 5, 7
- Word of the LORD v. 1
- Stirred the spirit of Cyrus, king of Persia v. 1
- Gave king of Persia all the kingdoms of the earth v. 2
- Fulfills His word v. 1
- God of heaven v. 2
- Charged king Cyrus to build Him a house at Jerusalem v. 2
- Stirs man's spirits v. 5

Ezra 2

- LORD v. 68

Ezra 3

- LORD vv. 3, 5, 6, 8, 10, 11
- God of Israel v. 3
- House of the LORD vv. 8, 9
- Praised v. 10
- Good v. 11
- Steadfast love endures forever v. 11

Ezra 4

- LORD vv. 1, 3
- God of Israel v. 1
- Temple of the LORD v. 1

Ezra 5

- House of God v. 5
- God of heaven and earth v. 11
- Anger v. 12

Ezra 6

- LORD vv. 21, 22
- House of God vv. 5, 7, 16, 22
- God of heaven v. 10
- Caused His name to dwell in Jerusalem v. 12
- Decrees v. 14
- God of Israel vv. 14, 21, 22
- Made His people joyful v. 22
- Turned the heart of the king of Assyria to them v. 22

Ezra 7

- LORD vv. 6, 10, 11, 27
- God of Israel vv. 6, 15
- House of God vv. 16, 19
- Wrath v. 23

Ezra 8

- LORD vv. 28, 29, 35
- The hand of God is for good on all who seek Him v. 22
- The power of His wrath is on those who forsake Him v. 22
- Listens to entreaties v. 23
- House of the LORD v. 29
- Delivers from the enemy v. 31
- God of Israel v. 35

Ezra 9

- LORD vv. 5, 8, 15
- God of Israel v. 4
- Steadfast love v. 9
- Didn't forsake His people v. 9
- Punishes evil less than it deserves (merciful) v. 13
- The guilty cannot stand before God v. 15

Ezra 10

- LORD vv. 3, 11
- House of God v. 1
- Counselor v. 3
- Wrath v. 14

Nehemiah 1

- "Yahweh has comforted" (Nehemiah) v. 1
- LORD vv. 5, 11
- Steadfast love toward those who love and obey Him v. 5
- Ear vv. 6, 11
- Eyes v. 6
- Sinned against v. 6
- Gave commands, statutes, and rules v. 7
- Redeemer v. 10
- Great power v. 10
- Strong hand v. 10

Nehemiah 2

- God of heaven vv. 4, 20
- His good hand was upon Nehemiah and granted him favor before King Artaxerxes vv. 8, 18
- Makes His servants prosper v. 20

Nehemiah 3

- LORD v. 5

Nehemiah 4

- LORD v. 14
- Anger v. 5
- Great v. 14
- Awesome v. 14
- Fights for His people v. 20

Nehemiah 5

- LORD v. 13
- Fear of Him leads to justice in the community vv. 9-13

Nehemiah 6

- Accomplishes work among His faithful people v. 16

Nehemiah 7

- Sets tasks in people's hearts v. 5

Nehemiah 8

- LORD vv. 1, 6, 9, 10, 14
- Word given to attentive ears v. 3
- Blessed v. 6
- Great God v. 6
- His joy is our strength v. 10

Nehemiah 9

- LORD vv. 3, 4, 5, 6, 7
- God of the people of Israel v. 3
- Blessed, exalted above all blessing and praise v. 5
- The LORD alone v. 6
- Maker of heaven, the heaven of heavens, with all their hosts v. 6
- Chose Abram v. 7
- Finds and makes covenants with faithful hearts v. 8
- Sees v. 9
- Hears vv. 9, 28
- Made a name for Himself v. 10
- Divided the Red Sea and cast the pursuers into the depths v. 11
- Led His people with pillars of cloud and fire vv. 12, 19
- Speaks v. 13
- Gave the law v. 13
- Provider v. 15
- Rejected vv. 16, 26
- Ready to forgive v. 17
- Gracious vv. 17, 31
- Merciful vv. 17, 19, 28, 31
- Slow to anger v. 17
- Abounding in steadfast love vv. 17, 31
- Faithful vv. 19, 33
- Gave His good Spirit to instruct v. 20
- Sustainer v. 21
- Giver of kingdoms and peoples v. 22
- Multiplies people and subdues enemies vv. 23, 24
- Great goodness vv. 25, 35
- Gives the disobedient over to enemies to suffer v. 27
- Abandons the evil v. 28

- Hears the cry of His people from heaven v. 28
- Delivers v. 28
- Warns vv. 29, 30, 34
- Spirit v. 30
- Sends prophets v. 30
- Righteous v. 33

Nehemiah 10

- LORD vv. 29, 34, 35
- House of God vv. 32, 36, 39
- Gave His law by Moses v. 29

Nehemiah 11

Nehemiah 12

- His people rejoice and are heard far away v. 43

Nehemiah 13

- Turned curse into blessing v. 2
- House of God vv. 4, 7, 8
- Remembers vv. 14, 22, 30
- Brings disaster v. 18

Esther 1

Esther 2

Esther 3

Esther 4

Esther 5

Esther 6

Esther 7

Esther 8

Esther 9

Esther 10

Job 1

- LORD vv. 6, 7, 8, 9, 12, 21
- Interacts with His sons as well as Satan v. 6
- Gave Job (blameless and upright) into Satan's hand v. 12
- Gives and takes away v. 21

Job 2

- LORD vv. 1, 2, 3, 4, 6, 7
- Interacts with His sons as well as Satan v. 1
- Allows Satan to test Job again v. 6

Job 3

Job 4

- By the breath of God the evil perish v. 9

Job 5

- Does great things and unsearchable, marvelous things without number v. 9
- Gives rains on the earth and sends waters on the fields v. 10
- Sets on high those who are lowly, and those who mourn are lifted to safety v. 11
- Frustrates the devices of the crafty, so that their hands achieve no success v. 12
- Catches the wise in their own craftiness, and the schemes of the wily are brought to a quick end v. 13
- Saves the needy from the sword of their mouth and from the hand of the mighty v. 15
- Gives hope to the poor, and shuts the mouth of injustice v. 16
- Those who He reproves are blessed v. 17
- He wounds, but He binds up v. 18
- In famine He will redeem you from death, and in war from the power of the sword v. 20

Job 6

Job 7

Job 8

- Almighty vv. 3, 5
- Doesn't pervert justice v. 3
- The hope of the Godless shall perish v. 13

- Will not reject a blameless man, nor take the hand of evil doers v. 20

Job 9

- Wise in heart, and mighty in strength v. 4
- Shakes the earth out of its place v. 6
- Commands the stars and sun v. 7
- Does great and marvelous things without number v. 10
- Not seen v. 11
- Doesn't turn back His anger v. 13
- Cannot be answered v. 14
- He crushes and multiplies wounds v. 17
- He is mighty v. 19
- Proves the blameless to be perverse v. 20
- Destroys blameless and the wicked v. 22

Job 10

- Fashions with His hands v. 8
- Knits humans together v. 11
- Grants life v. 12
- Steadfast love v. 12
- Preserves spirits with care v. 12

Job 11

- Manifold in understanding v. 6

Job 12

- LORD v. 9
- In His hand is the life of every living thing and the breath of mankind v. 10
- With Him are wisdom and might v. 13
- The deceived and deceivers are His v. 16
- Loosens the belt of the strong v. 21
- Controls nations v. 23

Job 13

- Almighty v. 3
- Cannot be deceived v. 9
- Watches every path v. 27
- Limits the soles of feet v. 27

Job 14

Job 15

Job 16

- Allows Job to be utterly broken vv. 11-12

Job 17

Job 18

- Job 19
- Redeemer v. 25
- Job 20
- Job 21
- Job 22
- Job 23
- Unchangeable v. 13
- Completes what He appoints v. 14
- Job 24
- Almighty v. 1
- Prolongs the life of the mighty by His power, and judgment is not immediately transparent on the earth v. 22
- Job 25
- Dominion and fear are with Him v. 1
- Job 26
- Sheol is naked before Him v. 6
- Creates clouds v. 8
- Job 27
- The ultimate hope v. 8
- Almighty vv. 10, 11, 13
- Job 28
- LORD v. 28
- Job 29
- Almighty v. 5
- Job 30
- Humbles Job, allows prosperity to pass away and calamity to pour in vv. 11-15
- Cast Job in the mire v. 19

Job 31

Job 32

- The spirit in man and the breath of the Almighty is what facilitates understanding v. 8

Job 33

- Breath and life come from the Almighty v. 4
- Greater than man v. 12

Job 34

- The Almighty will not pervert justice v. 12
- Sees all a man's steps v. 21

Job 35

Job 36

- Mighty v. 5
- Number of His years are unsearchable v. 26
- Commands lightning to strike its mark v. 32

Job 37

- Does great things that we cannot understand v. 5
- Clothed with awesome majesty v. 22
- Almighty v. 23
- Cannot simply be found v. 23
- Great in power v. 23
- Will not violate what is right v. 23

Job 38

- LORD v. 1
- Answered Job out of the whirlwind v. 1
- Commands Job to dress for action like a man v. 3
- Laid the foundation of the earth v. 4
- Determined the earth's measurements v. 5
- Laid the earth's cornerstone v. 6
- Shut in the sea with doors, making clouds its garment v. 8
- Commands the morning and caused the dawn to know its place v. 12
- Walked in the recesses of the deep v. 16
- Comprehends the expanse of the earth v. 18
- Entered the storehouses of snow v. 22
- Prepares the storehouses of hail for war v. 23
- Makes the ground sprout with grass v. 27
- Established the rule of heaven over the earth v. 33
- Gives understanding to the mind v. 36
- Satisfies the hunger of the animals v. 39
- Sends forth lightnings v. 35
- Job 39
- Knows when mountain goats give birth v. 1
- Observes the calving of does v. 1
- Lets the hardy, wild donkey go free v. 5
- Served by the wild ox v. 9
- Made the ostrich forget wisdom v. 17
- Gives the horse its might and clothes its neck with a mane v. 19
- The hawk soars by His understanding v. 26
- At His command the eagle mounts up and builds its nest on high v. 27

Job 40

- LORD vv. 1, 3, 6
- Spoke to Job v. 1
- Tells Job to dress for action like a man v. 7
- Cannot be put in the wrong or condemned v. 8

- Adorns Himself with majesty and dignity, glory and splendor v. 10
- Pours out the overflowings of His anger onto the proud and wicked vv. 11-13
- Provides behemoths with might with mere grass vv. 15-18

Job 41

- Doesn't owe anybody v. 11
- Everything under the whole heaven is His v. 11

Job 42

- LORD vv. 1, 7, 10, 11, 12
- Can do all things v. 2
- His purpose cannot be thwarted v. 2
- Seen v. 5
- Lied about v. 7
- Listens to intercession v. 8
- Restored Job two-fold v. 10

Psalm 1

- LORD vv. 2, 6
- Blesses those who do not sin, but delights in God's word vv. 1, 2
- Prospers the way of the righteous v. 3
- Drives away the wicked and causes them to perish vv. 5, 6

Psalm 2

- LORD vv. 2, 4, 7, 11
- Laughs at opposition v. 4
- Holds His enemies in derision v. 4
- Will speak to His enemies in His wrath and terrify them in His fury v. 5
- Set His King on Zion v. 6
- Blesses those who take refuge in His son v. 12

Psalm 3

- LORD vv. 1, 3, 4, 5, 7, 8
- Shield v. 3
- Glory v. 3
- Answers from His holy hill v. 4
- Sustains v. 5
- Strikes and breaks the teeth of the wicked v. 7
- Owns salvation v. 8

Psalm 4

- LORD vv. 3, 5, 6, 8
- Relieves the distressed v. 1
- Set apart the godly for Himself v. 3
- Hears those that call to Him v. 3
- Put more joy in David's heart than anyone else v. 7
- He alone makes one to dwell in safety v. 8

Psalm 5

- LORD vv. 3, 6, 8, 12
- Hears v. 3
- Does not delight in wickedness v. 4
- Evil may not dwell in Him v. 4
- Destroys liars v. 6
- Hates evil doers v. 5
- Abhors the bloodthirsty and deceitful man v. 6
- Steadfast love is abundant v. 7
- Makes ways straight v. 8
- Those who love Him exult in Him v. 11
- Blesses the righteous v. 12
- Covers the righteous with favor as with a shield v. 12

Psalm 6

- LORD vv. 1, 2, 3, 4, 8, 9
- Anger v. 1
- Wrath v. 1
- Steadfast love v. 4
- Hears pleas and accepts prayer v. 9

Psalm 7

- LORD vv. 1, 3, 6, 8, 17
- Anger v. 6
- Appointed a judgment v. 6
- Judges the people v. 8
- Tests the minds and hearts v. 9

- Saves the upright in heart v. 10
- Righteous judged v. 11
- Whets His sword and bends His bow against the unrepentant v. 12
- His righteousness is due thanks v. 17

Psalm 8

- LORD vv. 1, 9
- Name is majestic vv. 1, 9
- Establishes strength before His foes through the week v. 2
- Set His glory above the heavens v. 1
- Mindful and caring of man v. 4
- Made man a little lower than the heavenly beings and crowned him with glory and honor v. 5
- Gave man dominion over the works of His hands v. 6

Psalm 9

- LORD vv. 1, 7, 9, 10, 11, 13, 16, 19, 20
- Did wonderful deeds v. 1
- Exulted and praised v. 2
- Rebuked the nations v. 5
- Blotted out the wicked v. 5
- Sits enthroned forever v. 7
- Judges the world with righteousness v. 8
- Stronghold for the oppressed v. 9
- Does not forget the cry of the afflicted v. 12
- Lets the nations know that they are but men v. 20
- Psalm 10
- LORD vv. 1, 3, 12, 16, 17
- Cursed and renounced by the greedy and wicked v. 3
- Out of sight from His enemies v. 5
- Allows evil vv. 2-11
- King forever and ever v. 16
- Strengthens the hearts and inclines His ear to do justice to the fatherless and oppressed vv. 17, 18
- Psalm 11
- LORD vv. 1, 4, 5, 7
- In His holy temple v. 4
- His throne is in heaven v. 4
- Sees v. 4
- Tests v. 4
- His soul hates the wicked and lovers of violence v. 5
- Righteous v. 7
- Loves righteous deeds v. 7
- The upright shall behold His face v. 7

Psalm 12

- LORD vv. 1, 3, 5, 6, 7
- Arises v. 5
- His words are pure v. 6
- Keeps and guards his people from great opposition vv. 7, 8

Psalm 13

- LORD vv. 1, 3, 6
- Hides His face v. 1
- Allows persecution v. 2
- Steadfast love v. 5
- Hearts rejoice in His salvation v. 5
- Dealt bountifully with David v. 6

Psalm 14

- LORD vv. 2, 4, 6, 7
- Fools say in their heart, "There is no God." v. 1
- With the generation of the righteous v. 5
- Refuge of the poor v. 6
- Will restore the fortunes of His people v. 7

Psalm 15

- LORD vv. 1, 4

Psalm 16

- LORD vv. 2, 5, 7, 8
- Refuge v. 1
- No good without Him v. 2
- Multiplies sorrows of idolaters v. 4
- Makes secure v. 9

- Blessed v. 7
- Counsels and instructs v. 7
- Will not abandon souls to hell v. 10
- Makes known the path of life v. 11
- In His presence there is fullness of joy v. 11
- At His right hand are pleasures forevermore v. 11

Psalm 17

- LORD vv. 1, 13, 14
- Eyes v. 2
- Tries hearts, visits by night, and tests v. 3
- Answers v. 6
- Ear v. 6
- Steadfast love v. 7
- Savior of those who seek refuge v. 7
- Wings v. 8
- Satisfies with His likeness v. 15
- His face is beheld v. 15

Psalm 18

- LORD vv. 1, 2, 3, 6, 13, 15, 18, 20, 21, 24, 28, 30, 31, 41, 46, 49
- Loved v. 1
- Strength of David v. 1
- Rock v. 2
- Refuge v. 2
- Shield vv. 2, 30, 35
- Horn of salvation v. 2
- Stronghold v. 2
- Hears v. 6
- Angry v. 7
- Nostrils vv. 8, 15
- Mouth v. 8
- Rescues vv. 17, 19, 48
- Rewards v. 20, 24
- Merciful to the merciful v. 25
- Blameless to the blameless v. 25
- Pure to the purified v. 26
- Torturous to the cruel v. 26
- Brings down the haughty v. 27
- God alone v. 31
- Trains hands for war v. 34
- Equips with strength v. 39
- Delivers vv. 43, 48
- Shows steadfast love to His anointed v. 50

Psalm 19

- LORD vv. 7, 8, 9, 14
- The heavens declare His glory, and the sky above declares His handiwork v. 1
- All voices are heard that give Him glory v. 3
- His law is perfect, reviving the soul v. 7
- His testimony is sure, making wise the simple v. 7
- His commandment is pure, enlightening the eyes v. 8
- The fear of Him is clean, enduring forever v. 9
- His rules are true, and righteous altogether v. 9
- His rules warn His servants, and there is great reward in keeping them v. 11
- Rock v. 14
- Redeemer v. 14

Psalm 20

- LORD vv. 1, 5, 6, 7, 9
- Can answer in the day of trouble, protect you, send help from the sanctuary, give support from Zion, remember all your offerings, grant your heart's desire, fulfill all your plans, and fulfill all your petitions vv. 1-5
- Saves His anointed v. 6
- Answers from His holy heaven with the saving might of His right hand v. 6

Psalm 21

- LORD vv. 1, 7, 9, 13

- Strength v. 1
- Savior vv. 1, 5
- Gives hearts their desires, not withholding requests v. 2
- Meets with rich blessings v. 3
- Gives everlasting life v. 4
- Glory v. 5
- Makes blessed forever v. 6
- Makes glad with the joy of His presence v. 6
- Steadfast love v. 7
- Most High v. 7
- Sustains forever v. 7
- His right hand finds out enemies and those who hate Him v. 8
- Swallows His enemies in wrath v. 9
- Evil plans and mischief devised against Him will not succeed v. 11
- Aims at His enemies faces with His bows and puts them to flight v. 12
- Praised v. 13

<u>Psalm 22</u>

- LORD vv. 8, 19, 23, 26, 27, 28, 30
- Forsakes v. 1
- Holy and enthroned on praises v. 3
- Delivers v. 4
- Makes to trust v. 9
- Rescues v. 21
- Praised and glorified v. 23
- Has not despised or abhorred the affliction of the afflicted v. 24
- Hears cries v. 24
- Kingship belongs to Him v. 28
- All shall bow before Him to the dust v. 29
- Served by posterity v. 30
- Told of to the coming generation v. 30
- His righteousness is proclaimed v. 31

<u>Psalm 23</u>

- LORD vv. 1, 6
- Shepherd v. 1
- Leads v. 2
- Restores v. 3
- With His flock v. 4
- His name is His motivation v. 3
- Comforts v. 4
- Anoints v. 5
- House of the LORD v. 6

<u>Psalm 24</u>

- LORD vv. 1, 3, 5, 8, 10
- The earth is the LORD's and the fullness thereof, the world and those who dwell therein v. 1
- Founded and established the world v. 2
- Gives blessing and righteousness to those who seek the face of the God of Jacob vv. 5, 6
- King of glory vv. 8, 9, 10
- LORD of hosts v. 10

<u>Psalm 25</u>

- LORD vv. 1, 4, 6, 7, 8, 10, 11, 12, 14, 15
- Trusted v. 1
- None who wait for Him shall be put to shame v. 3
- God of salvation v. 5
- Steadfast love vv. 6, 10
- Good and upright v. 8
- Leads the humble in what is right v. 9
- Faithful to those who keep His testimonies v. 10
- Pardons guilt v. 11
- Instructs v. 12
- Befriends and makes known His covenant to those who fear Him v. 14
- Plucks feet from the net v. 15

<u>Psalm 26</u>

- LORD vv. 1, 2, 6, 8, 12
- Trusted v. 1
- Steadfast love v. 3
- Wondrous deeds v. 7
- Blessed v. 12

Psalm 27

- LORD vv. 1, 4, 6, 7, 8, 10, 11, 13, 14
- Light v. 1
- Salvation vv. 1, 9
- Stronghold v. 1
- Beautiful v. 4
- Hides in His shelter on the day of trouble, lifts up and conceals from enemies v. 5
- Sing and make melodies to Him v. 6
- Goodness v. 13

Psalm 28

- LORD vv. 1, 5, 6, 7, 8
- Called upon v. 1
- Cried to for help v. 2
- Drag off the wicked v. 3
- The wicked do not regard His works v. 5
- Blessed v. 6
- Strength v. 7
- Shield v. 7
- Saving refuge of His anointed v. 8

Psalm 29

- LORD vv. 1, 2, 3, 4, 5, 7, 8, 9, 10, 11
- Due glory v. 2
- His voice is powerful and full of majesty v. 4
- Shakes the wilderness v. 8
- Sits enthroned as King forever v. 10

Psalm 30

- LORD vv. 1, 2, 3, 4, 7, 8, 10, 12
- Drew David up v. 1
- Not let foes rejoice v. 1
- Heals v. 2
- Brings up souls from hell v. 3
- Restores from among those who go down into the pit v. 3
- His name is holy v. 4
- Anger is but for a moment v. 5
- Favor is for a lifetime v. 5
- Hides His face from the prosperous proud vv. 6, 7
- Turns mourning into dancing v. 11
- Loosens sackcloth and clothes with gladness v. 11

Psalm 31

- LORD vv. 1, 5, 6, 9, 14, 17, 21, 23, 24
- Refuge vv. 1, 4
- Righteous v. 1
- Ear v. 2
- Rock v. 3
- Fortress v. 3
- Redeemed v. 5
- Trusted v. 6
- Steadfast love makes glad and causes rejoicing v. 7
- Knows the distress of souls v. 7
- Trusted v. 14
- Times are in His hand v. 15
- Steadfast love v. 16
- Abundant goodness is stored up for those who fear Him v. 19
- Blessed v. 21
- Wondrously shown His steadfast love v. 21
- Hears the voice of pleas for mercy v. 22
- Preserves the faithful v. 23
- Abundantly repays the one who acts in pride v. 23

Psalm 32

- LORD vv. 2, 5, 10, 11
- Forgives transgression and covers sin v. 1
- Forgives the repentant after revealing their sin to them vv. 3, 4
- Hiding place v. 7
- Preserves from trouble v. 7
- Surrounds with shouts of deliverance v. 7
- Steadfast love surrounds those who trust Him v. 10

Psalm 33

- LORD vv. 1, 2, 4, 5, 6, 8, 10, 11, 12, 13, 18, 20, 22
- His word is upright v. 4
- All His work is done in faithfulness v. 4
- Loves righteousness and justice v. 5
- The earth is full of His steadfast love v. 5
- The heavens were made by His word, and their host by the breath of His mouth v. 6
- Gathers seas as a heap and puts the deep in storehouses v. 7
- Spoke, and it was v. 9
- Commanded, and it stood firm v. 9
- Brings the counsel of the nations to nothing, and frustrates the plans of the peoples v. 10
- His counsel stands forever, the plans of His heart to all generations v. 11
- Blessed is the nation whose God is the LORD, the people whom He has chosen as His heritage v. 12
- Looks down from heaven and sees all the children of man v. 13
- Fashions all hearts and observes all deeds v. 15
- The eye of the LORD is on those who fear Him, on those who hope in His steadfast love v. 18
- Delivers souls from death and keeps alive during famine v. 19
- Help. 20
- Shield v. 20
- Trusted v. 21
- Steadfast love is upon those who fear Him v. 22

Psalm 34

- LORD vv. 1, 2, 3, 4, 6, 7, 8, 9, 10, 11, 15, 16, 17, 18, 19, 22
- Blessed at all times v. 1
- Boasted in v. 2
- The humble hear His name and are glad v. 2
- Answers those who seek Him, and delivers from all fears v. 4
- Those who look to Him are radiant and shall never be ashamed v. 5
- Hears and delivers the poor v. 6
- Angel of the LORD encamps around those who fear Him and delivers them v. 7
- Good v. 8
- Blessed is the man who takes refuge in Him v. 8
- Those who fear Him have no lack v. 9
- Those who seek Him lack no good thing v. 10
- His eyes are toward the righteous and His ears hear their cry v. 15
- His face is against all who do evil, to cut their memory from the earth v. 16
- Hears when the righteous cry for help and delivers them out of all their troubles v. 17
- Near to the broken hearted and saves the crushed in spirit v. 18
- Delivers the righteous from their many afflictions v. 19
- Redeems v. 22
- None of those who take refuge in Him will be condemned v. 22

Psalm 35

- LORD vv. 1, 5, 6, 9, 10, 17, 22, 23, 24, 27
- Salvation is His v. 9
- No one is like Him v. 10
- Delivers the poor from him who is too strong for him v. 10
- Seen v. 22

- Righteous vv. 24, 28
- Great v. 27
- Delights in the welfare of His servant v. 27

Psalm 36

- LORD vv. 1, 5, 6
- Steadfast love extending to the heavens vv. 5, 7, 10
- Faithfulness extending to the clouds v. 5
- His righteousness is like mountains and His judgments, the great deep vv. 6, 10
- Saves man and beast v. 6
- The children of mankind take refuge in the shadow of His wings v. 7
- In Him is the fountain of life v. 9
- In His light do we see light v. 9

Psalm 37

- LORD vv. 3, 4, 5, 7, 9, 13, 17, 18, 20, 22, 23, 24, 28, 33, 34, 39, 40
- Gives the desires of the heart to those who delight in Him v. 4
- Acts when trusted v. 5
- Gives inheritance to those who wait on Him and who are humble v. 9
- Laughs at the wicked v. 12
- Knows the days of the blameless v. 18
- The enemies of the LORD vanish v. 20
- Establishes a man's steps when he delights in His way v. 23
- Faithful to the righteous v. 25
- Does not leave His children to beg for bread v. 25
- Lends generously v. 26
- His children become a blessing v. 26
- Loves justice v. 27
- Will not forsake His saints, who, unlike the wicked, shall be preserved forever v. 28
- His law is in the righteous man's heart, and his steps do not slip v. 31
- Does not abandon the righteous to the power of the wicked or let them be condemned under trial v. 33
- Exalts and looks on those who wait on the LORD and keep His way v. 34
- The salvation of the righteous is from the LORD v. 39
- Delivers and saves those who take refuge in Him v. 40

Psalm 38

- LORD vv. 1, 9, 15, 21, 22
- Anger v. 1
- Wrath v. 1
- Sighing of the repentant and distressed is not hidden from God v. 9
- Answers v. 15
- LORD of salvation v. 22

Psalm 39

- LORD vv. 4, 7, 12
- A lifetime is nothing before Him v. 5
- Rebukes man for sin and consumes what is dear to him v. 11

Psalm 40

- LORD vv. 1, 3, 4, 5, 9, 11, 13, 16, 17
- Inclines to and hears cries v. 1
- Draws up from the pit and out of the miry bog and onto a secure rock v. 2
- Put a new song in David's mouth, a song of praise v. 3
- Many will see and fear, and put their trust in the LORD v. 3
- Blesses the man who trusts in Him, rather than lies of the proud v. 4

- Multiplies His wondrous deeds toward us. More than can be told v. 5
- None can compare with Him v. 5
- Does not delight in or require offering and sacrifice for sin, but gives an open ear v. 6
- His law was in David's heart v. 8
- Delivers vv. 9, 10
- Steadfast love vv. 10, 11
- Faithfulness vv. 10, 11
- Will not restrain His mercy v. 11
- Preserves v. 11
- Salvation v. 16
- Great v. 16
- Takes thought for one, though he is poor and needy v. 17
- Help v. 17
- Deliverer v. 17

Psalm 41

- LORD vv. 1, 2, 3, 4, 10, 13
- Delivers, protects, keeps alive, does not give him up to the will of his enemies, sustains on his sickbed, and restores back to full health him who considers the poor vv. 1-3
- Blessed, from everlasting to everlasting v. 13
- God of Israel v. 13

Psalm 42

- LORD vv. 8
- Living v. 2
- Savior vv. 5, 11
- Commands His steadfast love v. 8
- Rock v. 9

Psalm 43

- Savior v. 5

Psalm 44

- LORD v. 23
- Performed deeds in the days of our fathers, planting and setting them free v. 1
- Drove out the nations with His hand, afflicting the peoples v. 2
- Delights in His people v. 3
- King v. 4
- Through Him foes are pushed down v. 5
- Saves v. 7
- Disciplines His people v. 10
- Scatters His disobedient people v. 11
- Made His people a laughing stock to other peoples v. 14
- Knows the secrets of the heart v. 21
- His people suffer at the hands of those who oppose God v. 22
- Steadfast love v. 26

Psalm 45

- LORD v. 11
- Blesses v. 2
- The scepter of His kingdom is of uprightness v. 6
- Loves righteousness v. 7
- Hates wickedness v. 7
- Anoints v. 7

Psalm 46

- LORD vv. 7, 8, 11
- Refuge v. 1
- Strength v. 1
- A very present help in trouble v. 1
- Makes wars cease to the end of the earth; He breaks the bow and shatters the spear; He burns chariots with fire v. 9
- Exalted among the nations and earth v. 10
- LORD of hosts v. 11
- Fortress v. 11
- God of Jacob v. 11

Psalm 47

- LORD vv. 2, 5
- To be loved by all peoples v. 1
- Most High v. 2

- Subdues peoples v. 3
- King of all the earth v. 7
- Reigns over the nations v. 8
- Sits on His holy throne v. 8
- God of Abraham v. 9
- The shields of the earth belong to Him v. 9
- He is highly exalted v. 9

Psalm 48

- LORD vv. 1, 8
- Great, and greatly to be praised v. 1
- His holy mountain, beautiful in all the earth, is the joy of all the earth v. 2
- Made Himself known as a fortress v. 3
- Shattered the ships of Tarshish by the east wind v. 7
- LORD of hosts v. 8
- Will establish His city forever v. 8
- Steadfast love v. 9
- His praise reaches the end of the earth v. 10
- His right hand is filled with righteousness v. 10
- Guides His people forever v. 14

Psalm 49

Psalm 50

- LORD v. 1
- The Mighty One v. 1
- Speaks and summons the earth v. 1
- Shines forth v. 2
- Does not keep silence; before Him is a devouring fire and around Him a mighty tempest v. 3
- Calls to the heavens above and to the earth that He may judge His people v. 4
- Gathers His faithful ones v. 5
- Made a covenant by sacrifice v. 5
- All that moves is His v. 11
- The world and its fullness are His v. 12
- Delivers v. 15
- Rebukes and lays charges v. 21
- The one who offers thanksgiving as his sacrifice glorifies Him and will be shown salvation v. 23

Psalm 51

- LORD vv. 15
- Steadfast love v. 1
- Abundant mercy v. 1
- Sinned against v. 4
- Justified v. 4
- Blameless in His judgment v. 4
- Delights in truth in the inward being v. 6
- Teaches wisdom in the secret heart v. 6
- Washes whiter than snow v. 7
- Holy Spirit v. 11
- Gives the joy of His salvation v. 12
- Savior v. 14
- Is not delighted or pleased with a burnt offering v. 16

Psalm 52

- His steadfast love endures all the day long vv. 1, 8
- Breaks evil doers down forever v. 5
- His name is good v. 9

Psalm 53

- Looks down from heaven on the children of man to see if there are any who understand, who seek after God v. 2
- Restores v. 6

Psalm 54

- LORD vv. 4, 6
- Mighty v. 1
- Hears v. 2
- Helper v. 4
- Upholder of life v. 4
- Returns evil to enemies v. 5

- Faithful v. 5
- Deliverer v. 7

Psalm 55
- LORD vv. 9, 16, 22
- Hears vv. 1, 17
- God's house v. 14
- Savior v. 16
- Redeemer v. 18
- Humbles those who do not fear Him v. 19
- Sustains when burdens are heavy v. 22
- He will never permit the righteous to be moved v. 22
- Trusted in v. 23
- Casts men of blood and treachery into the pit of destruction v. 23

Psalm 56
- LORD v. 10
- Trusted vv. 3, 4, 11
- Wrath v. 7
- Keeps count of wanderings v. 8
- God is for David v. 9
- His word is praised v. 10
- Delivers souls from death and feet from falling, that one may walk before God in the light of life v. 13

Psalm 57
- LORD v. 9
- In Him do souls take refuge v. 1
- God Most High v. 2
- Fulfills His purpose for His people v. 2
- Sends from heaven and saves v. 3
- Puts to shame those who trample the righteous v. 3
- Steadfast love vv. 3, 10
- Faithful vv. 3, 10
- Exalted above the heavens v. 5
- Praised v. 9

Psalm 58
- LORD v. 6
- Judges on earth v. 11

Psalm 59
- LORD vv. 3, 6, 8
- LORD God of hosts v. 5
- God of Israel v. 5
- Strength vv. 9, 16, 17
- Fortress vv. 9, 16, 17
- Steadfast love vv. 10, 16, 17
- Gives triumph v. 10
- Power v. 11
- Shield v. 11
- Rules over Jacob v. 13
- Refuge v. 16
- Praised v. 17

Psalm 60
- Rejected and broke the defenses of His people vv. 1, 10
- Anger v. 1
- Makes the land to quake, and tears it open v. 2
- Made His people see hard things v. 3
- Gave wine to make His people stagger v. 3
- Set up a banner for those who fear Him, that they may flee to it from the bow v. 4
- Has spoken in His holiness: "With exultation I will divide up Shechem and portion out the valley of Succoth. Gilead is mine; Manasseh is mine; Ephraim is my helmet; Judah is my scepter. Moab is my washbasin; upon Edom I cast my shoe; over Philistia I shout in triumph." vv. 6, 7, 8
- Treads down His people's foes v. 12

Psalm 61
- Called to from the end of the earth from a faint heart v. 2
- Refuge v. 3
- Strong tower v. 3
- Shelter of His wings v. 4

- Hears vows v. 5
- Gives the heritage of those who fear His name v. 5

Psalm 62
- LORD v. 12
- Source of salvation v. 1
- Rock vv. 2, 6, 7
- Salvation vv. 2, 6, 7
- Fortress vv. 2, 6
- Source of hope v. 5
- Refuge vv. 7, 8
- Power belongs to Him v. 11
- Steadfast love belongs to Him v. 12
- Renders to a man according to his work v. 12

Psalm 63
- David's God v. 1
- Earnestly sought v. 1
- Flesh faints for Him v. 1
- Power v. 2
- Glory v. 2
- His steadfast love is better than life v. 3
- Praised vv. 3, 5
- Hands are lifted in His name v. 4
- Help v. 7
- Wings v. 7
- His right hand upholds v. 8
- The king rejoices in God v. 11
- Those who swear by Him shall exult v. 11

Psalm 64
- LORD v. 10
- God shoots His arrows at those who shoot their arrows at the innocent, wounding them suddenly v. 7
- All mankind fears; they tell what God has brought about and ponder what He has done v. 9

Psalm 65
- Praise is due Him v. 1
- In Zion v. 1
- To Him vows shall be performed v. 1
- Atones for transgressions when iniquities prevail v. 3
- Blessed is the one He chooses to bring near, to dwell in His courts v. 4
- His people shall be satisfied with the goodness of His house, the holiness of His temple v. 4
- By awesome deeds He answers with righteousness v. 5
- Savior v. 5
- Hope of the ends of the earth and of the farthest seas v. 5
- By His strength He established the mountains, being girded with might v. 6
- Stills the roaring of the seas v. 7
- Those who dwell at the ends of the earth are in awe of His signs v. 8
- Makes dawn and dusk shout for joy v. 8
- Visits the earth, waters it, greatly enriches it, filling His river and providing grain v. 9

Psalm 66
- LORD v. 18
- His name is glorious v. 2
- So great in power that His enemies come cringing to Him v. 3
- All the earth worships and sings praises to Him v. 4
- Awesome v. 5
- His deeds are toward the children of man v. 5
- Turned the sea into dry land v. 6
- Rejoiced in Him v. 6
- Rules by His might forever v. 7
- His eyes keep watch on the nations v. 7
- Praised v. 8

- Keeps souls among the living and has not let feet slip v. 9
- Tests and tries v. 10
- Laid a crushing burden on His people's backs v. 11
- Let men ride over His people's heads, and brought them out of a place of abundance v. 12
- Has a house v. 13
- Offered sacrifice v. 15
- Cried to and praised v. 17
- Listens to those who forsake iniquity v. 19
- Blessed for not rejecting prayer or removing His steadfast love v. 20
- Steadfast love v. 20

Psalm 67

- Saving power v. 2
- Judges the peoples with equity and guides the nations upon earth v. 4
- Blesses vv. 6, 7

Psalm 68

- LORD vv. 4, 11, 16, 17, 18, 19, 20, 22, 26, 32
- Shall arise and His enemies shall be scattered, and those who hate Him shall flee before Him v. 1
- The wicked shall perish before God v. 2
- The righteous shall exult before God and be jubilant with joy v. 3
- Rides through the deserts v. 4
- Father of the fatherless and protector of widows v. 5
- In His holy habitation v. 5
- Settles the solitary in a home and leads prisoners to prosperity, but the rebellious dwell in a parched land v. 6
- Went out before His people, marching through the wilderness v. 7
- One of Sinai v. 8
- God of Israel v. 8
- Restored His inheritance as it languished v. 9
- Gave His flock a dwelling place v. 10
- Provided for the needy in His goodness v. 10
- Gives the word v. 11
- Almighty v. 14
- Will dwell forever at the mountain He desired for His abode v. 16
- The chariots of God are twice ten thousand v. 17
- Ascended on high, leading a host of captives on His train, receiving gifts among men, even among the rebellious, that He may dwell there v. 18
- Blessed v. 19
- Daily bears up v. 19
- Savior vv. 19, 20
- To Him belong deliverances from death v. 20
- Will strike the heads of His enemies v. 21
- His procession is seen v. 24
- Blessed v. 26
- Power v. 28
- Works power for His people v. 28
- Kings shall bear gifts to Him v. 29
- Praised v. 32
- Rides in the ancient heavens and sends out His mighty voice v. 33
- His majesty is over Israel, and His power is in the skies v. 34
- Awesome v. 35
- God of Israel v. 35
- Gives power and strength to His people v. 35
- Blessed v. 35

Psalm 69

- LORD vv. 6, 13, 16, 31, 33
- Knows one's folly v. 5

- LORD God of hosts v. 6
- God of Israel v. 6
- For His sake reproach is born v. 7
- Steadfast love vv. 13, 16
- Saving faithfulness v. 13
- Abundant in mercy v. 16
- Knows one's reproach v. 20
- Burning anger and indignation v. 24
- Enrolls among the righteous v. 28
- Savior v. 29
- Praised with a song and magnified with thanksgiving v. 30
- Hears the needy v. 33
- Does not despise the His own people who are prisoners v. 33
- Will save Zion and build up the cities of Judah v. 35
- Those who love Him shall dwell in their inheritance v. 36

Psalm 70

- LORD vv. 1, 5
- Help v. 5
- Deliverer v. 5

Psalm 71

- LORD vv. 1, 5, 16
- Righteous v. 2
- Given the command to save v. 3
- Rock v. 3
- Fortress v. 3
- Hope v. 5
- Trust v. 5
- Leaned on and continually praised v. 6
- Refuge v. 7
- Hoped in and praised continually v. 14
- His righteous acts and deeds of salvation are past knowledge v. 15
- Teaches v. 17
- His righteousness reaches to the high heavens v. 19
- Done great things v. 19
- Will revive again those who He has made to see many troubles and calamities v. 20
- Will increase His people's greatness and revive them v. 21
- Faithful v. 22
- Holy One of Israel v. 22
- Redeemer v. 23

Psalm 72

- LORD v. 18
- Just v. 1
- Righteousness v. 1
- Judge v. 2
- Delivers the needy when he calls, and the poor and him who has no helper v. 12
- Has pity on the weak and the needy, and saves the lives of the needy v. 13
- Redeems life from oppression and violence, and precious is their blood in His sight v. 14
- Blessed vv. 18, 19
- God of Israel v. 18
- He alone does wondrous things v. 18

Psalm 73

- LORD vv. 20, 28
- Good to Israel, to those who are pure in heart v. 1
- Most High v. 11
- Holds the pure in heart in His right hand v. 23
- Guides with His counsel v. 24
- Receives the pure heart to glory v. 24
- Strength of my heart, and my portion forever v. 26
- Those who are far from Him shall perish v. 27
- He puts an end to everyone who is unfaithful to Him v. 27
- Refuge v. 28

Psalm 74

- LORD v. 18
- Anger v. 1
- Purchased His congregation of old v. 2
- Redeemed the tribe of His heritage v. 2
- Dwelt in Mount Zion v. 2
- The enemy profaned the dwelling place of His name v. 7
- From of old, working salvation in the midst of the earth v. 12
- Divided the sea by His might, broke the heads of sea monsters on the waters v. 13
- His is the day as well as the night. He established the heavenly lights and the sun v. 16
- Fixed all the boundaries of the earth v. 17
- Made summer and winter v. 17
- The clamor of His foes goes up continually v. 23

Psalm 75

- LORD v. 8
- His name is near v. 1
- His deeds are wondrous v. 1
- Will judge with equity at the set time He has appointed v. 2
- Keeps steady the earth's pillars v. 3
- Tells the boastful not to boast and the wicked to not raise up their horn or speak with haughty neck v. 5
- It is God who executes judgment v. 7
- He puts down one and lifts up another v. 7
- All the wicked of the earth drink His cup of well mixed, foaming wine to the very dregs v. 8
- God of Jacob v. 9
- Cuts off the horns of the wicked, but lifts up the horns of the righteous v. 10

Psalm 76

- LORD v. 11
- Known in Judah, and His name is great in Israel v. 1
- His abode has been established in Salem, His dwelling place in Zion v. 2
- Glorious v. 4
- Majestic v. 4
- God of Jacob v. 6
- The rider and horse are stunned at His rebuke v. 6
- To be feared, for no one can stand once His anger is roused v. 7
- Uttered judgments from the heavens; the earth feared and was still v. 8
- Arose to establish judgment, to save all the humble of the earth v. 12

Psalm 77

- LORD vv. 7, 11
- Hears v. 1
- Steadfast love v. 8
- Promised v. 8
- Gracious v. 9
- Anger v. 9
- Compassion v. 9
- Right hand v. 10
- Most High v. 10
- Mighty deeds v. 12
- His way is holy v. 13
- Works wonders v. 14
- Made known His might among the peoples v. 14
- Redeemed His people with His arm v. 15
- When the waters saw Him they were afraid v. 16

- His way was through the sea, yet His footprints were unseen v. 19
- Led His people like a flock by the hand of Moses and Aaron v. 20

Psalm 78

- LORD v. 4, 21, 65
- Glorious deeds v. 4
- Might v. 4
- Done wonders v. 4
- Established a testimony in Jacob v. 5
- Appointed a law in Israel v. 5
- Commanded fathers to teach their children His law and testimony v. 5
- Made and keeps His covenant v. 10
- Forgotten by His people v. 11
- Performed wonders in His people's sight v. 12
- Divided the sea and let them pass through it, and made the waters stand like a heap v. 13
- Led with a cloud and a fiery light v. 14
- Made streams come out of the rock v. 16
- Sinned against v. 17
- Most High v. 17
- Tested v. 18
- Wrath v. 21
- His anger rose against Israel v. 21
- Rained down manna from the skies for His stubborn people eat v. 24
- Sent angel food in abundance v. 25
- Rained meat on His people like dust v. 27
- Gave His people what they craved v. 29
- In His anger He killed and laid low the strongest and young men of Israel v. 31
- Made His people's days vanish like a breath v. 33
- Sought after earnestly v. 34
- Rock v. 35
- Most High God vv. 35, 56
- Redeemer v. 35
- Lied to v. 36
- Compassionate v. 38
- Made atonement for His people's iniquity v. 38
- Restrains His anger often v. 38
- Did not stir up all His wrath v. 38
- Remembered that His people were but flesh, a wind that passes and comes not again v. 39
- Often rebelled against and grieved v. 40
- Tested again and again and provoked v. 41
- Holy One of Israel v. 41
- Powerful v. 42
- Redeems from the foe v. 42
- Performed His signs in Egypt and His marvels in the fields of Zoan v. 43
- Turned rivers to blood v. 44
- Sent swarms of flies to devour and frogs to destroy v. 45
- Gave crops and the fruit of labor to the destroying locust v. 46
- Destroyed vines with hail v. 48
- Let loose His burning anger v. 49
- Anger v. 50
- Struck down every firstborn in Egypt v. 51
- Led out His people like sheep and guided them in the wilderness like a flock v. 52
- Brought them to His holy land to the mountain which His right hand had won v. 54
- Drove out the nations before Israel and settled them in their tents v. 55

- Provoked to anger and moved to jealousy v. 58
- Wrath v. 59
- Utterly rejected Israel v. 59
- Gave His people over to the sword and vented His wrath on His heritage v. 62
- Awoke as from sleep, like a strong man shouting because of wine v. 65
- Put His adversaries to rout; He put them to everlasting shame v. 66
- Rejected the tent of Joseph; He did not choose the tribe of Ephraim v. 67
- Chose the tribe of Judah, Mount Zion, which He loves v. 68
- Built His sanctuary like the high heavens, like the earth, which He has founded forever v. 69
- Chose David His servant v. 70
- Brought David to Shepherd Jacob his people, Israel his inheritance v. 71
- With upright heart He shepherded them and guided them with His skillful hand v. 72

Psalm 79

- LORD vv. 5, 12
- The nations have come into His inheritance, defiled His holy temple, and laid Jerusalem in ruins v. 1
- Nations gave the bodies of His servants to the birds of the heavens for food, the flesh of His faithful to the beasts of the earth v. 2
- Anger vv. 5, 6
- Jealousy v. 5
- Compassion v. 8
- Savior v. 9
- Great power v. 11
- Taunted v. 12
- Praised from generation to generation v. 13

Psalm 80

- LORD vv. 4, 19
- Shepherd of Israel v. 1
- Lead Joseph like a flock v. 1
- Enthroned upon the cherubim v. 1
- Might v. 2
- Face vv. 3, 7, 19
- God of hosts vv. 4, 7, 14 19
- Anger v. 4
- Fed His people with the bread of tears and gave them tears to drink in full measure v. 5
- Made Israel an object of contention v. 6
- Brought a vine out of Egypt; drove out the nations and planted it vv. 8, 15
- Broke down Israel's walls v. 12
- In heaven v. 14

Psalm 81

- LORD vv. 10, 15
- Strength v. 1
- God of Jacob vv. 1, 4
- Relieves shoulders of burdens v. 6
- Delivers v. 7
- Answers v. 7
- Tests v. 7
- Admonishes His people v. 8
- Israel's God v. 10
- Brought Israel out of Egypt v. 10
- Gave Israel over to their stubborn hearts to follow their own counsels v. 12
- Subdues the enemies of those who listen to Him vv. 13, 14

Psalm 82

- Taken His place in the divine counsel; in the midst of the gods He holds judgment v. 1
- Most High v. 6
- Shall inherit all the nations v. 8

Psalm 83

- LORD vv. 16, 18
- His enemies make an uproar v. 2
- He alone is the Most High over all the earth v. 18
- Psalm 84
- LORD vv. 1, 2, 3, 11, 12
- LORD of hosts vv. 1, 8, 12
- Living v. 2
- Anoints v. 9
- A day in His courts are better than a thousand elsewhere v. 10
- Sun and shield v. 11
- Bestows favor and honor v. 11
- No good thing does He withhold from those who walk uprightly v. 11
- Psalm 85
- LORD vv. 1, 7, 8, 12
- Favorable to His land v. 1
- Restored the fortunes of Jacob v. 1
- Forgave the iniquity of His people; He covered all their sin v. 2
- Withdrew all His wrath; He turned from His hot anger v. 3
- Savior vv. 4, 7
- Indignant v. 4
- Anger vv. 3, 5
- Steadfast love v. 10
- Faithfulness vv. 10, 11
- Will give what is good v. 12
- Psalm 86
- LORD vv. 1, 3, 4, 5, 6, 8, 9, 11, 12, 15, 17
- Favorable to His land v. 1
- Restored the fortunes of Jacob v. 1
- Forgave the iniquity of His people, covering all their sin v. 2
- Withdrew all His wrath; turned from His hot anger v. 3
- Savior vv. 4, 7, 9
- Indignant v. 4
- Restores v. 4
- Anger v. 5
- Revives v. 6
- Steadfast love v. 7
- Will speak peace to His people, to His saints v. 8
- Glorious v. 9
- Righteousness will go before Him and make His footsteps a way v. 13

Psalm 87

- LORD vv. 2, 6
- Loves the gates of Zion, the city He founded v. 1
- Glorious things of His city are spoken v. 2
- Most High v. 5
- Singers and dancers alike say, "All my springs are in you." v. 7

Psalm 88

- LORD vv. 1, 9, 13, 14
- Savior v. 1
- Cuts people off from His hand and remembers them no more v. 5
- Wrath vv. 7, 16
- Steadfast love v. 11
- Faithful v. 11
- Does wonders v. 12
- Righteous v. 12
- Allows suffering vv. 13-18

Psalm 89

- LORD vv. 1, 5, 6, 8, 15, 18, 46, 49, 50, 51, 52
- Steadfast love vv. 1, 2, 28, 33, 49
- Faithful vv. 1, 5, 8, 33, 49
- Made a covenant with His chosen one, establishing his offspring forever and building his throne for all generations vv. 3, 4, 28, 34
- Does wonders v. 5
- Nobody can compare to Him v. 6
- Greatly to be feared v. 7
- Awesome v. 7
- Above all v. 7
- God of hosts v. 8

- Mighty vv. 8, 13
- Rules the raging of the sea v. 9
- Scatters enemies with His mighty arm v. 10
- Heaven and earth are His v. 11
- Founder of the world and all that is in it v. 11
- Praised joyously v. 12
- Strong v. 13
- High v. 13
- Blesses v. 15
- Righteous v. 16
- Holy One of Israel v. 18
- Anoints v. 20
- Establishes vv. 21, 29
- Strengthens v. 21
- Is not outwitted or humbled by the wicked v. 22
- Rock of salvation v. 26
- Punishes transgression with the rod and iniquity with stripes v. 32
- Wrath v. 46
- Blessed forever v. 52

Psalm 90

- LORD vv. 1, 13, 17
- Dwelling place v. 1
- Formed the world v. 2
- Returns man to dust v. 3
- A thousand years is like a day to Him v. 4
- Wrath vv. 9, 11
- Anger vv. 9, 11
- Steadfast love v. 14
- Afflicts v. 15
- Glorious power v. 16
- Gives favor v. 17

Psalm 91

- LORD vv. 2, 9
- Most High vv. 1, 9
- Almighty v. 1
- Refuge vv. 2, 9
- Fortress v. 2
- Delivers vv. 3, 14
- Faithful v. 4
- Dwelling place v. 9
- Guards with His angels v. 11
- Protector v. 14
- Answers v. 15
- Rescues v. 15
- Honors v. 15
- Satisfies v. 16
- Savior v. 16

Psalm 92

- LORD vv. 1, 4, 5, 8, 9, 13, 15
- Most High v. 1
- Steadfast love v. 2
- Makes glad by the work of His hands v. 4
- His thoughts are very deep v. 5
- On high forever v. 8
- His enemies will perish and be scattered v. 9
- Exalts v. 10
- Upright v. 15
- Righteous v. 15
- Rock v. 15

Psalm 93

- LORD vv. 1, 3, 5
- Reigns v. 1
- Robed in majesty v. 1
- Put on strength as His belt v. 1
- His throne is established from old v. 2
- Mighty v. 4
- His decrees are very trustworthy v. 5
- Holy v. 5

Psalm 94

- LORD vv. 1, 3, 5, 7, 11, 12, 14, 17, 18, 22, 23
- God of vengeance v. 1
- God of Jacob v. 7
- Planted the ear v. 9
- Hears v. 9

- Formed the eye v. 9
- Sees v. 9
- Disciplines the nations v. 10
- Rebukes v. 10
- Teaches man knowledge v. 10
- Knows the thoughts of man, that they are but a breath v. 11
- Blesses v. 12
- Teaches out of His law v. 12
- Will not forsake His people v. 14
- Will not abandon His heritage v. 14
- Steadfast love v. 18
- Consoles v. 19
- Stronghold v. 22
- Rock of one's refuge v. 22
- Wipes out the wicked v. 23

Psalm 95

- LORD vv. 1, 3, 6
- Rock of salvation v. 1
- Great v. 3
- The depths of the earth are in His hand v. 4
- Made the sea and formed the dry land with His hands v. 5
- Maker v. 6
- Speaks v. 7

Psalm 96

- LORD vv. 1, 2, 4, 5, 7, 8, 9, 10, 13
- Savior v. 2
- Glorious v. 3
- Marvelous works v. 3
- Great v. 4
- Made the heavens v. 5
- Splendor and majesty are before Him; strength and beauty are in His sanctuary v. 6
- Reigns v. 10
- Comes to judge the earth in righteousness and faithfulness v. 13

Psalm 97

- LORD vv. 1, 5, 8, 9, 10, 12
- Reigns v. 1
- Clouds and thick darkness are all around Him v. 2
- Righteousness and justice are the foundation of His throne v. 2
- Lights up the world v. 4
- The earth sees and trembles before Him v. 4
- All the peoples see His glory v. 6
- The heavens declare His righteousness v. 6
- Because of His judgments Zion is glad and the daughters of Judah rejoice v. 8
- Exalted far above all gods v. 9
- Preserves the lives of the saints, delivering them from the hand of the wicked v. 10

Psalm 98

- LORD vv. 1, 2, 4, 5, 6, 8, 9
- Has done marvelous things v. 1
- His right hand and holy arm worked salvation v. 1
- Made known His salvation v. 2
- Revealed His righteousness in the sight of the nations v. 2
- Remembered His steadfast love and faithfulness v. 3
- All the ends of the earth have seen the salvation of our God (benefits not limited to the Jews) v. 3
- King v. 6
- Comes to judge the earth v. 9
- Will judge with equity and righteousness v. 9

Psalm 99

- LORD vv. 1, 2, 5, 6, 8, 9
- Reigns v. 1
- Sits enthroned upon the cherubim v. 1
- Great in Zion v. 2
- Exalted over the peoples v. 2
- Holy vv. 3, 5
- King v. 5

- Mighty v. 5
- Loves justice v. 5
- Established equity v. 5
- Executed justice v. 5
- Answers vv. 6, 8
- Given testimonies and statutes v. 7
- Forgiving v. 8
- Avenger of wrongdoings v. 8
- Holy v. 9

Psalm 100

- LORD vv. 1, 2, 3, 5
- God v. 3
- Made and owns us v. 3
- Good v. 5
- His steadfast love and faithfulness endures forever to all generations v. 5

Psalm 101

- LORD vv. 1, 8

Psalm 102

- LORD vv. 1, 12, 15, 16, 18, 19, 21, 22
- Indignation v. 10
- Anger v. 10
- Enthroned forever (whereas man withers like grass) v. 12
- Remembered throughout all generations v. 12
- Regards prayer of the destitute v. 17
- Looked at the earth from heaven v. 19
- Heard the groans of prisoners v. 20
- Laid the foundation of the earth and the heavens are the work of His hands v. 25
- His years have no end vv. 24-27
- The children of His servants shall dwell secure and be established before Him v. 28

Psalm 103

- LORD vv. 1, 2, 6, 8, 13, 17, 19, 21, 22
- Forgives from all iniquity; heals all diseases v. 3
- Redeems life from the pit v. 4
- Crowns with steadfast love and mercy v. 4
- Satisfies with good, that youth is renewed like the eagle's v. 5
- Works righteousness and justice for all who are oppressed v. 6
- Made known His ways and acts to Israel and Moses v. 7
- Merciful v. 8
- Gracious v. 8
- Slow to anger v. 8
- Abounding in steadfast love v. 8
- Will not always chide nor keep His anger forever v. 9
- Does not deal with us according to our sins, nor repay us according to our iniquities v. 10
- As high as the heavens are above the earth, so great is His steadfast love toward those who fear Him. v. 11
- As far as the east is from the west, so far does He remove our transgressions from us v. 12
- Shows compassion as a father does His child to those who fear Him v. 13
- He knows our frame and remembers that we are dust v. 14
- His steadfast love is from everlasting to everlasting on those who fear Him, and His righteousness to children's children, to those who keep His covenant and remember to do His commandments v. 17
- Established His throne in the heavens, and His kingdom rules over all v. 19

Psalm 104

- LORD vv. 1, 16, 24, 31, 34, 35
- Very great v. 1

- Clothed with splendor and majesty v. 1
- Covers Himself with light as with a garment v. 2
- Stretches out the heavens like a tent v. 2
- Makes the clouds His chariot v. 3
- Set the earth on its foundations so it will never be moved v. 5
- Makes springs gush forth in the valleys and gives drink to every beast of the field v. 11
- The earth is satisfied with the fruit of His work v. 13
- Causes plants to grow for livestock and man's cultivation for food and wine to gladden and strengthen his heart v. 14
- Made the moon to mark the seasons and the sun to know its time for setting v. 19
- His works are manifold v. 24
- Creatures look to Him to give them their food in due season v. 27
- Sends forth His Spirit to create creatures and renew the face of the ground v. 30
- Glorious v. 31
- Praised v. 33
- Touches the mountains and they smoke; looks at the earth and it trembles v. 32

<u>Psalm 105</u>

- LORD vv. 1, 3, 4, 7, 19, 21, 24, 45
- Wondrous works v. 2
- Holy v. 3
- Strong v. 4
- His judgments are in all the earth v. 7
- Remembers His covenant forever v. 7
- Allowed no one to touch His anointed ones or to do His prophets harm v. 15
- Providentially and powerfully worked through individuals to accomplish His will vv. 1-45

<u>Psalm 106</u>

- LORD vv. 1, 2, 4, 16, 25, 29, 34, 40, 47, 48
- Good v. 1
- His steadfast love endures forever vv. 1, 7
- Mighty deeds v. 2
- Shows favor to His people and saves them v. 4
- Sinned against by His own people v. 6
- Rebuked the Red Sea v. 9
- Saves v. 10
- Redeems v. 10
- Believed v. 12
- Quickly forgotten v. 13
- Put to the test v. 14
- Provoked to anger v. 29
- Anger kindled against His people who whored against Him v. 40
- Holy v. 47
- Remembered His covenant v. 45
- Relents according to the abundance of His steadfast love v. 45

<u>Psalm 107</u>

- LORD vv. 1, 2, 6, 8, 13, 15, 19, 21, 24, 28, 31, 43
- Good v. 1
- Steadfast love vv. 1, 13, 21, 31, 43
- Redeems v. 2
- Delivers vv. 6, 13
- Leads v. 7
- Fills the hungry soul with good things v. 9
- Counsels v. 11
- Mistreated v. 11
- Most High v. 11
- Works wonders vv. 15, 21
- Delivers the repentant v. 20

- Works wonders v. 24
- Cried to v. 28
- Delivers v. 28
- Turns rivers into a desert v. 33
- Blesses v. 38
- Pours contempt v. 40

Psalm 108

- LORD v. 3
- Praised v. 3
- Steadfast love v. 4
- Faithfulness v. 4
- Glorious v. 5
- Promised v. 7

Psalm 109

- LORD vv. 14, 15, 20, 21, 26, 27, 30
- Praised v. 1
- Steadfast love vv. 21, 26
- Blesses v. 28
- Stands at the right hand of the needy one, to save him from those who would condemn his soul to death v. 31

Psalm 110

- LORD vv. 1, 2, 4, 5
- Will make His enemies His footstool v. 1
- Doesn't change His mind v. 4
- Will shatter kings on the day of His wrath v. 5
- Will execute judgments among the nations, filling them with corpses; He will shatter chiefs over the wide earth v. 6

Psalm 111

- LORD vv. 1, 2, 4, 10
- His works are great, full of majesty and splendor v. 3
- His righteousness endures forever v. 3
- Caused His wondrous works to be remembered forever v. 5
- Shown His people the power of His works, in giving them the inheritance of the nations v. 6
- The works of His hands are faithful and just; all His precepts are trustworthy v. 7
- His rules are established forever and ever, to be performed with faithfulness and uprightness v. 8
- Sent redemption to His people; has commanded His covenant forever v. 9
- Holy and awesome is His name v. 9
- His praise endures forever v. 10

Psalm 112

- LORD vv. 1, 7
- Blesses those who fear Him and greatly delight in His commandments v. 1

Psalm 113

- LORD vv. 1, 2, 3, 4, 5, 9
- Blessed forever v. 2
- High above all nations and His glory is above the heavens v. 4
- Raises the poor from the dust and lifts the needy from the ash heap to make them sit with princes v. 8
- Gives barren women a home, making her the joyous mother of children v. 7

Psalm 114

- LORD v. 7
- Judah became His sanctuary, Israel His dominion v. 2
- Turns rock into a pool of water, the flint into a spring of water v. 8

Psalm 115

- LORD vv. 1, 9, 10, 11, 12, 13, 14, 15, 16, 17, 18
- Help vv. 10, 11
- Shield vv. 10, 11

- Remembers His people; will bless them v. 12
- Blesses those who fear Him, both the small and great v. 13
- Made heaven and earth v. 15
- The heavens are His, but He gave the earth to the children of man v. 16
- Not praised by the dead and silent v. 17

Psalm 116

- LORD vv. 1, 4, 5, 6, 7, 9, 12, 13, 14, 15, 16, 17, 18, 19
- Hears pleas for mercy v. 1
- Gracious v. 5
- Righteous v. 5
- Merciful v. 5
- Preserves the simple v. 6
- Delivers souls from death, eyes from tears, feet from stumbling v. 8
- Called upon v. 13
- The death of His saints is precious in His sight v. 15
- Looses bonds v. 16

Psalm 117

- LORD vv. 1, 2
- Great is His steadfast love v. 2
- His faithfulness endures forever v. 2

Psalm 118

- LORD vv. 1, 2, 4, 5, 6, 7, 8, 9, 10, 11, 12, 13, 14, 15, 16, 17, 18, 19, 20, 23, 24, 25, 26, 27, 29
- Good v. 1
- Steadfast love vv. 2, 3, 4
- Answers v. 5
- Sets free v. 5
- Helper vv. 7, 13
- Salvation vv. 15, 21
- His right hand does valiantly and exalts v. 16
- Disciplines severely v. 18
- Answers v. 21
- His wisdom surpasses that of men, who in their own reasoning rejected the cornerstone He had willed to establish v. 22
- His doing is marvelous in man's eyes v. 23
- God v. 27
- Makes His light shine upon us v. 27
- His steadfast love endures forever v. 29

Psalm 119

- LORD vv. 1, 12, 31, 33, 41, 52, 55, 57, 64, 65, 75, 89, 107, 108, 126, 137, 145, 149, 151, 156, 166, 169, 174
- Commanded His precepts to be kept diligently v. 4
- Blessed v. 12
- Rebukes the insolent who wander from His commandments v. 21
- Answers v. 26
- Wondrous works v. 27
- Enlarges hearts v. 32
- Steadfast love vv. 41, 76, 88, 124, 149, 159
- Salvation vv. 41, 166
- Delight is found in His commandments v. 47
- His promise gives life v. 50
- Forsaken v. 51
- Portion v. 57
- The earth is full of His steadfast love v. 64
- Deals with His servants according to His word v. 65
- Believed v. 66
- His hands made and fashioned man v. 73
- His rules are righteous v. 75
- Afflicts in faithfulness v. 75
- Merciful vv. 77, 156
- Salvation vv. 81, 123, 174
- Promised vv. 82, 123, 133
- His word is forever, firmly fixed in the heavens v. 89

- His faithfulness endures to all generations v. 90
- He established the earth, and it stands fast v. 90
- All things are His servants v. 91
- Gives life by His precepts v. 94
- His commandment is exceedingly broad v. 96
- His words are sweeter than honey v. 103
- Source of true wisdom vv. 98, 99, 100
- His word is a light and lamp v. 105
- His rules are righteous v. 106
- Hiding place v. 114
- Shield v. 114
- Spurns all who go away from His statutes v. 118
- Discards the wicked like rubbish v. 119
- His law has been broken v. 126
- His testimonies are wonderful v. 129
- The unfolding of His words gives light, imparting understanding to the simple v. 130
- Turns and is gracious to those who love His name v. 132
- Righteous v. 137
- Savior v. 146
- Just v. 149
- All His commandments are true vv. 151, 172
- Founded His testimonies forever v. 152
- The sum of His word is truth v. 160
- Those who love His law have great peace v. 165
- Teacher v. 171

<u>Psalm 120</u>

- LORD vv. 1, 2
- Called upon v. 1
- Answers v. 1

<u>Psalm 121</u>

- LORD vv. 2, 5, 7, 8
- Helper v. 2
- Made heaven and earth v. 2
- He who keeps Israel with neither slumber nor sleep v. 4
- Keeper v. 5
- Shade on your right hand v. 5
- Will keep you from all evil v. 7

<u>Psalm 122</u>

- LORD vv. 1, 4, 9
- Decrees v. 4
- Set thrones for judgment v. 5

<u>Psalm 123</u>

- LORD vv. 2, 3
- Enthroned in the heavens v. 1
- Merciful v. 2

<u>Psalm 124</u>

- LORD vv. 1, 2, 6, 8
- On Israel's side vv. 1, 2
- Blessed v. 6
- Helps v. 8
- Made heaven and earth v. 8

<u>Psalm 125</u>

- LORD vv. 1, 2, 4, 5
- Surrounds His people as firmly as mountains forever v. 2
- Leads away with evildoers those who turn aside to their crooked ways v. 5

<u>Psalm 126</u>

- LORD vv. 1, 2, 3, 4
- Restored the fortunes of Zion v. 1
- Done great things v. 3

<u>Psalm 127</u>

- LORD vv. 1, 3
- Unless it is He that works, work is done in vain v. 1
- Gives to His beloved sleep v. 2
- Children are a heritage from the LORD v. 3

<u>Psalm 128</u>

- LORD vv. 1, 4, 5

- Blesses those who fear Him and walk in His ways vv. 1, 4
- Blesses from Zion v. 5

<u>Psalm 129</u>

- LORD vv. 4, 8
- Righteous v. 4
- Cut the cords of the wicked v. 4

<u>Psalm 130</u>

- LORD vv. 1, 2, 3, 5, 6, 7
- Cried to v. 1
- Ears v. 2
- No one could stand if He should mark their iniquities v. 3
- With Him there is forgiveness, that He may be feared v. 4
- Steadfast love v. 7
- With Him there is plentiful redemption v. 7
- Will redeem Israel from all his iniquities v. 8

<u>Psalm 131</u>

- LORD vv. 1, 3

<u>Psalm 132</u>

- LORD vv. 1, 2, 5, 8, 11, 13
- Mighty One of Jacob vv. 2, 5
- Might v. 8
- Anoints v. 10
- Swore to David that if His sons keep His covenant and testimonies then they shall sit on the throne forever vv. 11, 12
- Chose Zion, desiring it for a resting place v. 13
- Abundantly blessed Zion with provisions and satisfied her poor with bread v. 15
- Clothes Zion's priests with salvation v. 16
- Prepared a lamp for His anointed v. 17
- Clothes enemies with shame, but crowns His anointed v. 18

<u>Psalm 133</u>

- LORD v. 3
- Commanded the blessing, life forevermore v. 3

<u>Psalm 134</u>

- LORD vv. 1, 2, 3
- Made heaven and earth v. 3

<u>Psalm 135</u>

- LORD vv. 1, 2, 3, 4, 5, 6, 13, 14, 19, 20, 21
- Good v. 3
- His name is pleasant v. 3
- Chose Jacob and Israel for his own possession v. 4
- Great v. 5
- Above all gods v. 5
- Whatever He pleases, He does v. 6
- Makes the clouds rise, lightning strike, and winds blow v. 7
- Struck down the first born of both man and beast of Egypt v. 8
- Sent signs and wonders against Pharaoh and all his servants v. 9
- Struck down many nations and killed many kings, giving their land as heritage to His people v. 10
- His name endures forever v. 13
- His renown endures throughout all generations v. 13
- Will both vindicate His people and have compassion on His servants v. 14
- Dwells in Jerusalem v. 21

<u>Psalm 136</u>

- LORD vv. 1, 3, 4, 7
- Good v. 1
- His steadfast love endures forever vv. 1-26
- God of gods v. 2
- Lord of lords v. 3
- He alone does great wonders v. 4

- By understanding made the heavens v. 5
- Spread out the earth above the waters v. 6
- Made the great lights v. 7
- Made the sun to rule over the day v. 8
- Made the moon and stars to rule over the night v. 9
- Struck down the first born of Egypt v. 10
- Brought out Israel from slavery v. 11
- Strong hand and outstretched arm v. 12
- Divided the Red Sea in two v. 13
- Made Israel to pass through the middle of the Red Sea v. 14
- Overthrew Pharaoh and his host in the Red Sea v. 15
- Led His people through the wilderness v. 16
- Struck down great kings v. 17
- Killed mighty kings v. 18
- Gave the land of the mighty to Israel, His servant v. 22
- Remembered His people in their low estate v. 23
- Rescued His people from foes v. 24
- Gives food to all flesh v. 25
- God of heaven v. 26

<u>Psalm 137</u>

- LORD vv. 4, 7

<u>Psalm 138</u>

- LORD vv. 1, 4, 5, 6, 8
- Steadfast love v. 2
- Faithfulness v. 2
- Exalted above all things His name and His word v. 2
- Answers v. 3
- Increases strength of soul v. 3
- All the kings of the earth shall give Him thanks, for they have hear the words of His mouth v. 4
- Great is His glory v. 5
- Though He is high, He regards the lowly v. 6
- The haughty He knows from afar v. 6
- Preserves life v. 7
- Stretches out His hand against the wrath of His people's enemies, and His right hand delivers v. 7
- Will fulfill His purpose v. 8
- His steadfast love endures forever v. 8

<u>Psalm 139</u>

- LORD vv. 1, 4, 21
- Searches and knows v. 1
- Knows the sitting down and rising of His servants v. 2
- Discerns thoughts from afar v. 2
- Searches out one's path and is acquainted with all their ways v. 3
- Knows exactly what we're going to say v. 4
- Hems man in, laying His hand upon them v. 5
- We cannot flee from His presence v. 7
- Spirit v. 7
- He is in heaven and Sheol v. 8
- Even in the uttermost parts of the sea He will lead us and His right hand will hold us v. 10
- Darkness is not dark to Him v. 12
- Formed our inward parts v. 13
- His works are wonderful v. 14
- Children are not hidden from Him in their mother's wombs v. 15
- Wrote our days before they even existed v. 16

- His thoughts are vast, more than the sand if counted vv. 17, 18
- Strength of one's salvation v. 7
- Covers heads in the day of battle v. 7
- Maintains the cause of the afflicted v. 12
- Will execute justice for the needy v. 12
- The upright shall dwell in His presence v. 13

Psalm 140

- LORD vv. 1, 4, 6, 7, 8, 12

Psalm 141

- LORD vv. 1, 3, 8

Psalm 142

- LORD vv. 1, 5
- Merciful v. 1
- Knows our way v. 3
- Refuge v. 5
- Portion in the land of the living v. 5
- Will deal bountifully with His anointed v. 7

Psalm 143

- LORD vv. 1, 7, 9, 11
- Faithful v. 1
- Righteous v. 1
- Judgment v. 2
- Steadfast love vv. 8, 12
- Place for refuge and deliverance v. 9
- Good Spirit v. 10
- Righteous v. 11
- Will cut off enemies and destroy all the adversaries of one's soul v. 12

Psalm 144

- LORD vv. 1, 3, 5, 15
- Blessed v. 1
- Rock v. 1
- Trains hands for war and fingers for battle v. 1
- Steadfast love v. 2
- Fortress v. 2
- Stronghold v. 2
- Deliverer v. 2
- Shield v. 2
- Refuge v. 2
- Subdues people under His own v. 2
- Regards man, though he is a breath and his days are like a passing shadow vv. 3, 4
- Gives victory to kings v. 10
- Rescued David from the cruel sword v. 10
- Blesses His people v. 15

Psalm 145

- LORD vv. 3, 8, 9, 10, 13, 14, 17, 18, 20, 21
- Extolled v. 1
- Blessed forever v. 2
- Great and greatly to be praised v. 3
- One generation shall commend His works to another and shall declare His mighty acts v. 4
- The splendor of His majesty is glorious v. 5
- His wondrous works are worthy of meditation v. 5
- The might of His awesome deeds are spoken of v. 6
- Greatness v. 6
- His goodness is abundant v. 7
- Righteous v. 7
- Gracious v. 8
- Merciful v. 8
- Slow to anger v. 8
- Abounding in steadfast love v. 8
- Good to all v. 9
- His mercy is over all that He has made v. 9
- His works and saints shall bless and give Him thanks v. 10
- The glory of His kingdom and His power is spoken of v. 11

- Glorious splendor v. 12
- His kingdom is everlasting, and His dominion endures throughout all generations v. 13
- Faithful in all His words and kind in all His works v. 13
- Upholds all who are falling and raises up all who are bowed down v. 14
- The eyes of all look to Him, and He gives them their food in due season v. 15
- He opens His hand and satisfies the desire of every living thing v. 16
- Righteous in all His ways and kind in all His works v. 17
- Near to all who call on Him in truth v. 18
- Fulfills the desire of those who fear Him; He also hears their cry and saves them v. 19
- Preserve all who love Him, but al the wicked He will destroy v. 20

Psalm 146

- LORD vv. 1, 2, 5, 7, 8, 9, 10
- Blesses and helps those who hope in Him and are His v. 5
- Made heaven and earth, the sea, and all that is in them v. 6
- Keeps faith forever v. 6
- Executes justice for the oppressed v. 7
- Gives food to the hungry v. 7
- Sets prisoners free v. 7
- Opens the eyes of the blind v. 8
- Lifts up those who are bowed down v. 8
- Loves the righteous v. 8
- Watches over the sojourners v. 9
- Upholds the widow and the fatherless, but the way of the wicked He brings to ruin v. 9
- Will reign forever v. 10

Psalm 147

- LORD vv. 1, 2, 5, 6, 7, 11, 12, 20
- He is beautiful, and a song of praise is fitting for Him v. 1
- Builds up Jerusalem and gathers the outcast of Israel v. 2
- Heals the brokenhearted and binds up their wounds v. 3
- Determines the number of stars and gives them their names v. 4
- Great v. 5
- Abundant in power v. 5
- His understanding is beyond measure v. 5
- Lifts up the humble and casts the wicked to the ground v. 6
- Covers the heavens with clouds, prepares rain for the earth, and makes grass grow on the hills v. 8
- Gives beasts and crying ravens food v. 9
- His delight and pleasure are neither in the strength of the horse or the legs of a man v. 10
- Takes pleasure in those who fear Him and in those who hope in His steadfast love v. 11
- Blesses, strengthens, and heals v. 14
- His word runs swiftly v. 15
- Declares His word to Jacob and His statutes and rules to Israel v. 19

Psalm 148

- LORD vv. 1, 5, 7, 13, 14
- Praised v. 1
- Has angels and hosts v. 2
- Commanded all things into being v. 5
- His establishments and decrees are everlasting v. 6
- His name alone is exalted v. 13
- His majesty is above earth and heaven v. 13

- Lifts up the horn for (exalts) His people v. 14

Psalm 149

- LORD vv. 1, 4, 9
- Praised v. 1
- Maker v. 2
- Takes pleasure in His people v. 4
- He adorns the humble with salvation v. 4

Psalm 150

- LORD vv. 1, 6
- The mighty heavens are His v. 1
- His deeds are mighty v. 2
- His greatness is excellent v. 2

Proverbs 1

- LORD vv. 7, 29
- Has wisdom call out to the fools and simple that they might adhere to and understand words of insight, thereby dwelling securely and at ease, without dread of disaster vv. 1-33
- The fear of Him is the beginning of knowledge v. 7

Proverbs 2

- LORD vv. 5, 6
- Gives wisdom v. 6
- From His mouth come wisdom and understanding v. 6
- Stores up sound wisdom for the upright v. 7
- A shield about those who walk in integrity v. 7
- Guards the path of justice and watches over the way of His saints v. 8

Proverbs 3

- LORD vv. 5, 7, 9, 11, 12, 19, 26, 32, 33
- Will make straight the paths of those who trust in Him v. 6
- Gives healing and refreshment to those who fear Him vv. 7, 8
- Gives plenty to those who honor God with the first fruits of all their produce v. 9
- Reproves him whom He loves v. 12
- By wisdom founded the earth v. 19
- Established the heavens by understanding v. 19
- By His knowledge the deeps broke open and the clouds drop down the dew v. 20
- He will be your confidence and keep your foot from being caught if you do not lose sight of sound wisdom and discretion v. 26
- The devious person is an abomination to Him v. 32
- His curse is on the house of the wicked, but He will bless the dwelling of the righteous v. 33
- Toward the scorners He is scornful, but to the humble He gives favor v. 34

Proverbs 4

Proverbs 5

- LORD v. 21
- A man's ways are before the eyes of the LORD, and He ponders all His paths v. 21

Proverbs 6

- LORD v. 16
- There are six things He hates, seven that are abominations to Him: haughty eyes, a lying tongue, hands that shed innocent blood, a heart that devises wicked plans, feet that make haste to run to evil, a false witness who breaths out lies, and one who sows discord among brothers) vv. 16-19

Proverbs 7

Proverbs 8

- LORD vv. 13, 22, 35

- The fear of Him is hatred of evil v. 13
- The LORD possessed wisdom at the beginning of His work, the first acts of old v. 22
- Made earth, fields, and dust. Heavens, the deep, and skies vv. 26-30
- Wisdom is His daily delight v. 30
- Whoever finds wisdom obtains favor from the LORD v. 35

Proverbs 9

- LORD v. 3
- The fear of the LORD is the beginning of wisdom, and the knowledge of the Holy One is insight v. 10

Proverbs 10

- LORD vv. 3, 22, 27, 29
- Doesn't let the righteous go hungry v. 3
- Thwarts the craving of the wicked v. 3
- His blessing makes rich, and He adds no sorrow to it v. 22
- The fear of Him prolongs life v. 27
- The way of the LORD is a stronghold to the blameless v. 29

Proverbs 11

- LORD vv. 1, 20
- False balances are an abomination to Him v. 1
- Those of a crooked heart are an abomination to Him, but those of blameless ways are His delight v. 20

Proverbs 12

- LORD vv. 2, 22
- A good man obtains favor from Him, but He condemns a man of evil devices v. 2
- Lying lips are an abomination to Him, but those who act faithfully are His delight v. 22

Proverbs 13

Proverbs 14

- LORD vv. 2, 26, 27
- Whoever walks in uprightness fears the LORD, but he who is devious in his ways despises Him v. 2
- In the fear of the LORD one has strong confidence, and his children will have a refuge v. 26
- The fear of the LORD is a fountain of life, that one may turn from the snares of death v. 27
- Insulted by those who oppress the poor, but honored by those who are generous to the poor v. 31
- Maker v. 31

Proverbs 15

- LORD vv. 3, 8, 9, 11, 16, 25, 26, 29, 33
- Sees all things, keeping watch on the good and the evil v. 3
- The sacrifice of the wicked is an abomination to Him, but the prayer of the upright He finds acceptable v. 8
- The way of the wicked is an abomination to Him, but He loves those who pursue righteousness v. 9
- The hearts of man are open to Him v. 11
- Better is a little with fear of the LORD than great treasure and trouble with it v. 16
- Tears down the house of the proud, but maintains the widow's boundaries v. 25
- The thoughts of the wicked are an abomination to Him, but gracious words are pure v. 26
- Far from the wicked, but hears the prayer of the righteous v. 29

- The fear of Him is instruction in wisdom, and humility comes before honor v. 33

Proverbs 16

- LORD vv. 1, 2, 3, 4, 5, 6, 7, 9, 11, 20, 33
- Though the plans of the heart belong to man, the answer of the tongue is from the LORD v. 1
- All the ways of man are pure in his own eyes, but the LORD weighs the spirit v. 2
- Establishes work committed to Him v. 3
- Made everything for its purpose, even the wicked for the day of trouble v. 4
- All who are arrogant in heart are an abomination to Him and will not go unpunished v. 5
- By steadfast love and faithfulness iniquity is atoned for, and by the fear of the LORD one turns away from evil v. 6
- When a man's ways please the LORD, He makes even his enemies to be at peace with him v. 7
- The heart of a man plans his way, but the LORD establishes his steps v. 9
- A just balance and scales are the LORD's; all the weights in the bag are His work v. 11
- Establishes kings by righteousness v. 12
- Blessed is he who trusts in Him v. 20
- The lot is cast into the lap, but its every decision is from the LORD v. 33

Proverbs 17

- LORD vv. 3, 55
- Tests hearts v. 3
- Insulted by those who mock the poor v. 5
- Maker v. 5
- Hates those who justify the wicked and who condemn the righteous v. 15

Proverbs 18

- LORD vv. 10, 22
- His name is a strong tower; the righteous man runs into it and is safe v. 10
- He who finds a wife obtains favor from the LORD v. 22

Proverbs 19

- LORD vv. 3, 14, 17, 21, 23
- A prudent wife comes from Him v. 14
- Whoever keeps His commandments keeps his life v. 16
- Whoever is generous to the poor lends to the LORD v. 17
- His purpose stands in spite of the many plans in the mind of a man v. 21
- The fear of the LORD leads to life, and those who have it rests satisfied v. 23

Proverbs 20

- LORD vv. 10, 12, 22, 23, 24, 27
- Made both the seeing eye and the hearing ear v. 12
- Delivers those who wait on Him rather than repaying evil themselves v. 22
- Biased scales are an abomination to the LORD v. 23
- Sees the innermost parts of a man, and therefore has more effective judgment v. 27
- A man's steps are from the LORD v. 24

Proverbs 21

- LORD vv. 1, 2, 3, 30, 31

- Turns a king's heart wherever He will v. 1
- Weighs a man's heart v. 2
- Doing righteousness and justice are more acceptable to the LORD than sacrifice v. 3
- Righteous One v. 12
- Observes the house of the wicked; He throws the wicked down to ruin v. 12
- No wisdom, no understanding, no counsel can prevail against the LORD v. 30
- Victory belongs to the LORD, no matter the circumstances or odds v. 31

<u>Proverbs 22</u>

- LORD vv. 2, 4, 12, 14, 19, 23
- Maker of both the rich and the poor v. 2
- The reward of humility and fear of the LORD is riches and honor and life v. 4
- His eyes keep watch over knowledge, but He overthrows the words of the traitor v. 12
- Anger v. 14
- Lets him with whom He is angry fall into the mouth of the forbidden woman v. 14
- Pleads the cause of the poor and robs life from those who rob them v. 23

<u>Proverbs 23</u>

- LORD v. 17
- Redeemer v. 11
- Pleads the cause of the fatherless v. 11

<u>Proverbs 24</u>

- LORD vv. 18, 21
- Sees v. 18
- Displeased by those who rejoice at the falling and stumbling of his enemies vv. 17, 18

<u>Proverbs 25</u>

- LORD v. 22
- Rewards those who do good to their enemies v. 21

<u>Proverbs 26</u>

<u>Proverbs 27</u>

<u>Proverbs 28</u>

- LORD vv. 5, 14, 25
- Those who seek Him understand justice completely v. 5
- Whoever does not harden his heart but fears the LORD will be blessed v. 14
- Enriches those who trust in Him and are not greedy v. 25

<u>Proverbs 29</u>

- LORD vv. 13, 25, 26
- Shows no favoritism, but gives light to the eyes of both the strong and weak v. 13
- Whoever trusts in Him is safe v. 25
- Justice is found in Him v. 26

<u>Proverbs 30</u>

- LORD v. 9
- Holy One v. 3
- Every one of His words prove true v. 5
- Shield to those who take refuge in Him v. 5

<u>Proverbs 31</u>

- LORD v. 30

<u>Ecclesiastes 1</u>

<u>Ecclesiastes 2</u>

- Food, drink, and enjoyment is from the hand of God, and apart from Him no one eats or has enjoyment v. 24
- Gives to those who please Him v. 26

Ecclesiastes 3

- Gives business for the children of man to be busy with v. 10
- Made everything beautiful in its time v. 11
- Put eternity into man's heart v. 11
- Gifts man with food, drink, and pleasure v. 13

Ecclesiastes 4

Ecclesiastes 5

- The only one we must fear v. 5
- Divinely bestows blessings v. 20

Ecclesiastes 6

- The giver of possessions, but also the one who lets (or withholds) the owner of them enjoy them v. 2

Ecclesiastes 7

- No one can straighten what He has made crooked v. 13
- Made both the day of prosperity and adversity equally well v. 14
- He who pleases God escapes the temptress v. 26
- Made man upright, though they have sought out many schemes v. 29

Ecclesiastes 8

- Makes an oath to the king v. 2
- It will be well for those who fear Him v. 12
- Gives man each day of life that he has under the sun v. 15
- Man cannot find out His work, neither the wise nor those who toil v. 17

Ecclesiastes 9

- The deeds of the righteous and the wise are in the hand of God v. 1

Ecclesiastes 10

Ecclesiastes 11

- His work is not known to man v. 5

Ecclesiastes 12

- Spirits return to God who gives them v. 7
- Shepherd v. 11
- Obedience to God and keeping His commandments is the whole duty of man v. 13
- Will bring every deed into judgment with every secret thing, whether good or evil v. 14

Song of Solomon 1

Song of Solomon 2

Song of Solomon 3

Song of Solomon 4

Song of Solomon 5

Song of Solomon 6

Song of Solomon 7

Song of Solomon 8

- LORD v. 6

Isaiah 1

- LORD vv. 2, 4, 9, 10, 11, 18, 20, 24, 28
- Spoken v. 1
- Reared and brought up Israel, who did not know Him or understand v. 2
- Forsaken and despised by His people v. 4
- LORD of hosts vv. 9, 24
- Left survivors v. 9
- Burdened by hypocritical worship v. 14
- Hides His eyes from vain worship and does not listen to prayers of the corrupt v. 15
- Mighty One of Israel vv. 4, 24
- Redeems the repentant by justice and righteousness v. 27
- Consumes those who forsake Him v. 28

Isaiah 2

- LORD vv. 2, 3, 5, 10, 11, 12, 17, 19, 21

- The mountain of the house of the LORD shall be established as the highest of the mountains v. 2
- God of Jacob v. 3
- His word shall go out from Jerusalem v. 3
- Shall judge between the nations v. 4
- Rejected His people since they were full of greed, idolatry, pride, and oppression. They became saturated with the ways of the world v. 6
- Majestic splendor vv. 10, 19, 21
- Brings the haughty looks of man low and humbles their lofty pride v. 11
- He alone will be exalted vv. 11, 17
- LORD of hosts v. 1
- Has a day against all that is proud and lofty, against all that is lifted up vv. 12, 17
- Will rise to terrify the earth v. 19

Isaiah 3

- LORD vv. 1, 8, 13, 14, 15, 16, 17, 18
- God of hosts vv. 1, 15
- Takes away the support of those who have whored against Him v. 1
- Glorious presence v. 8
- Will enter to judgment with elders and princes of His people v. 14
- Speaks v. 16
- Will lay bare the secret parts of the haughty daughters of Zion v. 17

Isaiah 4

- LORD vv. 2, 4, 5
- Will cleanse the bloodstains of Jerusalem from its midst by a spirit of judgment and a spirit of burning v. 4
- Branch of the LORD (Messiah) v. 2
- His people will be forever protected from all distress v. 6

Isaiah 5

- LORD vv. 7, 9, 12, 16, 24
- LORD of hosts vv. 7, 9, 24
- Exalted in justice v. 16
- Holy vv. 16, 19, 24
- Anger v. 25

Isaiah 6

- LORD vv. 1, 3, 5, 8, 11, 12
- Sits on His throne v. 1
- High and lifted up v. 1
- Holy, holy, holy v. 3
- The whole earth is full of His glory v. 3
- LORD of hosts vv. 3, 5
- Calls, shaking the foundations of the thresholds v. 4
- Takes guilt away v. 7
- Atones for sin v. 7
- Personally applies the remedy of grace vv. 6, 7
- Qualified Isaiah to proclaim the only hope of the world v. 7
- Speaks v. 8
- Triune v. 8
- His discipline only leaves a remnant (holy seed) of His people and by the same grace that saved Isaiah He leaves heirs of His promise to Abraham to be only hope to the whole world vv. 11-13

Isaiah 7

- LORD vv. 3, 7, 10, 11, 12, 14, 17, 18, 20
- Spoke to King Ahaz though Isaiah vv. 3-9, 10
- Those without firm faith will not be firm at all v. 9
- Gives signs v. 14
- Immanuel v. 14

Isaiah 8

- LORD vv. 1, 3, 5, 7, 11, 13, 17, 18
- LORD of hosts vv. 13, 18

- Snare to those who do not fear Him v. 13
- Hides His face v. 17
- Dwells on Mount Zion v. 18
- Gives signs v. 18

Isaiah 9

- LORD vv. 7, 8, 11, 13, 14, 17, 19
- Wonderful Counselor v. 6
- Mighty God v. 6
- Everlasting Father v. 6
- Prince of Peace v. 6
- No end to the increase of His government and peace v. 7
- Established and upholds His kingdom on the throne of David with justice and righteousness v. 7
- Zeal v. 7
- Disciplines His children vv. 8, 14
- Anger vv. 12, 21

Isaiah 10

- LORD vv. 12, 16, 18, 20, 23, 24, 26, 33
- Only help v. 3
- Anger vv. 4, 5
- Wrath v. 6
- Punishes v. 12
- Strong hand v. 13
- Wise v. 13
- Understanding v. 13
- Plunders and brings down those who sit on thrones v. 13
- God of hosts vv. 16, 33
- Sovereign wielder of the instruments of His creation v. 15
- Holy One v. 16
- LORD of hosts vv. 13, 23, 24, 26, 33
- The land is scorched by His wrath v. 19
- The fury of His discipline is temporary v. 25
- Brings the lofty low v. 33

Isaiah 11

- LORD vv. 2, 3, 9, 11, 15
- Brought forth a Messiah from the same root of David v. 1
- Spirit of the LORD v. 2
- Spirit of wisdom and understanding v. 2
- Spirit of counsel and might v. 2
- Spirit of knowledge and the fear of the LORD v. 2
- The Messiah's delight is in the fear of the LORD, and does not judge by appearances or is swayed by things said v. 3
- Judges the poor with righteousness v. 4
- Decides equity for the meek of the earth v. 4
- Will strike the earth with the rod of His mouth and kill the wicked with the breath of His lips v. 5
- Righteous v. 5
- Faithful v. 5
- Will renew the earth from the curse v. 6
- The earth shall be full of the knowledge of the LORD as the waters cover the sea v. 9
- The nations shall inquire of the root of Jesse v. 10
- His resting place shall be glorious v. 10
- Will gather all His people vv. 11-16

Isaiah 12

- LORD vv. 1, 2, 4, 5
- Turned His anger away v. 1
- Comforts v. 1
- Salvation v. 2
- LORD God v. 2
- Strength v. 2
- Song v. 2

- Will joyfully draw water from the wells of salvation v. 3
- Speaks v. 4
- Exalted v. 4
- Has done gloriously v. 5
- Holy One of Israel v. 6
- Great in the inhabitant of Zion's midst v. 6

Isaiah 13

- LORD vv. 4, 5, 6, 9, 13
- Consecrates v. 3
- Summoned His mighty men and proudly exulting ones to execute His anger v. 3
- LORD of hosts v. 4
- Mustering a host for battle v. 4
- Almighty v. 6
- His destruction upon the whole land will come v. 6
- His day of cruel wrath and fierce anger will come and make desolation of the land and destroy its sinners from it v. 9
- Will punish the world for its evil, and the wicked for their iniquity v. 11
- Will put an end to the pomp of the arrogant v. 11
- Will lay low the pompous pride of the ruthless v. 11
- Will make people more rare than fine gold v. 12
- Will make the heavens tremble and the earth shake out of place at the wrath of the LORD of hosts in the day of His fierce anger v. 13

Isaiah 14

- LORD vv. 1, 2, 3, 5, 22, 23, 24, 27, 32
- Will have compassion on Jacob and Israel and have Gentiles join the house of Jacob v. 1
- Gives rest from pain and turmoil v. 3
- Broken the staff of the wicked v. 5
- Most High v. 14
- LORD of hosts vv. 22, 23, 24, 27
- Declares and vows to sweep Babylon into oblivion, preserving no remnant v. 25
- Sworn v. 24
- All He purposes stands v. 24
- There is no straggler in His ranks v. 31
- Founded Zion, and in her the afflicted of His people find refuge v. 32

Isaiah 15

Isaiah 16

- LORD vv. 13, 14
- The Messiah's throne will be established in steadfast love with faithfulness sitting on it, one who judges and seeks justice and is swift to do righteousness v. 5
- Put an end to the joyful shouting of Moab v. 10

Isaiah 17

- LORD vv. 3, 6
- LORD of hosts v. 3
- God of Israel v. 6
- Declares v. 6
- Maker v. 7
- Holy One of Israel v. 7
- God of salvation v. 10
- Rock of refuge v. 10
- Rebukes effectively v. 13

Isaiah 18

- LORD vv. 4, 7
- Speaks v. 4
- Sees v. 4

Isaiah 19

- LORD vv. 1, 4, 12, 14, 16, 17, 18, 19, 20, 21, 22, 25

- Approached Egypt with power above that of mankind v. 1
- LORD of hosts vv. 4, 18, 25
- Mingled Egypt with a spirit of confusion v. 14
- Purposed against Egypt v. 15
- Struck and healed Egypt v. 22
- His overflowing blessing unites the entire world as His own and receives praise from all v. 25

Isaiah 20

- LORD vv. 2, 3
- Spoke by Isaiah v. 2
- Exposes the futility of man-centered hopes vv. 3-5

Isaiah 21

- LORD vv. 6, 8, 10, 16, 17
- LORD of hosts v. 10
- God of Israel v. 10
- Speaks vv. 16, 17

Isaiah 22

- LORD vv. 5, 12, 14, 15, 17, 25
- God of hosts vv. 5, 11, 14, 25
- Revealed Himself in Isaiah's ears v. 14
- His words are reality v. 25

Isaiah 23

- LORD vv. 9, 11, 17, 18
- LORD of hosts v. 9
- Purposed the defilement of the pompous pride of all glory and the dishonoring of all the honored of the earth v. 9
- Stretched out His hand over the sea; He has shaken the kingdoms; has given command to destroy the strongholds of Canaan v. 11
- Makes whores holy unto Him and devoted to His people v. 18

Isaiah 24

- LORD vv. 1, 3, 14, 15, 21, 23
- He will empty the earth and make it desolate, and He will twist its surface and scatter its inhabitants v. 1
- No position of social rank can serve as protection against the judgment of God v. 2
- What He speaks happens v. 3
- God of Israel v. 15
- Righteous One v. 16
- Will punish the host of heaven in heaven and the kings of the earth on earth v. 21
- LORD of hosts v. 23
- Reigns on Mt Zion and in Jerusalem v. 23
- His glory will be before His elders v. 23

Isaiah 25

- LORD vv. 1, 6, 8, 9, 10, 11
- Done wonderful things v. 1
- Formed faithful and sure plans of old v. 1
- Made the city a heap and the fortified city a ruin v. 2
- Strong peoples and ruthless nations will glorify and fear Him v. 3
- Stronghold to the poor, and to the needy in his distress v. 4
- Shelter from the storm and shade from the heat v. 4
- LORD of hosts v. 6
- He will swallow up death forever v. 8
- LORD GOD v. 8
- Will wipe away tears from all faces v. 8
- Will take the reproach of his people away from all the earth v. 8
- Salvation v. 9
- Humbles human pride vv. 9-12

Isaiah 26

- LORD vv. 4, 8, 10, 11, 12, 13, 15, 16, 17, 21

- Sets up salvation as walls v. 1
- Keeps him in perfect peace whose mind is stayed on Him, because he trusts in Him v. 3
- LORD GOD v. 4
- Everlasting rock v. 4
- Humbled the inhabitants of the height, the lofty city. He lays it low and casts it to the dust v. 5
- Makes level the path of the righteous v. 7
- When His judgments are in the earth the inhabitants learn righteousness v. 9
- Majesty v. 10
- His hand is lifted up, but the wicked do not see it and do not learn righteousness when favor is given them v. 11
- Will ordain peace for His children, for He has indeed done for them all their works v. 12
- Wiped out the remembrance of all other lords v. 14
- He has increased the nation, and He is glorified v. 15
- Disciplines and is sought out by the distressed v. 16
- His dead shall live; their bodies shall rise v. 19
- His dew is a dew of light, and the earth will give birth to the dead v. 19
- Coming out from His place to punish sinners, and the earth will show the blood shed on it, and no more cover its stain v. 21

Isaiah 27

- LORD vv. 1, 3, 12
- Will destroy the fleeing, twisting, sea dragon, serpent of monstrous horror with His hard and great and strong sword v. 1
- Keeper of the vineyard v. 3
- Will gather His chosen people with his hand on each individual v. 13

Isaiah 28

- LORD vv. 2, 5, 11, 13, 14, 16, 21, 22, 29
- Gives the proud, complacent, and self-indulgent northern city of Samaria into the hands of the rising Assyrian Empire vv. 1-4
- LORD of hosts vv. 5, 22, 29
- Crown of glory v. 5
- Diadem of beauty v. 5
- Spirit of justice v. 6
- Strength v. 6
- Sets right and sweeps away lies v. 17
- Beats down those who take refuge and build for themselves shelters of lies and evil covenants v. 18
- Strangely rises to fight His own people v. 21
- Decreed destruction against the whole land v. 22
- LORD GOD vv. 16, 22
- Wonderful in counsel v. 29
- Excellent in wisdom v. 29

Isaiah 29

- LORD vv. 6, 10, 13, 15, 19, 22
- Humbles His disobedient people v. 4
- LORD of hosts v. 6
- Visits instantly and suddenly v. 5
- Both punishes and saves those who in their hypocrisy try to control Him through false worship vv. 1-14
- His purpose is not hindered by false and shallow obedience v. 13
- The poor, meek, blind, and deaf shall exult in Him v. 19
- Holy One of Israel v. 19

- Cuts off the ruthless, the scoffer, and those who watch to do evil v. 20
- Redeemed Abraham v. 22
- Speaks v. 22
- Holy One of Jacob v. 23
- Will redeem His chosen in need of awakening v. 24

Isaiah 30

- LORD vv. 1, 9, 15, 18, 20, 26, 27, 29, 30, 31, 32, 33
- Spirit v. 1
- Holy One of Israel vv. 11, 12, 15
- LORD GOD v. 15
- Saves and strengthens those who trust quietly in Him v. 15
- Waits to be gracious to those that wait for Him v. 18
- God of justice v. 18
- Exalts Himself to show mercy v. 18
- Gracious v. 19
- Answers cries v. 19
- Teacher v. 20
- Binds up the brokenness of His people v. 26
- Heals the wounds inflicted by His blow v. 26
- Burns with anger v. 27
- His tongue is like a devouring fire v. 27
- Rock of Israel v. 29
- Majestic voice v. 30
- Heard v. 30
- Descending blow of His arm v. 30
- Seen v. 30
- Furious anger v. 30
- His triumph is final against all his adversaries v. 33

Isaiah 31

- LORD vv. 1, 3, 4, 5, 9
- Holy One of Israel v. 1
- Those that do not look to Him or consult Him are brought to disaster. He is against the house of evildoers vv. 1-2
- Wise v. 2
- Brings disaster v. 2
- Does not call back His words v. 2
- He will protect, deliver, spare, and rescue Jerusalem v. 5

Isaiah 32

- LORD v. 6
- Spirit v. 15
- His people, though disciplined, will abide in a peaceful habitation, insecure dwellings, and in quiet resting places v. 18

Isaiah 33

- LORD vv. 2, 5, 6, 10, 21, 22
- Exalted v. 5
- Dwells on high v. 5
- Will fill Zion with justice and uprightness v. 5
- He will be the stability, abundance of salvation, wisdom, and knowledge v. 6
- The fear of the LORD is Zion's treasure v. 6
- He will arise, lift Himself up, and be exalted v. 10
- Mighty v. 13
- Majesty v. 21
- Judge v. 22
- Lawgiver v. 22
- King v. 22
- Savior v. 22
- God's sin-sick people will be forgiven their iniquity v. 24

Isaiah 34

- LORD vv. 2, 6, 8, 16
- Enraged against all the nations, and furious with all their host v. 2
- Has a day of vengeance v. 8
- Will reduce the nations to a wasteland v. 11
- Commanded v. 16
- Spirit v. 16
- Gathered v. 16

Isaiah 35

- LORD vv. 2, 10
- Glorious v. 2
- Majesty v. 2
- Will come and save v. 4
- Shall open the eyes of the blind and unstop the ears of the deaf v. 5
- The salvation God provides includes both spiritual well-being and physical healing and wholeness vv. 5-7
- Way of Holiness v. 8
- Ransoms, causes singing and everlasting joy, gladness and joy, and causes sorrow and sighing to flee away v. 10

Isaiah 36

- LORD vv. 7, 10, 15, 18, 20

Isaiah 37

- LORD vv. 1, 4, 6, 14, 15, 16, 17, 18, 20, 21, 22, 24, 32, 33, 34, 36
- Living v. 4
- Hears v, 4
- Made the king of Assyria turn away from His people and be destroyed in his own land when they trusted in Him v. 7
- LORD of hosts vv. 16, 32
- God of Israel v. 16
- Enthroned above the cherubim v. 16
- God alone v. 16
- Made heaven and earth v. 16
- Holy One of Israel v. 23
- Protects His own v. 29
- Omniscient v. 28
- Struck down 185,000 soldiers with His angel v. 36

Isaiah 38

- LORD vv. 1, 2, 3, 4, 5, 7, 11, 14, 16, 20, 22
- Compassion v. 5
- Hears v. 5
- Sees v. 5
- Delivers vv. 6, 17
- Defends v. 6
- Turned back the sun on the dial of Ahaz ten steps v. 8

Isaiah 39

- LORD vv. 5, 6, 8
- LORD of hosts v. 5

Isaiah 40

- LORD vv. 2, 3, 5, 7, 10, 13, 27, 28, 31
- His glory shall be revealed, and all flesh shall see it v. 5
- His word will stand forever v. 8
- LORD GOD v. 10
- Comes with might v. 10
- His arm rules before Him v. 10
- Will tend his flock like a shepherd v. 11
- Creator v. 12
- Spirit of the LORD v. 13
- Cannot be measured or instructed v. 13
- Knows justice and understanding v. 14
- All nations are counted as less than nothing and emptiness before Him v. 17
- Cannot be compared v. 18
- Sits above the circle of the earth v. 22
- Spreads the heavens like a tent to dwell in v. 22
- Brings princes to nothing and makes rulers of the earth as emptiness v. 23
- Holy One v. 25
- Strong in power v. 26
- Created the stars and calls them by name v. 26
- Everlasting v. 28
- Creator v. 28

- Gives power to the faint, and to him who has no might He increases strength v. 29
- Renews the strength of those who wait on Him v. 31

Isaiah 41

- LORD vv. 4, 13, 14, 16, 17, 20, 21
- He gives up nations before Him, so that He tramples kings underfoot v. 2
- Called generations from the beginning v. 4
- With the first and the last v. 4
- Chose for Him a people, calling them from the ends of the earth and taking them from the farthest corners v. 9
- Strengthens v. 10
- Helps vv. 10, 14
- Upholds with His righteous hand v. 10
- No human hostility can contend against God v. 13
- Redeemer v. 14
- Holy One of Israel vv. 14, 16, 20
- Answers the poor and needy's thirst v. 17
- Disgusted by idolatry v. 24

Isaiah 42

- LORD vv. 5, 6, 8, 10, 12, 13, 19, 21, 24
- Chose and delights in Jesus Christ v. 1
- Put His Spirit on Christ v. 1
- Brings forth justice to the nations v. 1
- Defender of the weak v. 3
- Faithfully established justice in the earth v. 4
- Speaks v. 5
- Created the heavens and stretched them out v. 5
- Spread out the earth and what comes from it v. 5
- Gives breath and spirit v. 5
- Called His children in righteousness; He will take them by the hand and keep them v. 6
- Gave Christ as a covenant for the people. A light for the nations to open the eyes of the blind vv. 6-7
- Gives His glory to no other, nor His praise to carved idols v. 8
- Goes out like a mighty man of war, shouting aloud and showing Himself mighty against His foes v. 13
- His grace is so unsearchable that those He lead in the path of salvation might as well be blind, in darkness, and on rough terrain v. 16
- Puts idolaters to shame v. 17
- Disciplines His people who neither obey nor understand v. 25

Isaiah 43

- LORD vv. 1, 3, 10, 11, 12, 14, 15, 16
- Speaks v. 1
- Created Jacob and formed Israel v. 1
- Redeemer vv. 1, 14
- Calls by name His people v. 1
- Defines His people not by their guilty blindness but the grace of the One who says, "You are mine." v. 1
- Holy One of Israel vv. 3, 14
- Savior v. 3
- Loving v. 4
- Honors His redeemed v. 4
- Ensures His people's restoration for His own glory vv. 1-7
- Only Savior v. 11
- Declared, saved, and proclaimed v. 12
- Creator of Israel v. 15
- King v. 15
- Gives drink to His chosen people v. 20
- Formed people for Himself that they might declare His praise v. 21

- Blots out transgressions for His own sake, and He will not remember sins v. 25

Isaiah 44

- LORD vv. 2, 5, 6, 23, 24
- Jacob is His servant, and Israel and His chosen v. 1
- Formed you in the womb vv. 2, 24
- Helps v. 2
- Chosen v. 2
- Will pour His Spirit and blessing on His chosen's offspring v. 3
- King of Israel v. 6
- Redeemer v. 6
- LORD of hosts v. 6
- The first and the last v. 6
- None like Him v. 7
- Declares the future events v. 7
- Removed understanding and sight from idolaters v. 18
- Formed His servant v. 21
- Will not forget Israel v. 21
- Redeemer vv. 22, 24
- Blotted out transgressions v. 22
- Will be glorified in Israel v. 23
- Creator v. 24
- Frustrates the signs of liars, makes fools of diviners, turns wise men back, and makes their knowledge foolish v. 25
- Confirms the word of His servant and fulfills the counsel of His messengers v. 26

Isaiah 45

- LORD vv. 1, 3, 5, 6, 7, 8, 11, 13, 14, 17, 18, 19, 21, 24, 25
- Anoints v. 1
- God of Israel v. 3
- Equips v. 5
- Calls by name v. 4
- None besides Him v. 6
- Forms light and creates darkness v. 7
- Makes well-being and creates calamity v. 7
- Creator vv. 8, 12
- Holy One of Israel v. 11
- Commands the host of heaven v. 13
- Hides Himself v. 15
- Savior v. 17
- God v. 18
- None besides Him vv. 5, 18, 21, 22
- Formed and made the earth. Established it and purposed it to be inhabited v. 19
- Speaks the truth v. 19
- Declares what is right v. 19
- Savior v. 21
- Righteous vv. 22, 24
- Looses the belts of kings v. 1
- Levels the exalted places v. 2
- Saves those who turn to Him v. 22
- Offers hope to the ends of the earth v. 22
- To Him every knee shall bow and every tongue shall swear allegiance v. 23
- Strength v. 24
- In Him all the offspring of Israel shall be justified and shall glory v. 25

Isaiah 46

- Carries His people their entire lives v. 4
- Made, bears, carries, and saves v. 4
- Has no equal v. 5
- None compares to Him or is like Him v. 5
- Brings to pass what He has purposed v. 11
- His righteousness is not far off v. 13
- His salvation will not delay v. 13

Isaiah 47

- LORD v. 4
- Redeemer v. 4
- LORD of hosts v. 4

- Holy One of Israel v. 4
- Anger v. 6
- Profaned His heritage v. 6
- Punishes the proud v. 9
- Sees all v. 10

Isaiah 48

- LORD vv. 1, 2, 14, 16, 17, 20, 22
- God of Israel v. 2
- LORD of hosts v. 2
- Prophesies and does v. 5
- Defers His anger and restrains it for His name's sake and for the sake of His praise v. 9
- He will not give His glory to another v. 11
- Calls v. 12
- The first and the last v. 12
- His hand laid the foundation of the earth, and His right hand spread out the heavens v. 13
- Loves v. 14
- Performs His purpose v. 14
- Calls, brings, and prospers v. 15
- LORD GOD v. 16
- Sent Jesus v. 16
- Sent His Spirit v. 16
- Redeemer v. 17
- Holy One of Israel v. 17
- Teaches to profit and leads in the way to go v. 17
- Obedience leads to abundant peace and righteousness v. 18
- Redeems v. 20
- Satisfies thirst v. 21
- Gives no peace to the wicked v. 22

Isaiah 49

- LORD vv. 1, 4, 5, 7, 8, 13, 14, 18, 22, 23, 25, 26
- Calls and names v. 1
- Forms His servants in the womb v. 5
- His Servant will be a Light to the nations, that His salvation will reach to the end of the earth v. 6
- Redeemer of Israel v. 7
- Deeply despised, abhorred by the nation, and the servant of rulers v. 7
- Kings see Him and arise; princes, and they shall prostrate themselves; because of the LORD, who is faithful, the Holy One of Israel, who has chosen you v. 7
- Conquers by His sufferings v. 7
- Answers in the time of favor and helps in a day of salvation v. 8
- Gave His son as a covenant to His people v. 8
- His people will not hunger or thirst, neither the scorching wind nor sun will strike them, for He who has pity on them will lead them v. 10
- Comforted His people v. 13
- Will have compassion on His afflicted v. 13
- He is less likely to forget His chosen than a mother is her nursing child v. 15
- Savior v. 26
- Redeemer v. 26
- Mighty one of Jacob v. 26

Isaiah 50

- LORD vv. 1, 4, 5, 7, 9. 10
- Redeems v. 2
- Delivers v. 2
- Has authority over the waters and the heavens vv. 2-3
- Accepts abusive opposition though He is innocent v. 6
- One either obeys the voice of His Servant or kindles the false light of his own wisdom and lies down in torment forever v. 11

Isaiah 51

- LORD vv. 1, 3, 9, 11, 13, 15, 17, 20, 22
- Blessed and multiplied Abraham v. 1
- Comforts Zion, making her wilderness and deserts like Eden, that joy and gladness might be found in her, thanksgiving and the voice of song v. 3
- His law has gone out and His arms will judge the peoples v. 5
- His salvation will be forever and His righteousness will never be dismayed v. 6
- His salvation will be to all generations v. 8
- His ransomed shall have everlasting joy v. 11
- Comforts v. 12
- Maker v. 13
- Stirs up the sea so that its waves roar v. 15
- LORD of hosts v. 15
- Wrath v. 20
- Rebukes v. 20

Isaiah 52

- LORD vv. 3, 4, 5, 8, 9, 10, 11, 12
- Comforted his people v. 9
- Redeemed Jerusalem v. 9
- God of Israel v. 12
- His servant shall act wisely, be high and lifted up, and be exalted v. 13
- Jesus' appearance was marred beyond human semblance v. 14

Isaiah 53

- LORD vv. 1, 6, 10
- Jesus had no form or majesty or beauty that we should look at or desire Him v. 2
- Despised and rejected by men v. 3
- Man of sorrows v. 3
- Acquainted with grief v. 3
- As one from whom men hide their faces v. 3
- Despised and not esteemed v. 3
- Bore our grieves and carried our sorrows; yet we esteemed Him stricken, smitten by God, and afflicted v. 4
- He was wounded for our transgressions; He was crushed for our iniquities; upon Him was the chastisement that brought us peace, and with His stripes we are healed v. 5
- All men foolishly have gone astray, but Jesus was uniquely qualified to bear our sins v. 6
- He was oppressed and afflicted, but didn't open His mouth v. 7
- It was his will to crush His Son; He has put Him to grief v. 10
- Satisfied His wrath on Jesus, and by Him will make many to be accounted righteous v. 11
- Bore our iniquities v. 11
- Given a portion and spoil with the great and numerous, because He poured out His soul to death and was numbered with the transgressors; yet He bore the sin of many, and makes intercession for the transgressors v. 12

Isaiah 54

- LORD vv. 1, 5, 6, 8, 10, 13, 17
- Maker v. 5
- LORD of Hosts v. 5
- Redeemer vv. 5, 8
- God of the whole earth v. 5
- Will gather with great compassion v. 7
- Hid His face for a moment in overflowing anger, but will have compassion with everlasting love v. 8

- Sworn that He will not be angry with or rebuke His people v. 9
- His steadfast love shall not depart v. 10
- His covenant of peace shall not be removed v. 10
- Compassion v. 10
- Will bless the afflicted who does not find comfort v. 11
- His people's children shall be taught by Him and great shall be their peace v. 13
- Shall establish His people in righteousness; they shall be far from oppression, for they shall not fear; terror shall not come near to them v. 14
- Any strife stirred up among his people is not from Him, and the one responsible shall fall because of His people v. 15
- No weapon fashioned against His people shall succeed, and they shall confute every tongue that rises against them in judgment v. 17

Isaiah 55

- LORD vv. 5, 6, 7, 8, 13
- Invites everyone to enter into His promised blessings vv. 1-13
- Those who come to Him have an everlasting covenant and steadfast love v. 3
- LORD your God v. 5
- Holy One of Israel v. 5
- Glorified His people v. 5
- Compassionate v. 7
- Pardons abundantly v. 7
- His thoughts are not our thoughts v. 8
- His ways are not our ways v. 8
- His thoughts and ways are above ours like the heavens are above the earth v. 9
- His word shall not return empty, but it will accomplish what He sent it to do v. 11

Isaiah 56

- LORD vv. 1, 3, 4, 6, 8
- Speaks v. 1
- Authority v. 1
- Commands justice and righteousness v. 1
- His salvation will come and His deliverance will be revealed v. 1
- Those that join themselves with Him receive an eternal place with God vv. 3-5
- Gives an everlasting name to His people v. 5
- Foreigners that join themselves to Him, minister to Him, and love his name and hold to His covenant will be brought to His holy mountain and be made joyful in His house of prayer vv. 6-7
- Lord GOD v. 8

Isaiah 57

- LORD v. 19
- Takes the righteous man away from calamity when he dies v. 1
- Revives the spirit of the lowly v. 15
- One v. 15
- Holy v. 15
- Struck and hid His face from the unjust for He was angry v. 17
- Leads, restores comfort to, and heals v. 18
- Heals in spite of iniquity, both the Jew and the Gentile v. 19
- Gives no peace for the wicked v. 21

Isaiah 58

- LORD vv. 5, 8, 9, 11, 13, 14

- Cannot be manipulated v. 3
- Glorious v. 8
- Answers v. 9
- Guides continually, satisfies the desires, makes the bones strong, and upholds those that forsake wickedness and help the hungry and afflicted vv. 10-12
- If one is not self-seeking, then their delight shall be taken in the LORD vv. 13-14
- Mouth v. 14

<u>Isaiah 59</u>

- LORD vv. 1, 13, 15, 19, 20, 21
- His hand is not shortened that it cannot save, or His ear dull, that it cannot hear v. 1
- Separated by iniquity v. 2
- Hides His face from sin so that He does not hear v. 2
- Perceives lies v. 4
- Repays wrath to His enemies v. 18
- Sees v. 15
- Displeased v. 15
- Salvation v. 16
- Glory v. 19
- Redeemer v. 20
- Spirit v. 21

<u>Isaiah 60</u>

- LORD vv. 1, 2, 6, 9, 14, 16, 19, 20, 22
- His glory has risen upon His people v. 2
- Seen v. 2
- Nations and kings come to His light v. 3
- Holy One of Israel v. 9
- Struck in His wrath v. 10
- Merciful v. 10
- Enemies bow before His majesty v. 15
- Savior v. 16
- Redeemer v. 16
- Mighty One of Jacob v. 16
- Everlasting Light v. 20
- Makes the smallest one a mighty nation v. 22

<u>Isaiah 61</u>

- LORD vv. 1, 2, 3, 6, 8, 9, 10, 11
- Spirit v. 1
- Proclaims good news to the oppressed, hungry, and poor v. 1
- Loves justice v. 8
- Hates robbery and wrong v. 8
- Faithfully gives recompense v. 8
- Made an everlasting covenant v. 8
- Clothes with garments of salvation v. 10
- Covers with the robe of righteousness v. 10
- Will cause righteousness and praise to sprout up before all the nations v. 11

<u>Isaiah 62</u>

- LORD vv. 2, 3, 4, 6, 8, 9, 11, 12
- Will not keep silent until His people's righteousness has gone forth v. 1
- His mouth will give v. 2
- Forsaken and Desolate are temporary names v. 4
- Will establish Jerusalem v. 7
- Makes His people holy and redeemed, sought out and not forsaken v. 12

<u>Isaiah 63</u>

- LORD vv. 7, 14, 16, 17
- Speaks in righteousness v. 1
- Mighty to save v. 1
- Trampled in wrath v. 3
- His own arm brought down salvation v. 5
- Steadfast love v. 7
- Savior v. 8
- Afflicted v. 9

- Enemy of those who grieved His Holy Spirit v. 10
- Spirit of the LORD gave rest v. 14
- Father v. 16
- Redeemer from of old v. 16
- Makes people to wander from His ways and hardens hearts that people may not fear Him v. 17

Isaiah 64

- LORD vv. 8, 9, 12
- Did awesome things not looked for v. 3
- No one has seen a God besides Him v. 4
- Angry v. 9
- Makes people to melt in the hand of their iniquities v. 7
- Meets joyfully those who work righteousness v. 5

Isaiah 65

- LORD vv. 7, 8, 11, 13, 15, 23, 25
- Ready to be found by those who did not seek Him v. 1
- Spread out His hands to those who spit in His face v. 2
- Will not keep silent, but will repay v. 6
- Brings forth offspring to bless v. 9
- Destines for the sword evildoers who choose what He does not delight in; lets them be hungry, thirsty, put to shame, broken, and put to death v. 13
- Creates new heavens and new earth and remembers not former things v. 17

Isaiah 66

- LORD vv. 1, 2, 5, 6, 9, 12, 14, 15, 16, 17, 20, 21, 22, 23
- Heaven is His throne and the earth His footstool v. 1
- Maker v. 1
- Looks to the humble who trembles at His word v. 2
- Brings fear upon those that did not listen to Him and did evil instead v. 4
- Extends peace like a river v. 12
- Comforts v. 13
- Will come in fire v. 15
- Will slay many v. 16
- Knows works and thoughts v. 18
- Will set a sign v. 18
- His glory shall be declared among the nations v. 20
- All flesh shall come to worship before Him v. 23

Jeremiah 1

- LORD vv. 2, 4, 6, 7, 8, 9, 11, 12, 13, 14, 15, 19
- Appointed the priest Jeremiah a prophet and knew and consecrated him before He formed him in the womb v. 5
- Commanded Jeremiah to go everywhere He would send Him and to speak everything He commanded without fear of man, in spite of his youth vv. 7-8
- Deliverer vv. 8, 19
- Touched and put words in Jeremiah's mouth v. 9
- Set Jeremiah over nations and kingdoms to destroy and to overthrow, to build and to plant v. 10
- Watches over His word to perform it v. 12
- Called nations to bring disaster on His disobedient people v. 14
- Declares judgment on the evil who forsake Him v. 16
- Protects and delivers Jeremiah, His servant v. 18

Jeremiah 2

- LORD vv. 1, 2, 3, 4, 5, 6, 8, 9, 12, 17, 19, 22, 29, 31, 37

- Intimate with His people v. 2
- Relational v. 2
- Contends with sinners v. 9
- His people forsook Him for lesser things v. 13
- Lord GOD vv. 19, 22
- Judges liars and puts them to shame as a thief when he is caught vv. 26, 35

Jeremiah 3

- LORD vv. 1, 6, 10, 11, 12, 13, 14, 16, 17, 20, 21, 22, 23, 25
- Sees past words to actions v. 5
- Will not be angry forever, but desires whores to acknowledge their guilt v. 13
- Will give shepherds with His own heart v. 15
- Merciful v. 12
- Salvation of Israel v. 23
- Voice v. 25

Jeremiah 4

- LORD vv. 1, 2, 3, 4, 8, 9, 10, 17, 26, 27
- Desires hearts v. 4
- Justly speaks in judgment v. 12
- Anguishes over Judah's desolation v. 19
- Fierce anger v. 26
- Brings the land into desolation v. 27

Jeremiah 5

- LORD vv. 2, 3, 4, 5, 9, 10, 11, 12, 14, 15, 18, 19, 22, 24, 29
- Avenges Himself vv. 9, 29
- Preserves a remnant v. 18
- Placed the sand as a barrier to the sea v. 22
- His people have rebellious hearts v. 23

Jeremiah 6

- LORD vv. 6, 9, 10, 11, 12, 15, 16, 21, 22, 30
- Will destroy the delicately bred daughter of Zion v. 2
- Turns in disgust to sin v. 9
- LORD of hosts v. 9
- Speaks warning to those that hear v. 10
- Wrath v. 11
- Rejects the impure v. 30

Jeremiah 7

- LORD vv. 1, 2, 3, 4, 11, 13, 19, 20, 21, 28, 29, 30, 32
- God of Israel v. 3
- LORD of hosts v. 3
- Lets the repentant dwell in His promised land v. 3
- Casts the evil out of His sight and will not hear interceding on their behalf v. 16
- Provoked to anger v. 18
- Pours our wrath and anger v. 20
- Commands obedience v. 23
- Sent prophets continuously, though the people were calloused and disobedient, not accepting discipline v. 28
- Silences the voices of mirth and gladness v. 34

Jeremiah 8

- LORD vv. 1, 3, 4, 7, 8, 9, 12, 13, 14, 17, 19
- Turns the greedy over to sin v. 10

Jeremiah 9

- LORD vv. 3, 6, 7, 9, 12, 13, 15, 17, 20, 22, 23, 24, 25
- LORD of hosts vv. 7, 15
- Punishes and avenges Himself v. 9
- God of Israel v. 15
- Scatters, poisons, and consumes with the sword the unfaithful v. 16
- Delights in men that does not boast in their wisdom, might, or riches,

but in that they understand and know Him v. 23
- Practices steadfast love, justice, and righteousness in the earth v. 24
- Will punish all those who are circumcised merely in the flesh, rather than the heart vv. 25-26

Jeremiah 10
- LORD vv. 1, 2, 6, 10, 16, 18, 21, 23, 24
- None like Him v. 6
- Made the earth by His power, established the world by His power, and by His understanding stretched out the heavens v. 12
- Formed all things v. 16
- LORD of hosts v. 16
- Israel is the tribe of His inheritance v. 16
- Anger v. 24

Jeremiah 11
- LORD vv. 1, 3, 5, 6, 9, 11, 16, 17, 18, 20, 21, 22
- Covenant v. 2
- Curses those that do not hear His hear the words of His covenant v. 3
- Solemnly warned v. 5
- Commands obedience v. 7
- Brings inescapable disaster v. 11
- LORD of hosts vv. 20, 22

Jeremiah 12
- LORD vv. 1, 3, 12, 13, 14, 16, 17
- Righteous v. 1
- If any nation will not listen to Him, then He will utterly pluck it up and destroy it v. 17

Jeremiah 13
- LORD vv. 1, 2, 3, 5, 6, 8, 9, 11, 12, 13, 14, 15, 16, 17, 25
- Will spoil those of pride and make them good for nothing v. 8
- Made His people a glory and as a garment to Him v. 11
- Demands glory v. 16
- Weeps bitterly in secret for people's pride v. 17
- Sees all His people's abominations, adulteries and neighings, and lewd whorings v. 27

Jeremiah 14
- LORD vv. 1, 7, 9, 10, 11, 13, 14, 15, 20, 22
- Hope of Israel v. 8
- Savior in time of trouble v. 8
- Does not help those who love to wander in self-seeking v. 10
- No knowledge outside of Him v. 18

Jeremiah 15
- LORD vv. 1, 2, 3, 6, 9, 11, 15, 16, 19, 20
- Increased sorrows upon sorrows on those that rejected Him v. 6
- God of hosts v. 16
- Will restore those who return to Him v. 19
- Saves and delivers from the wicked and ruthless v. 20

Jeremiah 16
- LORD vv. 1, 3, 5, 9, 10, 11, 14, 15, 16, 21
- Steadfast love and mercy taken away from the evil v. 5
- Gives no favor to idolaters v. 13
- Will restore Israel v. 15
- His eyes see all iniquity and sin and idolatry that fills His inheritance vv. 17-18
- Will make His people know His power and might, and that His name is the LORD v. 21

Jeremiah 17
- LORD vv. 5, 7, 10, 13, 14, 15, 19, 20, 21, 24, 26
- In His anger a fire shall burn forever v. 4

- Curses man who trusts in man and flesh v. 5
- Blesses the man who trusts in the LORD v. 7
- Hope of Israel v. 13
- Fountain of living water v. 13
- Healer v. 14
- Saves v. 14
- Refuge v. 17

Jeremiah 18

- LORD vv. 1, 5, 6, 11, 13, 19, 23
- Relents of His disaster if a nation repents, and relents of blessing if a nation does evil, not listening to His voice vv. 5-11
- Sees v. 23
- Anger v. 23
- Desires to rework His people like a spoiled vessel of clay v. 5

Jeremiah 19

- LORD vv. 1, 3, 6, 11, 12, 14, 15
- Brings disaster on those that have forsaken Him v. 4
- Breaks His people as a potter's vessel is broken v. 11
- Gives opportunity to repent and accept the covenant v. 15

Jeremiah 20

- LORD vv. 1, 2, 3, 4, 7, 8, 11, 12, 13, 16
- Strong v. 7
- With Jeremiah as a dread warrior v. 11
- LORD of hosts v. 12
- Tests the righteous v. 12
- Sees the heart and mind v. 12
- Delivered the life of the needy from the hand of evildoers v. 13

Jeremiah 21

- LORD vv. 1, 2, 4, 7, 8, 10, 11, 12, 13, 14
- Wonderful deeds v. 2
- Set His face against Israel v. 10
- Punishes according to the fruit of one's deeds v. 14

Jeremiah 22

- LORD vv. 1, 2, 3, 5, 6, 8, 9, 11, 16, 18, 24, 29, 30
- Commands justice and righteousness v. 3
- Makes one's house a desolation if they are disobedient v.5
- Dishonors the dishonorable v. 18

Jeremiah 23

- LORD vv. 1, 2, 4, 5, 6, 7, 8, 9, 11, 12, 15, 16, 17, 18, 19, 20, 23, 24, 28, 29, 30, 31, 32, 33, 34, 35, 36, 37, 38
- Judges leaders that do not judge well v. 2
- Promised up a righteous Branch v. 5
- Will save Judah v. 6
- Righteousness of His people v. 6
- Punishes v. 12
- LORD of hosts vv. 15, 16
- Will cast off false prophets and bring upon them everlasting reproach and perpetual shame vv. 33-40

Jeremiah 24

- LORD vv. 1, 3, 4, 5, 7, 8
- Gives saving knowledge according to His sovereign will v. 7

Jeremiah 25

- LORD vv. 3, 4, 5, 7, 8, 9, 12, 15, 17, 27, 28, 29, 30, 31, 32, 33, 36, 37
- Demands faithfulness v. 3
- Desires sinners to return to Him, persistently speaking to them v. 4
- Punishes those that do not listen or obey Him v. 7
- Roars from on high v. 30
- Has an indictment against the nations; He is entering into

judgment with all flesh, and the wicked He will put to the sword v.31
- Anger vv. 37, 38

Jeremiah 26
- LORD vv. 1, 2, 4, 7, 8, 9, 10, 12, 13, 15, 16, 18, 19, 20
- Offers opportunity for repentance by prophets v. 3
- Failure to obey means rejecting His grace vv. 4-5
- Commands sinners to mend their ways v. 13
- Protected Jeremiah from death and the hands of the people that would have killed him v. 24

Jeremiah 27
- LORD vv. 1, 2, 4, 8, 11, 13, 15, 16, 18, 19, 21, 22
- LORD of hosts vv. 4, 18, 21
- God of Israel vv. 4, 18
- Great power v. 5
- Outstretched arm v. 5
- Made the earth v. 5

Jeremiah 28
- LORD vv. 1, 2, 3, 4, 5, 6, 9, 11, 12, 13, 14, 15, 16
- LORD of hosts vv. 2, 14
- God of Israel vv. 2, 14

Jeremiah 29
- LORD vv. 4, 7, 8, 9, 10, 11, 14, 15, 16, 17, 19, 20, 21, 22, 23, 25, 26, 30, 31, 32
- Hears those that call on Him v. 12
- When one seeks Him with their whole heart they will find Him v. 13
- Restores v. 14
- LORD of hosts v. 25
- God of Israel v. 25

Jeremiah 30
- LORD vv. 1, 2, 3, 4, 5, 8, 9, 10, 11, 12, 17, 18, 21, 23, 24
- God of Israel v. 2
- Restores v. 3
- Saves v. 11
- Dealt the blow of an enemy because of flagrant sins v. 14
- Heals wounds v. 17
- Compassion v. 18
- God of His people v.22
- Anger v. 24

Jeremiah 31
- LORD vv. 1, 2, 3, 6, 7, 10, 11, 12, 14, 15, 16, 17, 18, 20, 22, 23, 27, 28, 31, 32, 33, 34, 35, 37, 38, 40
- God of all the clans of Israel v. 1
- Loved His people with an everlasting love and continued in faithfulness to them v. 3
- Builds His people v. 4
- Father to Israel v. 9
- Ransomed Jacob v. 11
- Scattered and gathers Israel v. 10
- Yearns v. 20
- Merciful v. 20
- Creates v. 22
- LORD of hosts v. 23
- God of Israel v. 23
- Restores fortunes v. 23
- Replenishes v. 25
- Husband v. 32
- Writes His laws on His people's hearts v. 33
- Forgives iniquity and remembers sin no more v. 34
- Stirs up the sea v. 35
- LORD of hosts v. 35
- Gives the sun for light by day, and the moon and stars for light by night v. 35

Jeremiah 32
- LORD vv. 1, 3, 5, 6, 8, 14, 15, 16, 17, 18, 25, 26, 27, 28, 30, 36, 42, 44
- LORD of hosts vv. 15, 18
- God of Israel v. 15

- Made the earth and the heavens v. 17
- Great power v. 17
- Outstretched arm v. 17
- Shows steadfast love to thousands v. 18
- Great and mighty God v. 18
- Great in counsel and mighty in deed v. 19
- His eyes are open to all the ways of man, rewarding each one according to all his ways and according to the fruit of his deeds v. 19
- Showed signs and wonders in the land of Egypt v. 20
- Made a name for Himself v. 20
- Brings terror v. 21
- Blesses v. 22
- Makes disaster v. 23
- What He speaks comes to pass v. 24
- Sees v. 24
- God of all flesh v. 27
- Nothing is too hard for Him v. 27
- Provoked to anger by His own people vv. 29, 30, 31, 32
- Taught persistently v. 33
- Anger and wrath v. 31
- I did not command them, nor did it enter into my mind, that they should do this abomination, to cause Judah to sin v. 35
- Gives His people one heart and one way and an everlasting covenant v. 40
- Gives His people a fear of Himself and brings good upon them as He promises v. 42
- Restores fortunes v. 44

<u>Jeremiah 33</u>

- LORD vv. 1, 2, 4, 10, 11, 12, 13, 14, 16, 17, 19, 20, 23, 24, 25
- Formed and established the earth v. 2
- Answers those who call and tells great things that they have not known v. 3
- God of Israel v. 4
- Anger and wrath v. 5
- Hides His face from evil v. 5
- Heals v. 6
- Reveals v. 6
- Restores fortunes vv. 7, 11, 26
- Cleanses from all the guilt of sin v. 8
- Does good v. 9
- Provides prosperity v. 9
- LORD of hosts vv. 11, 12
- Good v. 11
- His steadfast love endures forever v. 11
- Fulfills His promises v. 14
- Righteous Branch v. 15
- Executes righteousness and justice v. 15
- His people's righteous v. 16
- His covenants endure forever v. 21
- Merciful v. 26

<u>Jeremiah 34</u>

- LORD vv. 1, 2, 4, 5, 8, 12, 13, 17, 22
- God of Israel vv. 2, 13

<u>Jeremiah 35</u>

- LORD vv. 1, 2, 4, 12, 13, 17, 18, 19
- LORD of hosts vv. 13, 19
- God of Israel vv. 13, 19

<u>Jeremiah 36</u>

- LORD vv. 1, 4, 5, 6, 7, 8, 9, 10, 11, 26, 27, 29, 30
- Desires repentance v. 3
- Disciplines v. 3
- Forgives v. 3
- Great wrath and anger against His people v. 7
- Hid Baruch and Jeremiah v. 26

- Punishes v. 31
- Brings disaster v. 31

Jeremiah 37

- LORD vv. 2, 3, 6, 7, 9, 17, 20
- Was ignored v. 2
- Gave Jerusalem over to the Chaldeans v. 10
- Allows persecution of His beloved v. 15
- Gave the land of Benjamin into the hand of the King of Babylon v. 18

Jeremiah 38

- LORD vv. 2, 3, 9, 14, 16, 17, 20, 21
- God of hosts v. 17
- God of Israel v. 17
- Gives visions v. 21

Jeremiah 39

- LORD vv. 15, 16, 17, 18
- LORD of hosts v. 16
- God of Israel v. 16
- Saved Ebed-melech the Ethiopian for trusting in Him v. 18

Jeremiah 40

- LORD vv. 1, 2, 3

Jeremiah 41

- LORD v. 5

Jeremiah 42

- LORD vv. 2, 3, 4, 5, 6, 7, 9, 11, 13, 15, 18, 19, 20, 21
- God of Israel vv. 9, 15, 18
- Saves and delivers v. 11
- Grants mercy on the obedient v. 12
- LORD of hosts vv. 15, 18
- Brings disaster on those that do not trust in Him v. 17
- Anger and wrath v. 18

Jeremiah 43

- LORD vv. 1, 2, 4, 7, 8, 10
- LORD of hosts v. 10
- God of Israel v. 10

Jeremiah 44

- LORD vv. 2, 7, 11, 16, 21, 22, 23, 24, 25, 26, 29, 30
- LORD of hosts vv. 2, 7, 11, 25
- God of Israel vv. 2, 7, 11, 25
- Provoked to anger by evil vv. 3, 8
- Hates idolatry v. 4
- Wrath and anger v. 6
- Punishes with sword, famine, and pestilence v. 13
- Lord GOD v. 26
- Gave Egypt into the hand of Babylon v. 30

Jeremiah 45

- LORD vv. 2, 3, 4, 5
- God of Israel v. 2

Jeremiah 46

- LORD vv. 1, 5, 10, 13, 15, 18, 23, 25, 26, 28
- LORD of hosts vv. 10, 18, 25
- Avenges Himself on His foes v. 10
- God of Israel v. 25
- Punishes vv. 25, 28
- Disciplines His people in just measure v. 28

Jeremiah 47

- LORD vv. 1, 2, 4, 6, 7
- Destroyed the Philistines v. 4

Jeremiah 48

- LORD vv. 1, 8, 12, 15, 25, 26, 30, 35, 38, 40, 42, 43, 44, 47
- LORD of hosts vv. 1, 15
- God of Israel v. 1
- Destroys those that trust in their works and treasures v. 7
- Declares vv. 25, 30, 38, 43, 44, 47

Jeremiah 49

- LORD vv. 1, 2, 5, 6, 7, 12, 13, 14, 16, 18, 20, 26, 28, 30, 31, 32, 34, 35, 37, 38, 39
- Lord GOD of hosts v. 5
- LORD of hosts v. 7

- Punishes vv. 8, 12
- Scatters and brings calamity v. 32
- Restores fortunes v. 39

Jeremiah 50

- LORD vv. 1, 4, 5, 7, 10, 13, 14, 15, 18, 20, 21, 24, 25, 28, 29, 30, 31, 33, 34, 35, 40, 45
- God of the people of Israel v. 4
- His people sinned against Him and were led astray v. 6
- LORD of hosts vv. 18, 33, 34
- God of Israel v. 18
- Brought out His weapons of wrath v. 25
- Lord GOD of hosts vv. 25, 31
- Redeemer v. 34
- Pleads His people's cause v. 34
- None is like Him v. 44

Jeremiah 51

- LORD vv. 1, 5, 6, 7, 10, 11, 12, 14, 19, 24, 25, 26, 29, 33, 36, 39, 45, 48, 50, 51, 52, 53, 55, 56, 57, 58, 62
- Stirred up the spirit of a destroyer against Babylon v. 2
- Vengeance v. 11
- Made the earth by His power v. 15
- Established the world by His wisdom v. 15
- By His understanding He stretched out the heavens v. 15
- Makes the mist rise from the ends of the earth v. 16
- Makes lightning for the rain and brings forth wind from His storehouses v. 16
- Formed all things v. 19
- LORD of hosts vv. 19, 25, 57
- Stretches out His hand against evil v. 25
- His purposes stand v. 29
- God of Israel v. 33
- Fierce anger v. 45
- Will execute judgment v. 52

Jeremiah 52

- LORD vv. 2, 3, 13, 17, 20
- Cast out Jerusalem and Judah from His presence because of King Zedekiah's evil vv. 1-3

Lamentations 1

- LORD vv. 5, 9, 11, 12, 14, 15, 17, 18, 20
- Afflicted Judah for the multitude of her transgressions v. 5
- Inflicted sorrow on the day of His fierce anger v. 12
- Give disobedient into the hands of enemies v. 14

Lamentations 2

- LORD vv. 1, 2, 5, 6, 7, 8, 9, 17, 18, 19, 20, 22
- Set the daughter of Zion in a cloud in His anger v. 1
- Swallowed up without mercy v. 2
- Brought down to the ground in dishonor the kingdom v. 2
- Cut down in fierce anger all the might of Israel v. 3
- Poured out His fury like fire v. 4
- Became like an enemy to Israel v. 5
- Swallowed up and multiplied mourning and lamentation in the daughter of Judah v. 5
- Made Zion forget festival and Sabbath, and in His fierce anger spurned king and priest v. 6
- Scorned His altar and disowned His sanctuary v. 7
- Exalted the might of His people's foes v. 17
- Did what He purposed v. 17
- His anger is inescapable v. 22

Lamentations 3

- LORD vv. 18, 22, 24, 25, 26, 31, 36, 37, 40, 50, 55, 58, 59, 61, 64, 66
- Afflicts with wrath v. 1

- Besieges and envelops with bitterness and tribulation v. 5
- Makes chains heavy v. 7
- Shuts out prayer v. 8
- Blocks way and makes paths crooked v. 9
- Like a bear or lion lying in wait v. 10
- Fills with bitterness v. 15
- Makes teeth to grind on gravel v. 16
- The steadfast love of the LORD never ceases v. 22
- His mercies never come to an end v. 22
- Great faithfulness v. 23
- Good to those who wait for Him v. 25
- Salvation v. 26
- Causes grief, but has compassion according to the abundance of His steadfast love v. 32
- Does not willingly afflict or grieve the children of man v. 33
- Most High vv. 35, 38
- Does not approve of injustice v. 36
- Only what He speaks comes to pass v. 37
- From His mouth come good and bad, renewal and judgment v. 38
- In heaven v. 41
- Wrapped Himself with anger and pursued transgressors, killing without pity v. 43
- Wrapped Himself in a cloud so that no prayer can pass through v. 44
- Punishes His people, making them scum and garbage among the peoples v. 45
- Looks down and sees v. 50
- Hears pleas for help v. 56
- Comes near and says, "Do not fear!" v. 57
- Takes up causes v. 58
- Redeems lives v. 58
- Sees wrong done v. 59
- Hears v. 61
- Repays evildoers, giving them dullness of heart, putting His curse on them, and pursuing them in anger and destroying them from under His heavens vv. 64-66

Lamentations 4

- LORD vv. 11, 16, 20
- Gave full vent to His wrath; poured out His hot anger, and He kindled a fire in Zion that consumed its foundations v. 11
- Scatters and regards not, not honoring priests or favoring the elders v. 18
- Uncovers sins and punishes His anointed v. 22

Lamentations 5

- LORD vv. 1, 19, 21
- Reigns forever v. 19
- His throne endures to all generations v. 19

Ezekiel 1

- LORD vv. 3, 28
- Vision giver v. 1
- Word v. 3
- Hand v. 3
- Almighty v. 24
- Appearance of brightness all around v. 28

Ezekiel 2

- LORD v. 4
- Spirit v. 2
- Speaks v. 1
- Sends messengers (Ezekiel) v. 3

Ezekiel 3

- LORD vv. 11, 12, 14, 16, 22, 23, 27
- Spirit vv. 14, 24
- Blessed v. 12
- Hand strong upon Ezekiel vv. 14, 22
- Glory v. 23

Ezekiel 4

- LORD vv. 13, 14

Ezekiel 5

- LORD vv. 5, 7, 8, 11, 13, 15, 17
- Lord GOD v. 5
- Rebelled against and rejected vv. 6, 7, 11
- Satisfies Himself in fury v. 13
- Jealous v. 13
- Executes judgment with furious rebukes v. 15

Ezekiel 6

- LORD vv. 1, 3, 7, 10, 11, 13, 14
- Lord God vv. 3, 11
- Leaves a portion alive v. 8
- Brings a sword upon His people v. 3
- Stretches out His hand against His people v. 14

Ezekiel 7

- LORD vv. 1, 2, 4, 5, 9, 19
- Lord GOD says to Israel v. 1
- Judges according to one's ways and punishes according to their abominations v. 3
- Pours out His wrath and His eye will not spare or have pity v. 9
- His wrath is upon all the multitude, and because of his iniquity, none can maintain His life v. 13
- Face v. 22
- Does to His people according to their way, and judges them according to their judgments, and they shall know that He is the LORD v. 27

Ezekiel 8

- LORD vv. 1, 12, 14, 16
- His hand fell upon Ezekiel v. 1
- Spirit v. 3
- Ignores the cry for help v. 18

Ezekiel 9

- LORD vv. 4, 8, 9
- Does not spare those that disregard Him vv. 9-10

Ezekiel 10

- LORD vv. 4, 18, 19
- God of Israel vv. 19, 20
- Glory v. 19

Ezekiel 11

- LORD vv. 1, 5, 7, 8, 10, 12, 13, 14, 15, 16, 17, 21, 23, 25
- Spirit v. 1
- Judges v. 12
- Makes Himself known v. 12
- Lord GOD v. 17
- God of Israel v. 22
- Spirit of God gives visions v. 24

Ezekiel 12

- LORD vv. 1, 8, 10, 15, 16, 17, 19, 20, 21, 23, 25, 26, 28
- Allows a chance for His people to understand. Warns v. 3
- Both says and does vv. 26-28

Ezekiel 13

- LORD vv. 1, 2, 3, 5, 6, 7, 8, 9, 13, 14, 16, 18, 20, 21, 23
- Against those that utters lying divinations and false visions that mislead people v. 8
- Makes Himself known v. 14
- Lord GOD vv. 8, 9, 18, 20
- Watches out for His people v. 23

Ezekiel 14

- LORD vv. 2, 4, 6, 7, 8, 9, 11, 12, 14, 16, 18, 20, 21, 23
- Asks that people repent and turn from their idolatry and abominations v. 6
- Delivers the righteous v. 16
- Does not act without cause v. 23

Ezekiel 15

- LORD vv. 1, 6, 7, 8

- Compares Israel to a useless vine v. 6
- Makes Himself known v. 7
- Set His face to punish Israel v. 7
- Desolates the faithless v. 8

Ezekiel 16

- LORD vv. 1, 3, 8, 14, 19, 23, 30, 35, 36, 43, 48, 58, 59, 62, 63
- Lord GOD vv. 19, 36
- Provoked to anger v. 26
- Delivered His people to their enemies v. 28 Calls His people a prostitute v. 35
- Uncovers His people's nakedness to their neighbors v. 37
- Makes His people to stop playing the whore, that His anger may stop being provoked v. 42
- Satisfies His wrath v. 42
- Removes abominations v. 50
- Uncovers wickedness v. 57
- Remembers His covenant to His people, even though they despised the oath v. 60

Ezekiel 17

- LORD vv. 1, 3, 9, 11, 16, 19, 21, 22, 24
- Sovereign v. 24

Ezekiel 18

- LORD vv. 1, 3, 9, 23, 32
- Lets the righteous that keep His statutes live v. 9
- Kills the wicked v. 13
- Has pleasure in repentance v. 23
- Just v. 29
- Has no pleasure in the death of anyone v. 32

Ezekiel 19

Ezekiel 20

- LORD vv. 1, 2, 3, 5, 7, 12, 19, 20, 26, 27, 30, 31, 33, 36, 38, 39, 40, 42, 44, 45, 47, 48, 49
- Gave Israel His rules, but was rebelled against v. 21
- Lord GOD v. 33
- Withheld His hand from destroying His idolatrous people
- Does not share glory with other gods v. 39
- Deals with His people according to His name's sake and not according to their evil ways v. 44

Ezekiel 21

- LORD vv. 5, 7, 8, 9, 13, 17, 18, 24, 26, 28, 32
- Against idolaters, and His wrath splatters on the righteous v. 3
- Lord GOD vv. 7, 13
- Sending the one to whom judgment belongs v. 27
- Spoken v. 32

Ezekiel 22

- LORD vv. 1, 3, 12, 14, 16, 17, 19, 22, 23, 28, 31
- Lord GOD vv. 3, 12, 19, 31
- Made His people defiled who defiled Him v. 5
- Israel became dross to Him, and He breathed out the fire of wrath on them and they melted v. 20
- Consumed His people with the fire of His wrath, and poured out His indignation upon them v. 31

Ezekiel 23

- LORD vv. 1, 22, 28, 32, 34, 35, 36, 46, 49
- His people played the whore v. 5
- Delivered His people to their whoredoms which destroyed them v. 10
- Promised to put an end to his people's lewdness and whoring begun in Egypt, and gave them into the hands they hate vv. 27-28
- Makes Himself known v. 49
- Lord GOD v. 49

Ezekiel 24

- LORD vv. 1, 3, 9, 14, 15, 20, 21, 24, 27
- Lord GOD vv. 6, 14, 21
- Gives signs v. 24
- Makes Himself known v. 27

Ezekiel 25

- LORD vv. 1, 3, 5, 6, 7, 8, 11, 12, 13, 14, 15, 16, 17
- Lord GOD vv. 8, 12, 16
- Destroys Judah v. 7
- Vengeance v. 14
- Makes Himself known vv. 7, 11, 17

Ezekiel 26

- LORD vv. 1, 3, 5, 6, 7, 14, 15, 19, 21
- Lord GOD vv. 3, 7,15, 21
- Brought Tyre to a dreadful end, and though sought for, would never be found again v. 21

Ezekiel 27

- LORD vv. 1, 3
- Lord GOD v. 3

Ezekiel 28

- LORD vv. 1, 2, 6, 10, 11, 12, 20, 22, 23, 24, 25, 26
- Lord GOD vv. 6, 25
- Defiles the splendor of the proud vv. 6-7

Ezekiel 29

- LORD vv. 1, 3, 6, 8, 9, 13, 16, 17, 19, 20, 21
- Against Pharaoh, king of Egypt, so He made the Egyptians the most lowly of the kingdoms
- Makes Himself known v. 16
- Lord GOD vv. 16, 19
- Vindicates Ezekiel's prophetic ministry v. 21

Ezekiel 30

- LORD vv. 1, 2, 3, 6, 8, 10, 12, 13, 19, 20, 22, 25, 26
- Those that support God's enemies shall fall with them v. 5
- Destroys idols v. 13
- Executes judgment on Thebes v. 14
- Scattered the Egyptians throughout the countries v. 26
- Makes Himself known vv. 19, 26

Ezekiel 31

- LORD vv. 1, 10, 15, 18
- Lord GOD vv. 10, 15

Ezekiel 32

- LORD vv. 1, 3, 8, 11, 14, 15, 16, 17, 31, 32
- Judges Egypt v. 12
- Lord GOD vv. 3, 8, 11, 14, 16

Ezekiel 33

- LORD vv. 1, 11, 17, 20, 22, 23, 25, 27, 29, 30
- Lord GOD vv. 11, 25, 27
- Bids Israel repent of wickedness v. 11
- Gives life to the repentant v. 19
- Judges each according to his ways v. 20

Ezekiel 34

- LORD vv. 1, 2, 7, 8, 9, 10, 11, 15, 17, 20, 24, 27, 30, 31
- Lord GOD vv. 10, 11
- He searches and seeks out His sheep Himself in all places where they have been scattered, gathers them from their countries and feeds them with good pasture on the high mountains of Israel and He will be their shepherd. He will strengthen the weak, and the fat and strong He will destroy. He feeds sheep justice vv. 11-16
- Rescues His flock v. 22
- Makes His sheep to dwell securely and showers blessing on them v. 26
- Makes Himself known to His sheep v. 30

Ezekiel 35

- LORD vv. 1, 3, 4, 6, 9, 10, 11, 12, 14, 15
- Lord GOD v. 6
- Makes Himself known v. 15

Ezekiel 36

- LORD vv. 1, 2, 3, 4, 5, 6, 7, 11, 13, 14, 15, 16, 20, 23, 32, 33, 36, 37, 38
- Lord GOD vv. 2, 3, 4, 5, 6, 7, 13, 14, 15, 22, 32, 33, 37
- Spoke in His hot jealousy against proud idolaters v. 5
- Makes Himself known v. 11
- Takes out those that cause their nations to stumble v. 15
- Judge according to one's ways v. 19
- Acts for the sake of His holy name, which was profaned among the nations v. 22
- Vindicates the holiness of His great name v. 23
- The nations will know that He is the LORD v. 23
- Cleanses His people from all their idols, and give them a new heart and spirit, replacing the heart of stone with a heart of flesh vv. 25-26
- He puts His Spirit in His people, and causes them to walk in His statutes and to take care to obey all His rules v. 27
- The God of His people v. 28
- Will deliver His people from all uncleanness, summon all the grain and make it abundant and lay no famine before them v. 29
- His people see themselves as He sees them, and they see sin the way He sees it, and they are ashamed and confounded for their ways v. 32
- Will rebuild and till desolated cities and waste v. 36
- Does what He said He will do v. 36
- He will increase the splendor of the house of Israel and they will know that He is the Lord v. 38

Ezekiel 37

- LORD vv. 1, 3, 4, 5, 6, 9, 12, 13, 14, 15, 19, 21, 28
- Spirit of the LORD v. 1
- Led Ezekiel by His Spirit v. 1
- Raised an exceedingly great army from bones and breathed life into them v. 10
- Those who He puts His Spirit in live v. 14
- Does what He says v. 14
- Lord GOD vv. 18, 21
- His people shall cease to defile themselves with their idols and detestable things or transgressions, but will be saved from their backslidings in which they have sinned and be cleansed, and they shall be His people, and He shall be their God v. 23
- His people will have one ruler and shall walk in His rules v. 24
- Makes a covenant of peace with His people v. 25
- The LORD who sanctifies Israel, when His sanctuary is on their midst forevermore v. 28

Ezekiel 38

- LORD vv. 1, 3, 10, 14, 17, 18, 21, 23
- Lord GOD vv. 3, 10, 14, 17, 18, 21
- Uses Gog to punish Israel with His blazing wrath v. 19
- The earth shall quake at His presence v. 20
- Will show His greatness and holiness and make Himself known among the nations v. 23

Ezekiel 39

- LORD vv. 1, 5, 6, 7, 8, 10, 13, 17, 20, 22, 25, 28, 29

- Against Gog, and made him fall and be devoured vv. 3-4
- Spoken v. 5
- Makes Himself known vv. 6, 22, 28
- Lord GOD vv. 8, 17, 20, 25
- Hid His face from Israel according to their transgressions v. 24
- Restores the fortune of Jacob v. 25
- Pours His Spirit on the house of Israel and no longer hides His face from them v. 29

Ezekiel 40

- LORD vv. 1, 46
- Gives Ezekiel a vision of the new temple vv. 1-4

Ezekiel 41

- LORD v. 22
- Gives Ezekiel a vision of the inner temple vv. 1-4

Ezekiel 42

- LORD v. 13
- Gives Ezekiel a vision of the Temple's chambers vv. 1-20

Ezekiel 43

- LORD vv. 4, 5, 18, 19, 24, 27
- Glory of the God of His Israel, coming from the east with the sound of many rushing waters with the earth shining with His glory, and He entered the temple filling it with His glory vv. 1-5
- Will dwell in the midst of the people of Israel forever, the place of His throne and the soles of His feet v. 7
- Ends the defilement of His name v. 7
- Consumed in anger those who defiled His holy name by their abominations v. 8
- He will dwell in the midst of His people forever when they put away their whoring and dead bodies of their kings far from Him v. 9
- His people must undergo a purification process before being accepted by Him v. 27

Ezekiel 44

- LORD vv. 2, 3, 4, 5, 6, 9, 12, 15, 27
- Lord GOD vv. 6, 9, 12, 15, 27
- Glory v. 4
- Foreigners must be circumcised in the heart and flesh v. 9

Ezekiel 45

- LORD vv. 1, 4, 9, 15, 18, 23
- Lord GOD v. 9

Ezekiel 46

- LORD vv. 1, 3, 4, 9, 12, 13, 14, 16
- Lord GOD vv. 1, 16
- None of His people shall be scattered from his property v. 18

Ezekiel 47

- LORD vv. 13, 23
- Lord GOD v. 13
- Divides the land of the inheritance and gives the people of Israel as well as sojourners among them their allotments vv. 13-23

Ezekiel 48

- LORD vv. 9, 10, 14, 29, 35
- Divides the land of the inheritance and gives the people of Israel their portions vv. 1-29
- Lord GOD v. 9
- The name of His city shall be The LORD Is There v. 35

Daniel 1

- LORD vv. 2, 10
- Gave Daniel favor and compassion in the sight of the chief of the eunuchs v. 9

- Gave the four youths of Israel learning and skill in all literature and wisdom, and Daniel had understanding in all visions and dreams v. 17

Daniel 2

- LORD v. 47
- Gave Nebuchadnezzar dreams that troubled his spirit, causing his sleep to leave him v. 1
- God of heaven vv. 18, 19, 28, 37, 44
- Mercy v. 18
- Revealed mystery to Daniel in a vision of the night v. 19
- Blessed by Daniel v. 19
- Blessed is His name forever and ever v. 20
- To Him belong wisdom and might v. 20
- He changes times and seasons v. 21
- He removes and sets up kings v. 21
- Gives wisdom to the wise, and knowledge to those who have understanding v. 21
- Reveals deep and hidden things, knows what is in the darkness, and the light dwells with Him vv. 22, 28
- Thanked and praised v. 23
- Gave wisdom and might, and made known to Daniel what he asked of Him, for He made known to him the king's matter v. 23
- Gave the king of Babylon his kingdom, the power, and the might, and the glory v. 38
- Great God v. 45
- God of gods v. 47
- Lord of kings v. 47
- Revealer of mysteries v. 47
- Placed His people over the entire province of Babylon v. 49

Daniel 3

- Able to deliver from the burning fiery furnace v. 17
- Present with believers, ensuring that their trials and difficulties would not utterly overwhelm them v. 25
- Most High God v. 26
- Delivered His servants who trusted in Him, yielding up their bodies and setting aside the king's command rather than serve and worship an other god except their own God v. 28
- No other god is able to rescue as He is v. 29

Daniel 4

- LORD vv. 19, 24
- Most High God v. 2
- Great are His signs, and mighty are His wonders v. 3
- His kingdom is everlasting, and His dominion endures from generation to generation vv. 3, 34
- Watcher v. 24
- Most High vv. 17, 24, 25, 34
- Blessed v. 34
- Lives forever v. 34
- None can stay His hand or say to Him, "What have you done?" v. 35
- King of heaven v. 37
- All His works are right and His ways are just v. 37
- Those who walk in pride He is able to humble v. 37

Daniel 5

- In His own time He will vindicate His own name against those who defile it, no matter how powerful they are vv. 1-31
- Most High God vv. 18, 21
- Lord of Heaven v. 23

Daniel 6

- Delivered Daniel, who trusted in Him and had no fault in him, from the den of lions vv. 22, 27
- God of Daniel v. 26
- The Living God v. 26
- Enduring forever v. 26
- His kingdom shall never be destroyed, and His dominion shall be to the end v. 26
- He delivers and rescues v. 27
- He works signs and wonders v. 27

Daniel 7

- Gives Daniel a dream and visions as he lay on his bed v. 1
- Ancient of Days vv. 9, 13, 22
- Most High vv. 18, 22, 25, 27
- His saints shall receive and possess the kingdom forever, forever and ever v. 18

Daniel 8

- Gave Daniel another vision v. 1
- Sent Gabriel to interpret Daniel's vision v. 16
- Prince of princes v. 25

Daniel 9

- LORD vv. 2, 3, 4, 7, 8, 9, 10, 13, 14, 15, 16, 17, 19, 20
- Lord GOD v. 3
- Great and awesome God v. 4
- Keeps covenant and steadfast love with those who love Him and keep His commandments v. 4
- To Him belongs righteousness v. 7
- Sinned against by His people v. 8
- Mercy and forgiveness belong to Him, for He was rebelled against v. 9
- Set laws before His servants by the prophets v. 10
- Voice v. 11
- Pours His curse on law breakers v. 11
- Confirms His words v. 12
- Righteous in all the works He has done v. 14
- Brought His people out of Egypt with a mighty hand and made a name for Himself v. 15
- Anger and wrath v. 16

Daniel 10

- LORD vv. 16, 17, 19
- Revealed a word to Daniel v. 1
- Heard Daniel's words as he set his heart to understand and humbled himself before his God v. 12

Daniel 11

Daniel 12

- LORD v. 8
- God has an appointed time for the end, and no one knows when it is, and must simply persevere vv. 12-13

Hosea 1

- LORD vv. 1, 2, 4, 6, 7, 9
- His word came to Hosea v. 1
- Had Hosea take a wife of whoredom in order to represent the relationship between God and His people v. 2
- Gave Hosea's children prophetic names vv. 2-11

Hosea 2

- LORD vv. 13, 16, 20, 21
- Shows great mercy toward Israel vv. 14-23
- Will betroth His people to Him forever, in righteousness, justice, steadfast love, mercy, and faithfulness, and they shall know the LORD vv. 19, 20
- Takes back His people of whoredom v. 23

Hosea 3

- LORD vv. 1, 5
- Told Hosea to buy back Gomer, who was in a desperate situation v. 1
- God takes away from His people that they shall come in fear to Him and His goodness v. 4

Hosea 4

- LORD vv. 1, 10, 15, 16
- His contention was with the priest v. 4
- Rejected His priest for rejecting knowledge and letting His people be destroyed for lack of knowledge v. 6
- Changes the sinners' glory to shame v. 7
- Repays people for their deeds v. 9

Hosea 5

- LORD vv. 4, 6, 7
- Disciplines v. 2
- Nothing is hidden from Him v. 3
- Withdraws from the faithless vv. 6-7
- He withdraws in expectance of the unfaithful acknowledging their guilt and seeking His face, seeking Him earnestly in their distress v. 15

Hosea 6

- LORD vv. 1, 3
- Torn in order to heal, strikes down to bind up v. 1
- Revives and on the third day raises up to life that His people may live before Him v. 2
- Responds to those that press on to know Him v. 3
- Desires His people to love and know Him rather than polluted religious practice v. 6
- Has appointed a harvest and will restore the fortunes of His people v. 11

Hosea 7

- LORD v. 10
- Sees all evil deeds v. 2
- Disciplines v. 12
- Redeems the truthful v. 13

Hosea 8

- LORD vv. 1, 13
- His anger burns against the guilty v. 5
- Maker v. 14

Hosea 9

- LORD vv. 3, 4, 5, 14
- God will punish Israel by sending her people away from the land, to a place where they will not be able to make sacrifices to the Lord vv. 1-9
- His judgment is dramatic, when His grace is spurned vv. 11-12
- Rejects those who do not listen v. 17

Hosea 10

- LORD vv. 2, 3, 12
- False hearts bear their guilt v. 2
- Rains righteousness on those who seek Him v. 12
- Those who plow iniquity and trust in their own way reap injustice and eat lies v. 13

Hosea 11

- LORD vv. 10, 11
- God's love provided and provides the reinforcement for an ultimate relationship of care, guidance, and obedience vv. 2-4
- Faithful in spite of unfaithfulness. His affection weighs heavier than Israel's ingratitude, and He cannot bring Himself to renounce His people even though they renounce Him v. 8
- Cannot bear to destroy Israel, and in His great compassion and with a torn heart He restores a remnant of Israel and does not come in wrath vv. 8-9

Hosea 12

- LORD vv. 2, 5, 9, 13
- Repays according to deeds v. 2

- God of hosts v. 5
- Reassures of former promises when people comply to His commands vv. 3-6
- By His calling His people can be restored and exhibit the qualities of love and justice v. 6

Hosea 13

- LORD vv. 4, 15
- The idolatrous pass like smoke from a window v. 3
- There is no savior but Him v. 4
- Gave a king in His anger and took him away in His wrath v. 11
- His compassion is hidden from the unfaithful v. 14

Hosea 14

- LORD vv. 1, 2, 9
- The ways of the Lord are right, and the upright walk in them, but transgressors stumble in them v. 9

Joel 1

- LORD vv. 1, 9, 14, 15, 19
- Called Judah to lament as deeply as a betrothed virgin whose promised husband dies before the marriage is consummated v. 8
- Almighty v. 15
- The day of the LORD is near, and comes as destruction from Him v. 15

Joel 2

- LORD vv. 1, 11, 12, 13, 14, 17, 18, 19, 21, 23, 26, 27, 31, 32
- The day of the LORD is near v. 1
- Before Him peoples are in anguish and all faces grow pale v. 6
- His day is great and awesome. Who can endure it? v. 11
- There is still time to turn to Him with wholehearted devotion vv. 12-13
- Gracious v. 13
- Merciful v. 13
- Jealous v. 18
- Had pity on His people v. 18
- Answered and sent provision and blessing to His people v. 19
- The LORD has done great things v. 21
- The LORD your God calls for rejoicing v. 23
- Restores v. 25
- Dealt wondrously for His people v. 26
- His people shall never again be put to shame v. 27
- Will pour out His Spirit on all flesh; sons and daughters shall prophecy, old men shall dream dreams, and young men shall see visions v. 29
- Will pour out His Spirit on male and female servants v. 29
- Will show wonders in the heavens and on the earth, blood and fire and columns of smoke v. 30
- Will turn the sun into darkness, and the moon to blood, before the great day of the LORD comes v. 31
- Everyone who calls on the name of the LORD shall be saved, and those that escape to Mount Zion and in Jerusalem shall be ones whom the LORD calls v. 32

Joel 3

- LORD vv. 8, 11, 14, 16, 17, 18, 21
- When He restores the fortunes of Judah and Jerusalem He will gather all the nations and bring them to the valley of Jehoshaphat vv. 1-2
- Will enter into judgment on behalf of His people v. 2

- The day of the LORD is near in the valley of decision v. 14
- Roars from Zion, utters His voice from Jerusalem, and the heavens and the earth quake v. 16
- Refuge to His people, a stronghold to the people of Israel v. 16
- His people shall know that He is the LORD their God, who dwells in Zion, His holy mountain v. 17
- A fountain shall come forth from the house of the LORD v. 18
- Will avenge the blood of His people v. 21
- Dwells in Zion v. 21

Amos 1

- LORD vv. 2, 3, 5, 6, 8, 9, 11, 13, 15
- Entrusted a farmer and shepherd, Amos, with a divine message to give to the people of the northern kingdom v. 1
- Roars from Zion and utters His voice from Jerusalem; the pastures of the shepherds mourn, and the top of Carmel withers v. 2
- Sends a devouring fire v. 4
- Turns His hand against Ekron and makes the remnant of the Philistines to perish v. 8
- Destroys Tyre for not remembering the covenant of brotherhood v. 9
- Punished Edom for pursuing his brother with the sword, casting off all pity, perpetually tearing in his anger, and keeping his wrath forever v. 11
- Punished the Ammonites for ripping open pregnant women in Gilead to expand their border v. 13

Amos 2

- LORD vv. 1, 3, 4, 6, 11, 16
- Punished Moab for burning to lime the bones of the King of Edom v. 1
- Punished Judah for rejecting the law of the LORD, but led themselves astray with their lies v. 4
- Punished Israel because they sell the righteous for silver, the needy for a pair of sandals. For trampling the head of the poor into the dust of the earth and turn aside the way of the afflicted; a man and his father go in to the same girl, so that His holy name is profaned vv. 6-7
- Destroyed the mighty Amorite before Israel, brought them out of Egypt, led them in the wilderness for forty years to posses the land of the Amorite, raised up some of their sons for prophets, and some of their young men for Nazirites vv. 9-11
- Pressed down Israel in their place v. 13
- Makes the mighty, swift, and strong come to nothing vv. 14-16

Amos 3

- LORD vv. 1, 6, 7, 8, 10, 11, 12, 13, 15
- Spoke a word against Israel, punishing them for their iniquities vv. 2, 14
- Does nothing without revealing it first to His servants the prophets v. 7
- Declares v. 10
- Lord GOD v. 13
- God of hosts v. 13
- Strikes v. 15

Amos 4

- LORD vv. 2, 3, 5, 9, 10, 11, 13
- Swore by His holiness punishment v. 1
- Lord GOD v. 5

- Sent various natural and social calamities that His people might turn back (makes patient appeals) v. 5
- Forms the mountains and creates the wind v. 13
- Declares to man what is his thought v. 13
- Makes the morning darkness v. 13
- Treads on the heights of the earth v. 13
- God of hosts v. 13

Amos 5

- LORD vv. 3, 4, 6, 8, 14, 15, 16, 17, 18, 20, 27
- Gives a word to the house of Israel to be taken in lamentation v. 1
- Commands His people to seek Him and live vv. 5, 6
- Commands to seek good and not evil v. 14
- God of hosts vv. 15, 27
- Gracious to the remnant of Joseph who hate evil and love good, who establish justice v. 15
- Cannot be manipulated v. 22
- Lets justice roll down like waters, and righteousness like an overflowing stream v. 24
- Exiles v. 27

Amos 6

- LORD vv. 10, 11, 14
- Brings destruction on the self-indulgent and complacent vv. 4-14
- God of hosts vv. 8, 14
- Raised up a nation against Israel v. 14

Amos 7

- LORD vv. 1, 2, 3, 4, 5, 6, 7, 8, 15, 16, 17
- Relented vv. 3, 6
- Lord GOD vv. 4, 5, 6
- Punished Israel for rejecting His word vv. 12-17

Amos 8

- LORD vv. 1, 2, 3, 7, 9, 11, 12
- Israel is doomed after a long summer of opportunity from a patient Lord for a harvest of repentance vv. 1-2
- Pronounced the coming days of famine and mourning vv. 9-14

Amos 9

- LORD vv. 1, 5, 6, 7, 8, 12, 13, 15
- No one can escape from Him vv. 2-4
- Lord GOD vv. 5, 8
- God of hosts v. 5
- Touches the earth and it melts, and all who dwell in it mourn v. 5
- His eyes are upon the sinful kingdom, and He will destroy it from the surface of the ground, but not utterly v. 8
- The sinners of His people shall die by the sword, who are deceived and think that, "Disaster shall not overtake or meet us." v. 10
- Repairs, raises, and rebuilds v. 11
- Will bring great restoration to His people, and they shall never again be uprooted v. 15
- LORD your God v. 15

Obadiah 1

- LORD vv. 1, 4, 8, 15, 18, 21
- Lord GOD v. 1
- Brings down those deceived by the pride of their heart vv. 2-4
- Will cut off every man of Edom by slaughter v. 9
- Shame shall cover Edom for the violence done to their brother, Jacob v. 10

- His day is near upon all the nations v. 15
- Will return one's deeds on their own heads v. 15
- Saviors shall go up to Mount Zion to rule Mount Esau, and the kingdom shall be the LORD's v. 21

Jonah 1

- LORD vv. 1, 3, 4, 9, 10, 14, 16, 17
- His word came to Jonah, calling him to go to the great city of Nineveh and call out against it for the great evil that came up before Him vv. 1-2
- God of heaven, who made the sea and the dry land v. 9
- Feared by men v. 16
- Appointed a great fish to swallow up Jonah, where he stayed three days and three nights v. 17

Jonah 2

- LORD vv. 1, 2, 6, 7, 9, 10
- Answered Jonah v. 2
- Heard Jonah's voice from the belly of Sheol v. 2
- Brought up Jonah's life from the pit v. 6
- Salvation belongs to Him v. 9
- Spoke to the fish and it vomited Jonah out upon the dry land v. 10

Jonah 3

- LORD vv. 1, 3
- His word came to Jonah a second time, saying, "Arise, go to Nineveh, that great city, and call out against it the message that I tell you." vv. 1-2
- Believed by the people of Nineveh v. 5
- When God saw what the people of Nineveh turned from their evil way, God relented of the disaster that He had said He would do to them, and He did not do it v. 10

Jonah 4

- LORD vv. 2, 3, 4, 6, 10
- Gracious v. 2
- Merciful v. 2
- Slow to anger v. 2
- Abounding in steadfast love v. 2
- Relenting from disaster v. 2
- Asked Jonah if he did to well be angry v. 4
- Appointed a plant and made it to come up over Jonah, that it might be a shade over his head, to save him from his discomfort v. 6
- Appointed a worm to attack the tree v. 7
- Appointed a scorching east wind and the sun to beat down on Jonah so that he was faint v. 8
- Called Jonah to check his heart, since he pitied a plant over the great city of Nineveh vv. 8-11

Micah 1

- LORD vv. 1, 2, 3, 12
- His word came to Micah v. 1
- Witnesses everything on earth from His holy temple v. 2
- Will come out of His place and tread upon the high places of the earth v. 3
- The mountains will melt under Him, and the valleys will split open like wax before the fire, like waters poured down a steep place v. 4
- Lays waste to the His people for their sin vv. 5-7
- Laments and wails for Judah's incurable wound vv. 8-9
- Found the transgressions of Israel in neighboring communities, and

He again brought a conqueror to them vv. 13-15

Micah 2

- LORD vv. 2, 5, 7, 13
- Devises humbling disaster on the necks of the wicked vv. 1-3
- Changes the portion of His people v. 4
- His words do good to him who walks uprightly v. 7
- Assembles a remnant of Israel and leads them as the triumphant King v. 12

Micah 3

- LORD vv. 4, 5, 8, 11
- Spoke to the leaders of the house of Israel, who He expected the know justice v. 1
- Hides His face from those who do evil deeds. Silence is part of their sentence v. 4
- Takes away the supernatural gifts of the prophets, seers, and diviners, who misuse their office vv. 5-7
- Filled with power, the Spirit of the LORD, and justice and might, to declare to Jacob his transgression and to Israel his sin v. 8

Micah 4

- LORD vv. 1, 2, 4, 5, 6, 7, 10, 12, 13
- The mountain of the house of the LORD shall be established as the highest of mountains, and it shall be lifted up above the hills, and the peoples shall flow to it v. 1
- God of Jacob v. 2
- Teacher, guide, lawyer, with word of authority v. 2
- Shall judge between many peoples v. 3
- In the day His house is established, He declares He will assemble the lame and gather those whom He has afflicted; and the lame He will make the remnant, and those who were cast off, a strong nation vv. 6-7a
- He will reign over His people in Mount Zion from that day and forevermore v. 7b
- Kingship shall be given to the daughter of Jerusalem v. 8
- Disciplines His people v. 10
- Redeemer v. 10
- Many nations do not know the thoughts of the LORD, nor understand His plan, that He has gathered them as sheaves to the threshing floor v. 12
- Commands Zion to arise and thresh, and He will make their horn iron, their hooves bronze, and they shall beat in pieces many peoples; and they shall devote their gain to the LORD, their wealth to the LORD of the whole earth v. 13

Micah 5

- LORD vv. 4, 7, 10
- Calls troops to be mustered, and He shall raise up the ruler of Israel from the small town of Bethlehem, whose coming forth is from of old, from ancient days vv. 1-2
- Unity and peace will be established under the Messianic rule vv. 3-5
- In anger and wrath He will execute vengeance on the nations that did not obey v. 15

Micah 6

- LORD vv. 1, 2, 5, 6, 7, 8, 9
- Has an indictment against His people, and He will contend with Israel v. 2

- Calls His people to remember His righteous acts v. 5
- Judges the heart vv. 6-7
- He requires that you do justice, and to love kindness, and to walk humbly with your God v. 8
- Feared by the wise v. 9
- His voice cries to the city v. 9
- Doesn't forget the unrepentant v. 10
- Desolates the wicked v. 13

Micah 7

- LORD vv. 7, 8, 9, 10, 17
- God of salvation v. 7
- Hears v. 7
- A light to one who sits in darkness v. 8
- Enemies will see that He is God v. 10
- He shepherds His people with His staff, the flock of His inheritance v. 14
- The mighty shall come trembling out of their strongholds; they shall turn in dread to the LORD, and be in fear of Him v. 17
- There is no God like Him, pardoning iniquity and passing over transgression for the remnant of His inheritance v. 18
- He does not retain His anger forever, because He delights in steadfast love v. 18
- He will have compassion on His people, treading their iniquities underfoot v. 19
- He will cast all His people's sins into the depths of the sea v. 19
- He will show faithfulness to Jacob and steadfast love to Abraham, as He has sworn to His people's fathers from the days of old v. 20

Nahum 1

- LORD vv. 2, 3, 7, 9, 11, 12, 14
- Gave Nahum of Elkosh a vision concerning the great city of Nineveh v. 1
- Jealous and avenging; avenging and wrathful v. 2
- Takes vengeance on His adversaries and keeps wrath for His enemies v. 2
- Slow to anger v. 3
- Great in power v. 3
- Will by no means clear the guilty v. 3
- His way is in whirlwind and storm, and the clouds are the dust of His feet v. 3
- He rebukes the sea and makes it dry; He dries up all the rivers; cities wither v. 4
- The mountains quake before Him; the hills melt; the earth heaves before Him, the world and all who are in it v. 5
- None can stand before His indignation or endure the heat of His anger v. 6
- His wrath is poured out like fire, and the rocks are broken into pieces by Him v. 6
- Good v. 7
- A stronghold in the day of trouble v. 7
- He knows those who take refuge in Him v. 7
- With an overflowing flood He will make a complete end of His adversaries, and will pursue His enemies into darkness v. 8
- He will make a complete end to plots of trouble that they may not rise up a second time v. 9
- Makes graves v. 14

Nahum 2

- LORD vv. 2, 13
- The Scatterer v. 1
- Restoring the majesty of Jacob as the majesty of Israel v. 2
- Against Nineveh v. 13

Nahum 3

- LORD v. 5
- Against Nineveh v. 5
- LORD of hosts v. 5
- Declares v. 5
- Will lift up Nineveh's skirt over its face and make the nations look at its nakedness v. 5

Habakkuk 1

- LORD vv. 2, 12
- Gave Habakkuk the prophet an oracle to see v. 1
- His timing is not ours v. 2
- Allows wicked to surround the righteous and for justice to be perverted for a season v. 4
- Does unbelievable works v. 5
- From everlasting v. 12
- Habakkuk's God v. 12
- Holy One v. 12
- Rock v. 12
- Established the mighty and evil Chaldeans as a judgment and reproof against His people v. 12
- Uses corrupt people for His holy purpose v. 13

Habakkuk 2

- LORD vv. 2, 13, 14, 16, 20
- Visions from Him will not lie nor delay v. 3
- The righteous cling to His promises, and live by faith v. 4
- LORD of hosts v. 13
- The earth will be filled with the knowledge of the glory of the LORD as the waters cover the sea v. 14
- In His holy temple v. 20

Habakkuk 3

- LORD vv. 2, 8, 18, 19
- Works v. 2
- His splendor covered the heavens, and the earth was full of His praise v. 3
- His brightness was like the light; rays flashed from His hand v. 4
- Before Him went pestilence, and plague followed at His heels v. 5
- He stood and measured the earth; He looked and shook the nations v. 6
- His ways are everlasting v. 6
- Stripped the sheath from His bow, calling for many arrows v. 9
- Split the earth with rivers v. 9
- Marched through the earth in fury; threshed the nations in anger v. 12
- Went out for the salvation of His people, His anointed v. 13
- Crushed the head of the house of the wicked v. 13
- God of salvation v. 18
- Strength of the righteous: He makes their feet like the deer's, and makes them to tread on high places v. 19

Zephaniah 1

- LORD vv. 1, 2, 3, 5, 6, 7, 8, 10, 12, 14, 17, 18
- Will sweep away everything from the face of the earth: man, beast, birds, fish vv. 2-3
- He will cut off mankind from the face of the earth v. 3
- He will stretch out His hand against Judah and all the inhabitants of Jerusalem v. 4

- Will cut off the remnant of Baal and the name of the idolatrous priests along with the priests who have turned back from following the LORD, who do not seek the LORD or inquire of Him vv. 4-6
- The day of the LORD is near vv. 7, 14
- Prepared a sacrifice and consecrated His guests v. 7
- Commands respect and fear v. 7
- Will punish transgressors v. 8
- He will punish the complacent, who say in their hearts, "The LORD will not do good, nor will He do ill." v. 12
- The sound of the day of the LORD is bitter; the mighty man cries aloud there v. 14
- The day of the LORD is one of wrath, distress, anguish, ruin, devastation, darkness, gloom, clouds, thick darkness, trumpet blast, and battle cry vv. 15-16
- Will bring distress on mankind, so that they shall walk like the blind because they have sinned against Him; their blood shall be poured out like dust, and their flesh like dung, and neither their silver nor their gold shall be able to deliver them vv. 17, 18
- In the fire of His jealousy all the earth shall be consumed; for a full and sudden end He will make all the inhabitants of the earth v. 18

Zephaniah 2

- LORD vv. 2, 3, 5, 7, 9, 10, 11
- Anger vv. 2, 3
- Those who are humble and seek righteousness may be hidden on the day of the anger of the LORD v. 3
- The word of the LORD was against evil nations, and He destroyed them v. 5
- The LORD will be mindful of His people and restore their fortunes, making the seacoast a possession of the remnant of Judah v. 7
- Hears v. 8
- The people, who in their pride taunted and boasted against the people of the LORD of hosts, shall be plundered. The LORD will be awesome against them; for He will famish all the gods of the earth, and to Him shall bow down, each in its place, all the lands of the nations vv. 10-11
- Told the Cushites that they would be slain by His sword v. 12
- Will stretch out His hand against the north and destroy Assyria and make Nineveh a desolation, a dry waste like the desert v. 13

Zephaniah 3

- LORD vv. 2, 5, 8, 9, 12, 15, 17, 20
- Declares trouble over those who are rebellious and defiled, who listen to no voice, accept no correction, and do not trust in the LORD nor draw near to their God vv. 1-2
- Righteous v. 5
- Does no injustice v. 5
- Cuts off and makes nations desolate v. 6
- Disciplines so that people will fear Him and accept correction v. 7
- Will gather the nations, rise up to seize the prey, and pour on them His indignation, burning anger; for in the fire of His jealousy all the earth shall be consumed v. 8
- Shall convert the speech of the peoples to a pure one, that all may call upon His name and serve Him with one accord v. 9

- Exalts the humble but removes the proud vv. 11-13
- Taken away the judgments against His people, and calls them to sing aloud, shout, rejoice, and exult with all of their heart. He has cleared away their enemies and they shall never again fear evil vv. 14-15
- He is in the midst of His people, a mighty one who will save; He will rejoice over them with gladness; He will quiet them with His love; He will exult over them with loud singing v. 17
- He will gather those who mourn for a festival, so that they will no longer suffer reproach v. 18
- On His day He will deal with all His people's oppressors. And He will save the lame and gather the outcast, and He will change their shame into praise and renown in all the earth v. 19

Haggai 1

- LORD vv. 1, 2, 3, 5, 7, 8, 9, 12, 13, 14
- His word came to Haggai the prophet v. 1
- LORD of hosts vv. 2, 10, 14
- Calls people to consider their ways vv. 5, 7
- Commands His people to do work that He may take pleasure in it and that it may glorify Him v. 8
- Said to His obedient people, "I am with you, declares the LORD." v. 13

Haggai 2

- LORD vv. 1, 4, 6, 7, 8, 9, 10, 11, 14, 15, 17, 18, 20, 23
- Commands and encourages work, for He is with His people according to the covenant He made with them when they came out of Egypt vv. 4, 5
- LORD of hosts vv. 4, 6, 7, 8, 9, 11, 23
- His Spirit remains in His people's midst v. 5
- He will shake all the earth and all the nations vv. 6-7, 21
- Will fill His house with glory v. 7
- Claims the silver and gold v. 8
- Provides a good harvest to faithful sowing vv. 10-19
- Will overthrow the throne of kingdoms, the chariots and their riders v. 22
- Chooses v. 23

Zechariah 1

- LORD vv. 1, 2, 3, 4, 6, 7, 9, 10, 11, 12, 13, 14, 16, 17, 20
- His word came to the prophet Zechariah v. 1
- Was very angry with Zechariah's fathers v. 2
- LORD of hosts vv. 3, 4, 6, 14, 16, 17
- Calls His people to return to Him, and He will return to them v. 3
- Dealt with the ways of our fathers as He purposed vv. 4-6
- Gave Zechariah a vision of a horseman vv. 7-17
- The Abrahamic covenant to curse those who dishonor Abraham and his offspring is still in force vv. 18-21

Zechariah 2

- LORD vv. 5, 6, 8, 9, 10, 11, 12, 13
- Gave Zechariah a vision of a man with a measuring line vv. 1-13
- LORD of hosts vv. 8, 9
- Will dwell in Zion's midst v. 10
- Many nations shall join themselves to the LORD, both Jews and

Gentiles, and He will dwell in their midst v. 11
- Commands all flesh be silent before the LORD, for He has roused Himself from His holy dwelling v. 13

Zechariah 3
- LORD vv. 1, 2, 5, 6, 7, 9, 10
- Gave Zechariah a vision of Joshua the high priest vv. 1-10
- Removed Joshua's iniquity and clothed him in righteousness, making him suitable to be in the Lord's presence v. 4
- God graciously accepts Joshua and the people he represented v. 5
- Gave Joshua a task and a promise, to walk in His ways and keep His charge, and he will rule His house and have charge of His courts v. 7
- The Branch v. 8
- The Branch would reign with justice and establish salvation for His people v. 9
- The coming Branch would definitively restore fertility and peace for the land v. 10

Zechariah 4
- LORD vv. 4, 5, 6, 8, 9, 10, 13, 14
- Gave Zechariah a vision of a golden lampstand vv. 1-14
- Men please and obey God not by might or power, but by His Spirit, and when they do, mountains become plains before them vv. 6-7

Zechariah 5
- LORD v. 4
- Gave Zechariah a vision of a flying scroll vv. 1-4
- LORD of hosts v. 4
- Brings curses to bear on covenant breakers v. 3
- The house of the covenant breaker will be consumed out of the midst of the community v. 4
- Gave Zechariah a vision of a woman in a basket. Wickedness exists under the power and authority of God, and He shall remove it vv. 5-11

Zechariah 6
- LORD vv. 4, 5, 9, 12, 13, 14, 15
- Gives Zechariah a vision of four chariots vv. 1-8
- Spirit v. 8
- LORD of hosts vv. 12, 15
- Branch v. 13
- Promises aid in fulfilling His purposes if His voice is diligently obeyed v. 15

Zechariah 7
- LORD vv. 1, 2, 3, 4, 7, 8, 9, 12, 13
- LORD of hosts vv. 3, 4, 13
- Spirit v. 12
- Commands that true judgments are rendered, kindness and mercy is shown to one another, the widow, fatherless, sojourner, and poor are not oppressed, and that evil is not devised against one another in your heart vv. 8-10
- Great anger v. 12
- As He called and people would not hear, they shall call and He will not hear, and their pleasant land shall be made desolate vv. 13-14

Zechariah 8
- LORD vv. 1, 2, 3, 4, 6, 7, 9, 11, 14, 17, 18, 19, 20, 21, 22, 23
- LORD of hosts vv. 1, 2, 6, 9, 14, 18, 19, 20, 21, 22
- Jealous for Zion with great jealousy, with great wrath v. 2

- Returned to Zion and will dwell in the midst of Jerusalem, and it shall be called the faithful city, and the mountain of the LORD of hosts, the holy mountain v. 3
- Declared that old men and women shall once again sit in the streets of Jerusalem and they shall be full of boys and girls playing, and it will be marvelous in His sight as it is in His people's vv. 4-6
- He will save His people from the east and west country v. 7
- He will bring His people to dwell in the midst of Jerusalem. They shall be His people, and He shall be there God, in faithfulness and righteousness v. 8
- Preserves a remnant of His people v. 11
- He will restore, save, and bless His people v. 13
- Calls for courage vv. 9, 13, 15
- As He purposed to bring relentless disaster to the fathers of His people when they provoked Him to wrath, He has purposed to bring good to His people vv. 14-15
- Commands truth to be spoken, for He hates false oaths vv. 16-17
- Commands us to love truth and peace v. 19
- Many peoples and strong nations (Gentiles) shall come to seek God and entreat the favor of the LORD v. 22
- Finding its fulfillment on the day of Pentecost, a complete group from the nations of every tongue will recognize the God of the Jews v. 23

<u>Zechariah 9</u>

- LORD vv. 1, 4, 14, 15, 16
- Has an eye on mankind and on all the tribes of Israel v. 1
- Strikes down powerful and proud cities vv. 2-4
- Will strike His people's proud enemies and be their personal bodyguard vv. 5-8
- Calls His people to rejoice! v. 9
- King of His people, prophesied to humbly save His people v. 9
- The Messiah shall speak peace to the nations and His rule shall be from sea to sea v. 10
- God will make an end to war v. 10
- The result of God's rule will be universal peace v. 10
- Because of the blood of His covenant with His people, He will set His prisoners free from the waterless pit v. 11
- Lord GOD v. 14
- LORD of hosts v. 15
- He shall save His people, and they shall shine on His land v. 16
- His goodness and beauty is great v. 17

<u>Zechariah 10</u>

- LORD vv. 1, 3, 5, 6, 7, 12
- Maker of storm clouds v. 1
- His anger is hot against the bad shepherds and He will punish evil leaders v. 3
- The LORD of hosts cares for His flock, and will make them like His majestic steed in battle v. 3
- He will be with His warriors as they put their enemies to shame v. 5
- Will strengthen the house of Judah, and save the house of Joseph v. 6
- Compassion v. 6
- Mercy v. 6
- Answers v. 6

- Redeemed His people v. 8
- Will restore His people whom He punished and scattered in far countries v. 9
- His people shall be made strong and walk in His name v. 12

Zechariah 11

- LORD vv. 4, 5, 6, 11, 13, 15
- The fate of the community lies within God's sovereign hands, He reveals His will to His people, and His agents remain responsible for their own actions in response to the divine word vv. 1-17

Zechariah 12

- LORD vv. 1, 4, 5, 7, 8
- Stretched out the heavens v. 1
- Founded the earth v. 1
- Formed the spirit of man within him v. 1
- Made Israel a cup of staggering to all the surrounding peoples v. 2
- It shall be said, "The inhabitants of Jerusalem have strength through the LORD of hosts, their God." v. 5
- Salvation and strength shall come to Jerusalem and Judah vv. 7-9
- Will pour on the house of David a spirit of grace and pleas for mercy v. 10

Zechariah 13

- LORD vv. 2, 3, 7, 8, 9
- There shall be a fountain to cleanse His people from sin and uncleanness v. 1
- He will strike the good shepherd, His people will be scattered, put under trial, perish, and a third shall be tested and refined vv. 7-9

Zechariah 14

- LORD vv. 1, 3, 5, 7, 9, 12, 13, 16, 17, 18, 20, 21
- Will gather all the nations against Jerusalem to battle, plunder, and rape v. 2
- The LORD shall go out and fight against those nations v. 3
- Will be king over all the earth v. 9
- Will strike all the peoples that wage war on Jerusalem with a flesh-rotting plague v. 12
- Will one day have all traders eradicated from the house of the LORD of hosts, that it may finally become a place where the LORD dwells among His people v. 21

Malachi 1

- LORD vv. 1, 2, 4, 5, 6, 7, 8, 9, 10, 11, 12, 13, 14
- LORD of hosts vv. 4, 6, 8, 9, 10, 11, 13, 14
- Sent "His messenger", Malachi, to deliver an oracle just before the 400 years of silence as Israel grew stale and complacent v. 1
- Shows His greatness in His faithful and consistent character vv. 2-5
- Recognized as great beyond the border of Israel v. 5
- He deserves honor and fear v. 6
- Curses those who cheat God out of what is His due v. 14
- A great King v. 14
- His name will be feared among the nations v. 14

Malachi 2

- LORD vv. 2, 4, 7, 8, 11, 12, 13, 14, 16, 17
- LORD of hosts vv. 2, 4, 7, 8, 12, 16
- Curses the blessings of the priests that will not listen or take His word to heart v. 2
- Made corrupt priests despised and abased before all people inasmuch as they did not keep His ways but showed partiality in their instruction v. 9
- One vv. 10, 15
- Creator v. 10
- Loves v. 11

- Cuts off profaners of the covenant v. 12
- Makes husband and wife one with a portion of His Spirit in their union vv. 14-15
- God of Israel v. 16
- Charges husbands to be faithful to their wives v. 16
- Wearied by people saying that He is not just v. 17

Malachi 3

- LORD vv. 1, 3, 4, 5, 6, 7, 10, 11, 12, 13, 14, 16, 17
- LORD of hosts vv. 1, 5, 7, 10, 11, 12, 14, 17
- Sends a messenger v. 1
- Draws near to judge v. 5
- A swift witness against the sorcerers, adulterers, liars, cheaters and oppressors of the widow and the fatherless, and the inhospitable who do not fear Him v. 5
- Unchanging v. 6
- Faithful v. 6
- Will return to those that return to Him v. 7
- Curses v. 9
- Blesses v. 10
- Rebukes v. 11

Malachi 4

- LORD vv. 1, 3, 5
- LORD of hosts vv. 1, 3
- Will make all the arrogant to be stubble and set ablaze all the evildoers v. 1
- Heals those that fear Him v. 2

Matthew 1

- LORD vv. 20, 22, 24
- Jesus Christ v. 1
- Son of David v. 1
- Son of Abraham v. 1
- There were 42 generations from Abraham to Jesus v. 17
- Born as a human v. 18
- Had an earthly mother, Mary v. 18
- Holy Spirit vv. 18, 20
- Gave Mary a child by His Spirit while she was a virgin v. 18
- Prophesied by an angel that He would save His people from their sins v. 20
- Spoke through a prophet v. 22
- Immanuel v. 23

Matthew 2

- LORD vv. 13, 15, 19
- Jesus was born in Bethlehem of Judea in the days of Herod the king v. 1
- Born king of the Jews v. 2
- Worshiped by foreign wise men v. 11
- Warns v. 12
- Called His son out of Egypt vv. 13-15
- His words are fulfilled vv. 15, 17
- Prophesied and fulfilled His son being called a Nazarene v. 23

Matthew 3

- LORD vv. 3, 7, 10
- Able to raise children for Abraham from stones v. 9
- Jesus baptizes with the Holy Spirit and with fire v. 11
- Mighty v. 11
- Well pleased with His son v. 17
- Fulfilled all righteousness v. 15
- Was baptized v. 16
- The heavens were opened to Jesus v. 17
- The Spirit of God descended like a dove and came to rest on Jesus upon His baptism v. 17

Matthew 4

- LORD vv. 7, 10
- Jesus was led by the Spirit v. 1

- Fasted forty days and nights, and was hungry v. 2
- Tempted by the Devil v. 1
- Defended Himself from Satan with the Word of God vv. 4, 7, 10
- Only Him shall one worship and serve v. 10
- Angels ministered to Him v. 11
- Withdrew to Zebulun and Naphtali after John was arrested, fulfilling Isaiah's prophecy vv. 12-16
- Called disciples to Himself who followed Him immediately vv. 18-22
- Went throughout all Galilee, teaching in their synagogues and proclaiming the gospel of the kingdom and healing every disease and every affliction among the people v. 23
- His fame spread v. 24
- Healed the afflicted brought to Him v. 24
- Great crowds followed Him v. 25

<u>Matthew 5</u>

- LORD v. 33
- Taught v. 2
- Blesses the poor in spirit, those who mourn, the meek, those who hunger and thirst for righteousness, the merciful, the pure in heart, the peacemakers, those who are persecuted for righteousness sake, and those who are persecuted on His account vv. 3-10
- Did not come to abolish the law or the prophets, but to fulfill them v. 17
- Gives true translation to the OT, correcting the false interpretations of the religious leaders vv. 21-48
- Calls us to be perfect like our Heavenly father is perfect v. 48

<u>Matthew 6</u>

- Rewards those who practice righteousness with motives of glorifying God v. 1
- The Father is in heaven vv. 1, 9
- Rewards those who give to the needy in secret v. 4
- Rewards those who pray in secret v. 6
- Knows what you need before you ask Him v. 8
- Hallowed is His name v. 9
- His will is done in Heaven v. 10
- Forgives those who forgive others, and does not forgive those that do not forgive others vv. 14-15
- Sees and rewards good that is done in secret v. 18
- Does not share ownership v. 24
- Heavenly Father v. 32
- Knows our needs, so worry does no good v. 32
- Those who seek first His kingdom receive food, drink, and clothing v. 33

<u>Matthew 7</u>

- LORD vv. 21, 22
- Measures judgment according to the judgment one pronounces themselves v. 2
- Gives good things to those who ask Him v. 11
- Not everyone who says to Him, "Lord, Lord," will enter the kingdom of heaven, but the one who does the will of the Father who is in heaven v. 21
- Looks for a repentant heart, not mere actions v. 23
- Those who hear His words and does them are wise and do not fall, but those who do not experience a great fall when the storms come vv. 24-27
- Astonished crowds v. 28
- Jesus taught with authority v. 29

<u>Matthew 8</u>

- LORD vv. 2, 6, 8, 21, 25

- Touched and healed a man of leprosy who had faith v. 3
- Healed a centurion's servant v. 13
- Healed Peter's mother-in-law of a fever v. 15
- Cast out demonic spirits with a word and healed all who were sick, thereby fulfilling Isaiah's prophecy, "He took our illnesses and bore our diseases." vv. 16-17
- Son of Man v. 20
- Jesus had nowhere to lay His head v. 20
- Slept v. 24
- Rebuked the winds and the sea v. 26
- The winds and the sea obey Him v. 27
- Son of God v. 29
- Casted demons out of two men and into a herd of pigs v. 32

Matthew 9

- LORD vv. 28, 38
- Moved by faith v. 2
- Forgave sins v. 2
- Knows our thoughts v. 4
- Son of Man v. 6
- Healed a paralytic v. 6
- Given authority to man to heal and forgive sins vv. 6-8
- Called a tax collector to be His follower, Matthew v. 9
- Ate with sinners and tax collectors v. 11
- Came for the sick v. 13
- Physician v. 12
- Only those who realize their need to come to Jesus come to Him to receive the help they need v. 12
- Desires mercy, not sacrifice v. 13
- Came not to call the righteous, but sinners v. 13
- Mercy is more important to God than religious rituals v. 13
- Jesus came and offered real growth in kingdom righteousness, rather than patching up traditional, religious practices of righteousness vv. 16-17
- His power is available to those that believe in Him v. 22
- Raised a ruler's daughter to life v. 25
- Son of David v. 27
- Healed two blind men according to their faith v. 29
- Cast out a demon v. 33
- Called Satan by the Pharisees v. 34
- Taught and proclaimed the gospel of the kingdom throughout cities and villages and healed every disease and every affliction v. 35
- Had compassion on the crowds, because they were harassed and helpless, like sheep without a shepherd v. 36
- Called His disciples to pray earnestly to the Lord of the harvest to send out laborers into His harvest v. 38

Matthew 10

- Gave His disciples authority over unclean spirits, to cast them out, and to heal every disease and every affliction v. 1
- Betrayed v. 4
- Sent out his twelve to gather the lost sheep of Israel and proclaim that the kingdom of heaven is at hand and to heal the sick, raise the dead, cleanse lepers, and cast out demons, and to give without pay since they received without pay vv. 5-8

- Sent out His disciples as sheep among wolves, instructing them to be wise as serpents and innocent as doves v. 16
- The Spirit of His children's Father speaks through them v. 20
- His Apostles will be hated for His name's sake v. 22
- Son of Man v. 23
- Jesus was perversely accused of being Beelzebul, a reference to Satan meaning "master of the house" v. 25
- Not a single sparrow falls to the ground apart from the Father v. 29
- Numbers the hairs on one's head v. 30
- Humans are more valuable than sparrows, which God looks after v. 31
- Everyone who acknowledges Jesus before men shall be acknowledged before His Father who is in heaven, and vice versa v. 33
- Jesus came not to bring peace, but a sword v. 34
- Whoever loves his family more than Jesus is not worthy of Him v. 38
- A disciple of God must die to self and embrace God's will, no matter the cost v. 38
- Whoever receives Jesus' disciple receives Him, and whoever receives Him receives the Father v. 40
- Rewards those who receive a prophet or righteous person simply because they are righteous vv. 40-42

<u>Matthew 11</u>

- LORD v. 25
- Son of Man v. 19
- Taught and preached v. 1
- Christ v. 2
- Gave sight to the blind, healed the lame, the lepers, the deaf, and raised the dead, and gave the poor good news v. 5
- Blessed is the one who is not offended by Him v. 6
- Denounced the cities where most of His mighty works had been done, because they did not repent v. 20
- Jesus declared thanks to His Father, that He had hidden things from the understanding and the wise and revealed them to little children v. 25
- Lord of heaven v. 25
- Gracious v. 26
- All things have been handed over to Jesus by His Father, and only those to whom Jesus chooses to reveal the Father know Him v. 27
- Calls those who labor and are heavy laden to Himself, for He will give them rest v. 28
- Calls everyone to trust in Him with their personal lives v. 28
- His yoke is easy, and His burden is light v. 30

<u>Matthew 12</u>

- LORD v. 8
- Son of Man vv. 8, 32, 40
- Desires mercy, and not sacrifice v. 7
- LORD of the Sabbath v. 8
- Authority to interpret the law v. 8
- Declares it lawful to do good on the Sabbath v. 12
- Fully restored a man's withered hand v. 13
- Fulfilled Isaiah's prophecies by speaking in parables to the crowds vv. 17, 35
- Spirit v. 18

- Put His Spirit on His Servant, Jesus v. 18
- Jesus, as the Father willed, proclaimed justice to the Gentiles v. 18
- Jesus did not quarrel or cry aloud, nor will anyone to hear His voice in the streets v. 19
- In His name the Gentiles will hope v. 21
- Healed a blind and mute man oppressed by a demon v. 22
- Called the prince of demons by the Pharisees v. 24
- Does not forgive blasphemy against the Spirit v. 31
- By your words you will be justified or condemned v. 37
- Greater than both Jonah and Solomon vv. 41, 42
- Whoever does the will of His Father is Jesus' mother and brother v. 50

<u>Matthew 13</u>

- Son of Man vv. 37, 41
- Taught crowds in parables v. 3
- Gives ears to those whom He wills to reveal the secrets of the Kingdom vv. 9-11
- Allows believers and unbelievers to live in the world until the day of judgment v. 30
- Uses things that at first seem insignificant v. 32
- Sows sons of the kingdom in the world v. 38
- The righteous will shine like the sun in the Father's kingdom v. 43
- His angels will come and separate the good from the righteous v. 49
- Did not do many mighty works in hometown because of unbelief v. 58

<u>Matthew 14</u>

- LORD vv. 28, 30
- Herod the tetrarch heard about the fame of Jesus v. 1
- Withdrew in a desolate place by Himself after hearing the news about John the Baptist's death v. 13
- Compassion v. 14
- Ordered v. 19
- Fed five thousand men vv. 13-21
- Went on a mountain by Himself to pray v. 23
- Walked on the sea v. 25
- Mistaken for a ghost by His disciples v. 26
- Saved Peter from drowning after he had walked out on the water v. 28
- Worshipped by His disciples who confessed Him to be the Son (denoting equality) of God v. 33
- As many that touched the fringe of His garment were made well v. 36

<u>Matthew 15</u>

- LORD vv. 22, 25, 27
- States that His word is greater than tradition v. 6
- Calls Pharisees hypocrites v. 7
- Worshipped in vain by people whose hearts are far from Him and who teach as doctrines the commandments of men vv. 8-9
- Offended Pharisees v. 12
- Taught that what comes out of the mouth is what defiles a person rather than what goes into it, for what comes out of it proceeds from the heart: evil thoughts, murder, adultery, sexual immorality, theft, false witness, and slander vv. 18-19
- Was sent to the lost sheep of Israel v. 24
- Healed the daughter of a Canaanite woman of great faith v. 28

- Healed the lame, blind, cripple, mute, and many others that were brought to His feet v. 30
- The crowd wondered at His works and glorified Him v. 31
- God of Israel v. 31
- Fed four thousand people with seven loaves of bread and a few fish vv. 32-39

Matthew 16

- LORD v. 22
- Son of Man vv. 13, 27, 28
- Did not give a sign to His enemies who sought merely to test Him v. 4
- Called out His disciples for their lack of faith and perception vv. 8-9
- Warned His disciples about the teaching of the Pharisees v. 12
- The Father revealed to Simon Peter that Jesus is the Christ v. 17
- Strictly charged His disciples to keep His identity a secret v. 20
- Prophesied His suffering, death, and resurrection under the leaders and religious authority of Jerusalem vv. 22-23
- Rebuked Peter for allowing Satan to use His human thinking v. 23
- Those that set their minds on the things of man rather than God are a hindrance to Jesus as Satan is v. 23
- Calls His followers to deny themselves and to give up their lives for Him vv. 24-25
- The Son of Man is going to come with His angels in the glory of His Father, and then He will repay each person according to what He has done v. 27

Matthew 17

- LORD vv. 4, 15
- Son of Man vv. 9, 12, 22
- Jesus was transfigured from His earthly body to His exalted glory before Peter, James, and John. His face shown like the sun, and His clothes were as white as light. Moses and Elijah appeared with Him and talked with Him vv. 1-8
- The Father appeared in a white cloud saying, "This is my beloved Son, with whom I am well pleased; listen to Him." v. 5
- Men are terrified in the Father's presence v. 6
- Called His disciples to have no fear v. 7
- Rebuked a demon and it came out of an epileptic boy, who was healed instantly v. 18
- Jesus had Peter pay the religious tabernacle tax for both of them by taking a shekel out of the mouth of a fish v. 27

Matthew 18

- LORD v. 21
- Only allows those who have turned and humbled themselves like a child to enter the kingdom of heaven, and the greatest in the kingdom will be one who has done so v. 4
- Calls His disciples to radically remove sin from their lives vv. 6-9
- Does not wish for any of His disciples to perish, but rejoices when one that has went astray is found, more so than all the ones that never even went astray vv. 10-14
- The entire community of disciples is given authority as Peter was, in that whatever is bound or loosed on earth shall be so in heaven v. 18

- Puts no limit on forgiveness, and to not keep a record of sins v. 22
- Takes back His mercy from the merciless, who do not forgive their brother from their heart v. 35

Matthew 19

- Son of Man v. 28
- Large crowds followed Jesus, and He healed them v. 2
- God created male and female to become one flesh and not be separated, but because of man's hardness of heart Moses allowed divorce, but whoever divorces His wife for a reason other than sexual immorality and marries another commits adultery vv. 3-9
- The kingdom of heaven belongs to those such as little children v. 14
- The only One that is good v. 17
- Jesus will sit on His glorious throne v. 28

Matthew 20

- LORD vv. 25, 30, 31, 33
- Son of Man vv. 18, 28
- Fair (no one is right to begrudge His doings) v. 13
- Foretold His disciples a third time of His condemnation and death in Jerusalem vv. 17-19
- The Father grants who is to sit at His right and left hand in His kingdom v. 23
- Calls the great to servanthood, and the first to be last (servant leadership) vv. 26-27
- Jesus came to serve, rather than be served, and to give His life as ransom for many v. 28
- Son of David vv. 30, 31
- Pity v. 34
- Compassion v. 34

Matthew 21

- LORD vv. 3, 9, 42
- Fulfilled the prophecy of coming to His people mounted on a donkey and a colt, the foal of a beast of burden v. 5
- Came in the name of the Lord v. 9
- Praised v. 9
- Stirred up the whole city of Jerusalem when He entered it v. 10
- Prophet v. 11
- Nazarene v. 11
- Jesus cleansed the temple of robbers vv. 12-13
- Healed the blind and the lame that came to Him in the temple v. 14
- Offended the chief priests and scribes v. 15
- Was worshipped as the Son of David v. 15
- Prepared praise out of the mouths of infants and babes for His Son v. 16
- Cursed a fig tree v. 19
- Does what a person of enough faith asks v. 22
- Gives to those who ask Him in faith v. 22
- Teacher v. 23
- Stumped the chief priests and elders v. 27
- Tax collectors and prostitutes believed Him more so than the religious leaders v. 32
- Will take away the kingdom of God from the builders that reject the cornerstone and given to a people producing its fruits v. 43
- Religious leaders sought to arrest Him v. 45
- Held to be a prophet v. 46

Matthew 22

- LORD vv. 37, 43, 44, 45
- Spoke in parables v. 1

- Calls many, chooses few v. 14
- Teacher v. 16
- True v. 16
- Called out hypocrites who sought to test Him v. 18
- The Pharisees marveled at Him vv. 15-22
- Sadducees attempted to trap Him theologically v. 23
- Powerful v. 29
- God of Abraham, Isaac, and Jacob v. 32
- God of the living v. 32
- Astonished the Sadducees v. 33
- His greatest command is to love Him with all your heart, soul, and mind, and to love your neighbor as yourself vv. 34-40
- Spirit v. 43
- The Father will put the Son's enemies under His feet v. 44
- People did not dare to ask Him any more questions v. 46

Matthew 23

- LORD v. 39
- Instructor, the only one v. 11
- Christ v. 10
- Humbles the proud and exalts the humble v. 12
- Would have often gathered Jerusalem under his wings, but they would not v. 37
- Jesus identified Himself with God's Messiah and Savior who will once again come to His people v. 39

Matthew 24

- LORD v. 42
- Son of Man vv. 27, 30, 37, 39, 44
- Jesus prophesied the temple's destruction v. 2
- Prophet v. 2
- Warns His disciples of false teachers v. 4
- Prophesies the earth's birth pains v. 8
- His people will face death and tribulation v. 9
- The gospel of His kingdom will be proclaimed throughout the whole world to all nations, and then the end will come v. 14
- His second coming will come as obvious as a flash of lightning v. 27
- The sign of the Son of Man will appear in the heavens and all the tribes of the earth will mourn and see Him coming on the clouds of heaven with power and great glory v. 30
- Will send out His angels with a loud trumpet call and they will gather His elect v. 31
- His words will not pass away v. 35
- Only the Father knows when the last hour will be v. 36
- Calls His people to stay awake, for Jesus is coming at a time they will not expect v. 44
- Will set the faithful and wise servant over all His possessions v. 47
- He will destroy and put with the hypocrites the wicked servants vv. 48-51

Matthew 25

- LORD vv. 11, 37, 44
- Son of Man v. 31
- Warns us to be ready with a parable of ten virgins vv. 1-13
- Sets the faithful of little over much and lets him enter into the joy of his master vv. 21, 23
- Takes away from poor stewards and casts them into outer darkness

where there will be gnashing of teeth vv. 29-30
- Will come in glory with all the angels and sit on His glorious throne v. 31
- All the nations will be gathered before Him and He shall separate them v. 32
- King v. 34
- Will give the righteous their inheritance prepared for them from the foundation of the world v. 34
- Whatever we do to the least of Jesus' brothers we do to Him, and He will either utterly punish or exceedingly reward accordingly vv. 31-46

Matthew 26
- LORD v. 22
- Son of Man vv. 2, 24, 45, 64
- Jesus was delivered up to be crucified v. 2
- Prophet v. 2
- Plotted against by the chief priests and elders, who sought to stealthily arrest and then kill Him vv. 3-5
- Was here for a short time v. 11
- Betrayed by a disciple of His (Judas Iscariot) for thirty pieces of silver vv. 14-16
- Teacher v. 18
- Prophesied His betrayal v. 21
- Called Lord by all His disciples, but Judas was never recorded to do so vv. 22, 25
- Likened His body to bread and His blood to wine vv. 26-29
- His blood was poured out for many for the forgiveness of sins v. 28
- He will not drink wine until with His people in His Father's kingdom v. 29
- Struck the shepherd, and the flock was scattered v. 31
- Prophesied Peter's betrayal of Him v. 35
- Prayed alone in the garden of Gethsemane v. 36
- His soul was sorrowful, even to death v. 38
- Had human desires, but desired God's will above His own v. 39
- Repeated His prayers to the Father v. 44
- Betrayed into the hands of sinners v. 45
- Called His enemy an acquaintance v. 50
- Could have appealed to His Father to send more than twelve legions of angels, but was willingly arrested to fulfill the scriptures vv. 50-56
- Fulfilled the Scripture of the prophets v. 56
- Destroyed the temple of God and rebuilt it in three days v. 61
- Power v. 64
- Seated at the right hand of Power and coming on the clouds of heaven v. 64
- Humiliated vv. 65-68

Matthew 27
- LORD v. 10
- Directs v. 10
- King of the Jews v. 11
- Did not retaliate before His accusers v. 14
- Gave dreams of Jesus to Pilate's wife v. 19
- Scourged v. 26
- Mocked vv. 31, 41
- Jesus was forsaken by the Father v. 46
- Yielded up His spirit v. 50

- Called the Son of God by a centurion and other bystanders v. 54
- His tomb was sealed and guarded v. 66

Matthew 28

- LORD v. 2
- Rose from the dead v. 6
- Called the apostles His brothers v. 10
- Worshipped by the two Marys v. 9
- All authority in heaven and on earth was given to Him v. 18
- Commanded disciples to be made of all nations, and for them to be baptized in the name of the Father and of the Son and of the Holy Spirit, teaching them to observe all of His commandments vv. 19-20
- With His people always, to the end of the age v. 20

Mark 1

- LORD v. 3
- Jesus Christ, the Son of God v. 1
- Sent John the Baptist as His messenger to prepare the way vv. 2-3
- Mighty v. 7
- Baptizes with the Holy Spirit v. 8
- Jesus came from Nazareth of Galilee and was baptized by John in the Jordan v. 9
- Immediately upon coming up from the water at His baptism, Jesus saw the heavens being torn open and the Spirit descending on Him like a dove. And a voice came from heaven, "You are my beloved Son; with you I am well pleased." vv. 10-11
- The Spirit drove Jesus out into the wilderness v. 12
- Jesus spent forty days in the wilderness, being tempted by Satan, and was ministered to by angels afterward vv. 12-13
- Jesus proclaimed the gospel of God, saying, "The time is fulfilled, and the kingdom of God is at hand; repent and believe in the gospel." vv. 14-15
- Called twelve disciples to follow Him and become fishers of men, and they followed Him immediately vv. 16-20
- Jesus taught in the synagogue v. 21
- Taught with authority, astonishing those who heard it v. 22
- Jesus of Nazareth v. 24
- Holy One of God v. 24
- Commands unclean spirits, and they obey Him v. 27
- His fame spread v. 28
- Healed Simon's mother-in-law of a fever v. 31
- A whole city gathered at the door of the house where Jesus was, and He healed many who were sick with various diseases and cast out many demons vv. 33-34
- Rose and departed to pray in the dark of the morning v. 35
- Jesus went all throughout Galilee, preaching in synagogues and casting out demons v. 39
- Compassion v. 41
- Healed a leper who moved Him to pity v. 41
- Fame spread so much that He went to desolate places and people came to Him from every quarter v. 45

Mark 2

- LORD vv. 23, 28
- Son of Man vv. 10, 28
- Preached the word v. 2

- Moved by faith shown by friends of a paralytic v. 5
- Perceived immediately that some scribes were questioning His actions in their hearts, so He displayed His authority and power by healing a paralytic. All were amazed and glorified God vv. 6-12
- Teacher v. 13
- Called Levi the tax collector to follow Him v. 14
- Reclined at a table with many tax collectors and sinners, who followed Him v. 15
- Came to call not the righteous, but the sinners v. 17
- Jesus brought a new era with new ways v. 22
- Jesus is Lord over the Sabbath, which was made for mankind, and He is Lord of mankind v. 28

Mark 3

- Angered and grieved at the Pharisees' hardness of hearts v. 5
- Restored a man's withered hand v. 5
- Appointed twelve, naming them apostles so that they might be with Him and sent out to preach and have authority to cast out demons v. 15
- Named James and John the Sons of Thunder (Boanerges) vv. 16-17
- Never forgives one who blasphemes the Holy Spirit v. 29
- Whoever does the will of God is His mother and sister and brother v. 35

Mark 4

- Teacher v. 1
- Taught many things in parables v. 2
- Gives ears to hear v. 9
- Privately explained His parables to His disciples v. 34
- The wind and sea obey Jesus v. 41

Mark 5

- LORD v. 19
- Son of the Most High God v. 7
- Cast out Legion, an unclean spirit vv. 1-20
- Merciful v. 19
- His power healed a woman of a blood discharge who with faith simply touched His garments vv. 21-34
- Teacher v. 35
- Commanded courage and belief v. 36
- Raised a twelve year old from the dead v. 42

Mark 6

- Marveled at His hometown's unbelief v. 6
- Taught v. 6
- Astonished those who heard Him v. 2
- Carpenter v. 3
- Son of Mary and brother of James, Joses, Judas, and Simon v. 3
- Laid His hands on a few sick people and healed them v. 5
- Could do little mighty works with little faith v. 5
- Called and sent the twelve out by twos, and gave them authority over the unclean spirits v. 7
- Jesus' name had become known, and King Herod heard of Him v. 14
- Commanded His apostles to rest v. 31
- Compassion v. 34
- Fed five thousand men vv. 35-44
- Prayed v. 46
- Walked on the sea v. 48
- As many as touched the fringe of His garment were made well v. 56

Mark 7

- LORD v. 28
- His commandments transcend human tradition v. 9
- Called out the Pharisees and scribes for making void the word of God by their traditions v. 13
- Focuses on the heart vv. 14-23
- Declared all foods clean v. 19
- Cast out a demon from the daughter of a Gentile woman for her faith vv. 24-30
- Opened a man's ears and released his tongue, astonishing people beyond measure vv. 31-37

Mark 8

- Son of Man vv. 31, 38
- Compassion v. 2
- Fed four thousand people vv. 1-10
- Sighed deeply in His spirit v. 12
- Requires a fundamental change of heart v. 12
- Warned against the teaching of the Pharisees and of Herod v. 15
- Had to re-enlighten His disciples vv. 14-21
- Healed a blind man vv. 22-26
- Foretold His death and resurrection v. 31
- Rebuked Peter for not setting his mind on the things of God, but the things of man v. 33
- Ashamed of those who are ashamed of Him v. 38

Mark 9

- Son of Man vv. 9, 12, 31
- His kingdom will come in power v. 1
- Transfigured before Peter, James, and John v. 2
- Appeared with Moses and Elijah v. 5
- The Father loves His Son, and commands people to listen to Him v. 7
- Rose from the dead v. 9
- Prophet v. 9
- Called His generation faithless v. 19
- Cast out a mute and deaf spirit from a boy according to his father's belief vv. 14-29
- Teacher v. 31
- Prophesied His death and resurrection v. 31
- Defines serving and suffering as true leadership v. 35

Mark 10

- LORD v. 42
- Son of Man vv. 33, 45
- Came to Jericho v. 46
- Jesus v. 47
- Son of David v. 47
- Healed a blind man who was full of faith and eagerly sought Jesus while others only discouraged him, and Jesus healed him immediately vv. 46-52

Mark 11

- LORD vv. 3, 9
- Rode into Jerusalem on a colt amid exuberant praise from the city vv. 1-11
- Cursed a fig tree v. 14
- Cleansed the temple in Jerusalem, driving out the money-changers and salesmen, overturning their tables v. 15
- Grants the wishes of those who ask in faith vv. 20-25
- Countered the challenges of the chief priests and scribes vv. 27-33

Mark 12

- LORD vv. 11, 29, 30, 36, 37
- Spoke in parables, that only those with ears to hear could hear v. 1

- God sent many prophets and even His own beloved Son in hopes that His people would give Him His due, but they were all rejected, meriting destruction on themselves and giving up what God gave to them vv. 1-12
- The chief priests and scribes perceived that Jesus spoke against them, so they sent some of the Pharisees and Herodians to try to trap Him in His talk vv. 12-13
- Teacher vv. 14, 19, 32, 35, 38
- Does not care about anyone's opinion because He is not swayed by appearance, and truly teaches what is the way of God v. 14
- Caused the religious leaders to marvel by what He said v. 17
- Called out the Sadducees for knowing neither the scriptures nor the power of God v. 24
- God of the living v. 27
- The Lord is one v. 29
- His greatest commandment is to love Him with all of your heart, soul, mind, and strength, and the second is that you shall love your neighbor as yourself vv. 30-31
- There is no other besides Him v. 32
- Warns of the deceiving religious leadership vv. 38-40
- Loves those who give sacrificially vv. 41-44

<u>Mark 13</u>

- LORD v. 20
- Son of Man vv. 24, 26
- Teacher v. 1
- Prophet vv. 2-37
- Warns against impostors v. 6
- His people will be persecuted v. 9
- His gospel will be proclaimed to all nations v. 10
- His Spirit speaks through His people v. 11
- Saves those who endure to the end v. 13
- Elected individuals to be His v. 20
- Warns against false prophets and teachers v. 22
- Will gather His elect v. 27
- There will be signs to show of His coming v. 29
- Only the Father knows when the last day will be v. 32

<u>Mark 14</u>

- LORD v. 22
- Son of Man vv. 21, 41, 62
- Accepted an anointing of costly alabaster v. 6
- Teacher v. 14
- Instituted the Lord's supper vv. 22-25
- All things are possible for the Father v. 36
- Prayed in the garden of Gethsemane vv. 32-42
- Abba v. 36
- Warned against temptation v. 38
- Betrayed into the hands of sinners v. 42
- Rabbi v. 45
- Teacher v. 49
- Fulfilled scriptures v. 49
- Will be seen seated at the right hand of Power and coming in the clouds of heaven v. 62
- Prophet v. 72

<u>Mark 15</u>

- Son of Man v. 39
- King of the Jews vv. 2, 26
- Was silent before accusations v. 5

- Let men scourge Him and mock Him vv. 15, 17, 29, 31
- Let men crucify Him v. 24
- Jesus was forsaken by the Father v. 35
- Jesus died v. 37
- Son of God v. 39

Mark 16

- LORD vv. 19, 20
- Resurrected vv. 1-8
- Appeared to Mary, from whom He had cast out seven demons, and then two disciples vv. 9-13
- Jesus of Nazareth v. 6
- Rebuked the disciples who had not believed testimony of His resurrection v. 14
- Commanded His disciples to go into all the world and proclaim the gospel v. 15
- Saves whoever believes the gospel and is baptized v. 16
- In His name believers will cast out demons, speak in new tongues, pick up serpents with their hands, drink and not be hurt by deadly poison, and lay their hands on the sick and heal vv. 17-18
- Lord Jesus v. 19
- Taken up into heaven and sat down at the right hand of God v. 19
- Worked with His disciples as they preached everywhere, and confirmed the message by accompanying signs v. 20

Luke 1

- LORD vv. 6, 9, 11, 15, 16, 17, 25, 28, 32, 38, 43, 45, 46, 58, 66, 68, 76
- Gave commandments and statutes to follow v. 6
- Sent an angle to Zechariah v. 13
- Hears prayer v. 13
- His Holy Spirit fills man v. 15
- Gave a child to a barren Elizabeth v. 13
- God of Israel v. 16
- The angel Gabriel stands in His presence, and is sent to share good news v. 19
- Muted Zechariah for a season because of his unbelief v. 20
- Sent Gabriel to Mary in Nazareth v. 27
- Has favor on people v. 30
- Son of the Most High v. 32
- There is no end to His kingdom v. 33
- Holy Spirit v. 35
- Most High v. 35
- Holy v. 35
- Son of God v. 35
- The Holy Spirit filled Elizabeth v. 41
- Magnified v. 46
- Savior v. 47
- Looked on the humble estate of His servant v. 48
- Mighty v. 49
- His mercy is for those who fear Him from generation to generation v. 50
- He has shown strength with His arm v. 51
- Scattered the proud in the thoughts of their hearts v. 51
- Brought down the mighty from their thrones and exalted those of humble estate v. 52
- Filled the hungry with good things, an the rich He has sent away empty v. 53
- He has helped His servant Israel, in remembrance of His mercy, as He spoke to Abraham and his offspring forever vv. 54-55

- Showed great mercy to Elizabeth, and her neighbors heard of it v. 58
- His Holy Spirit filled Zechariah v. 67
- Blessed v. 68
- God of Israel v. 68
- Visited and redeemed His people v. 68
- Raised up a horn of salvation for the house of David as He spoke by the mouth of His holy prophets of old, that they should be saved from their enemies; to show the mercy promised to their fathers and to remember His holy covenant, the oath that He swore to their father Abraham, to grant them that they, being delivered from the hand of their enemies, might serve Him without fear, in holiness and righteousness before Him all their days vv. 69-75
- Raised up John as His prophet, the prophet of the Most High, who would go before the Lord to prepare His ways, to give knowledge of salvation to His people in the forgiveness of their sins, because of the tender mercy of their God, whereby the sunrise shall visit them from on high to give light to those that sit in darkness and in the shadow of death, to guide their feet into the way of peace vv. 76-79

Luke 2

- LORD vv. 9, 11, 15, 22, 23, 24, 26, 29, 39
- Jesus was born in a manger, an animal's feeding trough v. 7
- His glory shown around nearby shepherds at Jesus' birth, the Savior, the Christ and Lord, had come in humble flesh and brought peace on earth among those with whom He is pleased and bringing glory to God in the highest vv. 8-14
- Holy Spirit was upon Simeon, who was righteous and devout v. 25
- Prepared salvation in the presence of all peoples, a light for revelation to the Gentiles, and glory for His people Israel vv. 30-32
- The child Jesus was appointed for the fall and rising of many in Israel, and for a sign that is opposed v. 34
- Redemption v. 38
- Law of the Lord vv. 23, 39
- Jesus grew and became strong, filled with wisdom, and the favor of God was upon Him vv. 40, 52
- Amazed teachers at the age of twelve v. 47
- Submissive to His parents v. 51

Luke 3

- LORD v. 4
- All flesh shall see the salvation of God v. 6
- There is nothing that man can hold before God of themselves to be acceptable before Him, so we must bear fruits in keeping with repentance v. 7
- Cuts down every tree that does not bear good fruit v. 9
- Jesus baptizes with the Holy Spirit and with fire v. 16
- Jesus gathers His people to Himself and destroys the rest v. 17
- Jesus was baptized by John, and the heavens were opened and the Holy Spirit descended on Him in bodily form, like a dove, and a voice came from heaven, "You are

my beloved son; with you I am well pleased." vv. 21-22
- Jesus began His ministry at age thirty v. 23
- Son of David and Adam, the son of God vv. 23-38

Luke 4
- LORD vv. 8, 12, 18, 19
- Jesus was full of the Holy Spirit, and was led into the wilderness for forty days, being tempted by the devil vv. 1-2
- Hungry v. 2
- You shall worship the Lord your God, and Him only shall you serve v. 8
- Jesus returned in the power of the Spirit to Galilee v. 14
- Teacher, glorified by all vv. 14-15
- Jesus customarily went up to the synagogue on the Sabbath day v. 16
- The Spirit of the Lord was upon Him, because He had anointed Him to proclaim liberty to the captives and recovering of sight to the blind, to set at liberty those who are oppressed, to proclaim the year of the Lord's favor vv. 18-19
- Fulfilled Isaiah's prophecy of Himself v. 17
- Offended the people of His hometown v. 28
- Holy One of God v. 34
- Jesus of Nazareth v. 34
- Rebuked and cast out an unclean demon from a man v. 35
- Jesus healed many vv. 38-41
- Christ v. 41
- Preached the good news of the kingdom of God to several towns v. 43

Luke 5
- LORD vv. 8, 12, 17
- Son of Man v. 24
- People came to Jesus to hear the word of God v. 1
- Gave Simon Peter a huge catch of fish when he obeyed Jesus vv. 4-7
- Called Peter, James, and John to follow Him v. 10
- Cleansed a leper that came to Him v. 13
- The power of the Lord was with Jesus to heal v. 17
- Forgave sins v. 20
- Perceived thoughts v. 22
- Healed a paralyzed man v. 24
- Called a tax collector, Levi, to follow Him v. 27
- Came to call sinners, not the righteous v. 32
- Jesus brought a new covenant, requiring repentance, regeneration, and new forms of worship vv. 36-39

Luke 6
- LORD vv. 1, 5, 46
- Sōn of Man vv. 5, 22
- Lord of the Sabbath, which He gave for man's benefit v. 5
- Healed a man with a withered hand, doing good on the Sabbath vv. 6-11
- Went out to a mountain to pray all night v. 12
- Chose twelve men of His disciples to be his apostles v. 13
- Taught and healed people from a great multitude. Power came out from Him, that any who touched Him were healed vv. 17-19
- Blesses the poor with the kingdom, satisfies the hungry, makes those

who weep to laugh, and gives great reward to those who are persecuted for His sake vv. 20-23
- Curses the rich, the full, those who laugh, and those who are spoken well of vv. 24-26
- Calls everyone to love their enemies vv. 27-36
- Commands not condemnation, but forgiveness, for He will repay likewise v. 37

Luke 7
- LORD vv. 6, 13, 19
- Son of Man vv. 12, 34
- Healed a centurion's servant, because of the leader's great faith vv. 1-10
- Compassion v. 13
- Raised the son of a widow from the dead v. 15
- Healed many people of diseases, blindness, and paralysis v. 22
- Blesses those not offended by Him v. 23
- Makes the least in the kingdom of God the greatest v. 28
- Rejected by His people v. 32
- Forgives a sinful woman v. 47
- Saves according to one's faith v. 50

Luke 8
- Many women provided for Jesus and His apostles from out of their own means vv. 1-3
- Many crowds from many towns came to Jesus v. 4
- Taught in parables v. 10
- Those who do not listen carefully to the word of God will face the consequences, for it will be taken away v. 18
- His mother and brothers are those who hear the word of God and do it v. 21
- Calmed a storm v. 24
- Healed a man of demons vv. 26-39
- His power available for those of faith v. 48
- Teacher v. 49
- Raised a girl from the dead v. 54

Luke 9
- LORD vv. 54, 59, 61
- Son of Man vv. 22, 26, 44, 58
- Gave the twelve power and authority over all demons and to cure diseases v. 1
- Sent His apostles out to proclaim the kingdom of God and to heal v. 2
- Herod the tetrarch heard of what Jesus was doing v. 7
- Physician v. 11
- Fed five thousand men from just five loaves and two fish, with twelve baskets left over vv. 10-17
- The Christ of God v. 20
- Kept His identity a secret v. 21
- Calls His followers to deny themselves and make a dangerous commitment to Himself v. 23
- Whoever loses his life for Jesus' sake will save it v. 24
- The Son of Man, when He comes again in His glory, will be ashamed of anyone who was ashamed of Him and His word v. 26
- Was transfigured before Peter, John, and James vv. 28-36
- Chosen One v. 35
- The Father commands that we listen to Jesus v. 35
- Teacher v. 38
- Healed a boy of an unclean spirit vv. 37-43

- Majesty v. 43
- Foretold His death vv. 43-45
- Had nowhere to lay His head. Homeless v. 58

Luke 10

- LORD vv. 1, 2, 17, 21, 27, 39, 40, 41
- Sent seventy-two disciples ahead of Him to work the harvest. To heal and proclaim the kingdom vv. 1-12
- Saw Satan fall like lightning from heaven v. 18
- Reveals that true reason to rejoice is having one's name written in heaven v. 20
- Jesus rejoiced in the Holy Spirit v. 21
- Father v. 21
- Lord of heaven and earth v. 21
- Hidden things from the wise and revealed them to little children v. 21
- The Father handed all things down to Jesus v. 22
- Only those who know Jesus know God v. 22

Luke 11

- Son of Man v. 30
- Teacher v. 1
- Prayed v. 1
- Hallowed v. 2
- His kingdom is coming v. 2
- Forgives v. 4
- Gives the Holy Spirit to those who ask Him v. 13
- Casts out a mute demon v. 14
- Cast out demons by the finger of God v. 20
- Commands obedience when forgiving a person vv. 24-26
- Blesses those who hear His word and keep it v. 28
- A sign to His generation v. 30
- Gave woes to the Pharisees and lawyers vv. 37-53
- Teacher v. 45
- Wisdom of God v. 49
- Sent prophets and apostles v. 49
- Punishes those who do not walk in the light and lead others astray v. 52

Luke 12

- LORD vv. 41, 42
- Son of Man vv. 8, 10, 40
- Many thousands gathered together to hear Him v. 1
- Warns of false teaching v. 1
- Calls people to fear He who can both destroy the body and throw the soul into hell v. 5
- Knows the number of hairs on one's head v. 7
- Acknowledges those who acknowledge the Son v. 8
- Does not forgive those who blaspheme the Holy Spirit v. 10
- Feeds the birds, and so takes care of man who is much more valuable and there is no need to worry vv. 22-34
- It is the Father's good pleasure to give the everlasting kingdom vv. 32-33
- Will destroy the unfaithful v. 46
- Expects much from whom He entrusts much v. 48

Luke 13

- LORD vv. 15, 23, 25, 35
- All who fail to repent perish v. 5
- God's graciousness and patience should not be presumed upon v. 9
- Teacher vv. 10, 22
- Freed a woman from the bonds of Satan and called out the hypocrites v. 16
- Did glorious things v. 17
- Will cast out many who seek to enter the kingdom vv. 22-30
- Gathers people as a hen gathers her brood if they are willing v. 34

Luke 14

- Healed a man of dropsy on the Sabbath, asking the hypocrites would they not pull out their son that has fallen into a well on the Sabbath? vv. 1-6
- Exalts the humble and humbles him who exalts himself v. 11
- Calls people to bless those that cannot repay them, and promises future blessing at the resurrection of the just v. 14
- His followers must love Him more than everyone and everything, even their own life v. 26
- Tells potential disciples to consider the cost of following Him v. 26

Luke 15

- Son of Man v. 11
- Receives sinners and eats with them v. 2
- Rejoices more over one that repents than ninety-nine who do not v. 7
- Rejoices over those that are made alive and are found v. 32

Luke 16

- His disciples must choose Him over money v. 13
- Knows hearts v. 15
- What is exalted among men is an abomination in the sight of God v. 15
- His laws are permanent v. 17
- Sets a great chasm from which there is no getting out or relief in Hades vv. 19-31

Luke 17

- LORD vv. 5, 6, 37
- Son of Man vv. 22, 24, 26, 30
- Looks out for His own v. 2
- Calls us to rebuke sinners but to forgive those who repent as often as they do repent vv. 1-4
- Moved by faith v. 6
- Calls everyone to be a lowly and humble worker vv. 7-10
- Jesus v. 13
- Master v. 13
- His kingdom cannot be easily recognized, but is many times in our midst v. 21
- Jesus will return like a flash of lightning v. 24
- Jesus will come back unexpectedly v. 30

Luke 18

- LORD vv. 6, 41
- Son of Man vv. 8, 31
- Told a parable to the effect that one ought to always pray and not lose heart v. 1
- Gives justice to the elect speedily who cry to Him day and night v. 7
- Looks for faith v. 8
- Exalts the humble, but humbles the proud v. 14
- Gives the kingdom only to those that receive it like children v. 17
- Teacher v. 18
- Only God is good v. 19
- What is impossible with man is possible for God v. 27
- Gives many times more than what one forsakes on earth for the sake of the kingdom of God in this life and in the age to come eternal life v. 30
- Accomplished everything written about Him by the prophets v. 31
- Jesus v. 38
- Son of David v. 38
- Moved by faith v. 42

Luke 19

- LORD vv. 8, 16, 18, 20, 25, 31, 34, 38
- Son of Man v. 10

- Stayed at the chief tax collector's house v. 5
- Jesus came to seek and save the lost v. 10
- Gives more to the faithful, and takes away from the unfaithful v. 26
- Entered into Jerusalem triumphantly vv. 28-40
- Jesus went in the name of the Lord v. 38
- King v. 38
- Teacher vv. 39, 47
- He will be praised no matter what v. 40
- Wept v. 41
- Compassion v. 41
- Prophesied v. 44
- Cleansed the temple of robbers vv. 45-46
- The people hung on His words v. 48

<u>Luke 20</u>

- LORD vv. 37, 42, 44
- Teacher v. 1
- Jesus preached the gospel to the people in the temple v. 1
- Author v. 2
- Sent ambassadors and even His own son to gather His fruit, but the tenants were wicked vv. 9-18
- Caused scribes and chief priests to marvel when He answered their questions v. 26
- Warned of hypocrites who appear to be good but have wicked hearts and will receive greater condemnation vv. 45-47
- Has His Son sit at His right hand until He makes His enemies His footstool v. 43

<u>Luke 21</u>

- Son of Man vv. 25, 27, 36
- Loves when a person gives sacrificially vv. 1-4
- Prophet vv. 5-28
- Warns of false prophets and of persecution and wars vv. 10-19
- Gives life to those of endurance v. 19
- Jesus will come a second time, with power and great glory v. 27
- Redeems v. 28
- King v. 31
- Calls us to stay ready and to pray for strength to escape all the things that are going to take place and to stand before the Son of Man v. 36
- Taught in the temple daily v. 37

<u>Luke 22</u>

- LORD vv. 14, 33, 38, 49, 61
- Son of Man vv. 22, 48, 69
- Allowed Satan to enter Judas v. 3
- Earnestly desired to eat the Passover with His apostles before He suffered v. 15
- Gave His body and blood as a worthy sacrifice for His people's sins vv. 14-23
- Interceded for Simon Peter that His faith would not fail when Satan demanded to have him vv. 31-32
- Asked the Father to take His cup from Him if He was willing, but would do the Father's will no matter what v. 42
- Betrayed and arrested vv. 47-53
- Healed His persecutor v. 51
- Allowed His Son to be mocked vv. 63-65
- Shall be seated at the right hand of the power of God v. 69
- Admitted his sovereignty v. 70

<u>Luke 23</u>

- Christ v. 2

- King v. 2
- Stirred up people v. 5
- Remained silent before ridicule v. 9
- Asked His Father to forgive the very ones that crucified Him v. 34
- Sacrificed His son v. 33
- Christ v. 39
- Took a repentant criminal with Him to paradise v. 43
- Committed his Spirit into His Father's hands v. 46

Luke 24

- LORD vv. 3, 34
- Son of Man v. 7
- Rose from the dead v. 7
- Nazarene v. 19
- Prophet mighty in deed and word before God and all people v. 19
- Interpreted all the scriptures concerning Himself v. 27
- Ate with His disciples when He had risen v. 30
- Ate broiled fish in His resurrection body v. 43
- Sends the promise of the Father upon His disciples, clothing them in power from on high v. 49
- Ascended into heaven v. 51

John 1

- LORD vv. 7, 23
- Son of Man v. 51
- Word v. 1
- Jesus was in the beginning, He was with God, and He was God v. 1
- All things were made through Jesus, and nothing was made without Him v. 3
- In Jesus is life, the light of men v. 4
- Jesus' light shines in darkness, and the darkness has not overcome it v. 5
- Sent prophets to bear witness about the light v. 7
- The true light, which gives light to everyone, came into the world v. 9
- Jesus was in the world, and the world was made through Him, but didn't know Him v. 10
- He came to His own people, and they did not receive Him v. 11
- All who receive Jesus are given the right to become children of God v. 12
- His children are born not of blood nor the will of man, but of God v. 13
- Jesus became flesh and dwelt among us, allowing man to see His glory, glory as of the only Son of the Father, full of grace and truth v. 14
- From Christ's fullness we have all received grace upon grace v. 16
- God gave the law through Moses; grace and truth He brought to us Himself through Jesus Christ v. 17
- Nobody has ever seen God; the only God, who is at the Father's side, He has made Him known v. 18
- Prophet v. 21
- Lamb of God vv. 29, 36
- Takes away the sin of the world v. 29
- The Spirit descended like a dove from heaven onto Jesus v. 32
- Baptizes with the Holy Spirit v. 33
- Son of God v. 34
- Renamed Simon Peter, meaning rock v. 42
- Called Philip and Nathanael vv. 43-51
- Jesus of Nazareth v. 45
- Son of God v. 49
- Rabbi v. 49
- King of Israel v. 49
- Prophet v. 50

John 2

- Turned water into wine v. 9
- Manifested His glory v. 11
- Drove out money changers, pouring out coins and overturning their tables v. 15
- Prophesied v. 22
- Did signs, and many believed in His name v. 23
- Knows what is in man v. 25

John 3

- Son of Man vv. 3, 14
- Rabbi v. 2
- A teacher from God v. 2
- Only born again men can enter the kingdom of God v. 5
- Spirit v. 8
- Ascended into heaven v. 13
- Whoever believes in Him may have eternal life v. 15
- God so loved the world that He gave His only Son, that whoever believes in Him should not perish but have eternal life v. 16
- God did not send Jesus to condemn the world, but in order that the world might be saved through Him v. 17
- Whoever believes in Jesus is not condemned, but whoever does not believe in Him is already condemned since he has not believed in the name of God's only Son v. 18
- Carries His work out through men v. 21
- Came from above and is above all v. 31
- True v. 33
- He who is sent from God utters the words of God, for He gives the Spirit without measure v. 34
- The Father loves the Son and has given all things into His hand v. 35
- Whoever believes in the Son has eternal life; whoever does not obey the Son shall not see life, but the wrath of God remains on him v. 36

John 4

- Son of Man v. 47
- Jesus' disciples were baptizing more disciples than John v. 1
- Wearied v. 6
- Gives gifts v. 10
- Gives living water v. 10
- Gives "water" that quenches thirst v. 14
- Prophet v. 18
- The Father is seeking people to worship Him in spirit and truth v. 23
- God is spirit, so must be worshiped in spirit and truth v. 24
- Christ v. 25
- Jesus' food is to do the will of the Father, who sent Him to accomplish His work v. 34
- The one who "reaps" is receiving eternal wages v. 36
- Samaritans believed in Him because of His word v. 41
- Savior of the world v. 42
- Healed an official's son in Galilee vv. 53-54

John 5

- Son of Man v. 27
- Healed and invalid v. 8
- Called a man to sin no more lest something worse come upon Him v. 14
- Jesus, in calling God His Father, claims equality with God v. 17
- Jesus can do nothing except what He sees the Father doing, for whatever the Father does He does v. 19

- The Father loves the Son and shows Him all that He Himself is doing v. 20
- The Son raises the dead as He wills just as the Father does v. 21
- The Father leaves all the judging to the Son v. 22
- Desires the Son to be honored as He is honored v. 23
- Whoever hears Jesus' word and believes the Father has eternal life. He does not come into judgment, but has passed from death to life v. 24
- Son of God v. 25
- The dead hear Jesus' voice and live v. 25
- Has life in Himself v. 26
- Gave Jesus authority to execute judgment v. 27
- All will face either life or judgment from the Son v. 29
- Jesus only does as the Father wills v. 30
- The Father bears witness of Jesus, making His testimony true v. 31
- Jesus' testimony is greater than John's v. 36
- The Father's word abides in those who believe in Jesus v. 38
- The Scriptures bear witness about Jesus, in whom there is eternal life v. 39

<u>John 6</u>

- Son of Man vv. 27, 53, 62
- LORD vv. 23, 68
- Followed by a large crowd since they saw His miracles v. 2
- Fed five thousand vv. 1-15
- Prophet v. 14
- Withdrew by Himself v. 15
- Walked on water v. 19
- Rabbi v. 25
- God the Father v. 27
- God's work is that we believe in Jesus v. 29
- Whoever believes in Him will never hunger or thirst v. 35
- Whoever comes to and believes in the Son will never be cast out, but will have eternal life and will be raised up on the last day vv. 37-40
- Living bread that came down from heaven v. 51
- Whoever feeds on His flesh and drinks His blood abides in Christ and Christ abides in him, and he shall live forever vv. 52-59
- The Spirit gives life; the flesh is no help at all v. 63
- Jesus knew that Judas was going to betray Him v. 71

<u>John 7</u>

- Went to the Feast of Booths secretly v. 10
- Jesus' teaching was not from studying but from God, in whom there is no falsehood vv. 15-18
- Teacher v. 14
- Jesus came from God who sent Him v. 28
- Scripture v. 38
- Called the thirsty to believe in Him that they may have rivers of living water in their heart by the Spirit vv. 37-39

<u>John 8</u>

- Son of Man vv. 28
- LORD v. 11
- Teacher v. 5
- Light of the world, whoever follows Him will not walk in darkness, but will have the light of life v. 12

- Jesus knew where He came from and where He was going v. 14
- From above v. 23
- All die for their sins except ones that Jesus died for them v. 24
- Jesus heard from the Father v. 26
- Jesus only spoke with the Father's authority v. 28
- With those that please Him v. 29
- Many believed Jesus as He spoke v. 30
- Those who abide in His word will know the truth, and the truth will set them free vv. 31-32
- Whoever the Son frees is free indeed v. 36
- Told truths that He heard from God v. 40
- Those who love God love Jesus v. 42
- Those who are of Him hear Him v. 47
- Jesus honors the Father v. 49
- One v. 50
- All who keep His word live v. 51
- The Father glorifies Jesus v. 54
- Jesus knows God and keeps His word v. 55
- "Before Abraham was, I am." v. 58

John 9

- Son of Man v. 35
- LORD v. 38
- Rabbi v. 2
- Jesus is the light of the world v. 5
- Gave a blind man sight v. 11
- Listens to those who do His will and worship Him v. 31
- Came into the world to give sight to the blind and to blind those that see v. 39

John 10

- His sheep hear His voice and follow Him as He calls them by name v. 4
- Door. All who enter by Him are saved v. 7
- The good shepherd, who laid down His life for His sheep v. 11
- God has one flock, and He is the only shepherd v. 16
- Laid down His life that He may take it up again, and the Father loves Him for it v. 17
- No one takes His life, but He gives it freely v. 18
- The gospel is the will of the Father v. 18
- His works bear witness about Him, but only His sheep believe Him v. 25
- His sheep hear His voice, and He knows them, and they follow Him v. 27
- He gives His sheep eternal life, and they will never perish, and no one will snatch them from His hand v. 28
- The Father, who is greater than all, gave Jesus His sheep and no one can snatch them out of His hand v. 29
- Jesus and the Father are one v. 30
- Showed many good works from the Father v. 32

John 11

- Son of Man vv. 2, 3, 12, 21, 27, 32, 34, 39
- Loves vv. 3, 5
- Rabbi v. 8
- Walked in the light in obedience to the Father v. 9
- Whatever Jesus asks for His Father gives to Him v. 22
- The resurrection and the life v. 24
- Whoever believes in Jesus, though he die, yet he shall live v. 25

- Everyone who lives and believes in Jesus shall never die v. 26
- The Christ v. 27
- Son of God v. 27
- Teacher v. 28
- Jesus wept v. 35
- Those who believe will see the glory of God v. 40
- The Father hears Jesus v. 41
- Sent His Son v. 42
- Raised Lazarus from the dead v. 43
- Jesus died for His nation and all the children of God scattered abroad vv. 51-52

John 12

- LORD vv. 13, 23, 38
- Son of Man vv. 27, 34
- Came in His own name v. 13
- King of Israel v. 13
- Rode into Zion on a donkey's colt v. 15
- Fulfilled prophecies v. 16
- The world has gone after Him v. 19
- Greeks sought after Jesus v. 20
- Glorified v. 23
- Speaks truth v. 24
- Honors those who serve Jesus v. 26
- His soul was troubled v. 27
- Came to be a sacrifice v. 27
- Jesus came to glorify His Father's name v. 28
- He has glorified His name v. 28
- Light v. 35
- Those who walk in the Light become sons of light v. 36
- Fulfilled Isaiah's prophecies v. 38
- Hardens hearts v. 40
- Heals those that understand and turn to Him v. 40
- His glory is greater than that of man v. 43
- Whoever believes in Jesus believes in God who sent Him v. 44
- Whoever sees Jesus sees God v. 45
- Came into the world as light, so that whoever believes in Him may not remain in darkness v. 46
- Came to save the world, not judge it, but those who reject Him and do not keep His words have a Judge and His word will judge them on the last day vv. 47-48
- Jesus came to earth by God's authority, which He adhered to and walked in v. 49
- His commandment is eternal life v. 50

John 13

- LORD vv. 6, 9, 13, 14, 25, 36, 37
- Son of Man v. 31
- Jesus departed to His Father as He knew He would v. 1
- He loved His own who were in the world to the end v. 1
- God put all things into Jesus' hands v. 3
- Unless Christ cleans a person, they have no share with Him v. 8
- Teacher v. 13
- Lord v. 13
- Whoever receives the one He sends receives Him v. 20
- Troubled in His spirit v. 21
- Jesus is glorified and God is glorified in Him v. 31
- Commanded His disciples to love one another v. 34
- Prophet v. 38

John 14

- LORD vv. 5, 8, 22
- There are many rooms in the Father's house, and Jesus prepares a place for His people v. 2

- He will come and take His people to Himself v. 3
- The Way v. 6
- The Truth v. 6
- The Life v. 6
- No one comes to the Father except through Jesus v. 6
- Whoever knows Jesus knows the Father v. 7
- Christ and the Father are in one another v. 10
- Whoever believes in Jesus will also do the works that He does, greater works even v. 12
- He does whatever is asked in His name, that the Father may be glorified in the Son v. 13
- He will do anything asked in His name v. 14
- Those who love Him keep His commandments v. 15
- Helper vv. 16, 26
- Jesus promises the Holy Spirit forever to those who love Him v. 16
- He even gives the Spirit of truth, whom the world cannot receive because it neither sees nor knows Him v. 17
- Jesus did not leave His people as orphans v. 18
- His people see Him while the world does not v. 19
- Whoever loves Jesus keeps His word, and the Father will love him and God will make their home in him v. 23
- Whoever does not love Him does not keep His words, which are the Father's words v. 24
- The Helper, the Holy Spirit, whom the Father sends in Jesus' name, will teach His disciples all things and bring everything He has said to remembrance v. 26
- Gives peace, and calls us to not be afraid v. 27
- Prophet v. 29
- The Devil has no claim on Christ v. 30
- Jesus did as the Father willed that the world would know that Jesus loves the Father v. 31

John 15

- The true vine, of which the Father is the vinedresser v. 1
- He takes away every branch that does not bear fruit v. 2
- Every branch that does bear fruit He prunes to make it even more fruitful v. 2
- Only those that abide in Christ can bear fruit v. 4
- Jesus is the vine, and nobody can bear fruit apart from the vine v. 5
- Destroys all that are not in Jesus v. 6
- Does whatever they ask who abide in Him and He in them v. 7
- The Father is glorified by the fruit produced by those who abide in Jesus v. 8
- Loves His people as the Father has loved Him, and they are to abide in His love v. 9
- Keeping His commandments is abiding in His love v. 10
- He spoke for our joy, and that our joy may be full v. 11
- Commands that we love one another as He has loved us v. 12
- Makes His disciples His friends, and He makes all things known to His friends v. 15

- His people did not choose Him, but He chose them and appointed them that they should go bear fruit and give to them whatever they ask in His name v. 16
- Commands that we will love one another v. 17
- The world hates Jesus v. 18
- The world hates His people because He chose them out of the world v. 19
- The world persecutes His people, because they do not know God vv. 20-21
- Hated by the world without cause v. 25
- Sends the Helper from the Father, the Spirit of truth, who will bear witness about Christ v. 26
- His people will bear witness about Him v. 27

<u>John 16</u>

- Prophet v. 4
- His people will be killed v. 2
- Jesus left for the good of His people, sending the Spirit of truth that speaks from the Father, glorifying Jesus vv. 4-15
- His people's sorrow will turn to joy v. 20
- No one will take His people's joy from them v. 22
- Gives everything that one asks for in His name v. 24
- The Father loves those who love Jesus and know He is from God v. 27
- He came into the world and went back to the Father v. 28
- The Father is with Jesus v. 32
- He has overcome the world so those that belong to Him can take heart v. 33

<u>John 17</u>

- Prayed v. 1
- Eternal life is knowing God and His Son v. 3
- Jesus accomplished the work set before Him to do v. 4
- With God since before the world existed v. 5
- Came from God v. 8
- Prays for His people v. 9
- Desires His people to be one, and none shall be lost v. 11
- Jesus is one with the Father v. 11
- Not of the world v. 14
- His people are not of the world, though they are in the world v. 14
- Asks that the Father keeps His people from the evil one v. 15
- Sends His people into the world, but sanctifies them in truth vv. 16-17
- Gave His glory to His people, making them perfectly one vv. 21-22
- Jesus knows the Father, and He makes His people know the Father, that the love of God will be in them v. 26

<u>John 18</u>

- Often met with His disciples in the garden v. 2
- Allowed Himself to be betrayed and arrested vv. 1-11
- Lost not one of His people v. 9
- Jesus drank the cup that His Father gave to Him v. 11
- Spoke openly to the world, saying nothing in secret v. 20
- His kingdom is not of this world v. 36
- Came into the world to bear witness to the truth v. 37
- King of the Jews v. 39

John 19

- Allowed His Son to be crucified v.16
- Son of God v. 7
- Bore His own cross v. 17
- Jesus of Nazareth v. 19
- The King of the Jews v. 21
- Fulfills His word v. 24
- Died, giving up His spirit vv. 30, 36, 37
- Buried in a tomb v. 42

John 20

- LORD v. 2, 13, 18, 20, 25, 28
- Resurrected from the dead vv. 1-10
- Appeared to Mary v. 14
- Rabboni v. 16
- Father v. 17
- God v. 17
- Brother v. 17
- Appeared to His disciples v. 19
- Holy Spirit v. 22
- Locked doors cannot keep Jesus out v. 26
- God v. 28
- The Christ, the Son of God v. 31
- Whoever believes in Jesus may have eternal life v. 31

John 21

- LORD vv. 7, 12, 15, 16, 17, 20, 21
- Revealed Himself to seven disciples (third time to reveal Himself to His disciples) vv. 1-2
- Ate fish in His resurrected body v. 13
- Calls each individual to follow Him as an individual v. 22
- The world could not hold all of the recordings of the things Jesus did v. 25

Acts 1

- LORD vv. 6, 21, 24
- Jesus worked and taught v. 1
- Gave commands through the Holy Spirit to the apostles He chose v. 2
- Presented Himself alive after His suffering by many proofs, appearing to them during forty days and speaking about the kingdom of God v. 3
- Had His disciples stay in Jerusalem until the baptism of the Holy Spirit v. 5
- The times and seasons the Father has fixed by His own authority are for Him to know v. 7
- Those whom the Spirit comes upon receive power, and they are His witnesses to their people, their enemies, and to the whole world v. 8
- Ascended v. 9
- Jesus will come in the same way that He went into heaven v. 11
- Scripture v. 16
- As the Holy Spirit spoke by the mouth of David, so Judas' office was replaced v. 20
- Lord Jesus v. 21

Acts 2

- LORD vv. 34, 20, 21, 25, 36, 39, 47
- The Holy Spirit rushed upon the apostles like a mighty rushing wind, and they began to speak in tongues as the Spirit gave them utterance vv. 1-4
- The Spirit had the disciples speak to the multitude at Pentecost to those in their own language vv. 5-12
- In the last days, God will pour out His Spirit on all flesh, and people of all sorts will prophesy, see visions, and dream dreams. And He will show wonders in the heavens above and signs on the earth below, blood,

and fire, and vapor of smoke; the sun shall be turned to darkness and the moon to blood before the Lord comes the great and magnificent day. vv. 17-20

- And it shall come to pass that everyone who calls upon the name of the Lord shall be saved v. 21
- Jesus of Nazareth v. 22
- Jesus proved Himself by mighty works, wonders, and signs that God did through Him in the midst of the men of Israel v. 22
- Jesus was delivered up according to the definite plan and foreknowledge of God into the hands of lawless men to be crucified and killed v. 23
- God raised Jesus up, loosing the pangs of death, because it was not possible for Him to be held by it v. 24
- The Lord was always before Jesus v. 25
- God did not abandon Jesus' soul to Hades or let His Holy One see corruption v. 27
- God makes known the paths of life and fills with the gladness of His presence v. 28
- Raised Jesus up before many witnesses v. 32
- Jesus is exalted at the right hand of God, having received from the Father the promise of the Holy Spirit which He poured out onto His people v. 33
- God made Jesus both Lord and Christ v. 36
- Crucified by His own v. 36
- Calls many to His promise of forgiveness and the gift of the Holy Spirit vv. 38-39
- Saves three thousand souls, adding them to His family v. 41
- Causes awe among believers v. 42
- His Spirit endorses generosity, fellowship, praise, and increase vv. 45-47

<u>Acts 3</u>

- LORD vv. 20, 22
- Jesus Christ of Nazareth v. 6
- Heals through men v. 6
- God of Abraham, Isaac, and Jacob v. 13
- Servant v. 13
- Holy and Righteous One v. 14
- Author of life v. 15
- Raised Jesus from the dead v. 15
- Faith through Jesus gave a man perfect health in the sight of many v. 16
- Foretold Christ's suffering through the mouth of prophets v. 18
- Forgives those that repent and turn back from their sins, allowing them to be blotted out and times of refreshing may come from the presence of the Lord vv. 19-20
- Lord God v. 22
- Destroys all that do not listen to Jesus v. 23
- Made a covenant with mankind v. 25
- Raised Jesus from the dead to bless us by turning us from our wickedness v. 26

<u>Acts 4</u>

- LORD vv. 24, 26, 29, 33
- Saves five thousand souls, which heard the gospel and believed v. 4
- The Holy Spirit filled Peter v. 8

- Jesus Christ of Nazareth v. 10
- Salvation is in Christ alone, for there is no other name under heaven given among men by which we must be saved v. 12
- Jesus v. 13
- Sovereign Lord v. 24
- Made the heaven and the earth and the sea and everything in them v. 24
- Anointed v. 26
- It is pointless to plot against Him v. 25
- Jesus, God's holy and anointed servant v. 27
- His hand predestined all that takes place v. 28
- Looks v. 29
- Grants His servants to speak His word with all boldness, while He stretches out His hand to heal, and signs and wonders are performed through the name of Jesus v. 30
- Shook the place in which believers prayed, filling them all with the Holy Spirit, giving them boldness to continue to boldly speak the word of God v. 31
- His people have everything in common, and His great grace is upon us all, and there is no one needy vv. 32-37

Acts 5

- LORD vv. 9, 14, 19
- Killed Ananias and Sapphira for lying to Him and testing His Spirit about the proceeds of the land they sold and brought before the feet of the apostles vv. 1-11
- Added many believers to His kingdom as He performed many signs and wonders among the people by the hands of the apostles vv. 12-16
- Freed the apostles from prison supernaturally, and had them continue to teach His word vv. 17-21
- Life v. 20
- Raised Jesus v. 30
- Gives the Holy Spirit to those who obey Him v. 32
- Leader v. 31
- Savior v. 31
- His plans cannot be overtaken v. 39
- The Christ is Jesus v. 42

Acts 6

- Spirit vv. 3, 10
- Holy Spirit v. 5
- The word of God continues to increase, with the number of disciples multiplying and many priests becoming obedient to the faith v. 7
- Jesus of Nazareth v. 14

Acts 7

- LORD vv. 31, 33, 49, 59, 60
- God of glory v. 2
- Appeared to Abraham v. 2
- Promises v. 5
- Judges v. 7
- Gave the covenant of circumcision v. 8
- God was with Joseph as he was put in the worst of circumstances v. 9
- Rescues v. 10
- Gives favor and wisdom v. 10
- God of Abraham and of Isaac and of Jacob v. 32
- Performed signs and wonders through Moses v. 36
- The Most High does not dwell in houses made by hands v. 48
- Holy Spirit vv. 51, 55
- Righteous One v. 52
- Glorious v. 55

- Jesus stands at the right hand of God v. 56

Acts 8

- LORD vv. 16, 22, 24, 25, 26, 39
- Proclaimed by persecuted and scattered believers vv. 4-5
- Jesus Christ v. 12
- Has good news for everyone v. 12
- Holy Spirit (given to believers) vv. 15, 17, 19
- Lord Jesus v. 16
- The gift of God cannot be bought with money v. 20
- His Spirit speaks to believers v. 29
- Spirit of the Lord carried Philip away after baptizing an Ethiopian eunuch v. 39

Acts 9

- LORD vv. 1, 5, 10, 11, 13, 15, 17, 27, 28, 31, 35, 42
- The Way v. 2
- Personally encountered Saul vv. 1-9
- Blinded Saul for three days v. 9
- Lord Jesus v. 17
- The Holy Spirit filled Saul v. 17
- Jesus is the Son of God v. 20
- Jesus is the Christ v. 22
- His people are family v. 30
- His church multiplied as they walked in the fear of the Lord and the comfort of the Holy Spirit v. 31
- Jesus Christ healed a man bedridden for eight years through Peter, and all the residents of Lydda and Sharon turned to the Lord when they saw the man vv. 32-35
- Restored Tabitha to life v. 41

Acts 10

- LORD vv. 4, 14, 33, 36
- Sent an angel to a devout centurion v. 3
- Made all animals clean and good for eating v. 14
- The Spirit spoke to Peter v. 19
- Accepts anyone from any nation who fears Him and does what is right v. 35
- Jesus Christ v. 36
- Lord of all v. 36
- Anointed Jesus of Nazareth with the Holy Spirit and with power to do good and heal all who were oppressed by the devil v. 38
- Raised Jesus from the dead on the third day and made Him appear to witnesses v. 40
- Jesus was appointed by God to be judge of the living and the dead v. 42
- All the prophets bear witness that everyone who believes in Him receives forgiveness of sins through Jesus' name v. 43
- The Holy Spirit fell on all who heard Peter preach the Gospel (Gentiles) vv. 44-45

Acts 11

- LORD vv. 8, 16, 17, 20, 21, 23, 24
- God has granted to Jews and to Gentiles repentance that leads to life v. 18

Acts 12

- LORD vv. 7, 11, 17, 23
- Freed Peter from prison by an angel He sent v. 11
- Struck down Herod for not giving glory to God v. 23

Acts 13

- LORD vv. 2, 10, 11, 12, 44, 47, 48, 49
- The Holy Spirit spoke to prophets and teachers while they worshipped Him and fasted v. 2

- Sent out Barnabas and Saul by the Holy Spirit v. 4
- Filled Paul with His Spirit and opposed a magician, a "son of the devil," and blinded him for a time vv. 8-12
- God of Israel v. 17
- Brought Israel a Savior, Jesus, as He promised v. 23
- Raised Jesus from the dead v. 30
- Fulfilled His promise by raising Jesus v. 33
- Jesus was begotten from God v. 33
- Holy One v. 35
- Jesus did not see corruption v. 37
- By Jesus everyone who believes is freed from everything that obeying the law cannot free one from v. 39
- Gracious v. 43
- Fills faithful disciples with joy and the Holy Spirit v. 52

<u>Acts 14</u>

- LORD vv. 3, 23
- Bears witness to the word of His grace, granting signs and wonders to be done by the hands of His messengers v. 3
- Living v. 15
- Made the heavens and the earth and the sea and all that is in them v. 15
- Opened a door of faith among the Gentiles v. 27

<u>Acts 15</u>

- LORD vv. 11, 17, 26, 35, 36, 40
- Saves people by grace, not by works v. 11
- Did signs and wonders among the Gentiles v. 12
- Lord Jesus Christ v. 26
- Holy Spirit v. 28
- Raises up prophets, such as Judas and Silas, to encourage and strengthen other believers v. 32

<u>Acts 16</u>

- LORD vv. 14, 15, 31, 32
- Holy Spirit v. 6
- Forbids v. 6
- Spirit of Jesus v. 7
- Opened up a woman's heart to hear and believe the gospel vv. 11-15
- Most High God v. 17
- Saves all who believe in the Lord Jesus v. 31

<u>Acts 17</u>

- LORD v. 24
- Jesus is the Christ v. 3
- Uses men to turned the world upside down v. 6
- Jesus was resurrected v. 18
- Made the world and everything in it v. 24
- Lord of heaven and earth v. 24
- Does not live in temples made by man v. 24
- Not served by human hands v. 25
- Needs nothing from mankind, for He is the one that gives us all breath and life and everything v. 25
- Made every nation from one man to live on all the face of the earth v. 26
- Determines the allotted periods and places mankind lives v. 26
- Not far from each one of us, for in Him we live and move and have our being v. 28
- We are His offspring v. 28
- Divine, rather than something manmade v. 29
- Overlooked ignorance, but now commands all people to repent v. 30

- Fixed a day on which He will judge the world in righteousness by a man whom He has appointed (and He has assured us of this man by raising Him from the dead) v. 31

<u>Acts 18</u>

- LORD vv. 8, 9, 25
- Jesus is Christ v. 5
- Wills v. 21
- The Christ is Jesus v. 28

<u>Acts 19</u>

- LORD vv. 5, 10, 13, 17, 20
- Holy Spirit v. 2
- Lord Jesus v. 5
- Jesus came after John the Baptist, with a baptism not just of repentance but of the Holy Spirit v. 4
- The Way v. 9
- Did extraordinary miracles by the hands of Paul v. 11
- His word continues to increase and prevail mightily v. 20
- Spirit v. 21
- The Way v. 23

<u>Acts 20</u>

- LORD vv. 19, 21, 24, 35
- Raised Eutychus from the dead through Paul v. 10
- Lord Jesus Christ v. 21
- Constrains v. 22
- Spirit v. 22
- The Holy Spirit testifies truths and mysteries in believers v. 23
- The Lord Jesus calls believers to certain paths and ministries v. 24
- The Holy Spirit makes overseers of the flock, to care for the church that He purchased with His own blood v. 28
- God, and the word of his grace, is able to give us the inheritance of the sanctified v. 32
- Jesus helped the weak and taught that, "It is more blessed to give than to receive." v. 35

<u>Acts 21</u>

- LORD vv. 13, 14
- The Spirit spoke through people to tell Paul to not go to Jerusalem v. 4
- Raises up prophets and evangelists vv. 8-9
- Holy Spirit v. 11
- God worked among the Gentiles through Paul's ministry v. 19

<u>Acts 22</u>

- LORD vv. 8, 10, 19
- Way v. 4
- Powerfully encountered Paul v. 6
- Speaks v. 7
- Jesus of Nazareth v. 8
- Allows persecution against Himself v. 8
- Living v. 8
- The Righteous One v. 14
- Both shows and makes Himself heard v. 14
- Calls up witnesses and has them baptized and washes away the sins of those who call upon His name vv. 15-16
- Sent Paul far away to the Gentiles v. 21

<u>Acts 23</u>

- LORD v. 11
- Stood by Paul and said, "Take courage, for as you have testified to the facts about me in Jerusalem, so you must testify also in Rome." v. 11
- Delivered Paul's life vv. 12-35

<u>Acts 24</u>

- Turns the world upside down v. 5
- The Way vv. 14, 22
- Known by governors v. 22
- Christ Jesus v. 24

Acts 25
- LORD v. 26
- Took Paul before great rulers of His time vv. 1-27

Acts 26
- LORD v. 15
- Promises hope to His people v. 6
- Raises the dead v. 8
- Jesus of Nazareth v. 9
- Makes new creations v. 11
- Opens eyes, that people may "turn from darkness to light and from the power of Satan to God, that they may receive forgiveness of sins and a place among those who are sanctified by faith in me" v. 18
- Gives heavenly visions v. 19
- Helps v. 22
- Proclaims light to the world v. 23
- There is no law against God's purposes v. 32

Acts 27
- Saved 276 persons from perishing by shipwreck vv. 13-44

Acts 28
- LORD v. 31
- Justice v. 4
- Saved Paul from a viper bite v. 6
- Healed many through Paul, through laying his hands on them v. 9
- The Holy Spirit spoke truths through the prophet Isaiah v. 25
- Would heal those that hear and see and turn to Him v. 27
- His salvation is sent to the Gentiles v. 28
- Lord Jesus Christ v. 30

Romans 1
- LORD vv. 4, 7
- Christ Jesus v. 1
- Calls v. 1
- Sets apart people for His gospel v. 1
- Son vv. 2, 9
- Promises through prophecies v. 2
- Descended from David v. 3
- Became flesh v. 3
- Declared to be Son of God in power according to the Spirit of holiness by His resurrection from the dead v. 4
- Jesus Christ vv. 4, 6, 8
- Gives grace and apostleship to bring about the obedience of faith for the sake of His name among the nations v. 5
- Calls those who belong to His Son v. 6
- Loves v. 7
- Calls saints v. 7
- Grace and peace comes from the Father and the Lord Jesus Christ v. 7
- God v. 8
- Witnesses v. 9
- The gospel is the power of God for salvation to everyone who believes v. 16
- In the gospel the righteousness of God is revealed from faith for faith as the righteous live by faith v. 17
- His righteousness is revealed by faith v. 17
- His wrath is revealed from heaven against all ungodliness and unrighteousness of men, who suppress the truth by their unrighteousness v. 18
- Everyone knows about God's eternal power and divine nature by general revelation, so men are without excuse v. 20
- Immortal v. 23
- Glorious v. 23

- Gave men up in the lusts of their hearts to impurity, to dishonorable passions, and to a debased mind vv. 24-30
- Creator v. 25
- Blessed forever v. 25
- Just v. 27
- Demands acknowledgement v. 28
- Gives righteous decrees v. 32

Romans 2

- Judges rightly v. 2
- His rich kindness, forbearance, and patience is meant to lead us to repentance v. 4
- Will reveal His righteous judgment on the day of wrath v. 5
- Renders to each one according to His works v. 6
- Gives eternal life to those to those who by patience in well-doing seek for glory and honor and immortality v. 7
- Gives wrath and fury to those who are self-seeking and obey unrighteousness rather than truth v. 8
- Gives tribulation and distress for every human being who does evil v. 9
- Gives glory and honor and peace to everyone who does good v. 10
- Shows no partiality v. 11
- Justifies the doers of His law v. 13
- Writes the law on our hearts, to which our conscience bears witness v. 15
- Judges the secrets of men by Christ Jesus v. 16
- Circumcises hearts by the Spirit v. 29
- Praises the spiritually circumcised v. 29

Romans 3

- Entrusted the Jews with His oracles v. 2
- God is true no matter how much men lie v. 4
- Faithful in spite of our unfaithfulness v. 3
- Justified in His words, prevailing when He is judged v. 4
- Our unrighteousness serves to show the righteousness of God v. 5
- Incomprehensible v. 11
- Unsearchable v. 11
- The whole world is accountable to God v. 19
- No human being is justified in His sight through works; rather, through the law we have knowledge of our disobedience to God v. 20
- His righteousness has been shown apart from the law through faith in Jesus Christ in believers vv. 21-22
- Freely gives justification by His grace as a gift through the redemption that is in Jesus Christ v. 24
- Brought peace to mankind by the blood of His Son to be received by faith v. 25
- Passed over former sins by His divine forbearance v. 25
- He is just and the justifier of the one who has faith in Jesus v. 26
- Excludes boasting by the law of faith v. 27
- Justifies one by faith apart from works of the law v. 28
- One v. 30
- Justifies all through faith v. 30

Romans 4

- LORD vv. 8, 24
- Counted Abraham's faith as righteousness v. 3
- Counts faith in Christ's works alone as righteousness v. 5

- Blesses His children by counting them righteous apart from their deeds since all have sinned vv. 6-8
- God's promises of blessing come through the righteousness of faith v. 13
- His promise rests on grace by faith v. 16
- Gives life to the dead and calls into existence things that do not exist v. 17
- Spoke to Abraham v. 18
- His children grow strong in their faith as they give glory to God v. 20
- God is able to do as He promises v. 21
- When we believe God, we are counted as righteous v. 24
- Raised Jesus from the dead v. 24
- Delivered up for our trespasses and raised for our justification v. 25

Romans 5

- LORD vv. 1, 11, 21
- Justifies His people by faith, creating peace with Himself through the Lord Jesus Christ v. 1
- Through Christ we have obtained access by faith into His grace in which we stand, and we rejoice in hope of the glory of God v. 3
- His love has been poured into our hearts through the Holy Spirit that He gives to believers v. 5
- Christ died for the ungodly while we were still weak v. 6
- He died for sinners v. 8
- Justifies people by His blood and saves them from the wrath of God v. 9
- Reconciled His enemies to Himself by the death of His Son, and saved them by His life v. 10
- Believers rejoice in God through their Lord Jesus Christ, through whom they have received reconciliation v. 11
- God's free gift of grace abounds for many, eclipsing the death that entered the world through Adam's trespass v. 15
- His free gift justifies where Adam's sin condemns v. 16
- The abundance of grace and the free gift of righteousness reign in life through one man, Jesus Christ v. 17
- As one trespass led to condemnation for all men, so one act of righteousness leads to justification and life for all men v. 18
- As by one man's disobedience many were made sinners, so by one man's obedience many were made righteous v. 19
- Gave the law to increase the trespass, but where sin increased, His grace abounded all the more v. 20
- As sin reigns in death, grace also might reign through righteousness leading to eternal life through Jesus Christ our Lord v. 21

Romans 6

- LORD v. 23
- As Christ died and was raised to newness of life, His people have died and walk in newness of life vv. 1-4
- His followers are united with Him in His death and resurrection v. 5
- Frees believers from the slavery of sin v. 6
- Raised from the dead never to die again; death no longer has dominion over Him v. 9

- Those who believe in Jesus are alive to Him v. 11
- Brings the dead to life, that they might present their members to Him as instruments of righteousness v. 13
- Sets sinners free v. 18
- The wages of sin is death, but the free gift of God is eternal life in Christ Jesus our Lord v. 23

Romans 7

- LORD v. 25
- His law is only binding on the living v. 1
- His law is not binding on those who have died in Christ v. 4
- His Spirit is a new way of life for believers v. 6
- His law is holy, and the commandment is holy and righteous and good v. 12
- His law reveals sin to be sin v. 13
- Thanks is owed to God through Jesus Christ the Lord v. 25
- The living presence of Jesus Christ is the answer to man's problem of sin vv. 24-25

Romans 8

- LORD v. 39
- There is no condemnation for those who are in Christ Jesus v. 1
- The law of the Spirit of life has set believers free in Christ Jesus from the law of sin and death v. 2
- God did what the law, weakened by the flesh, could not do v. 3
- He condemned sin in the flesh by sending His own Son in the likeness of sinful flesh, in order that the righteous requirement of the law might be fulfilled by us who walk according to the Spirit and not the flesh vv. 3-4
- Setting one's mind on the Spirit is life and peace v. 6
- The mind set on the flesh is hostile to God, for it cannot not submit to God's law v. 7
- Those that are in the flesh cannot please God v. 8
- Those whom the Spirit dwells in are not in the flesh v. 9
- Anyone who does not have the Spirit of Christ does not belong to Him v. 9
- Though the body is dead because of sin, the Spirit is life because of righteousness v. 10
- If the Spirit of Him who raised Jesus from the dead dwells in a person, He who raised Christ Jesus from the dead will also give life to their mortal bodies through His indwelling Spirit v. 11
- Those who live by His Spirit live v. 13
- All who are led by the Spirit of God are sons of God v. 14
- Gives His Spirit of adoption as sons v. 15
- Abba v. 15
- Father v. 15
- The Spirit Himself bears witness with a believer's spirit that they are children of God v. 16
- His children are heirs with Christ, provided they suffer with Him in order that they may also be glorified with Him v. 17
- The sufferings of the present do not compare with the future glory that God is going to reveal in His people v. 18

- Creation waits eagerly for the revealing of the sons of God v. 19
- His whole creation groans together with the pains of childbirth under the bondage of corruption v. 22
- His people, who have the firstfruits of the Spirit, groan inwardly as they wait eagerly for adoption as sons, the redemption of their bodies v. 23
- The Spirit helps His people in their weakness v. 26
- The Spirit Himself intercedes for His people with groaning too deep for words and according to the will of God v. 26
- Searches hearts v. 27
- Causes all things to work together for good for those who love God and are called according to His purpose v. 28
- Those whom He foreknew He also predestined to be conformed to the image of His Son, in order that they might be the firstborn among many brothers v. 29
- Those whom He predestined He also called, and those whom He called He also justified, and those whom He justified He also glorified v. 30
- Graciously gives all things to His children, for He did not spare His own Son but gave Him up for them v. 32
- Those whom He justified cannot be condemned v. 33
- Christ died and was raised and sits at the right hand of God interceding for His chosen v. 34
- Nothing and nobody can separate the love of Christ from believers v. 35
- Those whom He loves are more than conquerors v. 37
- Nothing in all of creation can separate His people from His love in Christ Jesus their Lord v. 39

<u>Romans 9</u>

- LORD vv. 28, 29
- Christ v. 1
- Holy Spirit v. 1
- His adoption, glory, the covenants, the giving of the law, the worship, and the promises belong to His chosen people v. 4
- Christ came out of the race of the Israelites v. 5
- Christ is God over all v. 5
- Blessed forever v. 5
- Unfailing v. 6
- The children of promise are counted as His offspring v. 8
- His purpose of election is not dependent on works v. 11
- Has mercy on whom He wills, and it depends not on human will or exertion, but on Himself alone v. 16
- Hardens and has mercy on whomever He wills for His glory and to proclaim His name in all the earth vv. 17-18
- His will cannot be resisted v. 19
- Has the right to do as He pleases with man v. 21
- Righteousness is a gift v. 31
- Whoever does not believe in Jesus is put to shame v. 33

<u>Romans 10</u>

- LORD vv. 9, 12, 13, 16
- Knowing Christ is all it takes to be saved vv. 1-4

- Justifies believers because of what they believe in their hearts and confess with their mouths v. 10
- Everyone who believes in Jesus will not be put to shame v. 11
- Bestows riches on all that call on Him v. 12
- Everyone who calls on the name of the Lord will be saved v. 13
- Has shown Himself to people that did not ask for Him v. 20

<u>Romans 11</u>

- LORD vv. 3, 34
- Has not rejected His people v. 1
- Chosen a remnant of his people by grace v. 5
- Gives His elect His grace, but hardens others vv. 6-10
- Gives salvation to the Gentiles v. 11
- Uses jealousy to save people v. 14
- Calls His people to humbly stand fast by faith v. 20
- Severe toward the fallen and kind to those that continue in His kindness v. 22
- Grafts in people into His promise of life v. 24
- Deliverer v. 26
- Will come from Zion, He will banish ungodliness from His people v. 26
- Delivers all into disobedience that He may have mercy on all v. 32
- Deep and richly wise and knowledgeable v. 33
- His judgments are unsearchable v. 33
- His ways are inscrutable v. 33
- No one knows His mind v. 34
- Has no counselor v. 34
- Needs not repay anyone v. 35
- For Him and through Him and to Him are all things v. 36
- To Him is glory forever v. 36

<u>Romans 12</u>

- LORD vv. 11, 19
- Merciful v. 1
- Wills v. 2
- His people make up His body v. 5
- Gives a variety of gifts for His people to serve with vv. 6-8
- Commands honor, zeal, and fervency vv. 10-11

<u>Romans 13</u>

- LORD v. 14
- The only authority v. 1
- Institutes existing authorities v. 1
- Judges those who resist authority v. 2
- Rulers are His servants our good v. 4
- Authorities are His ministers v. 6
- Loving fulfills the law v. 10

<u>Romans 14</u>

- LORD vv. 4, 6, 8, 9, 11, 14
- Judge v. 4
- Lord of both the dead and the living v. 9
- All will stand before the judgment seat of God v. 10
- Every knee shall bow to Him and every tongue shall confess to God v. 11
- Everyone will give an account of themselves to God v. 12
- Lord Jesus v. 14
- Christ died v. 15
- His kingdom is a matter of righteousness and peace and joy in the Holy Spirit v. 17
- Whoever serves Christ is acceptable to God and approved by men v. 18

- Honored by faith and dishonored by lack thereof vv. 22-23

Romans 15

- LORD vv. 6, 11, 30
- Christ did not please Himself, but was reproached v. 3
- Gives hope through the endurance and encouragement of the Scriptures v. 4
- Endures v. 5
- Encourages v. 5
- Grants harmony in accord with the Lord Jesus Christ v. 6
- Christ welcomed believers for the glory of God v. 7
- Christ became a servant to the circumcised to show God's truthfulness, in order to confirm the promises given to the patriarchs, and in order that the Gentiles might glorify God for His mercy vv. 8-9
- In Him do the Gentiles hope v. 12
- God of hope v. 13
- The power of the Holy Spirit enables us to abound in hope v. 13
- Christ Jesus vv. 16, 17
- Holy Spirit v. 16
- Power v. 19
- Spirit of God v. 19
- Lord v. 30
- Jesus Christ v. 30

Romans 16

- LORD vv. 2, 8, 11, 12, 13, 18, 20, 22
- Christ Jesus v. 3
- Christ vv. 9, 10, 18
- Jesus Christ v. 27
- The God of peace will soon crush Satan under our feet v. 20
- Gracious v. 20
- Able to strengthen according to His gospel and the preaching of Jesus Christ, according to the mystery that was kept secret for long ages but has now been disclosed and through the prophetic writings has been made known to all nations, according to the command of the eternal God, to bring about the obedience of faith vv. 25-26
- The only wise God v. 27
- Forever glorious v. 27

1 Corinthians 1

- LORD vv. 2, 3, 7, 8, 9, 10, 31
- Wills v. 1
- Called Paul to be an apostle of Christ Jesus v. 1
- Sanctifies through Christ Jesus v. 2
- The Father and Son give grace and peace vv. 3, 4
- Enriches in all speech and knowledge v. 5
- Lord Jesus Christ vv. 7, 9, 10
- Sustains His people to the end, guiltless v. 8
- Faithful v. 9
- Calls believers into the fellowship of His Son v. 9
- Sent Paul to preach the gospel, and not in words of eloquent wisdom, lest the cross be emptied of its power v. 17
- The word of the cross is folly to those who are perishing, but to those that are being saved it is the power of God v. 18
- Destroys the wisdom of the wise and thwarts the discernment of the discerning v. 19
- Made foolish the wisdom of the world v. 20
- His foolishness is wiser than men and His weakness stronger v. 25

- Chose what is foolish in the world to shame the wise; He chose what is weak to shame the strong v. 27
- He chose what is low and despised and even what is not to bring to nothing the things that are v. 28
- No human being can boast in His presence v. 29
- To believers Jesus became wisdom from God, righteousness and sanctification and redemption, that one who boasts in the Lord vv. 30-31

1 Corinthians 2

- LORD vv. 8, 16
- Jesus Christ v. 2
- Spirit v. 4
- Decreed hidden wisdom before the ages of our glory v. 7
- Has prepared for those who love Him what no eye has seen, nor ear heard, nor the heart of man imagined v. 9
- Reveals mysteries through His Spirit, which searches everything, even the depths of God v. 10
- The Spirit discerns the thoughts of God v. 11
- Freely gives His Spirit to believers v. 12
- Spirit of God is revealed to and accepted by the supernatural/spiritual person vv. 14-15
- Gives the mind of Christ to believers v. 16

1 Corinthians 3

- LORD vv. 5, 20
- Gives solid food to those that are mature in Christ vv. 1-4
- Assigns servants v. 5
- Gives growth v. 6
- His people are His workers, His fields, and His buildings v. 9
- The Foundation v. 11
- Tests our work v. 13
- Believers are His temple and God's Spirit dwells in them v. 16
- Whoever destroys His temple He will destroy him, for His temple is holy v. 17
- Catches the wise in their craftiness v. 19
- Knows the thoughts of the wisdom that they are futile v. 20
- All things are believers', and they are Christ's, and Christ is God's vv. 22-23

1 Corinthians 4

- LORD vv. 4, 5, 17, 19
- Believers are servants of Christ and stewards of His mysteries v. 1
- Will bring light to things now hidden in darkness and will disclose the purposes of the heart v. 5
- Gives all things to believers vv. 7, 8
- His kingdom does not consist in talk but in power v. 20

1 Corinthians 5

- LORD vv. 4, 5
- Sexual immorality defiles His church vv. 1-13

1 Corinthians 6

- LORD vv. 11, 13, 14, 17
- The unrighteous will not inherit His kingdom v. 9
- Washes, sanctifies, and justifies in the name of the Lord Jesus Christ and by the Spirit of God v. 11
- Will raise up believers by His power as He raised Christ v. 14
- Believers' bodies are members of Christ v. 15
- A believer's body is a temple of the indwelling Holy Spirit from God, and he is not his own v. 19

- Bought each believer with a price, and they ought to glorify Him in their body v. 20

1 Corinthians 7

- LORD vv. 10, 12, 17, 22, 25, 32, 34, 35, 39
- Slaves are freedmen to Christ and freedmen are slaves to Him v. 22
- Spirit of God v. 40

1 Corinthians 8

- LORD v. 6
- If anyone loves God, he is known by God v. 3
- One vv. 4, 6
- From and for Him all things exist v. 6
- Sinning against a brother (making him stumble) is sinning against Christ v. 12

1 Corinthians 9

- LORD vv. 1, 2, 5, 14
- Freed, appointed to apostleship, and revealed Himself to Paul v. 1
- Speaks for man's sake v. 10
- Commands that those who proclaim the gospel should get their living by the gospel v. 14
- The gospel gives no ground for boasting v. 16

1 Corinthians 10

- LORD vv. 21, 22, 26
- Rock v. 4
- Made the Jewish nation an example for believers, that they might not desire evil like they did v. 6
- Destroyer v. 10
- Faithful v. 13
- Does not let one be tempted beyond his ability v. 13
- Provides escape from temptation v. 13
- His people are one body v. 17
- Believers are not under the law v. 23
- The earth is His, and the fullness thereof v. 26
- Everything is to be done for His glory v. 31

1 Corinthians 11

- LORD vv. 11, 20, 26
- Christ is the head of every man v. 3
- Created woman for man v. 9
- Judge v. 32

1 Corinthians 12

- LORD vv. 3, 5
- All who say "Jesus is Lord" say it in the Holy Spirit v. 3
- The same Spirit gives a variety of gifts v. 4
- The Lord can be served in various ways v. 5
- There are a variety of different activities, but it is the same God who empowers them all in everyone v. 6
- All believers are given a manifestation of the Spirit for the common good v. 7
- The Spirit gives utterances to people of wisdom and of knowledge; He also gives gifts of faith, healing, the working of miracles, prophecy, discernment, tongues, and interpretation of tongues vv. 8-11
- His body is one but comprises of many members v. 12
- Believers in one Spirit were all baptized into one body v. 13
- Gives great honor to those lacking v. 24

1 Corinthians 13

- Love (modeled perfectly by Christ) is patient and kind; He does not envy or boast; He is not arrogant or rude; He is not irritable or resentful; He does not rejoice at wrongdoing, but rejoices with the truth. He bears all things, hopes all things, and endures all things vv. 4-7

- He never ends v. 8
- When He comes, completion comes v. 10
- Will see His people face to face v. 12

1 Corinthians 14

- LORD vv. 21, 37
- Spirit v. 2
- Desires His church to be built up v. 5
- Not a God of confusion but of peace v. 33
- Created a general pattern of male leadership v. 34
- Gave commands through Paul v. 37
- Calls believers to desire prophesy and to not forbid speaking in tongues, so long as all things are done decently and in order vv. 39-40

1 Corinthians 15

- LORD vv. 31, 57, 58
- His gospel is preached, received, stood upon, saves, and held onto vv. 1-2
- Christ died for our sins in accordance with the Scriptures, was buried, and was raised on the third day, and appeared to the twelve and then to over five hundred brothers at one time, then to James and all the apostles and then to Paul vv. 3-8
- Graciously makes us what we are, and not in vain v. 10
- The last Adam became a life-giving spirit v. 45
- His people have borne the image of the man of dust, and shall also bear the image of the man of heaven v. 49
- Flesh and blood cannot inherit His kingdom, nor does the perishable inherit the imperishable v. 50
- In a twinkling of an eye His people shall be changed at the last trumpet v. 52
- Swallows death up in victory by putting immortality on the mortal v. 54
- Gives victory through the Lord Jesus Christ v. 57
- In the Lord labor is not in vain v. 58

1 Corinthians 16

- LORD vv. 7, 10, 19, 22, 23
- Commands watchfulness, firmness in the faith, behaving as a man, and strength v. 13
- Commands that in all things one does that it be done in love v. 14
- Desires recognition of those that refresh spirits v. 18
- His grace accompanies v. 23

2 Corinthians 1

- LORD vv. 2, 3, 14, 24
- Willed Paul to be an apostle of Jesus Christ v. 1
- Gives grace and peace v. 2
- Blessed v. 3
- Father of mercies v. 3
- God of all comfort v. 3
- Comforts His people in all their affliction, allowing them to comfort others in their afflictions with the same comfort from God v. 4
- Believers share both in His sufferings and comfort abundantly v. 5
- Lets His people know that they cannot rely on themselves, but on God who raises the dead v. 9

- Delivers from deadly peril as oft as required v. 10
- Grants blessings via the prayers of the saints v. 11
- Son of God, Jesus Christ v. 19
- All the promises of God find their Yes in Jesus v. 20
- Establishes v. 21
- Anoints v. 21
- Puts His seal on believers and gives His Spirit into their hearts as a guarantee v. 22
- 2 Corinthians 2
- LORD vv. 12
- Calls for forgiveness, that we not be outwitted by Satan vv. 5-11
- In Christ, He always leads believers in triumphal procession, and through them spreads the fragrance of the knowledge of Him everywhere v. 14
- Believers are the aroma of Christ to God among those that are being saved and among those that are perishing v. 15
- Commissions men of sincerity v. 17
- Sees v. 17

<u>2 Corinthians 3</u>

- LORD vv. 16, 17, 18
- Christ writes “letters” with the Spirit of the living God on the tablets of human hearts v. 3
- Makes believers sufficient to be ministers of the new covenant by the Spirit and not by the law v. 6
- The ministry of the Spirit has more glory than the ministry of death carved in letters on stone (which was brought to an end) vv. 7-8
- The glory of the ministry of righteousness far exceeds the glory of the ministry of condemnation v. 9
- If what was temporary came with glory, that which is permanent will have much more glory v. 11
- When one turns to the Lord, the veil is removed from before their hearts v. 16
- The Lord is the Spirit, and where the Spirit of the Lord is there is freedom v. 17
- Believers, with unveiled face, are being transformed into the same image of God from one degree of glory to another by the Lord who is the Spirit v. 18

<u>2 Corinthians 4</u>

- LORD vv. 5, 14
- Mercifully gives believers a ministry of glory v. 1
- Sees v. 2
- His gospel is veiled to those that are perishing v. 3
- Satan blinds the minds of unbelievers to keep them from seeing the gospel of the glory of Christ, who is the image of God v. 4
- Believers proclaim Him and serve for His sake v. 5
- He who raised Jesus will also raise believers with Him v. 14
- His grace extends to more and more people that it may increase thanksgiving, to His glory v. 15
- Renews the inner self of the believer day by day as their outer self wastes away v. 16
- Light momentary affliction prepares believers for His eternal weight of glory beyond all comparison v. 17

<u>2 Corinthians 5</u>

- LORD vv. 6, 11
- Builds a heavenly dwelling for believers v. 1

- Swallows up mortals with life v. 4
- Prepares by His Spirit v. 5
- Gives to all their due v. 10
- Knows His people, and teaches them fear v. 11
- The love of Christ controls believers v. 14
- Died for all, that those who live might no longer live for themselves but for Him who for their sake died and was raised v. 15
- Anyone that is in Christ is a new creation v. 17
- Reconciled believers to Himself and gave them the ministry of reconciliation v. 18
- Reconciled the world to Himself through Christ v. 19
- Raises up ambassadors for Christ and makes His appeal through them v. 20
- For mankind's sake He made Him to be sin who knew no sin, so that in Him we might become the righteousness of God v. 21

2 Corinthians 6

- LORD vv. 17, 18
- Saves v. 2
- Helps v. 2
- Favors v. 2
- Holy Spirit v. 6
- Power v. 7
- Has no accord with the Devil v. 15
- His temple has no agreement with idols v. 16
- His people are His temple v. 16
- Living v. 16
- Father v. 18
- Has sons and daughters v. 18
- Lord Almighty v. 18

2 Corinthians 7

- Promises v. 1
- Comforts the downcast v. 6
- Gives godly grief that leads to repentance v. 9
- His grief produces repentance that leads to salvation, whereas worldly grief produces death v. 10
- Sees v. 12

2 Corinthians 8

- LORD vv. 5, 9, 19, 21
- Gracious to His churches v. 1
- Tests v. 2
- Though He was rich, became poor for our sake that by His poverty we might become rich v. 9
- Sees v. 21
- Churches are the glory of Christ v. 23

2 Corinthians 9

- Loves a cheerful giver v. 7
- Able to make all grace abound in His believers, that they will have sufficiency in all things at all times and abound in all good work v. 8
- Distributed freely, given to the poor v. 9
- His righteousness endures forever v. 9
- Enriches in every way that one may be generous in every way, producing thanksgiving to God v. 11
- Gives inexpressible gifts v. 14

2 Corinthians 10

- LORD vv. 8, 17, 18
- Meek v. 1
- Gentle v. 1
- Christ v. 1
- Gives weapons of divine power to believers to destroy strongholds v. 4
- Gives weapons to destroy every lofty opinion raised against the knowledge of God and take every thought captive to obey Christ v. 5

- It is not the one who commends himself who is approved, but the one whom the Lord commends v. 18

2 Corinthians 11

- LORD vv. 17, 31
- Puts His truth in people v. 10
- The God and Father of the Lord Jesus is blessed forever v. 31

2 Corinthians 12

- LORD vv. 1, 8
- Gives visions and revelations v. 1
- His power is made perfect in weakness v. 9
- The power of Christ rests in human weakness, insults, hardships, persecutions, and calamities, and He makes strong the weak vv. 9-10
- Works signs and wonders and mighty works through believers v. 12
- Sees v. 19
- Humbles v. 21

2 Corinthians 13

- LORD vv. 10, 14
- Powerful in His dealings v. 3
- Crucified in weakness, but lives by the power of God v. 4
- Calls Christians to test themselves to see if they are in the faith and that Christ is in them or not v. 5
- Restores v. 9
- Gives authority v. 10
- Calls believers to rejoice, aim for restoration, comfort one another, agree with one another, and live in peace, and the God of love and peace will be with them v. 12
- Gracious v. 14
- Loving v. 14
- Fellowships with believers by the Holy Spirit v. 14

Galatians 1

- LORD vv. 3, 19
- Divinely made Paul an apostle v. 2
- Raised Jesus Christ from the dead v. 1
- Gives grace and peace v. 3
- Wills v. 4
- Gave Himself for the sins of believers to deliver them from the present evil age according to the will of the Father v. 4
- Delivers v. 4
- To Him is the glory forever and ever v. 5
- Calls believers into the grace of Christ v. 6
- Gives the only true gospel of Christ v. 7
- Curses those that preach a false gospel v. 9
- His servants do not worry themselves with trying to please man v. 10
- Personally reveals His gospel v. 12
- Set Paul apart before he was born and called him by His grace v. 15
- Was pleased to reveal His Son to Paul that he might preach Him to the Gentiles v. 16

Galatians 2

- Gives revelations v. 2
- Gives freedom in Christ v. 4
- Shows no partiality v. 6
- Worked through Peter and Paul in their ministries v. 8
- Gives grace v. 9
- Has a heart for the poor and instills it in believers v. 10
- There is neither Jew nor Gentile before Him v. 14
- Justifies through faith in Jesus rather than works of the law v. 16
- Loved and gave Himself for believers and lives in them v. 20

Galatians 3

- Was crucified publicly v. 1
- Gives the Spirit by hearing with faith and not by works of the law v. 2
- Supplies the Spirit to believers and works miracles among them with Him by hearing with faith v. 5
- Counts faith as righteousness v. 6
- Those of faith are sons of Abraham v. 7
- Justifies the Gentiles by faith v. 8
- Curses those who rely on works of the law v. 10
- No one is justified before Him by the law, for "The righteous shall live by faith." v. 11
- Christ redeemed believers from the curse of the law by becoming a curse for them v. 13
- In Christ Jesus the blessing of Abraham came to the Gentiles, so that they might receive the promised Spirit through faith v. 14
- Gave Abraham the inheritance by promise v. 18
- Gave the law because of transgressions v. 19
- Gave the law as our guardian until Christ came in order that we might be justified by faith v. 24
- All are one in Christ, and there is no Jew nor Greek, slave nor free, male nor female v. 28
- Believers are heirs according to promise v. 29

Galatians 4

- Sent His Son under the law to redeem those under the law that they might receive adoption as sons vv. 4-5
- God has sent the Spirit of his Son into His sons' hearts, crying, "Abba! Father!" v. 7
- Freed slaves into sonship, making them heirs through God v. 7
- Knows His people v. 9

Galatians 5

- LORD v. 10
- Set believers free for freedom v. 1
- Christ is no advantage to those who accept works-based salvation v. 2
- Through the Spirit by faith, believers eagerly await the hope of righteousness v. 5
- In Christ Jesus only faith counts working through love v. 6
- Calls to freedom and to serve through love v. 13
- Commands love to fulfill the whole law v. 14
- The desires of the Spirit are opposed to the desires of the flesh v. 17
- Those led by the Spirit are not under the law v. 18
- The fruit of the Spirit are love, joy, peace, patience, kindness, goodness, faithfulness, gentleness, and self-control vv. 22-23

Galatians 6

- LORD vv. 14, 18
- Calls us to bear one another's burdens v. 2
- He is not mocked v. 7
- One who sows to the Spirit will reap from the Spirit eternal life v. 8
- Gracious v. 18

Ephesians 1

- LORD vv. 2, 3, 15, 17
- Willed Paul to be an apostle of Christ Jesus v. 1
- Blessed v. 3

- Blessed believers in Christ with every spiritual blessing in the heavenly places v. 3
- Chose believers to be in Him before the foundation of the world that they should be holy and blameless before Him v. 4
- Lovingly predestined believers for adoption as sons through Jesus Christ according to the purpose of His will v. 6
- In Christ believers have redemption through His blood, the forgiveness of our trespasses according to the riches of His grace, which He lavished upon them, in all wisdom and insight making known to them the mystery of His will, according to His purpose, which He set forth in Christ as a plan for the fullness of time to unite all things to Him, things in heaven and things on earth vv. 7-10
- Gives an inheritance to believers, having predestined them according to the purpose of Him who works all things according to the counsel of His will v. 11
- Seals believers with the promised Holy Spirit v. 13
- Guarantees believers' inheritance with the Holy Spirit until they acquire possession of it, to the praise of His glory v. 14
- God of our Lord Jesus Christ v. 17
- Father of glory v. 17
- Gives the Spirit of wisdom and revelation in the knowledge of Him v. 17
- Enlightens the eyes of the heart to know what is the hope to which He has called believers, what are the riches of His glorious inheritance in the saints v. 18
- Has an immeasurable greatness of power toward believers, according to the work of His great might that He worked in Christ when He raised Him from the dead and seated Him at His right hand in the heavenly places, far above all rule and authority and power and dominion, and above every name that is named in every age, past, present, and future vv. 19-21
- Put all things under Jesus' feet and gave Him as head over all things to the church, which is His body, the fullness of Him who fills all in all vv. 22-23

<u>Ephesians 2</u>

- LORD v. 21
- Rich in mercy v. 4
- Loves with a great love v. 4
- Brings those dead in sin to life together with Christ and saves them by grace v. 5
- Raises up believers and seats them in the heavenly places in Christ Jesus v. 6
- Will show the immeasurable riches of His grace in kindness toward believers in Christ Jesus in the ages to come v. 7
- By grace He has saved believers through faith as a free gift v. 8
- His grace is undeserved v. 9
- Believers are His workmanship, created in Christ Jesus to walk in the good works that He prepared beforehand v. 10
- Promises v. 12
- Gives hope to the world v. 12

- Brings near those who are far off by the blood of Christ v. 13
- The peace of believers, having broken down the walls of hostility between man and God and creating life and reconciliation through the cross vv. 15-17
- Through Him access is granted to the Father in the Spirit v. 18
- Made strangers and aliens members of the household of God v. 19
- Cornerstone of the holy temple in the Lord v. 21
- Builds believers together into a dwelling place for God by the Spirit v. 22

Ephesians 3

- LORD v. 11
- Gave Paul stewardship of His grace v. 2
- Reveals mysteries v. 3
- Mysterious v. 4
- Makes known His mysteries to men of different generations by the Spirit v. 5
- Extends the promise of the gospel of Christ to Gentiles, making them fellow heirs v. 6
- Made Paul a minister of the gospel according to the gift of His grace given by the working of His power v. 7
- Brings to light His plan of mysteries hidden for ages in Himself v. 9
- Created all things v. 9
- Makes His manifold wisdom known to the rulers and authorities in the heavenly places through the church v. 10
- Eternally purposeful v. 11
- Gives boldness and access into Himself through Himself v. 12
- Names every family in heaven and on earth v. 15
- Gloriously rich v. 16
- Grants strengthening of power through His Spirit in the inner being v. 16
- Dwells in a person's heart through faith v. 17
- Roots and grounds His people in love v. 17
- His love is long, wide, tall, and deep v. 18
- The love of Christ surpasses knowledge and fills believers up with His fullness v. 19
- Able to do far more abundantly than on can ask or think according to the power at work in believers v. 20
- All the glory in the church and in Christ Jesus is to Him throughout all generations forever and ever v. 21

Ephesians 4

- LORD vv. 1, 5, 17
- Calls v. 1
- The Spirit causes unity and a bond of peace v. 3
- One v. 4
- He alone is the Father of all v. 6
- Over all and through all and in all v. 6
- Gives gifts to men v. 8
- Ascended after having descended into the lower regions, the earth v. 9
- Ascended far above the heavens that He might fill all things v. 10
- Gave the apostles, the prophets, the evangelists, the shepherds, and the teachers to equip the saints for the work of the ministry, for the

building up of the body of Christ vv. 11-12
- His children are to grow up into He who is the head, Jesus v. 15
- The truth is in Jesus v. 21
- Truly righteous and holy, and makes His children like Him as they take off the old and put on the new self vv. 23-24
- Holy Spirit of God v. 30
- Grieves v. 30
- Seals believers for the day of redemption v. 30
- Forgives v. 32

<u>Ephesians 5</u>
- LORD vv. 8, 10, 17, 19, 20, 22
- Loves His children v. 1
- Loves believers, and gave Himself up for them v. 2
- Idolaters have no place in His kingdom v. 5
- Creates children of light v. 8
- Pleased by His children v. 10
- Shines on the consecrated v. 14
- Fills with His Spirit as one fills himself with wine v. 18
- Commands submission to Himself and to each other vv. 21, 22, 24
- Head of the church v. 23
- Savior v. 23
- Christ loved the church and gave Himself up for her v. 25
- Sanctified the church, having cleansed her by the washing of water with the word so that He might present the church to Himself in splendor, holy and without any blemish vv. 26-27
- Example for how every husband should love his wife as his own body v. 28
- Nourishes and cherishes the church v. 29
- The church makes up the members of His body v. 30
- Is mysteriously one with the church as man and women mysteriously become one by marriage v. 32

<u>Ephesians 6</u>
- LORD vv. 1, 4, 7, 8, 10, 21, 23, 24
- Commands that the right thing is for children to obey their parents in the Lord v. 1
- Disciplines and instructs, and has earthly fathers do the same with their children v. 4
- Desires a sincere heart v. 5
- Wills v. 6
- Gives to man what man gives to others v. 8
- Looks down on threatening from masters v. 9
- Not partial v. 9
- Strong v. 10
- Mighty v. 10
- Supplies for believers the belt of truth, the breastplate of righteousness, the readiness given by the gospel of peace, the shield of faith, the helmet of salvation, and the sword of the Spirit, which is the word of God vv. 14-17
- God the Father v. 23
- Lord Jesus Christ v. 23
- Gracious to all who love Him v. 24
- His love is incorruptible v. 24

<u>Philippians 1</u>
- LORD vv. 2, 14
- Gives grace and peace v. 2
- He who starts a good work in a person will bring it to completion at the day of Jesus Christ v. 6
- Believers partake in His grace v. 7

- Witnesses v. 8
- Affectionate v. 8
- Makes pure and blameless those that approve what is excellent v. 10
- Fills with the fruit of righteousness that comes through Jesus Christ v. 11
- Glorious and praiseworthy v. 11
- The Spirit of Christ helps v. 19
- Delivers v. 19

<u>Philippians 2</u>

- LORD vv. 11, 19, 24, 29
- Encourages v. 1
- Comforts v. 1
- Loves v. 1
- Affectionate v. 1
- Sympathetic v. 1
- Gives believers His mind v. 5
- Christ was in the form of God, but did not count equality with God a thing to be grasped v. 6
- Christ emptied Himself by taking on the form of a servant, being born in the likeness of men v. 7
- Christ humbled Himself by becoming obedient to the point of death, even death on a cross v. 8
- God exalted the Son and bestowed on Him the name that is above every name v. 9
- At the name of Jesus every knee will bow, in heaven, on earth, and under the earth v. 10
- Every tongue will confess that Jesus Christ is Lord v. 11
- Receives glory v. 11
- Works in believers in order for them to will and to work for His good pleasure v. 13
- Has interests for the welfare of others v. 21

<u>Philippians 3</u>

- LORD vv. 1, 8, 20
- Spirit of God v. 3
- Worthy v. 8
- Gives righteousness to those of faith, instead of depending on obedience v. 9
- Makes people His own, that they may make Him their own v. 12
- Calls believers to press toward the prize of the upward call of Him in Jesus Christ v. 14
- Reveals the Way v. 15
- Makes His followers citizens of heaven, and the enemies of His cross He destroys vv. 19-20
- Savior v. 20
- Transforms the lowly bodies of man into glorious ones like His own, by the power that enables Him to even to subject all things to Himself v. 21

<u>Philippians 4</u>

- LORD vv. 1, 2, 4, 5, 10, 23
- Writes names in the book of life v. 3
- At hand, and there is no place for anxiety, but instead for thanksgiving in everything vv. 5-6
- His peace surpasses all understanding and guards His people's hearts and minds in Christ Jesus v. 7
- With those who do whatever is true, honorable, just, pure, lovely, commendable, excellent, and praiseworthy vv. 8-9
- God of peace v. 9
- Believers are to be content in every situation v. 11
- Enables believers to do all things through Him v. 13
- Strengthens v. 13

- Supplies every need of ours according to the riches of His glory in Jesus Christ v. 19
- Gracious v. 23

Colossians 1

- LORD vv. 3, 10
- Willed Paul to be an apostle of Christ Jesus v. 1
- Gives grace and peace v. 2
- Father of Jesus v. 3
- His word of truth, the gospel, is bearing fruit and increasing v. 6
- Gracious v. 6
- Spirit v. 8
- Wills and fills with spiritual wisdom and understanding v. 9
- Pleased v. 10
- Gloriously mighty v. 11
- Qualifies believers to share in the inheritance of the saints of light v. 12
- Delivered believers from the domain of darkness and transferred them to the kingdom of His beloved Son, in whom they have redemption, the forgiveness of sins vv. 13-14
- Deliverer v. 13
- Loves His Son v. 13
- Redeems v. 14
- Forgives v. 14
- Jesus is the image of the invisible God, the firstborn of all creation v. 15
- All things were created by Jesus in heaven and on earth, visible and invisible, whether thrones or dominions or rulers or authorities: all things were created through Him and for Him v. 16
- Before all things, and in Him all things hold together v. 17
- Head of the body, the church v. 18
- The beginning, the first born from the dead, that in everything He might be preeminent v. 18
- In Him all the fullness of God was pleased to dwell v. 19
- Through Christ God reconciles to Himself all things, whether on earth or in heaven, making peace by the blood of His cross v. 20
- Reconciles believers who were once evil enemies and presents them before Himself holy and blameless and above reproach vv. 21-22
- Rewards the stable and steadfast v. 23
- Made Paul a steward of His church v. 25
- Reveals mysteries hidden for ages and generations to the saints v. 26
- Chose to make known to the Gentiles the riches of His glorious mystery, which is Christ in you, the hope of glory v. 27
- Powerfully works His energy in His saints v. 29

Colossians 2

- LORD v. 6
- His mystery is Christ, in whom are hidden all the treasures of wisdom and knowledge v. 3
- Gives Himself that believers may walk in Him, rooted and built up in Him and established in the faith as taught and abounding in thanksgiving vv. 6-7
- In Christ the whole fullness of deity dwells bodily v. 9
- Head of all rule and authority v. 10
- Circumcises the spirit in Himself v. 11
- Buries believers in baptism and raises them through faith in the

powerful working of God who raised Christ from the dead v. 12
- Makes the dead alive, forgiving all their trespasses v. 13
- Cancelled the record of debt that stood against believers with its legal demands v. 14
- Set the record of debt against believers aside, nailing it to the cross v. 14
- Disarmed the rulers and authorities and put them to open shame by triumphing over them in Christ v. 15
- All things belong to Christ v. 17
- The Head v. 19
- The body of Christ grows with a growth that is from God v. 19
- Believers died with Christ to the elemental spirits of the world and no longer are to submit to their empty regulations v. 20
- Only His supernatural power is of help for humans in order to defeat the indulgence of the flesh v. 23

<u>Colossians 3</u>
- LORD vv. 13, 17, 18, 20, 22, 24
- Above, seated at the right hand of God v. 1
- Hides the lives of believers with Christ in Himself v. 3
- The life of believers v. 4
- Will appear in glory v. 4
- Creator v. 10
- Renews v. 10
- Christ is all, and in all v. 11
- Forgives and expects believers to forgive v. 13
- Calls believers into Christ, in one body v. 15
- Not partial v. 25
- Pays back wrongdoers their due v. 25

<u>Colossians 4</u>
- LORD vv. 7, 17
- Master v. 1
- Opens doors of opportunity for His word to go forth through His children v. 3
- Mysterious v. 3
- Served v. 7
- Christ Jesus v. 12
- Wills v. 12
- Assures v. 12
- Gives ministries v. 17

<u>1 Thessalonians 1</u>
- LORD vv. 1, 3, 6, 8
- Father vv. 1, 3
- Jesus Christ is Lord vv. 1, 3
- Loves Christians v. 4
- Chooses v. 4
- Holy Spirit vv. 5, 6
- His gospel comes in power and in the Spirit and with full conviction v. 5
- Living v. 9
- True v. 9
- Son v. 10
- From heaven v. 10
- Raised Jesus from the dead v. 10
- Jesus delivers believers from the wrath to come v. 10

<u>1 Thessalonians 2</u>
- LORD vv. 15, 19
- Dependable v. 2
- Approves and entrusts v. 4
- Tests hearts v. 4
- Calls believers into His own kingdom and glory v. 12
- Speaks v. 13
- His word is at work in believers v. 13
- His church exists in Christ Jesus v. 14

- Wrath v. 16
- Allows Satan to hinder people v. 18

1 Thessalonians 3

- LORD vv. 8, 11, 12, 13
- Father vv. 11, 13
- Lord Jesus vv. 11, 13
- Makes people abound in love for one another and for all v. 12
- Establishes hearts as blameless in holiness before the Father at the coming of the Lord Jesus with all His saints v. 13

1 Thessalonians 4

- LORD vv. 1, 2, 6, 13, 15, 16, 17
- Lord Jesus v. 1
- Instructs v. 2
- Wills our sanctification: that we abstain from sexual immorality; that each one know how to control his own body in holiness and honor rather than passion and lust as a heathen; that no one transgress and wrong his brother in this matter vv. 3-6
- Avenger v. 6
- Called His saints to holiness, not impurity v. 7
- Gives His Holy Spirit to people v. 8
- Teaches to love one another v. 9
- Desires people to be independent as far as they are able, rather than merely depending on the charity of wealthier people vv. 11-12
- Jesus died and rose again, and brings with Him others who have fallen asleep v. 14
- The dead in Christ will rise first v. 16
- The Lord Himself will descend from heaven with a cry of command, with the voice of an archangel, and with the sound of the trumpet of God v. 16
- His people will always be with Him v. 18

1 Thessalonians 5

- LORD vv. 1, 2, 9, 12, 23, 27, 28
- His day will come like a thief in the night v. 2
- Will send sudden destruction, such as labor pains come upon a pregnant woman, from which there is no escape v. 3
- Has not destined His children for wrath, but to obtain salvation through Christ v. 9
- Died so that whether we are awake or asleep we might live with Him v. 10
- Wills that in Christ we rejoice always, pray without ceasing, and give thanks in all circumstances v. 18
- God of peace v. 23
- Sanctifies v. 23
- Coming v. 23
- Calls v. 24
- Faithful v. 24
- Surely does what He says v. 24
- Gracious v. 28

2 Thessalonians 1

- LORD vv. 1, 2, 7, 8, 9, 12
- Father vv. 1, 2
- Lord Jesus Christ vv. 1, 2
- Gives grace and peace v. 2
- Causes faith and love of everyone to grow abundantly and increase v. 3
- His judgment is righteous v. 5
- The Lord Jesus will be revealed from heaven with His mighty angels in flaming fire, inflicting vengeance on those who do not

know God and on those who do not obey the gospel of our Lord Jesus vv. 7-8

- Will cause His enemies to suffer the punishment of eternal destruction, away from the presence of the Lord and from the glory of His might v. 9
- Coming to glorify His saints and to be marveled at among all who have believed the testimony of His gospel v. 10
- Makes those He has called worthy of it and able to fulfill every resolve for good and every work of faith by His power, that the name of Jesus may be glorified in them and they in Him, according to His grace vv. 11-12

<u>2 Thessalonians 2</u>

- LORD vv. 1, 2, 8, 13, 14, 16
- The day of His return will come after rebellion and the man of lawlessness is revealed, the son of destruction, who opposes and exalts himself against every so-called god or object of worship and proclaims himself to be God vv. 3-4
- Lord Jesus will kill the lawless one with the breath of His mouth and bring to nothing by the appearance of His coming v. 8
- Sends a strong delusion to those that do not love His truth but have pleasure in unrighteousness that they may be condemned v. 12
- Chose people as the first fruits to be saved through sanctification by the Spirit and belief in truth v. 13
- Calls people through His gospel that they may obtain the glory of the Lord Jesus Christ v. 14
- Father v. 16
- Loves believers, and gives them eternal comfort and good hope through grace v. 16
- Comforts hearts and establishes them in every good work and deed v. 17

<u>2 Thessalonians 3</u>

- LORD vv. 1, 3, 4, 5, 6, 12, 16, 18
- Though not all have faith, He is faithful vv. 2-3
- Establishes believers and guards them from the evil one v. 3
- Directs hearts to the love of God and to the steadfastness of Christ v. 5
- Steadfast v. 5
- Loving v. 5
- Desires that one works rather than be a busybody and still partake in charity vv. 6-12
- Lord of peace v. 16
- Gives peace at all times and in every way v. 16
- Gracious v. 18

<u>1 Timothy 1</u>

- LORD vv. 2, 12, 14
- Commanded Paul to be an apostle v. 1
- Savior v. 1
- Hope v. 1
- Gracious v. 2
- Merciful v. 2
- Peace-giving v. 2
- Father v. 2
- Christ Jesus vv. 1, 2, 12, 14-16
- Charges love that issues from a pure heart, a good conscience, and a sincere faith v. 5
- Lays down the law for the lawless and disobedient, for the ungodly and sinners, for the unholy and

profane, for those who strike their fathers and mothers, for murderers, the sexually immoral, men who practice homosexuality, enslavers, liars, perjurers, and whatever else is contrary to sound doctrine, in accordance with the gospel of the glory of the blessed God vv. 9-10

- Entrusted Paul with the gospel v. 11
- Gives strength v. 12
- Judges v. 12
- Appoints insolent opponents to His service v. 13
- Came into the world to save sinners v. 15
- Perfectly patient v. 16
- King of the ages v. 17
- Immortal v. 17
- Invisible v. 17
- The only God v. 17
- To Him be glory and honor forever and ever v. 17

<u>1 Timothy 2</u>

- Urges supplications, prayers, intercessions, and thanksgivings be made for all people v. 1
- Pleased when He sees peaceful, godly, quiet, and dignified lives vv. 2-3
- Savior v. 3
- Desires all people to be saved and come to the knowledge of the truth v. 4
- One v. 5
- The only mediator between God and man, Christ Jesus v. 5
- Gave Himself as a ransom for all v. 6
- Appointed Paul to be a preacher, apostle, and teacher of the Gentiles in faith and truth v. 7
- Desires that in every place men should pray, lifting holy hands without anger or quarreling v. 8
- Desires women adorn themselves in respectable apparel, with modesty and self-control, not with braided hair and gold or pearls or costly attire v. 9

<u>1 Timothy 3</u>

- Requires the leaders of His people to be the husband of one wife, sober-minded, self-controlled, respectable, hospitable, able to teach, not a drunkard, not violent but gentle, not quarrelsome, not a lover of money, a good manager of His household, keep his children submissive with all dignity, not a recent convert, well thought of by outsiders, dignified, truthful, not greedy, hold the mystery of the faith with a clear conscience, tested and proven blameless, and have dignified, faithful, and sober wives vv. 2-12
- The church is His household, a pillar and buttress of truth v. 15
- Living v. 15
- His godliness is a great mystery v. 16
- Manifested in the flesh v. 16
- Vindicated by the Spirit v. 16
- Seen by angels v. 16
- Proclaimed among the nations v. 16
- Believed on in the world v. 16
- Taken up in glory v. 16

<u>1 Timothy 4</u>

- The Spirit says some will depart from the faith by devoting themselves to deceitful spirits and teachings of demons v. 1

- Created marriage and food to be received with thanksgiving, for it is made holy by the word of God and prayer v. 5
- Christ Jesus v. 6
- His good servants are trained in words of faith and of good doctrine v. 6
- Living v. 10
- Savior of all people, especially those who believe v. 10

1 Timothy 5

- Desires we encourage rather than rebuke v. 1
- Christ Jesus v. 21

1 Timothy 6

- LORD vv. 3, 14, 15
- Those who revile their masters revile the name of God and His teaching v. 1
- Only in Christ Jesus is there any understanding at all vv. 3-4
- Calls the man of God to eternal life v. 12
- Made the good confession before Pontius Pilate v. 13
- Will appear again v. 14
- Blessed v. 15
- The only Sovereign v. 15
- He alone has immortality v. 16
- Dwells in unapproachable light v. 16
- No one has ever seen or can see v. 16
- To Him is honor and eternal dominion v. 16
- Charges the rich to not be haughty and to set their hope on God instead v. 17
- Richly provides us with everything to enjoy v. 17

2 Timothy 1

- LORD vv. 2, 8, 16, 18
- Willed Paul to be an apostle v. 1
- Christ Jesus vv. 1, 2
- Promises life in Himself v. 1
- Gracious v. 2
- Merciful v. 2
- Peace-giving v. 2
- Father v. 2
- Worthy of thanks v. 3
- Gives gifts v. 6
- Gives Christians a spirit not of fear, but of power and love and self-control v. 7
- Powerful v. 8
- Saved believers and called them into a holy calling, not because of their works, but because of His own purpose and grace, which He gave them in Christ Jesus before the ages began v. 9
- The purpose of Christianity was manifested through the appearing of the Savior Christ Jesus v. 10
- Savior v. 10
- Abolished death v. 10
- Brought life and immortality to light through the gospel v. 10
- Appointed Paul to be a preacher, apostle, and teacher v. 11
- Able to guard what He has entrusted Christians with v. 12
- Faith and love are in Christ Jesus v. 13
- The Holy Spirit dwells within Christians, allowing them to guard the good deposit entrusted to them v. 14
- Grants mercy v. 18

2 Timothy 2

- LORD vv. 7, 19, 22, 24
- Christians are strengthened by the grace that is in Christ Jesus v. 1

- Gives understanding in everything v. 7
- Risen from the dead v. 8
- Offspring of David v. 8
- His word is not bound v. 9
- Salvation is in Jesus with eternal glory v. 10
- Those who die with Him shall live with Him; if they endure, they will also reign with Him; if they deny Him, He will also deny them; if they are faithless, He is faithful vv. 11-13
- He cannot deny Himself v. 13
- His firm foundation stands, bearing this seal: "The Lord knows those who are His," and, "Let everyone who names the name of the Lord depart from iniquity." v. 19
- Sets apart for good use those who cleanse themselves from what is dishonorable v. 21
- His truth allows people to escape from the snare of the devil, after being captured by him to do his will v. 26

<u>2 Timothy 3</u>

- LORD v. 11
- His sacred writings are able to make one wise for salvation through Jesus Christ v. 15
- All Scripture is breathed out by God and profitable for teaching, for reproof, for correction, and for training in righteousness, that the man of God may be complete, equipped for every good work vv. 16-17

<u>2 Timothy 4</u>

- LORD vv. 8, 14, 17, 18, 22
- Is to judge the living and the dead v. 1
- Christ Jesus v. 1
- King v. 1
- Lays up for the faithful believer the crown of righteousness, which the Lord, the righteous Judge, will award to him on that Day, and to all who have loved His appearing vv. 7-8
- Repays people according to their deeds v. 14
- Stands by and strengthens believers v. 17
- Rescues believers from every evil deed and safely brings them into His heavenly kingdom v. 18
- To Him is the glory forever and ever v. 18

<u>Titus 1</u>

- Elects v. 1
- Promised eternal life before the ages began v. 2
- Never lies v. 2
- Manifested his word at the proper time through the preaching with which He entrusts to certain people by the command of God v. 3
- Savior v. 3
- Gives grace and peace v. 4
- His stewards, overseers, must be above reproach v. 7
- His word is trustworthy v. 9

<u>Titus 2</u>

- Savior v. 10
- His grace has appeared, bringing salvation to all people, training people to renounce ungodliness and worldly passions, and to live self-controlled, upright, and godly lives in the present age, waiting for the blessed hope, the appearing of the glory of the great God and Savior Jesus Christ, who gave Himself for us to redeem us from lawlessness and to purify for

Himself a people for His own possession who are zealous for good works vv. 11-14

Titus 3

- When His goodness and loving-kindness appeared, He saved His people, not because of anything they had done, but according to His own mercy, by the washing and renewal of the Holy Spirit, whom He poured out on believers richly through Jesus Christ their Savior vv. 4-6
- Those justified by His grace might become heirs according to the hope of eternal life v. 7
- Only His grace gives one worth vv. 7-9

Philemon

- LORD vv. 3, 5, 16, 20, 25
- Imprisoned Paul v. 1
- Gives grace and peace v. 3
- His grace accompanies a person's spirit v. 25

Hebrews 1

- LORD v. 10
- Spoke to the Fathers of the Jewish people long ago at many times and in many ways by the prophets v. 1
- Spoke to mankind by His Son v. 2
- Appointed His Son the heir of all things v. 2
- Created the world though His Son v. 2
- Jesus is the radiance of the glory of God and the exact imprint of His nature v. 3
- He upholds the universe by the word of His power v. 3
- Made purification for sins, then sat down at the right hand of the Majesty on high v. 3
- As superior to the angel as the name He inherited is greater than theirs v. 4
- Called Jesus His Son v. 5
- Begot His Son v. 5
- Father of Jesus (equality) v. 5
- Son of God v. 5
- All the angels worship Jesus v. 6
- Makes His angels winds and His ministers a flame of fire v. 7
- Son v. 8
- Made Jesus' throne forever and ever, and the scepter of uprightness the scepter of His kingdom v. 8
- Loves righteousness v. 9
- Hates wickedness v. 9
- Anointed Jesus with the oil of gladness v. 10
- Christ laid the foundation of the earth in the beginning, and the heavens are the work of His hands v. 10
- The heavens and earth will perish, but He will remain v. 11
- Unchanging v. 12
- Immortal v. 12
- Makes His Son's enemies a footstool for His feet v. 13
- Sends out angels to serve for the sake of those who are to inherit salvation v. 14

Hebrews 2

- LORD v. 3
- Bore witness to His salvation by signs and wonders and by gifts of the Holy Spirit distributed according to His will v. 4
- Made the Son for a little while lower than the angels vv. 7, 9
- Crowned Christ with glory and honor, and put everything in subjection under His feet vv. 7-8

- Put everything in subjection to Jesus, leaving nothing outside His control v. 8
- Crowned with glory and honor because of the suffering of death, so that by the grace of God He might taste death for everyone v. 9
- All things exist for Him and by Him v. 10
- Brings many sons to glory v. 10
- Perfected Jesus through suffering v. 10
- Source of sanctification v. 11
- Not ashamed to call believers brothers v. 11
- Not ashamed of His children, since He is the source of salvation vv. 11-18
- Partook in flesh and blood, that through death that He might destroy the one who has the power of death, the devil v. 14
- Deliverer v. 15
- Helps the offspring of Abraham personally v. 16
- Made like His brothers in every respect, that He might become a merciful and faithful high priest in the service of God, to make propitiation for the sins of the people v. 17
- Since He Himself suffered when tempted, He is able to help those who are being tempted v. 18

<u>Hebrews 3</u>

- Calls v. 1
- High priest v. 1
- Apostle v. 1
- Faithful to God v. 2
- Jesus has been counted worthy of more glory than Moses, as much more glory as the builder of a house has than the house itself v. 3
- Builder of all things v. 4
- Speaks vv. 7, 15
- Faithful in all God's house as a Son v. 6
- Holy Spirit v. 7
- Provokable vv. 10, 17
- Wrath v. 11
- Living v. 12

<u>Hebrews 4</u>

- The promise of entering His rest still stands v. 1
- Does not give his rest to the disobedient and unbelieving v. 6
- Whoever has entered God's rest has also rested from His works as God did from His v. 10
- His word is living and active, sharper than any two-edged sword, piercing to the division of souls and of spirit, of joints and of marrow, and discerning the thoughts an intentions of the heart v. 12
- No creature is hidden from His sight, but all are naked and exposed to the eyes of Him to whom we must give account v. 13
- Believers have a great high priest who has passed though the heavens, Jesus, allowing them to hold fast to their confession v. 14
- Son of God v. 14
- High Priest v. 15
- Able to sympathize with our weakness, since He in every respect has been tempted as man is, yet is without sin v. 15
- His throne of grace can be approached confidently, that believers may receive mercy and find grace to help in time of need v. 16

Hebrews 5

- Accepts gifts and sacrifices from priests appointed from among men v. 1
- Calls priests for Himself v. 4
- Christ did not exalt Himself as high priest, but the Father did v. 5
- Made Jesus a priest forever, according to the order of Melchizedek v. 6
- Became flesh v. 7
- Offered up prayers and supplications to the Father, who was able to save Him from death, and He was heard because of His reverence v. 7
- Although He was a Son, He learned obedience through what He suffered v. 8
- Made perfect, becoming the source of eternal salvation to all who obey Him, being designated by God a high priest after the order of Melchizedek v. 10

Hebrews 6

- Holy Spirit v. 4
- Good v. 5
- Just v. 10
- Does not overlook one's work and the love shown for His name in serving the saints v. 10
- Promises v. 12
- Made a promise to Abraham, swearing by Himself, since there is no one greater, promising to bless and multiply him vv. 13-14
- Guaranteed His promise with an oath v. 17
- Impossible for Him to lie v. 18
- Supplies believers with a sure and steadfast anchor of the soul, a hope that enters into the inner place behind the curtain v. 19
- Became a high priest forever after the order of Melchizedek v. 20

Hebrews 7

- LORD vv. 14, 21
- Most High God v. 1
- Blesses the inferior v. 7
- Receives tithes v. 8
- Lives v. 8
- Descended from the tribe of Judah v. 14
- Indestructible v. 16
- Priest forever, after the order of Melchizedek v. 17
- Produced a better hope than the law v. 19
- Made Jesus a priest by His personal oath and swearing v. 21
- Jesus is the guarantor of a better covenant v. 22
- Holds His priesthood permanently, because He continues forever v. 24
- Since He lives forever to intercede before the Father, He is able to save to the uttermost those who draw near to Him v. 25
- High priest v. 26
- Holy v. 26
- Innocent v. 26
- Unstained v. 26
- Separated from sinners v. 26
- Exalted above the heavens v. 26
- Has no need to offer sacrifices daily, since He offered one sacrifice, Himself personally, for all v. 27
- Gave a word of oath after the law with His own perfect and immortal Son as high priest v. 28

Hebrews 8

- LORD vv. 2, 8, 9, 10, 11
- Majesty v. 1
- In heaven v. 1
- High Priest v. 1

- Jesus is seated at the right hand of the Father's throne in heaven v. 1
- Minister in the holy places v. 2
- Mediates the new covenant v. 6
- Made a second, faultless covenant v. 7
- Finds fault v. 8
- Established a new covenant v. 8
- Merciful v. 12
- Spoke a new covenant, making the first one obsolete v. 13

Hebrews 9

- Holy Spirit v. 8
- Christ appeared as a high priest of the good things that have come v. 11
- Entered once for all into the holy places by means of His own blood, thus securing an eternal redemption v. 12
- The blood of Christ, through the eternal Spirit offered Himself without blemish to God, purification of our conscience from dead works to serve the living God v. 14
- Living v. 14
- Purifies v. 14
- Mediator v. 15
- Calls v. 15
- Gives His promised eternal inheritance, where His death redeems sinners v. 16
- Made His will effective by His death v. 17
- Forgives sins by the shedding of blood v. 22
- Christ has entered into the holy places in heaven to appear in the presence of God on the behalf of believers v. 24
- Appeared once for all at the end of the ages to put away sin by the sacrifice of Himself v. 26
- Will appear a second time to save those who are eagerly waiting for Him v. 28

Hebrews 10

- LORD vv. 16, 30
- Jesus came to do the Father's will vv. 7, 9
- Neither desired nor took pleasure in sacrifices and offerings and burnt offerings and sin offerings v. 8
- Sanctifies believers through the offering of the body of Jesus Christ once for all v. 10
- Offered a single time a sacrifice for sins, then sat down at the right hand of God v. 12
- Waiting for His enemies to be made a footstool for His feet v. 13
- By a single offering He has perfected for all time those who are being sanctified v. 14
- The Holy Spirit bears witness to us v. 15
- Makes a covenant with His people and puts His laws on their hearts and writes them on their minds v. 16
- Remembers His people's sins and their lawless deeds no more v. 17
- No longer needs an offering for which He has already forgiven v. 18
- His blood allows believers to enter into the holy places with confidence, by the new and living way that He opened for us through the curtain, that is, through His flesh vv. 19-20
- Great priest over the house of God v. 21
- Faithful to His promises v. 23
- Judge vv. 27, 30

- Vengeance is His; He will repay v. 30
- Living v. 31
- Enlightens v. 32
- Gives better possessions than physical ones v. 34
- Destroys those who shrink back v. 39
- His soul takes pleasure in those of faith v. 39

Hebrews 11

- Made things seen out of things invisible v. 3
- Without faith it is impossible to please Him v. 6
- Exists v. 6
- Rewards those who seek Him v. 6
- Warns v. 7
- Calls v. 8
- Designs and builds v. 10
- Unashamed to be called the God of those who are faithful v. 16
- Gives promises v. 17
- Able to raise people from the dead v. 19
- The reproach of Christ is of greater wealth than the treasures of the world v. 26
- Invisible v. 27
- Destroyer v. 28
- Empowers His people to conquer kingdoms, enforce justice, obtain promises, stop the mouths of lions, quench the power of fire, escape the edge of the sword, become strong out of weakness, become mighty in war, and put foreign armies to flight vv. 33, 34

Hebrews 12

- LORD vv. 5, 6, 14
- Founder and Perfector of the believer's faith v. 2
- For the joy that was set before Him He endured the cross v. 2
- Seated at the right hand of the throne of God v. 2
- Endured from sinners great hostility against Himself v. 3
- Disciplines v. 5
- Disciplines the one He loves, and chastises every son whom He receives v. 6
- Treats His people as sons v. 7
- Disciplines for one's own good, that they may share His holiness v. 10
- Only holiness allows one to see the Lord v. 14
- Living God v. 22
- Jesus, mediator of the new covenant v. 24
- There is no escape from Him v. 25
- His voice shook the earth, but next time He will shake the heavens with it v. 26
- Gives a kingdom that cannot be shaken v. 28
- A consuming fire v. 29

Hebrews 13

- LORD vv. 6, 20
- Will judge the sexually immoral and adulterous v. 4
- Never leaves nor forsakes His people v. 5
- Helper v. 6
- Sacrificial charity is pleasing to Him v. 16
- God of peace v. 20
- Raised Jesus to life v. 20
- Fully equips to do His will v. 21
- Works in His people that which is pleasing in His sight through Jesus Christ, to whom is the glory forever and ever v. 21

James 1

- LORD vv. 1, 7
- Jesus Christ v. 1
- Tests faith and allows trials v. 2
- Gives generously without reproach to those who ask in faith with no doubting vv. 5-6
- Cannot be tempted with evil and He Himself tempts no one v. 13
- Every good gift and every perfect gift comes from above v. 17
- Father of lights v. 17
- Doesn't vary or change v. 17
- Of His own will He brought His people forth by the word of truth, that they should be a kind of first-fruits of his creatures v. 18
- His righteousness is not produced by the anger of men v. 20
- Blesses those who do, rather than merely hear v. 25

James 2

- LORD v. 1
- Jesus Christ v. 1
- Lord of glory v. 1
- Chosen the poor in the world to be rich in faith and heirs of the kingdom v. 5
- Promised the kingdom to those who love Him v. 5
- Commands us to love our neighbor v. 8
- Justifies a man by his faith with his works v. 24

James 3

- LORD v. 9
- Judges teachers with greater strictness v. 1
- Father v. 9
- Gives wisdom that does not lead to boasting or lying v. 14
- The wisdom He gives is pure, impartial, and sincere v. 17

James 4

- LORD vv. 10, 15
- Gives to those who ask rightly and selflessly v. 3
- Jealous over the spirit He has made to dwell within us v. 5
- Gives more grace v. 6
- Opposes the proud but gives grace to the humble v. 6
- Draws near to those who draw near to Him v. 8
- Exalts the humble v. 10
- Lawgiver v. 12
- Judge v. 12
- Able to save and to destroy v. 12
- Wills v. 15

James 5

- LORD vv. 4, 7, 8, 10, 11, 14, 15
- Lord of hosts v. 4
- Hears cries v. 4
- Coming v. 7
- His coming is at hand v. 8
- Judge v. 9
- Purposes v. 11
- Compassionate v. 11
- Merciful v. 11
- Raises up the sick who are prayed over in faith v. 15
- Forgives sins v. 15
- His power is available to the righteous when they pray to Him v. 16
- Saves those who are brought back after wandering from the truth v. 19

1 Peter 1

- LORD vv. 3, 25
- Elects v. 1
- Foreknows v. 2
- Father vv. 2, 3, 17
- Sanctifies v. 2
- Spirit v. 2

- Jesus Christ vv. 2, 3, 7, 13
- Multiplies grace and peace to His people v. 2
- Blessed v. 3
- Greatly merciful v. 3
- Causes believers to be born again to a living hope through the resurrection of Christ from the dead v. 3
- Gives an inheritance that does not perish, is not defiled, and does not fade in heaven v. 4
- By His power He guards believers through faith for a salvation ready to be revealed in the last time v. 5
- Christ will reveal Himself v. 7
- Loved v. 8
- Gives inexpressible joy and fills with glory v. 8
- Saves souls v. 9
- Spirit of Christ v. 11
- Suffered v. 11
- Sends the Holy Spirit from heaven v. 12
- Bringing grace fully at the revelation of Jesus Christ v. 13
- Holy v. 15
- Judges impartially according to each one's deeds v. 17
- Ransoms from futile ways by the precious blood of Jesus, like that of a lamb without blemish or spot v. 18
- Foreknown before the foundation of the world, but was made manifest in the last times v. 20
- Believers in Christ are in God v. 21
- Raised Jesus from the dead and gave Him glory v. 21
- Believers are purified by their obedience to the truth v. 22
- Believers are born again by the imperishable seed, the word of God v. 23
- His word remains forever v. 25

<u>1 Peter 2</u>

- LORD vv. 3, 13
- Good v. 3
- Living stone, rejected by men but in the sight of God chosen and precious v. 4
- Makes believers a part of His holy priesthood, to offer spiritual sacrifices acceptable to God through Jesus Christ v. 5
- Laid a stone in Zion v. 6
- Whoever believes in Jesus will not be put to shame v. 6
- Jesus is a stone of stumbling and a rock of offense to unbelievers v. 8
- Chose a people for His own possession v. 9
- Excellent v. 9
- Gives mercy to His people v. 10
- Wills subjection to human institutions v. 13
- Sees endurance of suffering for doing good as a gracious thing v. 20
- Calls Christians to suffer, since Christ suffered for them v. 21
- Committed no sin and no deceit was found in His mouth v. 22
- Did not revile against those who reviled against Him v. 23
- Entrusted Himself to He who judges justly, rather than threatening those who caused Him suffering v. 23
- Bore sins in His body on the tree, that we might die to sin and live to righteousness v. 24
- By His wounds believers are healed v. 24
- Shepherd v. 25
- Overseer of souls v. 25

<u>1 Peter 3</u>

- LORD vv. 6, 12, 15
- Holds very precious in His sight wives who adorn themselves in the hidden person of the heart with the imperishable beauty of a gentle and quiet spirit v. 4
- His eyes are on the righteous, and His ears open to their prayer v. 12
- His face is against those who do evil v. 12
- Holy v. 15
- Jesus is Lord v. 15
- Christ suffered once for sins: the righteous for the unrighteous, that He might bring us to God, being put to death in the flesh but made alive in the spirit v. 18
- Resurrected v. 21
- Jesus Christ v. 21
- In heaven and at the right hand of God, with angels, authorities, and powers having been subjected to Him v. 22

<u>1 Peter 4</u>

- Suffered in the flesh v. 1
- Wills that man would not live for human passions v. 2
- Ready to judge the living and the dead v. 5
- Lives in the spirit and empowers others to do the same v. 6
- Gives varied grace v. 10
- Gives oracles v. 11
- Supplies strength v. 11
- Glorified through Jesus Christ v. 11
- To Him belong glory and dominion forever and ever v. 11
- Suffered v. 13
- Spirit of glory and of God rests on those insulted for the name of Christ v. 14
- Faithful Creator v. 19

<u>1 Peter 5</u>

- Suffered v. 1
- Reveals glory v. 1
- Chief Shepherd v. 4
- Will the unfading crown of glory to believers v. 4
- Opposes the proud but gives grace to the humble v. 5
- Mighty v. 6
- Exalts the humble v. 6
- Cares for people v. 7
- God of all grace v. 10
- Calls His people to His eternal glory in Christ, and He Himself restores, confirms, strengthens, and establishes them v. 10
- To Him is the dominion forever and ever v. 11
- Truly gracious v. 12
- Gives peace through Christ v. 14

<u>2 Peter 1</u>

- LORD vv. 2, 8, 11, 14, 16
- Savior v. 1
- Jesus Christ v. 1
- Multiplies grace and peace to His people v. 2
- Divine power v. 3
- Grants all things that pertain to life and godliness through the knowledge of Him who called believers to His own glory and excellence, by which He has granted to them His precious and very great promises, so that through them they may become partakers of the divine nature, having escaped from the corruption that is in the world because of sinful desire vv. 3-4
- Jesus Christ vv. 8, 11, 14
- Savior v. 11

- Made clear to Peter that his death was nearing v. 14
- Powerful v. 16
- Coming v. 16
- Real v. 16
- Jesus received glory and honor from God the Father v. 17
- Majestic Glory v. 17
- Well pleased with His beloved Son v. 17
- Prophecy comes from Him alone, which goes forth by the Holy Spirit v. 21

2 Peter 2

- LORD vv. 9, 11, 20
- Master v. 1
- Swiftly destroys those who deny Him v. 1
- Did not spare angels when they sinned, but cast them into hell and committed them to chains of gloomy darkness to be kept until the judgment v. 4
- Only spared Noah and His family from the ancient world v. 5
- Turned the cities of Sodom and Gomorrah to ashes, making them an example of what is going to happen to the ungodly v. 6
- Knows how to rescue the godly from trials and how to keep the unrighteous under punishment until the day of judgment v. 9
- Savior v. 20
- Jesus Christ v. 20

2 Peter 3

- LORD vv. 1, 2, 8, 9, 10, 15, 18
- Savior vv. 2, 18
- The heavens and earth that now exist are being stored up for fire, being kept until the day of judgment and destruction of the ungodly v. 7
- With Him one day is as a thousand years and a thousand years as one day v. 8
- Not slow to fulfill His promise, but patient v. 9
- Does not wish that any should perish, but that all should reach repentance v. 9
- His day will come like a thief v. 10
- Promised a new heavens and a new earth in which righteousness dwells v. 13
- Patience v. 15
- Saves v. 15
- Jesus Christ v. 18
- To Him is the glory both now and to the day of eternity v. 18

1 John 1

- Gave the word of life, making it manifest vv. 1-2
- Fellowships v. 3
- Father v. 3
- Son v. 3
- Jesus Christ v. 3
- God is light, and in Him is no darkness at all v. 5
- The blood of His Son Jesus cleanses from all sin those who walk in the light v. 7
- Faithful and just to forgive the sins and all the unrighteousness of those that confess their sins v. 9

1 John 2

- Advocate v. 1
- Father vv. 1, 24
- Jesus Christ vv. 1, 24
- Propitiation for the believer's sins, and also for the sins of the whole world v. 2

- His truth is in those who keep His commandments v. 4
- His love is perfected in those who keep His word v. 5
- Abides in those who walk in the same way in which He walked v. 6
- Forgives sins for His name's sake v. 12
- From the beginning vv. 13, 14
- His word abides in people v. 14
- Empowers people to overcome the evil one v. 14
- His love is not in those who love the world v. 15
- All that is in the world is not from the Father v. 16
- Whoever does His will abides forever v. 17
- Anoints v. 20
- Holy One v. 20
- Jesus is the Christ v. 22
- One must confess the Son to have the Father v. 23
- Promised eternal life v. 25
- His anointing teaches a person v. 27
- Coming back v. 28
- Righteous v. 29
- Everyone who practices righteousness has been born of Him v. 29

1 John 3

- Gave His love by making people His children v. 1
- Everyone who hopes in Him purifies himself as He is pure v. 3
- Appeared to take away sins v. 5
- In Him is no sin v. 5
- No one who abides in Him keeps on sinning v. 6
- No one who has seen or knows Him keeps on sinning v. 6
- Righteous v. 7
- Son of God v. 8
- Appeared to destroy the works of the devil v. 8
- Those born of Him have His seed abiding in them v. 9
- His people practice righteousness and love their brothers v. 10
- Laid down His life for us v. 16
- Greater than our heart v. 20
- Commands that we believe in the name of His Son, Jesus Christ, and love one another v. 23
- Given His Spirit to His children and abides in them v. 24

1 John 4

- Jesus Christ has come in the flesh v. 2
- In His people v. 4
- Greater than he who is in the world, Satan v. 4
- Spirit of truth v. 6
- Love is from Him v. 7
- Love v. 8
- His love was made manifest to us, that His Son was sent into the world that we might live through Him v. 9
- Loved us first and sent His Son to be the propitiation for our sins v. 10
- Loves us v. 11
- No one has ever seen God v. 12
- Abides in those who love one another and His love is perfected in them v. 12
- Has given of His Spirit to those that abide in Him and He in them v. 13
- Sent His Son to be the Savior of the world v. 14
- Abides in whoever confesses that Jesus is His Son v. 15
- Love v. 16
- Abides in those who abide in love v. 16

- Makes people like Him v. 17
- His perfect love casts out all fear v. 18
- First loved us v. 19

1 John 5

- Jesus is the Christ v. 1
- Father v. 1
- Commands v. 2
- His commandments are not burdensome v. 3
- His children overcome the world v. 4
- Jesus is the Son of God v. 5
- Jesus Christ v. 6
- Came by water and the blood, and the Spirit testifies this, for the Spirit is the truth v. 6
- The Spirit and the water and the blood all agree v. 8
- Son of God v. 10
- Son v. 10
- Gave man eternal life, and this life is in His Son v. 11
- Whoever has the Son has life; whoever does not have the Son does not have life v. 12
- Son of God v. 13
- Gives eternal life to those who believe in His Son v. 13
- Hears everything that a person asks according to His will, and those who ask in His will receive vv. 14-15
- The Son of God has come and given understanding v. 20
- True v. 20
- Son, Jesus Christ v. 20

2 John

- His truth abides in believers forever v. 2
- Gives grace, mercy, and peace in truth and love v. 3
- God the Father v. 3
- Jesus Christ, the Father's Son v. 3
- Commands us to walk in truth v. 4
- Jesus Christ came in the flesh v. 7
- Whoever abides in the teaching of Jesus has both the Father and the Son v. 9

3 John

- Whoever does good is from Him, and whoever does evil is not from Him v. 11

Jude

- LORD vv. 4, 9, 14, 17, 21, 25
- Served by Jude v. 1
- Jesus Christ vv. 1, 4
- Calls v. 1
- Multiplies mercy, peace, and love to believers v. 2
- Gracious v. 4
- Delivered faith to all the saints v. 3
- The only Master, Jesus Christ v. 4
- Saved the people out of Egypt, afterward destroying those who did not believe v. 5
- Kept the angels, who did not stay within their own position of authority, in eternal chains under gloomy darkness until the judgment of the great day v. 6
- Made an example of Sodom and Gomorrah for the ungodly with the punishment of eternal fire v. 7
- Rebukes v. 9
- Reserved the gloom of utter darkness forever for sinners v. 13
- Coming with ten thousands of His holy ones to execute judgment on all and to convict all the ungodly vv. 14-15
- His Spirit is not in the ungodly v. 19
- Holy Spirit v. 20

- Mercifully and lovingly leads people to eternal life through Jesus v. 21
- Able to keep one from stumbling and to present him blameless before the presence of glory with great joy v. 24
- The only God v. 25
- Savior v. 25
- Jesus Christ v. 25
- To Him be glory, majesty, dominion, and authority, before all time and now and forever v. 25

<u>Revelation 1</u>

- LORD vv. 8, 10
- Gave revelation to Jesus Christ to show to His servants the things that must take place soon v. 1
- Made known revelation by sending His angel to His servant, John v. 1
- Jesus Christ vv. 2, 5
- Gives grace and peace v. 4
- Was and is and is to come vv. 4, 8
- The faithful witness v. 5
- Firstborn of the dead v. 5
- Ruler of kings on earth v. 5
- Loves His people and has freed them from their sins by His blood v. 5
- To Him is glory and dominion forever v. 6
- Coming with the clouds, and every eye will see Him, even those who pierced Him, and all the tribes of the earth will wail on account of Him v. 7
- The Alpha and the Omega v. 8
- Lord God v. 8
- The Almighty v. 8
- Jesus v. 9
- Spirit v. 10
- The Son of Man appeared to John in a vision vv. 9-20
- Although He is exalted in heaven, He is also present with His churches on earth and knows their needs better than they themselves do vv. 9-20
- Conquered death forever, and there is no place for fear in His church v. 17
- Died and is alive forevermore v. 18
- Has the keys of Death and Hades v. 18

<u>Revelation 2</u>

- Holds the seven stars in His hands and walks among the seven golden lampstands v. 1
- Omniscient v. 2
- Hates v. 6
- His Spirit speaks to the churches vv. 7, 11, 17, 29
- Grants the one who conquers to eat of the tree of life, which is in the paradise of God v. 7
- The first and the last v. 8
- Died and came to life v. 8
- Crowns with life those who are faithful unto death v. 10
- Has the sharp, two-edged sword v. 12
- Gives hidden manna to the one who conquers v. 17
- Has eyes like a flame of fire v. 18
- Has feet like burnished bronze v. 18
- Searches minds and hearts v. 23
- Gives to one according to his works v. 23
- Gives authority over the nations to the one who conquers and obeys His words v. 26
- Jesus received authority from the Father v. 27

Revelation 3

- has the seven spirits of God and the seven stars v. 1
- To the one who conquers He clothes in white garments and will never blot his name from the book of life. He will confess his name before His Father and before His angels v. 5
- The Spirit speaks to the churches vv. 6, 13, 22
- Holy One v. 7
- True One v. 7
- Has the key of David v. 7
- Opens and no one will shut, and closes and no one will open vv. 7, 8
- Makes the conqueror a pillar in the temple of God, and He shall write on Him God's name, and the name of His city v. 12
- Will make a new Jerusalem come down from heaven and His own new name v. 12
- The Amen v. 14
- The faithful and true witness v. 14
- The beginning of God's creation v. 14
- Would rather one be cold or hot, rather than lukewarm v. 16
- Reproves and disciplines those whom He loves v. 19
- Stands at the door and knocks, waiting for someone to open to Him and let Him come in and fellowship with him v. 20
- Grants the conqueror to sit with Him on His throne, as Jesus also conquered and sat down with His Father on His throne v. 21

Revelation 4

- LORD vv. 8, 11
- Voice like a trumpet v. 1
- Holy, holy, holy, is the Lord God Almighty v. 11
- Was and is and is to come v. 8
- Glory, honor, and thanks are given to Him v. 9
- Lives forever and ever vv. 9, 10
- Worthy to receive glory and honor and power v. 11
- Created all things v. 11
- By His will creation exists v. 11

Revelation 5

- The Lion of the tribe of Judah v. 5
- The Root of David v. 5
- Conquered v. 5
- Can open the scroll and its seven seals v. 5
- Lamb v. 6
- Worthy to take the scroll and open its seven seals v. 9
- Slain, and by His blood He ransomed people tribe and language and people and nation, making them a kingdom and priests to God vv. 9-10

Revelation 6

- LORD vv. 10
- Conquers v. 2
- Takes peace from the earth v. 4
- Sovereign Lord v. 10
- Holy v. 10
- True v. 10
- Will judge and avenge the blood of His martyrs v. 11
- Seated on the throne v. 16
- Wrath of the Lamb v. 16

Revelation 7

- Living v. 2
- Served v. 3
- Seals 144,000 on the forehead from among every tribe of the sons of Israel v. 4

- Will save a great multitude that no one can number, from every nation, from all tribes and peoples and languages, and they will stand before His throne and before the Lamb v. 9
- Salvation belongs to God who sits on the throne, and to the Lamb v. 10
- Worshipped v. 11
- Blessing and glory and wisdom and thanksgiving and honor and power and might is His forever and ever v. 12
- His people shall be before His throne day and night in His temple; and He who sits on the throne will shelter them with His presence. The Lamb will be their Shepherd, and He will guide them to springs of living water, and God will wipe away every tear from their eyes vv. 15, 17

<u>Revelation 8</u>

- Brings woe to the earth vv. 1-13

<u>Revelation 9</u>

- God's patient restraint will come to a close, and plagues will come upon the unrepentant vv. 1-21
- Revelation 10
- Lives forever and ever v. 6
- Created heaven, earth, and sea and what is in them v. 6
- The mystery of God will be fulfilled, just as He announced to His servants the prophets v. 7
- Revelation 11
- LORD vv. 4, 8, 15, 17
- Grants authority v. 3
- Gives the breath of life v. 11
- The kingdom of the world will become the kingdom of God and His Christ, and He shall reign forever and ever v. 15
- Lord God Almighty v. 17
- Is and was v. 17
- Taken His great power and begun to reign v. 17
- His wrath came v. 18
- Judges the dead and rewards His servants, the prophets and saints, and those who fear His name, both great and small v. 18
- Destroys the destroyers of the earth v. 18
- His temple in heaven is opened v. 19
- Revelation 12
- Prepares v. 6
- Threw Satan down from heaven v. 9
- His salvation and power and kingdom and authority of His Christ comes v. 10
- Lamb v. 11
- Jesus v. 17

<u>Revelation 13</u>

- Dwells in heaven v. 7
- Wrote names before the foundation of the world in the book of life of the Lamb who was slain v. 8

<u>Revelation 14</u>

- LORD v. 13
- Lamb v. 1
- Stood with its 144,000 who had His name and His Father's name written on their foreheads v. 1
- Voice like the roar of many waters and like the sound of thunder v. 2
- Redeems people vv. 3, 4
- To be feared and given glory and worship v. 7
- Made the heaven and earth and the sea and the springs of water v. 7
- Gives the wine of wrath to idolaters to drink, poured full strength from the cup of His anger v. 10

- Calls the saints to endurance, those who keep the commandments of God and their faith in Jesus v. 12
- Blesses the dead who die in Jesus, that they may rest from their labors, for their deeds follow them v. 13
- Spirit v. 13
- Reaps the earth v. 16
- Wrath v. 19

Revelation 15

- LORD vv. 3, 4
- Wrath v. 1
- Lamb v. 3
- Great and amazing are His deeds v. 3
- Lord God Almighty v. 3
- His ways are just and true v. 3
- King of the nations v. 3
- All will fear and glorify His name v. 4
- He alone is holy v. 4
- All nations will come and worship Him, for His righteous acts have been revealed v. 4
- Wrath v. 7
- Lives forever and ever v. 7
- Glorious v. 8
- Powerful v. 8

Revelation 16

- LORD vv. 7, 17
- Loud voice v. 1
- Wrath v. 1
- Just v. 5
- Holy One v. 5
- Is and was v. 5
- Gives blood for His enemies to drink v. 6
- Lord God the Almighty v. 7
- True and just are His judgments v.7
- Has power over plagues v. 9
- God Almighty v. 14
- Comes like a thief v. 15
- Finishes v. 17
- Sends a plague of great hailstones, about a hundred pounds each, to fall on people v. 21

Revelation 17

- LORD v. 14
- Spirit v. 3
- Writes the names of some people in the book of life v. 8
- War will be made against the Lamb, and the Lamb will conquer the enemy v. 14
- The Lamb is the Lord of lords and King of kings, and those with Him are called and chosen and faithful v. 14
- Puts it into His enemies' hearts to do His will v. 17

Revelation 18

- LORD v. 8
- Delegates authority v. 1
- Calls His people to come out of sin v. 4
- Remembers iniquities of the unrepentant v. 5
- Given judgment over Babylon for His people v. 20

Revelation 19

- LORD vv. 6, 16
- Salvation and glory and power belong to God v. 1
- His judgments are true and just v. 2
- He has judged the great prostitute who corrupted the earth with her immorality, and has avenged the blood of His servants v. 2
- Worshipped by His servants v. 4
- Seated on the throne v. 4
- The Almighty v. 6
- Reigns v. 6
- Given glory v. 7

- Lamb v. 7
- Bride v. 7
- The righteous deeds of the saints clothe Him v. 8
- Lamb v. 9
- The testimony of Jesus is the spirit of prophecy v. 10
- Will ride on a white horse v. 11
- Faithful and True v. 11
- In righteousness He judges and makes war v. 11
- His eyes are like a flame of fire, and on His head are many diadems, and He has a name written that no one knows but Himself v. 12
- Clothed in a robe dipped in blood v. 13
- The Word of God v. 13
- The armies of heaven, arrayed in fine linen, white and pure, follow Him on white horses v. 14
- From His mouth comes a sharp sword with which to strike down the nations, and He will rule them with an iron rod v. 15
- He will tread the winepress of the fury of the wrath of God v. 15
- The Almighty v. 15
- On His robe and on His thigh He has a name written, "King of kings and Lord of lords" v. 16
- Throws the beast and the false prophet into the lake of fire that burns with sulfur vv. 20-21
- Slays His enemies v. 21

Revelation 20

- His people will reign with Him for a thousand years vv. 4, 6
- Consumes Satan and those whom he deceives from the nations, and they will be tormented day and night forever and ever vv. 7-10
- Seated on a great white throne v. 11
- Judges all according to what they have done and all whose names are not found in the book of life are thrown into the lake of fire vv. 11-15

Revelation 21

- LORD v. 22
- Created a new heaven and new earth and new Jerusalem prepared as a bride for Him vv. 1-2
- Will dwell with man, wiping away all tears vv. 3-4
- Seated on the throne v. 5
- Makes all things new v. 5
- Alpha and Omega v. 6
- God of the one who conquers v. 7
- Throws sinners into the lake of fire, the second death vv. 7-8
- Lamb v. 9
- Lord God v. 22
- Almighty v. 22
- Lamb v. 22
- Gloriously gives off light v. 23
- Those written in the Lamb's book of life will live in the new Jerusalem v. 27

Revelation 22

- LORD vv. 5, 6, 20, 21
- The river of life flows, bright as crystal, from the throne of God and of the Lamb through the middle of the street of the city vv. 1-2
- His servants will worship Him and see His face, and have His name written on their foreheads vv. 3-4
- The Lord will be the light in the new Jerusalem v. 5
- Will reign forever and ever v. 5
- His words are trustworthy and true v. 6

- God of the spirits of the prophets v. 6
- Sent His angel to show His servants what soon must take place v. 6
- Coming soon vv. 7, 12, 20
- Blesses those who keep the words of the prophecy of the book of Revelation v. 7
- Only He is worthy of worship v. 9
- The Alpha and the Omega, the first and the last, the beginning and the end v. 13
- Does not let evildoers inside v. 15
- Jesus sent His angel to testify things about the churches v. 16
- The root and descendent of David v. 16
- The bright morning star v. 16
- The Spirit and Bride say come v. 17
- Lets the thirsty and those who desire take the water of life without price v. 17
- Will add the plagues described in Revelation to any who add to His word, and will take away one's share in the tree of life if they take away the words addressed in His book of prophecy vv. 18-19
- His grace is with all v. 21
- Jesus is Lord v. 21

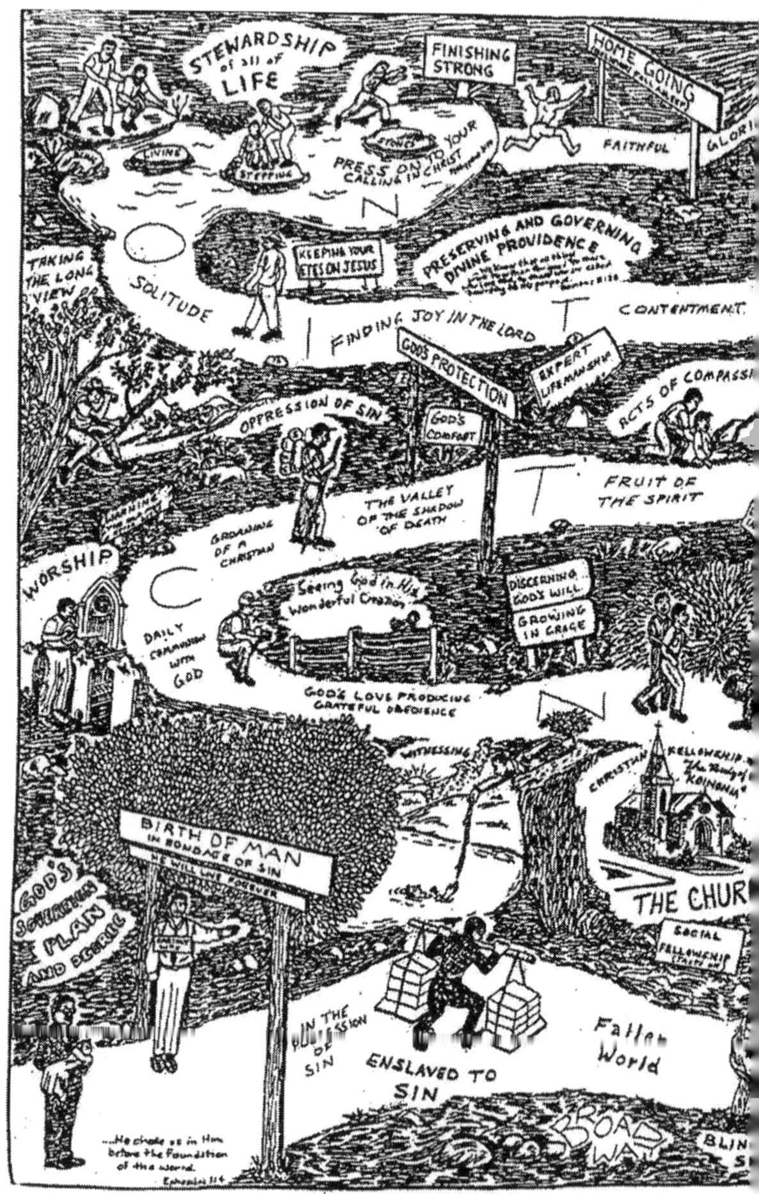

Guideposts and Miles

of the Christian Life

Appendix 4

THE 19 SIGNIFICANT ATTRIBUTES OF GOD WITH RELATED ATTRIBUTES

I. Constitutional Attributes

Infiniteness (0)

Boundless (0)

Immeasurable (4)
Ps 147:5; Eph 1:19, 2:7; John 3:34

Eph 1:19
...and what is the immeasurable greatness of his power toward us who believe, according to the working of his great might...

Eph 2:7
...so that in the coming ages he might show the immeasurable riches of his grace in kindness toward us in Christ Jesus.

Incomprehensible (0)

Mysterious (0)

Omnipresent (0)

Ubiquitous (0)

Unfathomable (0)

Unimaginable (0)

Unique (0)

Unknowable (0)

Unsearchable (6)

Job 5:9, 36:26; Ps 145:3; Isa 40:28; Rom 11:33; Eph 3:8

Ps 145:3

Great is the Lord, and greatly to be praised,
and his greatness is unsearchable.

Isa 40:28

Have you not known? Have you not heard?
The Lord is the everlasting God,
the Creator of the ends of the earth.
He does not faint or grow weary;
his understanding is unsearchable.

Rom 11:33

Oh, the depth of the riches and wisdom and knowledge of God! How unsearchable are his judgments and how inscrutable his ways!

Spirit (300)

Gen 1:2, 6:3, 41:38; Exod 31:3, 35:31; Num 11:17, 11:25, 11:26, 11:29, 24:2, 27:18; Judg 3:10, 6:34, 11:29, 13:25, 14:6, 14:19, 15:14; 1 Sam 10:6, 10:10, 11:6, 16:13, 16:14, 19:20, 19:23; 2 Sam 23:2; 1 Kings 18:12, 22:24; 2 Kings 2:16; 1 Chron 12:18; 2 Chron 15:1, 18:23, 20:14, 24:20; Neh 9:20, 9:30; Job 33:4; Ps 51:1, 104:30, 139:7, 143:10; Isa 11:2, 30:1, 32:15, 34:16, 40:13, 42:1, 44:3, 48:16, 59:21, 61:1, 63:10, 63:11, 63:14; Ezek 2:2, 3:12, 3:14, 3:24, 8:3, 11:1, 11:5, 11:24, 36:27, 37:1, 37:14, 39:29, 43:5; Joel 2:28, 2:29; Micah 3:8; Haggai 2:5; Zech 4:6, 6:8, 7:12; Mal 2:15; Matt 1:18, 1:20, 3:11, 3:16, 4:1, 10:20, 12:18, 12:28, 12:31, 12:32, 22:43, 28:19; Mark 1:8, 1:10, 1:12, 3:29, 12:36, 13:11; Luke 1:15, 1:35, 1:41, 1:67, 2:25, 2:26, 2:27, 3:16, 3:22, 4:1, 4:14, 4:18, 10:21, 11:13, 12:10, 12:12; John 1:32, 1:33, 3:5, 3:6, 3:8, 3:34, 6:63, 7:39, 14:17, 14:26, 15:26, 16:13, 20:22; Acts 1:2, 1:5, 1:8, 1:16, 2:4, 2:17, 2:18, 2:33, 2:38, 4:8, 4:25, 4:31, 5:3, 5:9, 5:32, 6:3, 6:5, 6:10, 7:51, 7:55, 8:15, 8;17, 8:18, 8:19, 8:29, 8:39, 9:17, 9:31, 10:19, 10:38, 10:44, 10:45, 10:47, 11:12, 11:15, 11:16, 11:24, 11:28, 13:2, 13:4, 13:9, 13:52, 15:8, 15:28, 16:6, 16:7, 19:2, 19:6, 19:21, 20:22, 20:23, 20:28, 21:4, 21:11, 28:25; Rom 1:4, 2:29, 5:5, 7:6, 8:2, 8:4, 8:5, 8:6, 8:9, 8:10, 8:11, 8:13, 8:14, 8:15, 8:16, 8:23, 8:26, 8:27, 9:1, 14:17, 15:13, 15:16, 15:19, 15:30; 1 Cor 2:4, 2:10, 2:11, 2:12, 2:13, 2:14, 3:16, 6:11, 6:19, 7:40, 12:3, 12:4, 12:7, 12:8, 12:9, 12:11, 12:13, 14:2, 14:12; 2 Cor 1:22, 3:3, 3:6, 3:8, 3:17, 3:18, 5:5, 6:6, 13:14; Gal 3:2, 3:3, 3:5, 3:14, 4:6, 4:29, 5:5, 5:16, 5:17, 5:18, 5:22, 5:25, 6:8; Eph 1:13, 1:17, 2:18, 2:22, 3:5, 3:16, 4:3, 4:4, 4:30, 5:18, 6:17, 6:18; Phil 1:19, 2:1, 3:3; Col 1:8; 1 Thess 1:5, 1:6, 4:8, 5:19; 2 Thess 2:13; 1 Tim 3:16, 4:1; 2 Tim 1:14; Titus 3:5; Heb 2:4, 3:7, 6:4, 9:8, 9:14, 10:15, 10:29; 1 Pet 1:2, 1:11, 1:12, 4:14; 2 Pet 1:21; 1 John 3:24, 4:2, 4:6, 4:13, 5:6, 5:8; Jude 19, 20; Rev 1:10, 2:7, 2:11, 2:17, 2:29, 3:6, 3:13, 3:22, 4:2, 14:13, 17:3, 21:10, 22:17

Isa 11:2

And the Spirit of the Lord shall rest upon him,
the Spirit of wisdom and understanding,

the Spirit of counsel and might,
the Spirit of knowledge and the fear of the Lord.

Ezek 36:27

And I will put my Spirit within you, and cause you to walk in my statutes and be careful to obey my rules.

Rom 8:14-16

For all who are led by the Spirit of God are sons of God. For you did not receive the spirit of slavery to fall back into fear, but you have received the Spirit of adoption as sons, by whom we cry, "Abba! Father!" The Spirit himself bears witness with our spirit that we are children of God.

Rom 8:26-27

Likewise the Spirit helps us in our weakness. For we do not know what to pray for as we ought, but the Spirit himself intercedes for us with groanings too deep for words. And he who searches hearts knows what is the mind of the Spirit, because the Spirit intercedes for the saints according to the will of God.

1 Cor 2:10

...these things God has revealed to us through the Spirit. For the Spirit searches everything, even the depths of God.

Distinct in Being (0)

Immaterial (0)

Invisible (4)

Rom 1:20; Col 1:15; 1 Tim 1:17; Heb 11:27

Col 1:15

He is the image of the invisible God, the firstborn of all creation.

1 Tim 1:17

To the King of the ages, immortal, invisible, the only God, be honor and glory forever and ever. Amen.

Non-corporeal (0)

Supernatural (0)

Transcendent (0)

Triunity (12)

Matt 3:16-17, 28:19; Acts 7:55; Rom 1:4; 1 Cor 6:11; 2 Cor 13:14; Gal 4:6; Eph 1:17; Heb 9:14, 10:29; 1 Pet 1:2

Matt 3:16-17

And when Jesus was baptized, immediately he went up from the water, and behold, the heavens were opened to him, and he saw the Spirit of God descending like a dove and coming to rest on him; and behold, a voice from heaven said, "This is my beloved Son, with whom I am well pleased.

Matt 28:19

Go therefore and make disciples of all nations, baptizing them in the name of the Father and of the Son and of the Holy Spirit,..

1 Pet 1:2

...according to the foreknowledge of God the Father, in the sanctification of the Spirit, for obedience to Jesus Christ and for sprinkling with his blood:
May grace and peace be multiplied to you.

Fellowship (1)

2 Cor 13:14

2 Cor 13:14

The grace of the Lord Jesus Christ and the love of God and the fellowship of the Holy Spirit be with you all.

One (45)

Deut 6:4; Josh 22:22; Judg 13:19; Ps 50:1, 68:8, 71:22, 78:41, 89:18, 132:2, 132:5; Prov 9:10; Eccles 5:7; Isa 1:4, 1:24, 5:24, 28:16, 29:19, 29:23, 30:15, 41:13, 43:3, 48:17, 54:5, 55:5, 60:9; Jer 51:5; Hos 11:9, 11:12; Hab 1:12, 3:3; Zeph 3:17; Mal 2:10, 2:15; Mark 1:24, 12:29; Luke 4:34; John 8:41; Acts 22:14; Rom 3:29-30; 1 Cor 8:4, 8:6; Gal 3:20; Eph 4:3-6; 1 Tim 2:5; James 2:19

1 Cor 8:6

...yet for us there is one God, the Father, from whom are all things and for whom we exist, and one Lord, Jesus Christ, through whom are all things and through whom we exist.

Eph 4:3-6

...eager to maintain the unity of the Spirit in the bond of peace. There is one body and one Spirit—just as you were called to the one hope that belongs to your call—one Lord, one faith, one baptism, one God and Father of all, who is over all and through all and in all.

Person (0)

Simple (0)

Trinity (0)

Unity (1)

Eph 4:3

Eph 4:3

...eager to maintain the unity of the Spirit in the bond of peace.

Unchangeableness (5)

Job 23:13; Heb 6:17; Mal 3:6; Heb 7:21; James 1:17

Job 23:13

But he is unchangeable, and who can turn him back?
What he desires, that he does.

Heb 6:17

So when God desired to show more convincingly to the heirs of the promise the unchangeable character of his purpose, he guaranteed it with an oath,..

Mal 3:6

For I the Lord do not change; therefore you, O children of Jacob, are not consumed.

James 1:17

Every good gift and every perfect gift is from above, coming down from the Father of lights with whom there is no variation or shadow due to change.

Consistent (0)

Everlasting (16)

Gen 21:33; 1 Chron 16:36; Neh 9:5; Ps 41:13, 90:2, 93:2, 103:17, 106:48; Isa 9:6, 26:4, 40:28, 60:19-20, 63:12; Jer 10:10; Hab 1:12, 3:6

Ps 103:17

But the steadfast love of the Lord is from everlasting to everlasting on those who fear him,
and his righteousness to children's children,..

Isa 9:6

For to us a child is born,
to us a son is given;
and the government shall be upon his shoulder,
and his name shall be called
Wonderful Counselor, Mighty God,
Everlasting Father, Prince of Peace.

Isa 40:28

Have you not known? Have you not heard?
The Lord is the everlasting God,
the Creator of the ends of the earth.
He does not faint or grow weary;
his understanding is unsearchable.

Firm (2)

Ps 119:89; 2 Tim 2:19

Ps 119:89

Forever, O Lord, your word
is firmly fixed in the heavens.

2 Tim 2:19

But God's firm foundation stands, bearing this seal: "The Lord knows those who are his," and, "Let everyone who names the name of the Lord depart from iniquity."

Forever (79)

Exod 3:15, 15:18; Deut 32:40; 1 Sam 20:23, 20:42; 1 Chron 16:34, 16:41, 17:17; 2 Chron 5:13, 7:3, 7:6, 20:21; Ezra 3:11; Ps 9:7, 10:16, 12:7, 16:11, 18:50, 21:6, 29:10, 33:11, 45:6, 48:8, 48:14, 52:5, 52:8, 66:7, 72:17, 72:19, 89:28-29, 92:8, 93:5, 100:5, 105:8, 106:1, 107:1, 111:3, 111:5, 111:9, 112:3, 117:2, 118:29, 119:142, 119:144, 119:152, 119:160, 121:8, 125:2, 135:13, 136:1-26, 138:8, 146:6, 146:10, 148:6; Eccles 3:14; Isa 26:4, 40:8, 57:16, 59:21; Jer 3:12, 15:14, 17:4, 33:11; Lam 3:31, 5:19; Dan 6:26; Micah 7:18; Mal 1:4; 2 Cor 9:9; Heb 7:24, 7:28, 13:8; 1 Pet 1:25; Rev 1:18, 4:9-10, 11:15, 15:7

Ps 93:5

Your decrees are very trustworthy;
holiness befits your house,
O Lord, forevermore.

Ps 100:5

For the Lord is good;
his steadfast love endures forever,
and his faithfulness to all generations.

Heb 13:8

Jesus Christ is the same yesterday and today and forever.

Immutable (0)

Rock (31)

Deut 32:4, 32:15, 32:18, 32:31; 1 Sam 2:2; 2 Sam 22:2-3, 22:32, 22:47, 23:3; Ps 18:2, 18:31, 18:46, 19:14, 28:1, 31:2-3, 42:9, 62:2, 62:6-7, 71:3, 78:35, 89:26, 92:15, 94:22, 95:1, 144:1; Isa 17:10, 26:4, 30:29, 44:8; Hab 1:12; 1 Cor 10:4

2 Sam 22:2-3

The Lord is my rock and my fortress and my deliverer,
my God, my rock, in whom I take refuge,
my shield, and the horn of my salvation,
my stronghold and my refuge,
my savior; you save me from violence.

Isa 26:4

Trust in the Lord forever,
for the Lord God is an everlasting rock.

Unrepentant (0)

Self-Existence (3)

Exod 3:14; John 17:5; Heb 11:6

Exod 3:14

God said to Moses, "I am who I am." And he said, "Say this to the people of Israel, 'I am has sent me to you.'"

Appendix 4

John 17:5

And now, Father, glorify me in your own presence with the glory that I had with you before the world existed.

Heb 11:6

And without faith it is impossible to please him, for whoever would draw near to God must believe that he exists and that he rewards those who seek him.

Alone (28)

Exod 22:20; Deut 32:12; 2 Kings 19:15, 19:19; Neh 9:6; Job 9:8; Ps 4:8, 62:1-2, 62:5, 71:16, 72:18, 83:18, 86:10, 136:4, 148:13; Isa 2:11, 2:17, 26:13, 37:16, 37:20, 44:24, 63:3; Mark 2:7, 10:18; Luke 5:21, 18:19; 1 Tim 6:16; Rev 15:4

Isa 44:24

Thus says the Lord, your Redeemer,
who formed you from the womb:
"I am the Lord, who made all things,
who alone stretched out the heavens,
who spread out the earth by myself,..

1 Tim 6:15-16

...which he will display at the proper time—he who is the blessed and only Sovereign, the King of kings and Lord of lords, 16 who alone has immortality, who dwells in unapproachable light, whom no one has ever seen or can see. To him be honor and eternal dominion. Amen.

Being (0)

Eternal (10)

Deut 33:27; Isa 57:15; Rom 1:20, 16:26; 1 Tim 6:16; Titus 1:2; Heb 9:14; 1 Pet 5:10; 2 Pet 3:18; 1 John 5:20

Isa 57:15

For thus says the One who is high and lifted up,
who inhabits eternity, whose name is Holy:
"I dwell in the high and holy place,
and also with him who is of a contrite and lowly spirit,
to revive the spirit of the lowly,
and to revive the heart of the contrite.

Essence (0)

Free (0)

Immortal (3)

Rom 1:23; 1 Tim 1:17, 6:16

1 Tim 1:17

To the King of the ages, immortal, invisible, the only God, be honor and glory forever and ever. Amen.

Omniscience (21)

1 Kings 8:39; 1 Chron 28:9; Job 37:16, 42:1-2; Ps 94:7-11, 147:5; Eccles 12:14; Isa 29:15-16; Jer 16:17, 32:19; Ezek 11:5; Dan 2:22; Matt 9:4, 12:25; Luke 6:8; John 2:24-25, 4:29, 6:64, 16:30

1 Kings 8:39

...then hear in heaven your dwelling place and forgive and act and render to each whose heart you know, according to all his ways (for you, you only, know the hearts of all the children of mankind),..

Ps 147:5

Great is our Lord, and abundant in power;
his understanding is beyond measure.

Only (14)

Matt 4:10; Luke 4:8; John 1:18, 3:16, 3:18, 5:44, 17:3; Rom 16:27; 1 Cor 3:7; 1 Tim 1:17, 6:15; 1 John 4:9; Jude 4, 25

John 17:3

And this is eternal life, that they know you the only true God, and Jesus Christ whom you have sent.

Jude 25

...to the only God, our Savior, through Jesus Christ our Lord, be glory, majesty, dominion, and authority, before all time and now and forever. Amen.

Self-sufficient (0)

Personal (0)

Accessible (4)

Zech 3:7; Rom 5:1-2; Eph 2:17-19, 3:12

Rom 5:1-2

Therefore, since we have been justified by faith, we have peace with God through our Lord Jesus Christ. Through him we have also obtained access by faith into this grace in which we stand, and we rejoice in hope of the glory of God.

Eph 2:17-19

And he came and preached peace to you who were far off and peace to those who were near. For through him we both have access in one Spirit to the Father. So then you are no longer strangers and aliens, but you are fellow citizens with the saints and members of the household of God,..

Immanent (2)

Ps 23:4; Matt 1:23

Ps 23:4

Even though I walk through the valley of the shadow of death,
I will fear no evil,

for you are with me;
your rod and your staff,
they comfort me.

Matt 1:23

"Behold, the virgin shall conceive and bear a son,
and they shall call his name Immanuel"
(which means, God with us).

Intimate (1)

1 Pet 3:4

1 Pet 3:4

...but let your adorning be the hidden person of the heart with the imperishable beauty of a gentle and quiet spirit, which in God's sight is very precious.

Knowable (41)

Deut 7:9; 1 Chron 28:9, 29:7; Ps 46:10, 56:9, 100:3; Isa 45:4-5; Jer 5:5, 9:6, 9:24, 22:16, 31:34; Ezek 20:20, 28:26, 34:30, 39:22, 39:28; Dan 11:32; Hos 8:2, 13:4; Luke 8:10; John 6:69, 10:14-15, 14:7, 14:16-17, 17:3; Acts 22:14; 1 Cor 3:16; Gal 4:8-9; Phil 3:10; Titus 1:16; Heb 8:11; 1 John 2:3-5, 2:13-14, 3:1, 3:24, 4:6, 4:7-8, 4:16, 5:2, 5:20

Ps 100:3

Know that the Lord, he is God!
It is he who made us, and we are his;
we are his people, and the sheep of his pasture.

John 10:14-15

I am the good shepherd. I know my own and my own know me, just as the Father knows me and I know the Father; and I lay down my life for the sheep.

John 14:16-17

And I will ask the Father, and he will give you another Helper, to be with you forever, even the Spirit of truth, whom the world cannot receive, because it neither sees him nor knows him. You know him, for he dwells with you and will be in you.

1 John 5:20

And we know that the Son of God has come and has given us understanding, so that we may know him who is true; and we are in him who is true, in his Son Jesus Christ. He is the true God and eternal life.

Near (30)

Exod 16:9, 19:22, 22:8, 24:2; Lev 9:5, 10:3; Deut 4:7; 1 Sam 14:36; Ps 34:18, 65:4, 69:18, 73:28, 75:1, 85:9, 119:151, 145:18, 148:14; Isa 29:13, 50:8, 55:6, 58:2; Ezek 40:46, 43:19, 44:15; Mal 3:5; Heb 4:16, 7:19, 7:25, 11:6; James 4:8

Ps 34:18

The Lord is near to the brokenhearted
and saves the crushed in spirit.

Heb 4:16

Let us then with confidence draw near to the throne of grace, that we may receive mercy and find grace to help in time of need.

Revealer (15)

1 Sam 3:7, 3:21; 1 Chron 17:25; Ps 98:2; Isa 22:14, 40:5, 56:1; Jer 33:6; Dan 2:19-22; Amos 3:7; Matt 11:25-27, 16:16-17; Luke 10:21-22; 1 Cor 2:9-10; Eph 3:5

Matt 11:25-27

At that time Jesus declared, "I thank you, Father, Lord of heaven and earth, that you have hidden these things from the wise and understanding and revealed them to little children; yes, Father, for such was your gracious will. All things have been handed over to me by my Father, and no one knows the Son except the Father, and no one knows the Father except the Son and anyone to whom the Son chooses to reveal him.

Matt 16:16-17

Simon Peter replied, "You are the Christ, the Son of the living God." And Jesus answered him, "Blessed are you, Simon Bar-Jonah! For flesh and blood has not revealed this to you, but my Father who is in heaven.

1 Cor 2:9-10

But, as it is written,
"What no eye has seen, nor ear heard,
nor the heart of man imagined,
what God has prepared for those who love him"—
these things God has revealed to us through the Spirit. For the Spirit searches everything, even the depths of God.

II. Moral Attributes

Truth (39)

1 Kings 17:24; Job 34:12; Ps 25:5, 43:3, 45:4, 51;6, 86:11, 119:43, 119:160, 145:18; Isa 10:20, 45:19, 65:16; Jer 5:3, 7:28; Zech 8:19; Matt 22:16; John 1:14, 1:17, 4:23-24, 8:32, 8:40, 14:6, 14:17, 15:26, 16:13, 17:17, 18:37; Rom 15:8; 1 Cor 2:13; 2 Cor 11:10; Eph 1:13, 4:21, 6:14; 2 Thess 2:13; 2 Tim 2:25; James 1:17-18; 1 John 5:6; 2 John 3

Job 34:12

Of a truth, God will not do wickedly,
and the Almighty will not pervert justice.

Ps 86:11

Teach me your way, O Lord,
that I may walk in your truth;
unite my heart to fear your name.

Ps 119:160

The sum of your word is truth,
and every one of your righteous rules endures forever.

Appendix 4

John 1:14

And the Word became flesh and dwelt among us, and we have seen his glory, glory as of the only Son from the Father, full of grace and truth.

John 14:6

Jesus said to him, "I am the way, and the truth, and the life. No one comes to the Father except through me.

Honest (0)

Illuminating (0)

Righteous (116)

Judg 5:11; 1 Sam 12:7; 2 Chron 12:6; Neh 9:8, 9:33; Job 36:3, 37:23; Ps 4:1, 5:8, 7:9, 7:11, 11:7, 19:9, 22:31, 23:3, 24:5, 31:1, 35:24, 35:28, 36:6, 36:10, 45:4, 45:7, 48:10, 50:6, 51:14, 65:5, 71:2, 71:15-16, 71:19, 71:24, 72:1, 85:10-13, 88:12, 89:14, 89:16, 96:13, 97:2, 97:6, 98:2, 98:9, 99:4, 103:6, 103:17, 111:3, 116:5, 119:7, 119:40, 119:62, 119:75, 119:106, 119:123, 119:137-138, 119:142, 119:144, 119:164, 129:4, 143:1, 143:11, 145:7, 145:17; Prov 21:12; Isa 5:16, 9:7, 11:4-5, 24:16, 18:17, 33:5, 41:10, 42:6, 42:21, 45:21, 45:23-24, 51:5-8, 56:1, 59:16-17; Jer 9:24, 11:20, 12:1, 23:5-6, 33:15-16; Dan 9:7, 9:14, 9:16, Hos 10:12; Micah 6:5; Zeph 3:5; Zech 8:8, 9:9; Matt 633; John 16:8, 17:25; Acts 3:14, 7:52, 17:31, 22:14; Rom 1:17, 1:32, 2:5, 3:5, 3:21-22, 3:25-26, 5:17-18, 5:21, 8:10, 10:3; 1 Cor 1:30; 2 Cor 3:9, 5:21; 2 Thess 1:5; 2 Tim 4:8; 1 Pet 3:18; 2 Pet 1:1; 1 John 2:1, 2:29; Rev 15:4, 19:11

Ps 50:6

The heavens declare his righteousness,
for God himself is judge! Selah

Ps 89:14

Righteousness and justice are the foundation of your throne;
steadfast love and faithfulness go before you.

Rev 15:4

Who will not fear, O Lord,
and glorify your name?
For you alone are holy.
All nations will come
and worship you,
for your righteous acts have been revealed."

True (33)

2 Sam 22:31; 2 Chron 15:3; Ps 18:30, 19:9, 119:142, 119:151; Prov 30:5; Jer 10:10, 42:5; Matt 22:16; Mark 12:14; John 1:9, 3:33, 7:18, 7:28, 8:14, 8:16, 8:26, 15:1, 17:3; Rom 3:4; 1 Thess 1:9; 1 Pet 5:12; 1 John 5:20; Rev 3:7, 3:14, 6:10, 15:3, 16:7, 19:2, 19:9, 19:11, 21:5

Prov 30:5

Every word of God proves true;
he is a shield to those who take refuge in him.

1 John 5:20

And we know that the Son of God has come and has given us understanding, so that we may know him who is true; and we are in him who is true, in his Son Jesus Christ. He is the true God and eternal life.

Rev 19:11

Then I saw heaven opened, and behold, a white horse! The one sitting on it is called Faithful and True, and in righteousness he judges and makes war.

Upright (6)

Ps 9:8, 25:8, 33:4, 45:6, 92:15; Heb 1:28

Ps 9:8

...and he judges the world with righteousness;
he judges the peoples with uprightness.

Ps 25:8

Good and upright is the Lord;
therefore he instructs sinners in the way.

Ps 33:4

For the word of the Lord is upright,
and all his work is done in faithfulness.

Virtue (0)

Zealous (0)

Goodness (73)

Exod 33:19; Josh 21:45, 23:14, 23:15-16, 24:20; 1 Kings 8:56; 1 Chron 16:34; 2 Chron 5:13, 6:41, 7:3, 30:18; Ezra 3:11, 7:9, 8:18, 8:22; Neh 2:8, 9:13, 9:20, 9:35; Ps 16:2, 25:7, 25:8, 27:13, 31:19, 34:8, 51:18, 52:9, 54:6, 68:10, 69:16, 73:1, 84:11, 85:12, 86:5, 100:5, 103:5, 104:28, 106:1, 107:1, 107:9, 109:21, 118:1, 118:29, 119:39, 119:68, 119:122, 125:4, 135:3, 136:1, 143:10, 145:7, 145:9; Jer 31:12, 31:14, 32:40-42, 33:9, 33:11; Lam 3:25, 3:38; Hos 3:5; Nah 1:7; Zech 9:17; Matt 7:11, 19:16-17; Mark 10:17-18; Luke 18:18-19; John 10:11, 10:14; Gal 5:22; Phil 2:13; Titus 3:4; Heb 6:5; 1 Pet 2:3

Josh 21:45

Not one word of all the good promises that the Lord had made to the house of Israel had failed; all came to pass.

Ps 25:7-8

Remember not the sins of my youth or my transgressions;
according to your steadfast love remember me,
for the sake of your goodness, O Lord!
Good and upright is the Lord;
therefore he instructs sinners in the way.

Ps 145:7-9

They shall pour forth the fame of your abundant goodness
and shall sing aloud of your righteousness.

The Lord is gracious and merciful,
slow to anger and abounding in steadfast love.
The Lord is good to all,
and his mercy is over all that he has made.

Jer 32:40-42

I will make with them an everlasting covenant, that I will not turn away from doing good to them. And I will put the fear of me in their hearts, that they may not turn from me. I will rejoice in doing them good, and I will plant them in this land in faithfulness, with all my heart and all my soul.

"For thus says the Lord: Just as I have brought all this great disaster upon this people, so I will bring upon them all the good that I promise them.

Lam 3:25

The Lord is good to those who wait for him,
to the soul who seeks him.

Mark 10:17-18

And as he was setting out on his journey, a man ran up and knelt before him and asked him,

"Good Teacher, what must I do to inherit eternal life?" And Jesus said to him, "Why do you call me good? No one is good except God alone."

Benevolent (0)

Encourager (3)

Rom 15:4-6; Phil 2:1-2; Heb 6:17-18

Rom 15:4-6

For whatever was written in former days was written for our instruction, that through endurance and through the encouragement of the Scriptures we might have hope. May the God of endurance and encouragement grant you to live in such harmony with one another, in accord with Christ Jesus, that together you may with one voice glorify the God and Father of our Lord Jesus Christ.

Favor (41)

Gen 6:8, 18:3, 39:21; Exod 3:21, 11:3, 12:36, 33:12-13, 33:16-17, 34:9; Deut 33:16, 33:23; 1 Sam 2:26; 1 Kings 13:6; 2 Kings 13:4; 2 Chron 33:12-13; Ezra 9:8; Ps 5:12, 30:5, 30:7, 84:11, 85:1, 89:17, 90:17, 102:13; Prov 3:3-4, 3:32-34, 8:35, 12:12, 18:22; Isa 49:8, 60:10, 61:2; Dan 1:9; Luke 1:28, 1:30, 2:40, 2:52, 4:19; Acts 7:9-10, 7:45-46; 2 Cor 6:2

Ps 5:12

For you bless the righteous, O Lord;
you cover him with favor as with a shield.

Ps 30:5

For his anger is but for a moment,
and his favor is for a lifetime.

Weeping may tarry for the night,
but joy comes with the morning.

Ps 84:11
For the Lord God is a sun and shield;
the Lord bestows favor and honor.
No good thing does he withhold
from those who walk uprightly.

For Us (20)
1 Sam 14:6; Neh 4:20; Ps 47:4, 62:8, 68:28, 126:3; Isa 26:12, 33:21; Luke 1:68-69; Rom 5:8, 8:26, 8:31-34; Gal 3:13; Eph 5:2; 1 Thess 5:9-10; Titus 2:14; Heb 10:20, 11:40; 1 John 3:16, 4:16

Neh 4:20
In the place where you hear the sound of the trumpet, rally to us there. Our God will fight for us.

Isa 26:12
O Lord, you will ordain peace for us,
for you have indeed done for us all our works.

Rom 8:26
Likewise the Spirit helps us in our weakness. For we do not know what to pray for as we ought, but the Spirit himself intercedes for us with groanings too deep for words.

Rom 8:31-35
What then shall we say to these things? If God is for us, who can be against us? He who did not spare his own Son but gave him up for us all, how will he not also with him graciously give us all things? Who shall bring any charge against God's elect? It is God who justifies. Who is to condemn? Christ Jesus is the one who died—more than that, who was raised—who is at the right hand of God, who indeed is interceding for us.

Giver (177)
Gen 17:8, 24:7, 27:28, 28:4, 28:13, 28:22, 41:16; Exod 6:8, 12:25, 16:8, 20:12; Lev 20:24, 25:2, 25:38; Num 6:26, 10:29, 11:18, 18:12, 18:19; Deut 1:20, 1:25, 2:29-31, 3:20, 4:1, 4:21, 4:40, 5:16, 6:10, 6:18, 7:2, 7:16, 7:23, 8:1, 8:18, 11:9, 11:17, 11:21, 11:31, 12:9-10, 13:12, 15:4, 15:7, 16:5, 16:18, 16:20, 17:2, 17:14, 18;9, 19;1-3, 19:8, 19:10, 19:14, 20:4, 20:13, 20:16 21:1, 21:10, 21:23, 23:14, 24:4, 25:15, 25:19, 26:1-3, 27:2-3, 28:8, 28:11, 28:65, 30:20, 31:5, 31:7, 31:20; Josh 1:11, 1;13, 1:15, 2:14, 5:6, 8:7, 21:46; Judg 11:9, 20:28; 2 Sam 5:19; 1 Kings 3:5, 11:31, 20:28, 22:6, 22:12, 22:15; 2 Kings 3:10, 3:13, 3:18; 1 Chron 14:10, 22:12; 2 Chron1:7, 18:5, 18:11, 19:6, 20:7, 25:9, 25;20, 30:12; Ezra 9:8-9; Neh 4:4; Job 16:11, 33:4, 35:10; Ps 16:7, 29:11, 37:4, 55:19, 68:11, 68:35, 72:1 85:12, 119:107, 119:149, 119:169, 146:7; Prov 2:6, 29:13; Eccles 2:26, 6:2; Isa 7:14, 19:4, 30:20, 42:5, 42:8, 43:3, 45:3, 62:2; Jer 5:24, 9:15, 21:7, 24:7, 29:11, 31:35, 32:3, 32:28, 34:2, 44:30, 45:5; Ezek 11:17, 29:19, 33:27; Haggai 2:9; Zech 10:1, 12:7; Luke 1:32, 18:7; John

3:34-35, 6:27, 6:33, 6:37-39, 11:22; Acts 5:31, 7:25, 15:8, 20:32; Romans 4:17; 1 Cor 3:7, 15:38, 15:57; 2 Cor 4:6; Eph 1:17; 1 Thess 4:8; 2 Thess 3:16; 1 Tim 6:13; 2 Tim 2:7; James 1:5, 4:6; 1 Pet 5:5; 1 John 5:16; Rev 21:23

Num 6:24-26

The Lord bless you and keep you;
the Lord make his face to shine upon you and be gracious to you;
the Lord lift up his countenance upon you and give you peace.

Job 33:4

The Spirit of God has made me,
and the breath of the Almighty gives me life.

Ps 37:4

Delight yourself in the Lord,
and he will give you the desires of your heart.

Jer 24:7

I will give them a heart to know that I am the Lord, and they shall be my people and I will be their God, for they shall return to me with their whole heart.

John 3:34-35

For he whom God has sent utters the words of God, for he gives the Spirit without measure. The Father loves the Son and has given all things into his hand.

John 6:37-39

All that the Father gives me will come to me, and whoever comes to me I will never cast out. For I have come down from heaven, not to do my own will but the will of him who sent me. And this is the will of him who sent me, that I should lose nothing of all that he has given me, but raise it up on the last day.

Acts 5:31

God exalted him at his right hand as Leader and Savior, to give repentance to Israel and forgiveness of sins.

2 Cor 4:6

For God, who said, "Let light shine out of darkness," has shone in our hearts to give the light of the knowledge of the glory of God in the face of Jesus Christ.

James 1:5

If any of you lacks wisdom, let him ask God, who gives generously to all without reproach, and it will be given him.

Helper (67)

Gen 4:1, 49:25; Exod 18:4; Deut 33:7, 33:26, 33:29; 1 Sam 7:12; 1 Chron 12:8, 12:18, 15:26; 2 Chron 14:11, 18:31, 25:8, 26:7, 32:8; Neh 6:16; Ps 10:14, 18:6, 22:19, 27:9, 28:7, 30:2, 30:10, 31:22, 33:20, 37:17, 37:40, 40:17, 46:1, 46:5, 54:4, 63:7, 70:5, 71:24, 72:12, 86:17, 89:19, 94:17, 106:4, 115:9-11, 118:13, 118:17, 121:1-2, 124:8, 146:5; Isa 41:10, 41:13-14, 44:2, 49:8, 50:7, 50:9; Hos 12:6, 13:8; Mark 9:22-24; Luke 1:54; John 14:16,

14:26, 15:26, 16:7; Acts 26:22; Rom 8:26; 2 Cor 6:2; Phil 1:19; Heb 2:16, 2:18, 4:16, 13:6

Ps 10:14

But you do see, for you note mischief and vexation,
that you may take it into your hands;
to you the helpless commits himself;
you have been the helper of the fatherless.

Ps 33:20

Our soul waits for the Lord;
he is our help and our shield.

Isa 41:10

Fear not, for I am with you;
be not dismayed, for I am your God;
I will strengthen you, I will help you,
I will uphold you with my righteous right hand.

Mark 9:22b-24

"...But if you can do anything, have compassion on us and help us." And Jesus said to him, "'If you can'! All things are possible for one who believes." Immediately the father of the child cried out and said, "I believe; help my unbelief!"

John 14:16

And I will ask the Father, and he will give you another Helper, to be with you forever...

Heb 2:18

For because he himself has suffered when tempted, he is able to help those who are being tempted.

Hope (53)

Ps 33:18, 33:22, 39:7, 42:5, 42:11, 43:5, 62:5, 65:5, 71:5, 78:7, 119:43, 119:49, 119:74, 119:81, 119:114, 119:147, 119:166, 130:5, 130:7, 131:3, 146:5, 147:11; Isa 8:17; Jer 14:22, 17:13, 29:11, 50:7; Lam 3:24; Matt 12:20-21; Acts 2:25-26, 24:15, 26:6; Rom 5:2, 15:12, 15:13; 2 Cor 1:10; Eph 1:12; Phil 2:19; 1 Thess 1:3, 5:8; 2 Thess 2:16-17; 1 Tim 1:1, 4:10, 5:5, 6:17; Titus 1:2, 2:13; Heb 3:6; 1 Pet 1:3, 1:13, 1:21, 3:5; 1 John 3:2-3

Ps 42:11

Why are you cast down, O my soul,
and why are you in turmoil within me?
Hope in God; for I shall again praise him,
my salvation and my God.

Ps 62:5

For God alone, O my soul, wait in silence,
for my hope is from him.

Ps 65:5

By awesome deeds you answer us with righteousness,
O God of our salvation,
the hope of all the ends of the earth
and of the farthest seas;

Jer 29:11

For I know the plans I have for you, declares the Lord, plans for welfare and not for evil, to give you a future and a hope.

Rom 15:13

May the God of hope fill you with all joy and peace in believing, so that by the power of the Holy Spirit you may abound in hope.

2 Thess 2:16-17

Now may our Lord Jesus Christ himself, and God our Father, who loved us and gave us eternal comfort and good hope through grace, comfort your hearts and establish them in every good work and word.

Kind (12)

Ruth 1:8, 2:20; Ps 145:13, 145:17; Hos 11:4; Luke 6:35; Rom 2:4, 11:22; Gal 5:22-23; Eph 2:7, 4:32; Titus 3:4

Ps 145:17

The Lord is righteous in all his ways
and kind in all his works.

Rom 2:4

Or do you presume on the riches of his kindness and forbearance and patience, not knowing that God's kindness is meant to lead you to repentance?

Gal 5:22-23

But the fruit of the Spirit is love, joy, peace, patience, kindness, goodness, faithfulness, gentleness, self-control; against such things there is no law.

Eph 2:7

...so that in the coming ages he might show the immeasurable riches of his grace in kindness toward us in Christ Jesus.

Holiness (210)

Exod 15:11, 26:33; Lev 11:44-45, 19:2, 20:26, 21:8, 22:2, 22:32; Num 20:13; Josh 24:19; 1 Sam 2:2, 6:20; 2 Kings 19:22; 1 Chron 16:10, 16:29, 16:35, 29:16; Job 6:10; Ps 22:3, 29:2, 30:4, 33:21, 51:11, 60:6, 71:22, 77:13, 78:41, 89:18, 89:35, 96:9, 97:12, 98:1, 99:3, 99:5, 99:9, 103:1, 105:3, 106:47, 108:7, 111:9, 145:21; Prov 9:10, 30:3; Isa 1:4, 5:16, 5:19, 5:24, 6:3, 8:3, 10:17, 10:20, 12:6, 17:7, 29:19, 29:33, 30:11, 30:12, 30:15, 31:1, 37:23, 40:25, 41:14, 41:16, 41:20, 43:3, 43:14-15, 45:11, 47:4, 48:17, 49:7, 52:10, 54;5, 55:5, 57:15, 60:9, 60:14, 63:10, 63:11; Jer 23:9, 50:29, 51:5; Ezek 20:39, 20:41, 28:22, 28:25, 36:20-23, 38:16, 38:23, 39:7, 39:25, 39:27, 43:7-8; Hos 11:9, 11:12; Amos 2:7, 4:2; Hab 1:12, Hab 3:3;

Zech 14:20; Matt 1:18, 1:20, 3:11, 12:32, 28:19; Mark 1:8, 1:24, 3:29, 12:36, 13:11; Luke 1:15, 1:35, 1:41, 1:49, 1:67, 2:25, 2:26, 3:16, 3:22, 4:1, 4:34, 10:21, 11:13, 12:10, 12:12; John 1:33, 6:69, 14:26, 17:11, 20:22; Acts 1:2, 1:5, 1:8, 1:16, 2:4, 2:27, 2:33, 2:38, 3:14, 4:8, 4:25, 4:27, 4:30, 4:31, 5:3, 5:32, 6:5, 7:51, 7:55, 8:15, 8:17, 8:19, 9:17, 9:31, 10:38, 10:44, 10:45, 10:47, 11:15, 11:16, 11:24, 13:2, 13:4, 13:9, 13:35, 13:52, 15:8, 15:28, 16:6, 19:2, 19:6, 20;23, 20:28, 21:11, 28:25; Rom 1:4, 5:5, 9;1, 14:17, 15:13, 15:16; 1 Cor 6:19, 12:3; 2 Cor 6:6, 13:14; Eph 1:13, 4:20; 1 Thess 1:5, 1:6, 4:8; 2 Tim 1:14; Titus 3:5; Heb 2:4, 3:7, 6:4, 7:26, 9:8, 10:15, 12:10; 1 Pet 1:12, 1:15, 1:16, 3:15; 2 Pet 1:21; 1 John 2:20; Jude 20; Rev 3:7, 4:8, 6:10, 15:4, 16:5

Lev 11:45

For I am the Lord who brought you up out of the land of Egypt to be your God. You shall therefore be holy, for I am holy.

1 Chron 16:29

Ascribe to the Lord the glory due his name;
bring an offering and come before him!
Worship the Lord in the splendor of holiness;

Ps 89:35

Once for all I have sworn by my holiness;
I will not lie to David.

Isa 5:16

But the Lord of hosts is exalted in justice,
and the Holy God shows himself holy in righteousness.

Isa 6:3

And one called to another and said:
"Holy, holy, holy is the Lord of hosts;
the whole earth is full of his glory!"

Isa 8:13

But the Lord of hosts, him you shall honor as holy. Let him be your fear, and let him be your dread.

Isa 29:19

The meek shall obtain fresh joy in the Lord,
and the poor among mankind shall exult in the Holy One of Israel.

Isa 49:7

Thus says the Lord,
the Redeemer of Israel and his Holy One,
to one deeply despised, abhorred by the nation,
the servant of rulers:
"Kings shall see and arise;
princes, and they shall prostrate themselves;
because of the Lord, who is faithful,

the Holy One of Israel, who has chosen you."

Isa 52:10

The Lord has bared his holy arm
before the eyes of all the nations,
and all the ends of the earth shall see
the salvation of our God.

Isa 60:9

For the coastlands shall hope for me,
the ships of Tarshish first,
to bring your children from afar,
their silver and gold with them,
for the name of the Lord your God,
and for the Holy One of Israel,
because he has made you beautiful.

Ezek 28:22

And say, Thus says the Lord God:
"Behold, I am against you, O Sidon,
and I will manifest my glory in your midst.
And they shall know that I am the Lord
when I execute judgments in her
and manifest my holiness in her;

Ezek 28:25

Thus says the Lord God: When I gather the house of Israel from the peoples among whom they are scattered, and manifest my holiness in them in the sight of the nations, then they shall dwell in their own land that I gave to my servant Jacob.

John 17:11

And I am no longer in the world, but they are in the world, and I am coming to you. Holy Father, keep them in your name, which you have given me, that they may be one, even as we are one.

Heb 12:10

For they disciplined us for a short time as it seemed best to them, but he disciplines us for our good, that we may share his holiness.

Rev 15:4

Who will not fear, O Lord,
and glorify your name?
For you alone are holy.
All nations will come
and worship you,
for your righteous acts have been revealed.

Blameless (2)
Ps 18:25, 51:4

Ps 51:4
Against you, you only, have I sinned
and done what is evil in your sight,
so that you may be justified in your words
and blameless in your judgment.

Blessedness (85)
Gen 9:26, 14:20, 24:27, 24:48; Exod 18:10; Deut 8:10; Josh 22:33; Judg 5:2, 5:9; 1 Sam 25:32, 25:39; 2 Sam 18:28, 22:47; 1 Kings 1:48, 5:7, 8:15, 8:56, 10:9; 1 Chron 16:36, 29:10; 2 Chron 2:12, 6:4, 9:8, 20:26, 31:8; Ezra 7:27; Neh 8:6, 9:5; Job 1:21; Ps 16:7, 18:46, 26:12, 28:6, 31:21, 34:1, 41:13, 63:4, 66:8, 66:20, 68:19, 68:35, 72:17, 72:18-19, 89:52, 96:2, 100:4, 103:1-2,103:20-22, 104:1, 104:35, 106:48, 113:2, 115:18, 119:12, 124:6, 134:1-2, 135:19-21, 144:1, 145:1-2, 145:10, 145:21; Ezek 3:12; Dan 2:19-20, 3:28, 4:34; Zech 11:5; Mark 11:9, 14:61; Luke 1:64, 1:68, 2:28, 19:38, 24:53; John 12:13; Rom 1:25, 9:5; 2 Cor 1:3, 11:31; Eph 1:3; 1 Tim 1:11, 6:15-16; James 3:9; 1 Pet 1:3; Rev 5:12-13, 7:12

Ps 72:18-19
Blessed be the Lord, the God of Israel,
who alone does wondrous things.
Blessed be his glorious name forever;
may the whole earth be filled with his glory!
Amen and Amen!

Ps 104:1
Bless the Lord, O my soul!
O Lord my God, you are very great!
You are clothed with splendor and majesty,

Mark 14:61
But he remained silent and made no answer. Again the high priest asked him, "Are you the Christ, the Son of the Blessed?"

Incomparable (6)
Ps 40:5, 89:6; Isa 40:18, 40:25, 46:5; Rom 8:18

Ps 40:5
You have multiplied, O Lord my God,
your wondrous deeds and your thoughts toward us;
none can compare with you!
I will proclaim and tell of them,
yet they are more than can be told.

Ps 89:5-7
Let the heavens praise your wonders, O Lord,
your faithfulness in the assembly of the holy ones!

For who in the skies can be compared to the Lord?
Who among the heavenly beings is like the Lord,
a God greatly to be feared in the council of the holy ones,
and awesome above all who are around him?

Incorruptible (6)

Ps 16:10; Acts 2:27, 2:31, 13:34-37; Gal 6:8; 2 Pet 1:4

Acts 2:31

...he foresaw and spoke about the resurrection of the Christ, that he was not abandoned to Hades, nor did his flesh see corruption.

Gal 6:8

For the one who sows to his own flesh will from the flesh reap corruption, but the one who sows to the Spirit will from the Spirit reap eternal life.

2 Pet 1:4

...by which he has granted to us his precious and very great promises, so that through them you may become partakers of the divine nature, having escaped from the corruption that is in the world because of sinful desire.

Light (45)

Gen 1:3-4; Exod 13:21; Ps 18:28, 27:1, 36:9, 43:3, 44:3, 56:13, 89:15, 90:8, 104:2, 118:27, 119:105, 119:130; Prov 6:23, 29:13; Isa 2:5, 10:17, 45:7, 60;1, 60:19-20; Micah 7:8; Hab 3:4; Mal 4:2; John 1:4-5, 1:9, 3:19-21, 8:12, 9:5, 12:35-36, 12:46; Acts 22:6-11, 26:13; 2 Cor 4:6; Eph 5:8-9, 5:14; 1 Tim 6:16; James 1:17; 1 Pet 2:9; 1 John 1:5, 2:8; Rev 21:23-24, 22:5

Isa 60:19

The sun shall be no more
your light by day,
nor for brightness shall the moon
give you light;
but the Lord will be your everlasting light,
and your God will be your glory.

Hab 3:4

His brightness was like the light;
rays flashed from his hand;
and there he veiled his power.

John 1:4-5

In him was life, and the life was the light of men. The light shines in the darkness, and the darkness has not overcome it.

John 3:19-21

And this is the judgment: the light has come into the world, and people loved the darkness rather than the light because their works were evil. For everyone who does wicked things hates the light and does not come to the light, lest his works should be exposed. But whoever does what is true comes to the light, so that it may be clearly seen that his works have been carried out in God."

John 8:12

Again Jesus spoke to them, saying, "I am the light of the world. Whoever follows me will not walk in darkness, but will have the light of life."

1 Tim 6:15-16

...which he will display at the proper time—he who is the blessed and only Sovereign, the King of kings and Lord of lords, who alone has immortality, who dwells in unapproachable light, whom no one has ever seen or can see. To him be honor and eternal dominion. Amen.

James 1:17

Every good gift and every perfect gift is from above, coming down from the Father of lights with whom there is no variation or shadow due to change.

Rev 21:23-24

And the city has no need of sun or moon to shine on it, for the glory of God gives it light, and its lamp is the Lamb. By its light will the nations walk, and the kings of the earth will bring their glory into it,

Perfect (17)

Deut 32:4; 2 Sam 22:31; Job 36:4, 37:16; Ps 18:30, 19:7, 119:96; Matt 5:48; 1 Tim 1:16; Heb 2:10, 5:9, 7:28, 12:2; James 1:25; 1 John 2:5, 4:12, 4:17-18

Deut 32:4

The Rock, his work is perfect,
for all his ways are justice.
A God of faithfulness and without iniquity,
just and upright is he.

Ps 18:30

This God—his way is perfect;
the word of the Lord proves true;
he is a shield for all those who take refuge in him.

Heb 2:10

For it was fitting that he, for whom and by whom all things exist, in bringing many sons to glory, should make the founder of their salvation perfect through suffering.

Pure (2)

Dan 7:9; 1 John 3:3

1 John 3:2-3

Beloved, we are God's children now, and what we will be has not yet appeared; but we know that when he appears we shall be like him, because we shall see him as he is. And everyone who thus hopes in him purifies himself as he is pure.

Sinlessness (4)

2 Cor 5:21; Heb 4:15; 1 Pet 2:22; 1 John 3:5

2 Cor 5:21

For our sake he made him to be sin who knew no sin, so that in him we might become the righteousness of God.

Heb 4:15

For we do not have a high priest who is unable to sympathize with our weaknesses, but one who in every respect has been tempted as we are, yet without sin.

1 John 3:5

You know that he appeared in order to take away sins, and in him there is no sin.

Unapproachable (3)

Lev 21:17; Jer 30:21; 1 Tim 6:16

Lev 21:17

Speak to Aaron, saying, None of your offspring throughout their generations who has a blemish may approach to offer the bread of his God.

Jer 30:21

Their prince shall be one of themselves;
their ruler shall come out from their midst;
I will make him draw near, and he shall approach me,
for who would dare of himself to approach me?
declares the Lord.

1 Tim 6:16

...which he will display at the proper time—he who is the blessed and only Sovereign, the King of kings and Lord of lords, who alone has immortality, who dwells in unapproachable light, whom no one has ever seen or can see. To him be honor and eternal dominion. Amen.

Love (121)

Gen 39:21; Num 14:18; Deut 7:7-9, 10:15, 23:5; 1 Sam 20:14-15; 2 Sam 2:6, 12:24, 15:20; 1 Kings 10:9; 1 Chron 16:41; 2 Chron 1:8, 2:11, 5:13, 7:3, 7:6, 9:8, 20:21; Ezra 3:11; Neh 1:5, 9:32; Job 10:12; Ps 11:7, 21:7, 25:6, 25:10, 31:21, 32:10, 33:5, 33:22, 36:5, 36:7, 37:28, 42:8, 48:9, 51:1, 52:1, 52:8, 57:3, 59:10, 59:17, 61:7, 62:12, 69:13, 69:16, 85:7, 87:2, 89:1, 89:49, 94:18, 100:5,101:1, 103:17, 106:1, 107:1, 107:8, 107:15, 107:21, 107:31, 107:43, 109:26, 109:29, 117:2, 118:1, 118:4, 118:29, 119:41, 119:64, 119:149, 130:7, 136:1-3, 136:26, 138:8, 146:8; Prov 3:12, 15:9; Isa 48:14, 54:8, 56:6, 61:8, 63:7; Jer 9:24, 16:5, 31:3, 33:11; Lam 3:22; Dan 9:4; Hos 3:1; Mal 1:2; Mark 10:21; John 3:16, 11:3, 11:5, 13:23, 19:26, 20:2, 20:6, 21:7, 21:20; Rom 1:7, 5:5, 5:8, 8:37-39, 15:30; 1 Cor 9:7; 2 Cor 13:11, 13:14; Gal 2:20; Eph 6:23; 1 Thess 1:4; 2 Thess 2:16, 3:5; 1 Tim 1:14; 2 Tim 1:13; Titus 3:4; Heb 12:6; 1 John 3:17, 4:7-12, 4:16; 2 John 3; Jude 21

Ps 51:1

Have mercy on me, O God,
according to your steadfast love;

according to your abundant mercy
blot out my transgressions.

Ps 100:5
For the Lord is good;
his steadfast love endures forever,
and his faithfulness to all generations.

Rom 5:8
...but God shows his love for us in that while we were still sinners, Christ died for us.

Rom 8:37-39
No, in all these things we are more than conquerors through him who loved us. For I am sure that neither death nor life, nor angels nor rulers, nor things present nor things to come, nor powers, nor height nor depth, nor anything else in all creation, will be able to separate us from the love of God in Christ Jesus our Lord.

1 John 4:7-12
Beloved, let us love one another, for love is from God, and whoever loves has been born of God and knows God. Anyone who does not love does not know God, because God is love. In this the love of God was made manifest among us, that God sent his only Son into the world, so that we might live through him. In this is love, not that we have loved God but that he loved us and sent his Son to be the propitiation for our sins. Beloved, if God so loved us, we also ought to love one another. No one has ever seen God; if we love one another, God abides in us and his love is perfected in us.

Caring (7)
Deut 11:12, 32:10; 1 Sam 25:29; Job 10:12; Ps 8:4; Zech 10:3; 1 Pet 5:7

Deut 32:10
He found him in a desert land,
and in the howling waste of the wilderness;
he encircled him, he cared for him,
he kept him as the apple of his eye.

Job 10:12
You have granted me life and steadfast love,
and your care has preserved my spirit.

1 Pet 5:6-7
Humble yourselves, therefore, under the mighty hand of God so that at the proper time he may exalt you, casting all your anxieties on him, because he cares for you.

Generous (1)
James 1:5

James 1:5

If any of you lacks wisdom, let him ask God, who gives generously to all without reproach, and it will be given him.

Gentle (7)

2 Sam 22:36; Job 15:11; Ps 18:35; Isa 40:11; Matt 11:29; 2 Cor 10:1; Gal 5:22-23

Ps 18:35

You have given me the shield of your salvation,
and your right hand supported me,
and your gentleness made me great.

Isa 40:11

He will tend his flock like a shepherd;
he will gather the lambs in his arms;
he will carry them in his bosom,
and gently lead those that are with young.

Matt 11:28-30

Come to me, all who labor and are heavy laden, and I will give you rest. Take my yoke upon you, and learn from me, for I am gentle and lowly in heart, and you will find rest for your souls. For my yoke is easy, and my burden is light.

Gracious (143)

Gen 33:5, 33:11, 43:29; Exod 33:19, 34:6; Num 6:25; 2 Sam 12:22; 2 Kings 13:23; 2 Chron 30:9; Neh 9:17, 9:31; Ps 4:1, 6:2, 9:13, 25:16, 26:11, 27:7, 31:9, 41:4, 41:10, 56:1, 67:1, 77:9, 86:3, 86:15-16, 103:8, 111:4, 112:4, 116:5, 119:29, 119:58, 119:132, 145:8; Isa 30:18-19, 33:2; Jer 31:2; Joel 2:13; Amos 5:15; Jonah 4:2; Zech 1:13; Mal 1:9; Matt 11:26; Luke 4:22, 10:21; John 1:14, 1:16-17; Acts 11:23, 13:43, 14:3, 14:26, 15:11, 15:40, 20:24, 20:32; Rom 1:5, 1:7, 3:24, 5:2, 5:15, 5:17, 5:20-21, 8:32, 11:5-6, 12:3, 12:6-8, 15:15, 16:20, 1 Cor 1:3-4, 3:10, 15:10, 16:23; 2 Cor 1:2, 1:12, 1:15, 2 Cor 14:15, 6:1, 8:1, 8:9, 9:8, 9:14, 12:9, 13:14; Gal 1:3, 1:6, 1:15, 2:9, 2:21, 5:4, 6:18; Eph 1:2, 1:6-7, 2:5-8, 3:2, 3:7-8, 4:7, 4:29, 6:24; Phil 1:2, 1:7, 4:23; Col 1:2, 1:6, 4:18; 1 Thess 1:1, 5:28; 2 Thess 1:2, 1:12, 2:16, 3:18; 1 Tim 1:2, 1:14, 6:21; 2 Tim 1:2, 1:9, 2:1, 4:22; Titus 1:4, 2:11, 3:7, 3:15; Philem 3, 25; Heb 2:9, 4:16, 10:29, 12:15, 13:9, 13:25; James 4:6; 1 Pet 1:2, 1:10, 1:13, 3:7, 4:10, 5:5, 5:10, 5:12; 2 Pet 1:2, 3:18; 2 John 3; Jude 4; Rev 1:4, 22:21

Exod 34:6

The Lord passed before him and proclaimed, "The Lord, the Lord, a God merciful and gracious, slow to anger, and abounding in steadfast love and faithfulness,

Num 6:24-26

The Lord bless you and keep you;
the Lord make his face to shine upon you and be gracious to you;
the Lord lift up his countenance upon you and give you peace.

Rom 8:32

He who did not spare his own Son but gave him up for us all, how will he not also with him graciously give us all things?

2 Cor 9:8

And God is able to make all grace abound to you, so that having all sufficiency in all things at all times, you may abound in every good work.

2 Cor 12:9

But he said to me, "My grace is sufficient for you, for my power is made perfect in weakness." Therefore I will boast all the more gladly of my weaknesses, so that the power of Christ may rest upon me.

Grieving (5)

Gen 6:6; Isa 63:10; Mark 3:5; John 11:35; Eph 4:30

Gen 6:6

And the Lord regretted that he had made man on the earth, and it grieved him to his heart.

Mark 3:5

And he looked around at them with anger, grieved at their hardness of heart, and said to the man, "Stretch out your hand." He stretched it out, and his hand was restored.

Eph 4:30

And do not grieve the Holy Spirit of God, by whom you were sealed for the day of redemption.

Long-suffering, "Slow to Anger" (9)

Exod 34:6; Num 14:18; Neh 9:17; Ps 86:15, 103:8, 145:8; Joel 2:13; Jonah 4:2; Nah 1:3

Exod 34:6-7

The Lord passed before him and proclaimed, "The Lord, the Lord, a God merciful and gracious, slow to anger, and abounding in steadfast love and faithfulness, keeping steadfast love for thousands, forgiving iniquity and transgression and sin, but who will by no means clear the guilty, visiting the iniquity of the fathers on the children and the children's children, to the third and the fourth generation."

Nah 1:2-3

The Lord is a jealous and avenging God;
the Lord is avenging and wrathful;
the Lord takes vengeance on his adversaries
and keeps wrath for his enemies.
The Lord is slow to anger and great in power,
and the Lord will by no means clear the guilty.
His way is in whirlwind and storm,
and the clouds are the dust of his feet.

Merciful (119)

Gen 19:16, 43:14; Exod 33:19; Deut 4:31, 30:3; 2 Sam 22:26, 24:14; 1 Chron 21:13; 2 Chron 30:9; Neh 1:11, 9:17, 9:19, 9:27-28, 9:31; Job 33:24; Ps 18:25, 23:6, Ps 25:6, 28:2,

28:6, 30:8, 30:10, 31:22, 40:11, 51:1, 55:1, 57:1, 69:16, 86:15, 103:4, 103:8, 111:4, 112:4, 116:1, 116:5, 119:77, 119:156, 123:2-3, 130:2, 140:6, 142:1, 143:1, 145:8, 145:9; Isa 19:22, 30:18, 60:10; Jer 3:12, 16:5, 31:9, 31:20, 33:26, 36:7, 42:2, 42:9, 42:12; Lam 3:22; Ezek 39:25; Dan 2:18, 4:27, 9:3, 9:9, 9:17-18, 9:23; Hos 1:6-7, 2:4, 2:19, 2:23, 14:3; Joel 2:13; Jonah 4:2; Hab 3:2; Zech 1:12, 1:16, 7:9, 12:10; Matt 9:27, 15:22, 17:15, 20:30-31; Mark 5:19, 10:47-48; Luke 1:50, 1:54, 1:58, 1:72, 1:78, 6:36, 17:13, 18:13, 18:38-39; Rom 9:15-18, 11:30-32, 12:1, 15:9; 1 Cor 7:25; 2 Cor 4:1; Gal 6:16; Eph 2:4; Phil 2:27; 1 Tim 1:2, 1:13, 1:16; 2 Tim 1:2, 1:16, 1:18; Titus 3:5; Heb 2:17, 4:16, 8:12, 10:28; James 2:13, 3:17, 5:11; 1 Pet 1:3, 2:10; 2 John 3; Jude 2, 21

Job 33:24

...and he is merciful to him, and says,
'Deliver him from going down into the pit;
I have found a ransom;'

Ps 51:1

Have mercy on me, O God,
according to your steadfast love;
according to your abundant mercy
blot out my transgressions.

Ps 119:156

Great is your mercy, O Lord;
give me life according to your rules.

Jer 31:20

Is Ephraim my dear son?
Is he my darling child?
For as often as I speak against him,
I do remember him still.
Therefore my heart yearns for him;
I will surely have mercy on him,
declares the Lord.

Hos 2:19-20

And I will betroth you to me forever. I will betroth you to me in righteousness and in justice, in steadfast love and in mercy. I will betroth you to me in faithfulness. And you shall know the Lord.

Eph 2:4-7

But God, being rich in mercy, because of the great love with which he loved us, even when we were dead in our trespasses, made us alive together with Christ—by grace you have been saved— and raised us up with him and seated us with him in the heavenly places in Christ Jesus, so that in the coming ages he might show the immeasurable riches of his grace in kindness toward us in Christ Jesus.

Patient (1)
2 Pet 3:9

2 Pet 3:9
The Lord is not slow to fulfill his promise as some count slowness, but is patient toward you, not wishing that any should perish, but that all should reach repentance.

Sympathetic (2)
Phil 2:1-2; Heb 4:15

Phil 2:1-2
So if there is any encouragement in Christ, any comfort from love, any participation in the Spirit, any affection and sympathy, complete my joy by being of the same mind, having the same love, being in full accord and of one mind.

Heb 4:14-15
Since then we have a great high priest who has passed through the heavens, Jesus, the Son of God, let us hold fast our confession. For we do not have a high priest who is unable to sympathize with our weaknesses, but one who in every respect has been tempted as we are, yet without sin.

Wrath (162)
Exod 22:24, 32:10-11; Lev 10:6; Num 1:53, 16:46, 18:5, 25:11; Deut 9:7-8, 9:22, 29:23, 29:28; Josh 9:20, 22:20; 1 Sam 28:18; 2 Kings 3:27, 22:13, 22:17, 23:26; 1 Chron 27:24; 2 Chron 12:7, 12:12, 19:2, 19:10, 24:18, 28:11, 28:13, 29:8, 32:25-26, 34:21, 34:21, 34:25, 36:16; Ezra 7:23, 8:22, 10:14; Neh 13:18; Job 14:13, 16:9, 19:11, 19:29, 20:28, 21:20; Ps 2:5, 2:12, 6:1, 21:9, 38:1, 56:7, 59:13, 78:21, 78:38, 78:49, 78:59, 78:62, 85:3, 88:7, 88:16, 89:38, 89:46, 90:7, 90:9, 90:11, 95:11, 106:23, 110:5; Isa 9:19, 10:6, 13:9, 13:13, 51:17, 51:20, 51:22, 59:18, 60:10, 63:3, 63:5-6; Jer 4:4, 6:11, 7:20, 7:29, 10:10, 10:25, 18:20, 21:5, 21:12, 23:19, 25:15, 30:23, 32:31, 32:37, 33:5, 36:7, 42:18, 44:6, 50:13, 50:25; Lam 2:2, 3:1, 4:11; Ezek 7:8, 7:12, 7:14, 7:19, 8:18, 9:8, 13:13, 14:19, 16:38, 16:42, 20:8, 20:13, 20:21, 20:33-34, 21:31, 22:20-22, 22:31, 24:8, 25:14, 25:17, 30:15, 36:6, 36:18, 38:18-19; Dan 9:16; Hos 5:10, 11:9, 13:11; Micah 5:8; Nah 1:2, 1:6; Hab 3:2, 3:8; Zeph 1:15, 1:18; Zech 8:2, 8:14; John 3:36; Rom 1:18, 2:5, 2:8, 3:5, 4:15, 5:9, 9:22, 12:19, 13:4-5; Eph 5:6; Col 3:6; 1 Thess 1:10, 2:16, 5:9; Heb 3:11, 4:3; Rev 6:16-17, 11:18, 14:10, 14:19, 15:1, 15:7, 16:1, 16:19, 19:15

Ps 78:38
Yet he, being compassionate,
atoned for their iniquity
and did not destroy them;
he restrained his anger often
and did not stir up all his wrath.

Ps 78:49
He let loose on them his burning anger,

wrath, indignation, and distress,
a company of destroying angels.

Isa 60:10

Foreigners shall build up your walls,
and their kings shall minister to you;
for in my wrath I struck you,
but in my favor I have had mercy on you.

Isa 63:3

I have trodden the winepress alone,
and from the peoples no one was with me;
I trod them in my anger
and trampled them in my wrath;
their lifeblood spattered on my garments,
and stained all my apparel.

Jer 7:20

Therefore thus says the Lord God: Behold, my anger and my wrath will be poured out on this place, upon man and beast, upon the trees of the field and the fruit of the ground; it will burn and not be quenched."

Jer 23:19

Behold, the storm of the Lord!
Wrath has gone forth,
a whirling tempest;
it will burst upon the head of the wicked.

Jer 50:25

The Lord has opened his armory
and brought out the weapons of his wrath,
for the Lord God of hosts has a work to do
in the land of the Chaldeans.

Lam 4:11

The Lord gave full vent to his wrath;
he poured out his hot anger,
and he kindled a fire in Zion
that consumed its foundations.

Ezek 7:8-9

Now I will soon pour out my wrath upon you, and spend my anger against you, and judge you according to your ways, and I will punish you for all your abominations. And my eye will not spare, nor will I have pity. I will punish you according to your ways, while your abominations are in your midst. Then you will know that I am the Lord, who strikes.

Nah 1:2

The Lord is a jealous and avenging God;

the Lord is avenging and wrathful;
the Lord takes vengeance on his adversaries
and keeps wrath for his enemies.

Zech 8:2

Thus says the Lord of hosts: I am jealous for Zion with great jealousy, and I am jealous for her with great wrath.

John 3:36

Whoever believes in the Son has eternal life; whoever does not obey the Son shall not see life, but the wrath of God remains on him.

Rom 2:3-5

Do you suppose, O man—you who judge those who practice such things and yet do them yourself—that you will escape the judgment of God? Or do you presume on the riches of his kindness and forbearance and patience, not knowing that God's kindness is meant to lead you to repentance? But because of your hard and impenitent heart you are storing up wrath for yourself on the day of wrath when God's righteous judgment will be revealed.

Rom 5:8-9

...but God shows his love for us in that while we were still sinners, Christ died for us. Since, therefore, we have now been justified by his blood, much more shall we be saved by him from the wrath of God.

Rev 14:19

So the angel swung his sickle across the earth and gathered the grape harvest of the earth and threw it into the great winepress of the wrath of God.

Anger (214)

Exod 4:14, 32:12, 34:6; Num 11:1, 11:10, 11:33, 12:9, 14:18, 22:22, 25:3-4, 32:10, 32:13-14; Deut 1:34, 1:37, 3:26, 4:21, 4:25, 6:15, 7:4, 9:8, 9:18-20, 11:17, 13:17, 29:20, 29:23-24, 29:27-28, 31:17, 31:29, 32:16, 32:21; Josh 7:1, 7:26, 22:18, 23:16; Judg 2:12, 2:14, 2:20, 3:8, 6:39, 10:7; 2 Sam 6:7, 24:1; 1 Kings 11:9, 14:9, 14:15, 15:30, 16:2, 16:7, 16:13, 16:26, 16:33, 21:22, 22:53; 2 Kings 13:3, 17:11, 17:17-18, 21:6, 21:15, 22:17, 23:19, 23:26, 24:20; 1 Chron 13:10; 2 Chron 6:36, 25:15, 28:9, 28:25, 29:10, 30:8, 33:6, 34:25; Ezra 5:12, 9:14; Neh 4:5, 9:17; Job 4:9, 9:5, 9:13, 20:23, 21:17, 42:7; Ps 2:12, 6:1, 7:6, 18:7, 27:9, 30:5, 38:1, 60:1, 69:24, 74:1, 76:7, 77:9, 78:21, 78:31, 78:38, 78:49, 78:50, 78:58, 79:5-6, 80:4, 85:3, 85:5, 86:15, 90:7, 90:11, 102:10, 103:8-9, 106:29, 106:32, 106:40, 145:8; Prov 22:14, 24:18; Eccles 5:6; Isa 5:25, 9:12, 9:17, 9:21, 10:4-5, 10:25, 12:1, 13:3, 13:9, 13:13, 30:27, 30:30, 42:25, 47:6, 48:9, 54:8-9, 57:16-17, 63:3, 63:6, 64:5, 64:9, 66:15; Jer 3:5, 3:12, 4:8, 4:26, 7:18, 7:20, 8:19, 10:24, 11:17, 12:13, 15:14, 17:4, 18:23, 21:5, 23:20, 25:6-7, 25:37-38, 30:24, 32:29, 32:30-32, 32:37, 33:5, 36:7, 42:18, 44:3, 44:6, 44:8, 49:37, 51:45, 52:3; Lam 1:12, 2:1, 2:3, 2:21-22, 3:43, 4:11, 5:22; Ezek 5:13, 5:15, 7:3, 7:8, 8:17, 13:13, 16:26, 16:42, 20:8, 20:21, 22:20, 25:14, 35:11, 38:18, 43:8; Dan 9:16; Hos 8:5, 11:9, 13:11, 14:4; Joel 2:13; Amos

1:11; Jonah 3:9, 4:2; Micah 5:15, 7:18; Nah 1:3, 1:6; Hab 3:8, 3:12; Zeph 2:2-3, 3:8; Zech 1:2, 1:12, 1:15, 7:12, 10:3; Mal 1:4; Mark 3:5; Rev 14:10

Deut 6:14-15

You shall not go after other gods, the gods of the peoples who are around you—for the Lord your God in your midst is a jealous God—lest the anger of the Lord your God be kindled against you, and he destroy you from off the face of the earth.

Deut 9:19-20

For I was afraid of the anger and hot displeasure that the Lord bore against you, so that he was ready to destroy you. But the Lord listened to me that time also. And the Lord was so angry with Aaron that he was ready to destroy him. And I prayed for Aaron also at the same time.

Deut 32:16

They stirred him to jealousy with strange gods;
with abominations they provoked him to anger.

Neh 9:17

They refused to obey and were not mindful of the wonders that you performed among them, but they stiffened their neck and appointed a leader to return to their slavery in Egypt. But you are a God ready to forgive, gracious and merciful, slow to anger and abounding in steadfast love, and did not forsake them.

Ps 30:5

For his anger is but for a moment,
and his favor is for a lifetime.
Weeping may tarry for the night,
but joy comes with the morning.

Ps 78:49

He let loose on them his burning anger,
wrath, indignation, and distress,
a company of destroying angels.

Ps 103:8-9

The Lord is merciful and gracious,
slow to anger and abounding in steadfast love.
He will not always chide,
nor will he keep his anger forever.

Isa 12:1

You will say in that day:
"I will give thanks to you, O Lord,
for though you were angry with me,
your anger turned away,
that you might comfort me."

Isa 30:30

And the Lord will cause his majestic voice to be heard and the descending blow of his arm to be seen, in furious anger and a flame of devouring fire, with a cloudburst and storm and hailstones.

Isa 48:9-11

For my name's sake I defer my anger,
for the sake of my praise I restrain it for you,
that I may not cut you off.
Behold, I have refined you, but not as silver;
I have tried you in the furnace of affliction.
For my own sake, for my own sake, I do it,
for how should my name be profaned?
My glory I will not give to another.

Isa 54:8-9

"In overflowing anger for a moment
I hid my face from you,
but with everlasting love I will have compassion on you,"
says the Lord, your Redeemer.
"This is like the days of Noah to me:
as I swore that the waters of Noah
should no more go over the earth,
so I have sworn that I will not be angry with you,
and will not rebuke you."

Isa 63:6

"I trampled down the peoples in my anger;
I made them drunk in my wrath,
and I poured out their lifeblood on the earth."

Jer 23:20

The anger of the Lord will not turn back
until he has executed and accomplished
the intents of his heart.
In the latter days you will understand it clearly.

Ezek 5:13

Thus shall my anger spend itself, and I will vent my fury upon them and satisfy myself. And they shall know that I am the Lord—that I have spoken in my jealousy—when I spend my fury upon them.

Hos 14:4

I will heal their apostasy;
I will love them freely,
for my anger has turned from them.

Hab 3:12-13

You marched through the earth in fury;
you threshed the nations in anger.
You went out for the salvation of your people,
for the salvation of your anointed.
You crushed the head of the house of the wicked,
laying him bare from thigh to neck. Selah

Mark 3:5

And he looked around at them with anger, grieved at their hardness of heart, and said to the man, "Stretch out your hand." He stretched it out, and his hand was restored.

Rev 14:9-10

And another angel, a third, followed them, saying with a loud voice, "If anyone worships the beast and its image and receives a mark on his forehead or on his hand, he also will drink the wine of God's wrath, poured full strength into the cup of his anger, and he will be tormented with fire and sulfur in the presence of the holy angels and in the presence of the Lamb.

Fiery (15)

Exod 24:17; Deut 4:24, 9:3, 32:22, 33:2; Ps 78:21, 79:5; Song 8:6; Isa 66:15; Jer 23:29; Amos 5:6; Zeph 1:18; Zech 2:5; Heb 12:29; Rev 2:18

Exod 24:17

Now the appearance of the glory of the Lord was like a devouring fire on the top of the mountain in the sight of the people of Israel.

Deut 4:24

For the Lord your God is a consuming fire, a jealous God.

Song 8:6

Set me as a seal upon your heart,
as a seal upon your arm,
for love is strong as death,
jealousy is fierce as the grave.
Its flashes are flashes of fire,
the very flame of the Lord.

Isa 66:15-16

For behold, the Lord will come in fire,
and his chariots like the whirlwind,
to render his anger in fury,
and his rebuke with flames of fire.
For by fire will the Lord enter into judgment,
and by his sword, with all flesh;
and those slain by the Lord shall be many.

Rev 2:18

And to the angel of the church in Thyatira write: "The words of the Son of God, who has eyes like a flame of fire, and whose feet are like burnished bronze."

Remembering (33)

Gen 8:1, 9:15-16, 19:29, 30:22; Exod 2:24, 6:5; Lev 26:42, 26:45; 1 Sam 1:19; Ps 78:39, 98:3, 103:14, 105:8, 105:42, 106:45, 111:5, 136:23; Isa 43:25, 44:21, 65:17; Jer 2:2, 31:20; Lam 2:1; Ezek 16:60, Hos 7:2; 8:13, 9:9; Luke 1:72; Heb 10:17; Rev 16:19, 18:5

Ps 105:8

He remembers his covenant forever,
the word that he commanded, for a thousand generations,

Ps 136:23

It is he who remembered us in our low estate,
for his steadfast love endures forever;

Isa 43:25

"I, I am he
who blots out your transgressions for my own sake,
and I will not remember your sins.

Isa 44:21

Remember these things, O Jacob,
and Israel, for you are my servant;
I formed you; you are my servant;
O Israel, you will not be forgotten by me.

Jer 31:20

Is Ephraim my dear son?
Is he my darling child?
For as often as I speak against him,
I do remember him still.
Therefore my heart yearns for him;
I will surely have mercy on him,
declares the Lord.

Revenging (51)

Gen 4:15; Lev 26:25; Num 31:3; Deut 32:35, 32:41, 32:43; Josh 22:23; Judg 11:36; 1 Sam 20:16, 24:12, 25:39; 2 Sam 4:8, 22:48; 2 Kings 9:7; 2 Chron 24:22; Ps 9:12, 18:47, 79:10, 94:1, 99:8; Isa 1:24, 34:8, 35:4, 47:3, 59:17, 61:2, 63:4; Jer 5:9, 5:29, 9:9, 11:20, 15:15, 20:12, 46:10, 50:15, 50:28, 51:6, 51:11, 51:36; Ezek 24:8, 25:14, 25:17; Joel 3:21; Micah 5:15; Nah 1:2; Rom 12:19; 1 Thess 4:6; 2 Thess 1:8; Heb 10:30; Rev 6:10, 19:2

Deut 32:35

Vengeance is mine, and recompense,
for the time when their foot shall slip;
for the day of their calamity is at hand,

and their doom comes swiftly.

1 Sam 24:12

May the Lord judge between me and you, may the Lord avenge me against you, but my hand shall not be against you.

Isa 59:17

He put on righteousness as a breastplate,
and a helmet of salvation on his head;
he put on garments of vengeance for clothing,
and wrapped himself in zeal as a cloak.

Nah 1:2

The Lord is a jealous and avenging God;
the Lord is avenging and wrathful;
the Lord takes vengeance on his adversaries
and keeps wrath for his enemies.

Rom 12:19

Beloved, never avenge yourselves, but leave it to the wrath of God, for it is written, "Vengeance is mine, I will repay, says the Lord."

Self-control (1)

Gal 5:22-23

Gal 5:22-23

But the fruit of the Spirit is love, joy, peace, patience, kindness, goodness, faithfulness, gentleness, self-control; against such things there is no law.

Unforgiving (8)

Deut 29:18-20; Josh 24:19; Isa 2:9; Jer 18:23; Lam 3:42; Matt 6:15, 12:31-32; Luke 12:10

Deut 29:18-20

Beware lest there be among you a man or woman or clan or tribe whose heart is turning away today from the Lord our God to go and serve the gods of those nations. Beware lest there be among you a root bearing poisonous and bitter fruit, one who, when he hears the words of this sworn covenant, blesses himself in his heart, saying, 'I shall be safe, though I walk in the stubbornness of my heart.' This will lead to the sweeping away of moist and dry alike. The Lord will not be willing to forgive him, but rather the anger of the Lord and his jealousy will smoke against that man, and the curses written in this book will settle upon him, and the Lord will blot out his name from under heaven.

Matt 6:14-15

For if you forgive others their trespasses, your heavenly Father will also forgive you, but if you do not forgive others their trespasses, neither will your Father forgive your trespasses.

Matt 12:31-32

Therefore I tell you, every sin and blasphemy will be forgiven people, but the blasphemy against the Spirit will not be forgiven. And whoever speaks a word against the Son of Man will be forgiven, but whoever speaks against the Holy Spirit will not be forgiven, either in this age or in the age to come.

Faithfulness (79)

Gen 24:27, 32:10; Exod 34:6; Deut 7:9, 32:4; Josh 2:14; 1 Sam 2:9; 2 Sam 2:6, 15:20; Ps 25:10, 26:3, 31:5, 33:4, 36:5, 40:10-11, 54:5, 57:3, 57:10, 61:7, 69:13, 71:22, 85:10-13, 86:15, 88:11, 89:1-2, 89:5, 89:8, 89:14, 89:24, 89:33, 89:49, 91:4, 92:2, 96:13, 98:3, 100:5, 108:4, 111:7-8, 115:1, 117:2, 119:30, 119:75, 119:90, 119:138, 138:2, 143:1, 145:13, 146:6; Isa 11:5, 16:5, 25:1, 38:18-19, 42:3, 49:7, 61:8; Jer 31:3, 32:41, 42:5; Lam 3:22-23; Hos 2:20; Micah 7:20; Zech 8:8; Rom 3:3; 1 Cor 1:9, 10:13; 2 Cor 1:18; Gal 5:22; 2 Thess 3:3; 2 Tim 2:13; Heb 2:17, 3:2, 3:6, 10:23, 11:11; 1 Pet 4:19; 1 John 1:9;
Rev 1:5, 3:14, 19:11

Ps 31:5

Into your hand I commit my spirit;
you have redeemed me, O Lord, faithful God.

Ps 111:7-8

The works of his hands are faithful and just;
all his precepts are trustworthy;
they are established forever and ever,
to be performed with faithfulness and uprightness.

Ps 119:75

I know, O Lord, that your rules are righteous,
and that in faithfulness you have afflicted me.

Jer 31:3

the Lord appeared to him from far away.
I have loved you with an everlasting love;
therefore I have continued my faithfulness to you.

Jer 32:40-41

I will make with them an everlasting covenant, that I will not turn away from doing good to them. And I will put the fear of me in their hearts, that they may not turn from me. I will rejoice in doing them good, and I will plant them in this land in faithfulness, with all my heart and all my soul.

2 Thess 3:3

But the Lord is faithful. He will establish you and guard you against the evil one.

2 Tim 2:13

if we are faithless, he remains faithful—
for he cannot deny himself.

1 Pet 4:19

Therefore let those who suffer according to God's will entrust their souls to a faithful Creator while doing good.

1 John 1:9

If we confess our sins, he is faithful and just to forgive us our sins and to cleanse us from all unrighteousness.

Rev 19:11

Then I saw heaven opened, and behold, a white horse! The one sitting on it is called Faithful and True, and in righteousness he judges and makes war.

Dependable (0)

Loyal (0)

Persistence (9)

2 Chron 36:15; Jer 7:13, 7:25, 11:7, 25:3-4, 29:19, 32:33, 35:14-15, 44:4

2 Chron 36:15-16

The Lord, the God of their fathers, sent persistently to them by his messengers, because he had compassion on his people and on his dwelling place. But they kept mocking the messengers of God, despising his words and scoffing at his prophets, until the wrath of the Lord rose against his people, until there was no remedy.

Jer 25:3-4

For twenty-three years, from the thirteenth year of Josiah the son of Amon, king of Judah, to this day, the word of the Lord has come to me, and I have spoken persistently to you, but you have not listened. You have neither listened nor inclined your ears to hear, although the Lord persistently sent to you all his servants the prophets,

Jer 32:33

They have turned to me their back and not their face. And though I have taught them persistently, they have not listened to receive instruction.

Reliable (5)

2 Chron 13:18, 14:11, 16:7-8; 2 Cor 1:9; Heb 2:2

2 Chron 13:18

Thus the men of Israel were subdued at that time, and the men of Judah prevailed, because they relied on the Lord, the God of their fathers.

2 Chron 14:11-12

And Asa cried to the Lord his God, "O Lord, there is none like you to help, between the mighty and the weak. Help us, O Lord our God, for we rely on you, and in your name we have come against this multitude. O Lord, you are our God; let not man prevail against you." So the Lord defeated the Ethiopians before Asa and before Judah, and the Ethiopians fled.

Steadfast (142)

Gen 24:12, 24:14, 24:27, 32:10, 39:21; Exod 15:13, 20:6, 34:6-7; Num 14:18-19; Deut 5:10, 7:9, 7:12; 1 Sam 20:14-15; 2 Sam 2:6, 3:8, 7:15, 15:20, 22:51; 1 Kings 3:6, 8:23; 1 Chron 16:34, 16:41, 17:13; 2 Chron 1:8, 5:13, 6:14, 6:42, 7:3, 7:6, 20:21; Ezra 3:11, 7:28, 9:9; Neh 1:5, 9:17, 9:32; 13:22; Job 10:12; Ps 5:7, 6:4, 13:5, 17:7, 18:50, 21:7, 25:6-7, 25:10, 26:3, 31:7, 31:16, 31:21, 32:10, 33:5, 33:18, 33:22, 36:5, 36:7, 40:10-11, 42:8, 44:26, 48:9, 51:1, 52:1, 52:8, 57:3, 57:7, 57:10, 59:10, 59:17, 61:7, 62:12, 63:3, 66:20, 69:13, 69:16, 77:8, 85:7, 86:5, 86:13, 86:15, 89:1-2, 89:14, 89:24, 89:28, 89:49, 90:14, 92:2, 94:18, 98:3, 100:5, 101:1, 103:4, 103:8, 103:11, 103:17, 106:1, 106:7, 106:45, 107:1, 107:8, 107:15, 107:21, 107:31, 107:43, 108:1, 108:4, 109:21, 109:26, 115:1, 117:2, 118:1-4, 119:41, 119:64, 119:76, 119:88, 119:124, 119:149, 119:159, 130:7, 136:1-26, 138:2, 138:8, 143:8, 143:12, 144:2, 145:8, 147:11; Isa 54:10, 55:3, 63:7; Jer 9:24, 16:5, 32:18, 33:11; Lam 3:22, 3:32; Dan 9:4; Hos 2:19; Joel 2:13; Jonah 4:2; Micah 7:18, 7:20; 2 Thess 3:5

Ps 25:6-7

Remember your mercy, O Lord, and your steadfast love,
for they have been from of old.
Remember not the sins of my youth or my transgressions;
according to your steadfast love remember me,
for the sake of your goodness, O Lord!

Ps 25:10

All the paths of the Lord are steadfast love and faithfulness,
for those who keep his covenant and his testimonies.

Ps 86:5

For you, O Lord, are good and forgiving,
abounding in steadfast love to all who call upon you.

Ps 106:1

Praise the Lord!
Oh give thanks to the Lord, for he is good,
for his steadfast love endures forever!

Ps 108:4

For your steadfast love is great above the heavens;
your faithfulness reaches to the clouds.

Ps 138:8

The Lord will fulfill his purpose for me;
your steadfast love, O Lord, endures forever.
Do not forsake the work of your hands.

Lam 3:22-24

The steadfast love of the Lord never ceases;
his mercies never come to an end;

they are new every morning;
great is your faithfulness.
"The Lord is my portion," says my soul,
"therefore I will hope in him."

Micah 7:18-19
Who is a God like you, pardoning iniquity
and passing over transgression
for the remnant of his inheritance?
He does not retain his anger forever,
because he delights in steadfast love.
He will again have compassion on us;
he will tread our iniquities underfoot.
You will cast all our sins
into the depths of the sea.

Trustworthy (52)
2 Kings 18:5; 1 Chron 5:20; Ps 4:5, 9:10, 13:5, 20:7, 21:7, 22:4-5, 22:8-9, 25:2, 26:1, 28:7, 31:6, 31:14, 32:10, 33:21, 37:5, 40:3-4, 52:8, 55:23, 56:3-4, 56:11, 62:8, 71:5, 84:12, 86:2, 91:2, 93:5, 111:7, 112:7, 115:8-11, 118:8, 118:9, 119:42, 125:1, 143:8; Prov 3:5, 16:20, 22:19, 28:25, 29:25; Isa 12:2, 26:3, 26:4, 50:10; Jer 17:7, 39:18; Dan 3:28, 6:23; Matt 27:43; Phil 2:24; Heb 2:13

Ps 9:10
And those who know your name put their trust in you,
for you, O Lord, have not forsaken those who seek you.

Ps 20:7
Some trust in chariots and some in horses,
but we trust in the name of the Lord our God.

Ps 52:8
But I am like a green olive tree
in the house of God.
I trust in the steadfast love of God
forever and ever.

Ps 56:3-4
When I am afraid,
I put my trust in you.
In God, whose word I praise,
in God I trust; I shall not be afraid.
What can flesh do to me?

Ps 93:5
Your decrees are very trustworthy;
holiness befits your house,

O Lord, forevermore.

Ps 111:7-8

The works of his hands are faithful and just;
all his precepts are trustworthy;
they are established forever and ever,
to be performed with faithfulness and uprightness.

Prov 3:5-6

Trust in the Lord with all your heart,
and do not lean on your own understanding.
In all your ways acknowledge him,
and he will make straight your paths.

Isa 12:2

Behold, God is my salvation;
I will trust, and will not be afraid;
for the Lord God is my strength and my song,
and he has become my salvation.

Dan 6:23

Then the king was exceedingly glad, and commanded that Daniel be taken up out of the den. So Daniel was taken up out of the den, and no kind of harm was found on him, because he had trusted in his God.

Unfailing (5)

Josh 3:10, 21:45, 23:14; 1 Kings 8:56; Zeph 3:5;

Josh 23:14

And now I am about to go the way of all the earth, and you know in your hearts and souls, all of you, that not one word has failed of all the good things that the Lord your God promised concerning you. All have come to pass for you; not one of them has failed.

Zeph 3:5

The Lord within her is righteous;
he does no injustice;
every morning he shows forth his justice;
each dawn he does not fail;
but the unjust knows no shame.

III. Positional Attributes

Sovereignty (3)

Acts 4:24; 1 Tim 6:15; Rev 6:10

Acts 4:24

And when they heard it, they lifted their voices together to God and said, "Sovereign Lord, who made the heaven and the earth and the sea and everything in them,

1 Tim 6:15

...which he will display at the proper time—he who is the blessed and only Sovereign, the King of kings and Lord of lords,

Rev 6:10

They cried out with a loud voice, "O Sovereign Lord, holy and true, how long before you will judge and avenge our blood on those who dwell on the earth?"

Almighty (58)

Gen 17:1, 28:3, 35:11, 43:14, 48:3, 49:25; Exod 6:3; Num 24:4, 24:16; Ruth 1:20-21; Job 5:17, 6:4, 6:14, 8:3, 8;5, 11:7, 13:3, 15:25, 21:15, 21:20, 22:3, 22:17, 22:23, 22:25-26, 23:16, 24:1, 27:2, 27:10-11, 27:13, 29:5, 31:2, 31:35, 32:8, 33:4, 34:10, 34:12, 35:13, 37:23, 40:2; Ps 68:14, 91:1; Isa 13:6; Ezek 1:24, 10:5; Joel 1:15; 2 Cor 6:18; Rev 1:8, 4:8, 11:17, 15:3, 16:7, 16:14, 19;6, 19:15, 21:22

Gen 17:1-2

When Abram was ninety-nine years old the Lord appeared to Abram and said to him, "I am God Almighty; walk before me, and be blameless, that I may make my covenant between me and you, and may multiply you greatly."

Job 37:22-23

Out of the north comes golden splendor;
God is clothed with awesome majesty.
The Almighty—we cannot find him;
he is great in power;
justice and abundant righteousness he will not violate.

Joel 1:15

Alas for the day!
For the day of the Lord is near,
and as destruction from the Almighty it comes.

Rev 1:8

"I am the Alpha and the Omega," says the Lord God, "who is and who was and who is to come, the Almighty."

Rev 15:3

Great and amazing are your deeds,
O Lord God the Almighty!
Just and true are your ways,
O King of the nations!

Divine (5)

Ps 82:1; Acts 17:29; Rom 1:20, 3:25; 2 Pet 1:3-4

Ps 82:1

God has taken his place in the divine council;
in the midst of the gods he holds judgment:

Acts 17:29

Being then God's offspring, we ought not to think that the divine being is like gold or silver or stone, an image formed by the art and imagination of man.

Rom 1:20

For his invisible attributes, namely, his eternal power and divine nature, have been clearly perceived, ever since the creation of the world, in the things that have been made. So they are without excuse.

Dominion (13)

Job 25:2; Ps 103:22, 145:13; Dan 4:3, 4:34, 6:26, 7:13-14; Rom 6:9; 1 Tim 6:16, 1 Pet 4:11, 5:11; Jude 25; Rev 1:6

Dan 4:3

How great are his signs,
how mighty his wonders!
His kingdom is an everlasting kingdom,
and his dominion endures from generation to generation.

Dan 7:13-14

I saw in the night visions,
and behold, with the clouds of heaven
there came one like a son of man,
and he came to the Ancient of Days
and was presented before him.
And to him was given dominion
and glory and a kingdom,
that all peoples, nations, and languages
should serve him;
his dominion is an everlasting dominion,
which shall not pass away,
and his kingdom one
that shall not be destroyed.

Rom 6:9

We know that Christ, being raised from the dead, will never die again; death no longer has dominion over him.

Exalted (33)

Exod 15:2; 2 Sam 22:47; 1 Chron 29:11; Neh 9:5; Job 36:22; Ps 18:46, 21:13, 34:3, 46:10, 47:9, 57:5, 57:11, 97:9, 99:2, 99:5, 99:9, 108:5, Ps 138:2, 148:13; Isa 2:11, 2:17, 5:16, 12:4, 25:1, 30:18, 33:5, 33:10, 52:13; Acts 2:32-33, 5:31; Phil 2:9; Heb 5:5, 7:26

2 Sam 22:47

The Lord lives, and blessed be my rock,
and exalted be my God, the rock of my salvation,

Appendix 4

1 Chron 29:11

Yours, O Lord, is the greatness and the power and the glory and the victory and the majesty, for all that is in the heavens and in the earth is yours. Yours is the kingdom, O Lord, and you are exalted as head above all.

Ps 46:10

Be still, and know that I am God.
I will be exalted among the nations,
I will be exalted in the earth!

Isa 30:18

Therefore the Lord waits to be gracious to you,
and therefore he exalts himself to show mercy to you.
For the Lord is a God of justice;
blessed are all those who wait for him.

Acts 5:31

God exalted him at his right hand as Leader and Savior, to give repentance to Israel and forgiveness of sins.

Heb 7:26

For it was indeed fitting that we should have such a high priest, holy, innocent, unstained, separated from sinners, and exalted above the heavens.

Fortress (13)

2 Sam 22:2, Ps 18:2, 31:2-3, 46:7, 46:11, 48:3, 59:9, 59:16-17, 62:2, 62:6, 71:3, 91:2, 144:2

Ps 18:2

The Lord is my rock and my fortress and my deliverer,
my God, my rock, in whom I take refuge,
my shield, and the horn of my salvation, my stronghold.

Ps 48:3

Within her citadels God
has made himself known as a fortress.

Ps 59:16-17

But I will sing of your strength;
I will sing aloud of your steadfast love in the morning.
For you have been to me a fortress
and a refuge in the day of my distress.
O my Strength, I will sing praises to you,
for you, O God, are my fortress,
the God who shows me steadfast love.

Great (110)

Exod 6:6, 14:31, 15:16, 32:11; Num 14:17; Deut 3:24, 4:34, 5:24-25, 6:22, 7:21, 9:26, 10:17, 10:21, 11:2, 11:7, 26:8, 29:24, 29:28, 32:3; Josh 24:17; Judg 2:7; 1 Sam 6:19, 12:16, 12:22, 12:24,

19:5; 2 Sam 7:22-23, 23:10, 23:12, 24:14; 2 Kings 17:36, 22:13, 23:26; 1 Chron 11:14, 16:25, 17:19, 17:21, 21:13, 29:11; 2 Chron 1:8, 2:5, 21:14, 34:21; Ezra 5:8; Neh 1:5, 4:14, 8:6, 9:31-32, 13:22; Job 36:26, 37:5; Ps 35:27, 36:6, 40:16, 47:2, 48:1, 66:3, 70:4, 71:19, 76:1, 77:13, 86:10, 89:7, 92:5, 95:3, 96:4, 99:2, 104:1, 106:21, 111:2, 117:2, 119:156, 126:2-3, 135:5, 138:5, 145:3, 147:5; Isa 61:10; Jer 10:6, 32:17-18, 36:7, 44:26; Ezek 36:23, 38:23; Dan 2:45, 9:4, 9:18; Joel 2:11, 2:21, 2:31; Micah 5:4; Nahum 1:3; Zeph 1:14; Zech 7:12, 8:2; Mal 1:5, 1:11, 1:14, 4:5; Luke 1:32, 7:16; Acts 2:20; Eph 2:4; Col 1:27; Titus 2:13; Heb 2:3, 4:14, 10:21, 13:20, 1 Pet 1:3; Rev 11:17, 14:19, 15:3

Deut 3:24

O Lord God, you have only begun to show your servant your greatness and your mighty hand. For what god is there in heaven or on earth who can do such works and mighty acts as yours?

Ps 66:3-4

Say to God, "How awesome are your deeds!
So great is your power that your enemies come cringing to you.
All the earth worships you
and sings praises to you;
they sing praises to your name." Selah

Jer 32:17-19

Ah, Lord God! It is you who have made the heavens and the earth by your great power and by your outstretched arm! Nothing is too hard for you. You show steadfast love to thousands, but you repay the guilt of fathers to their children after them, O great and mighty God, whose name is the Lord of hosts, great in counsel and mighty in deed, whose eyes are open to all the ways of the children of man, rewarding each one according to his ways and according to the fruit of his deeds.

Micah 5:4

And he shall stand and shepherd his flock in the strength of the Lord,
in the majesty of the name of the Lord his God.
And they shall dwell secure, for now he shall be great
to the ends of the earth.

Luke 1:32-33

He will be great and will be called the Son of the Most High. And the Lord God will give to him the throne of his father David, and he will reign over the house of Jacob forever, and of his kingdom there will be no end."

Eph 2:4-5

But God, being rich in mercy, because of the great love with which he loved us, even when we were dead in our trespasses, made us alive together with Christ—by grace you have been saved...

King (60)

Ps 5:2, 10:6, 24:7-10, 29:10, 44:4, 47:2, 47:6-7, 48:2, 68:24, 74:12, 84:3, 95:3, 98:6, 99:4, 145:1, 149:2; Isa 6:5, 33:22, 41:21, 43:15, 44:6; Jer 8:19, 10:7, 10:10; Ezek 20:33;

Zeph 3:15; Zech 14:9, 14:16-17; Mal 1:14; Matt 21:5, 25:34, 25:40, 27:11, 27:29, 27:37, 27:42; Mark 15:2, 15:9, 15:12, 15:18, 15:26, 15:32; Luke 19:38, 23:2-3, 23:37-38; John 1:49, 12:13, 12:15, 18:33, 18:37, 18:39, 19:3, 19:14-15, 19:19-21; Acts 17:7; 1 Tim 1:17, 6:15; Rev 15:3, 17:14, 19:16

Ps 47:6-8

Sing praises to God, sing praises!
Sing praises to our King, sing praises!
For God is the King of all the earth;
sing praises with a psalm!
God reigns over the nations;
God sits on his holy throne.

Jer 10:10

But the Lord is the true God;
he is the living God and the everlasting King.
At his wrath the earth quakes,
and the nations cannot endure his indignation.

John 1:49

Nathanael answered him, "Rabbi, you are the Son of God! You are the King of Israel!"

Rev 17:14

They will make war on the Lamb, and the Lamb will conquer them, for he is Lord of lords and King of kings, and those with him are called and chosen and faithful.

Lofty (1)

Ps 104:13

Ps 104:13

From your lofty abode you water the mountains;
the earth is satisfied with the fruit of your work.

Mighty (46)

Exod 32:11; Deut 3:24, 4:34, 5:15, 6:21, 7:8, 7:19, 9:26, 10:17, 11:2, 26:8; Josh 4:24, 6:2, 22:22; Neh 9:32; Job 36:5; Ps 24:8, 50:1, 50:3, 62:7, 71:16, 89:8, 93:4, 106:2, 132:2, 132:5, 150:1; Isa 1:24, 9:6, 10:21, 28:2, 42:13, 49:26, 60:16, 62:8; Jer 32:18; Ezek 20:33; Dan 9:15; Zeph 3:17; Luke 19:37, 24:19; Acts 2:11, 2:22; 1 Pet 5:6; Rev 18:8, 19:6

Deut 10:17

For the Lord your God is God of gods and Lord of lords, the great, the mighty, and the awesome God, who is not partial and takes no bribe.

Deut 26:8

And the Lord brought us out of Egypt with a mighty hand and an outstretched arm, with great deeds of terror, with signs and wonders.

Ps 50:1
The Mighty One, God the Lord,
speaks and summons the earth
from the rising of the sun to its setting.

Ps 93:4
Mightier than the thunders of many waters,
mightier than the waves of the sea,
the Lord on high is mighty!

Isa 9:6
For to us a child is born,
to us a son is given;
and the government shall be upon his shoulder,
and his name shall be called
Wonderful Counselor, Mighty God,
Everlasting Father, Prince of Peace.

Isa 42:13
The Lord goes out like a mighty man,
like a man of war he stirs up his zeal;
he cries out, he shouts aloud,
he shows himself mighty against his foes.

Omnipotent (0)

Providence (14)

Gen 22:8, 22:14; Josh 1:13; 1 Sam 16:1; 2 Chron 29:36, 32:22; Ps 65:9, 68:10, 111:5; Jer 33:9; Ezek 34:29; 1 Cor 10:13; 1 Tim 6:17; Heb 11:40

Ps 68:10
...your flock found a dwelling in it;
in your goodness, O God, you provided for the needy.

1 Cor 10:13

No temptation has overtaken you that is not common to man. God is faithful, and he will not let you be tempted beyond your ability, but with the temptation he will also provide the way of escape, that you may be able to endure it.

1 Tim 6:17

As for the rich in this present age, charge them not to be haughty, nor to set their hopes on the uncertainty of riches, but on God, who richly provides us with everything to enjoy.

Purposeful (41)

Exod 9:16; 1 Chron 29:18; Job 42:2; Ps 57:2, 138:8; Prov 16:4, 19:21; Isa 14:24, 14:26-27, 19:12, 19:17, 23:8-9, 44:28, 46:10-12, 48:14, 55:11; Jer 4:28, 49:20, 50:45,

51:11, 51:29; Lam 2:17; Zech 1:6, 8:14-15; Luke 4:43, 7:30; John 12:27, 18:37; Acts 13:36, 26:16; Rom 8:28, 9:11, 9:17; Eph 1:5, 1:9, 1:11, 3:11; 2 Tim 1:9; Heb 6:17; James 5:11; Rev 17:17

Exod 9:16

But for this purpose I have raised you up, to show you my power, so that my name may be proclaimed in all the earth.

Ps 138:8

The Lord will fulfill his purpose for me;
your steadfast love, O Lord, endures forever.
Do not forsake the work of your hands.

Prov 16:4

The Lord has made everything for its purpose,
even the wicked for the day of trouble.

Isa 14:24

The Lord of hosts has sworn:
"As I have planned,
so shall it be,
and as I have purposed,
so shall it stand,

Rom 8:28

And we know that for those who love God all things work together for good, for those who are called according to his purpose.

Eph 1:5-10

...he predestined us for adoption as sons through Jesus Christ, according to the purpose of his will, to the praise of his glorious grace, with which he has blessed us in the Beloved. In him we have redemption through his blood, the forgiveness of our trespasses, according to the riches of his grace, which he lavished upon us, in all wisdom and insight making known to us the mystery of his will, according to his purpose, which he set forth in Christ as a plan for the fullness of time, to unite all things in him, things in heaven and things on earth.

Rock (32)

Deut 32:4, 32:15, 32:18, 32:30-31; 1 Sam 2:2; 2 Sam 22:2-3, 22:32, 22:47, 23:3; Ps 18:2, 18:31, 18:46, 19:14, 28:1, 31:2-3, 42:9, 61:2, 62:2, 62:6-7, 71:3, 78:35, 89:26, 92:15, 94:22, 95:1, 144:1; Isa 17:10, 26:4, 30:29, 44:8; Hab 1:12; 1 Cor 10:4

Deut 32:4

The Rock, his work is perfect,
for all his ways are justice.
A God of faithfulness and without iniquity,
just and upright is he.

Deut 32:31
For their rock is not as our Rock;
our enemies are by themselves.

Ps 144:1-2
Blessed be the Lord, my rock,
who trains my hands for war,
and my fingers for battle;
he is my steadfast love and my fortress,
my stronghold and my deliverer,
my shield and he in whom I take refuge,
who subdues peoples under me.

1 Cor 10:4
...and all drank the same spiritual drink. For they drank from the spiritual Rock that followed them, and the Rock was Christ.

Ruler (1)
Rev 1:5

Rev 1:5
...and from Jesus Christ the faithful witness, the firstborn of the dead, and the ruler of kings on earth.

Strong Tower (2)
Ps 61:3; Prov 18:10

Ps 61:3
Hear my cry, O God,
listen to my prayer;
from the end of the earth I call to you
when my heart is faint.
Lead me to the rock
that is higher than I,
for you have been my refuge,
a strong tower against the enemy.

Prov 18:10
The name of the Lord is a strong tower;
the righteous man runs into it and is safe.

Supreme (0)

Creator (47)

Gen 1:1, 1:21, 1:27, 2:4, 5:1-2, 6:7; Num 16:30; Deut 4:32, 32:6; Ps 51:10, 89:12, 89:47, 104:30, 148:5; Eccles 12:1; Isa 4:5, 40:26, 40:28, 41:20, 42:5, 43:1, 43:7, 43:15, 45:7-8, 45:12, 45:18, 54:16, 57:19, 65:17-18; Jer 31:22; Amos 4:13; Mal 2:10; Matt 19:4; Mark 13:19; Rom 1:25; Eph 2:10, 2:15, 3:9, 4:24; Col 1:16, 3:10; 1 Tim 4:3-4; Heb 1:2, Heb 11:3; 1 Pet 4:19; Rev 4:11, 10:6

Isa 40:28
Have you not known? Have you not heard?
The Lord is the everlasting God,
the Creator of the ends of the earth.
He does not faint or grow weary;
his understanding is unsearchable.

Isa 45:7-12
I form light and create darkness,
I make well-being and create calamity,
I am the Lord, who does all these things.
"Shower, O heavens, from above,
and let the clouds rain down righteousness;
let the earth open, that salvation and righteousness may bear fruit;
let the earth cause them both to sprout;
I the Lord have created it.
"Woe to him who strives with him who formed him,
a pot among earthen pots!
Does the clay say to him who forms it, 'What are you making?'
or 'Your work has no handles'?
Woe to him who says to a father, 'What are you begetting?'
or to a woman, 'With what are you in labor?'"
Thus says the Lord,
the Holy One of Israel, and the one who formed him:
"Ask me of things to come;
will you command me concerning my children and the work of my hands?
I made the earth
and created man on it;
it was my hands that stretched out the heavens,
and I commanded all their host.

Isa 45:18
For thus says the Lord,
who created the heavens
(he is God!),
who formed the earth and made it
(he established it;
he did not create it empty,
he formed it to be inhabited!):
"I am the Lord, and there is no other."

Isa 65:17-18
For behold, I create new heavens
and a new earth,
and the former things shall not be remembered

or come into mind.
But be glad and rejoice forever
in that which I create;
for behold, I create Jerusalem to be a joy,
and her people to be a gladness.

Eph 2:10

For we are his workmanship, created in Christ Jesus for good works, which God prepared beforehand, that we should walk in them.

Eph 4:22-24

...to put off your old self, which belongs to your former manner of life and is corrupt through deceitful desires, and to be renewed in the spirit of your minds, and to put on the new self, created after the likeness of God in true righteousness and holiness.

Healer (83)

Gen 20:17; Exod 15:26; Deut 32:39; 2 Kings 2:21-22, 20:5; 2 Chron 7:14, 30:20; Job 5:18; Ps 6:2, 30:2, 41:4, 103:3, 107:20, 147:3; Isa 19:22, 30:26, 53:5, 57:18-19; Jer 3:22, 17:14, 30:17, 33:6; Hos 6:1, 7:1, 11:3, 14:4; Mal 4:2; Matt 4:23-24, 8:7-8, 8:13, 8:16, 9:35, 10:1, 12:15, 12:22, 13:15, 14:14, 15:28, 15:30, 17:18, 19:2, 21:14; Mark 1:34, 3:10, 5:29, 5:34, 6:5, 6:13; Luke 4:40, 5:15, 5:17, 6:18-19, 7:3, 7:7, 7:21, 8:2, 8:36, 8:47, 9:2, 9:6, 9:11, 9:42, 14:4, 17:15, 22:51; John 4:47, 5:9, 5:11, 5:15, 12:40; Acts 4:30, 5:16, 8:7, 9:34, 10:38, 28:8, 28:27; 1 Cor 12:9, 12:28; Heb 12:13; James 5:16; 1 Pet 2:24; Rev 22:1

Deut 32:39

See now that I, even I, am he,
and there is no god beside me;
I kill and I make alive;
I wound and I heal;
and there is none that can deliver out of my hand.

Job 5:17-18

Behold, blessed is the one whom God reproves;
therefore despise not the discipline of the Almighty.
For he wounds, but he binds up;
he shatters, but his hands heal.

Ps 147:3

He heals the brokenhearted
and binds up their wounds.

Isa 30:18

Moreover, the light of the moon will be as the light of the sun, and the light of the sun will be sevenfold, as the light of seven days, in the day when the Lord binds up the brokenness of his people, and heals the wounds inflicted by his blow.

Isa 53:4-5

Surely he has borne our griefs
and carried our sorrows;
yet we esteemed him stricken,
smitten by God, and afflicted.
But he was pierced for our transgressions;
he was crushed for our iniquities;
upon him was the chastisement that brought us peace,
and with his wounds we are healed.

Hos 6:1

Come, let us return to the Lord;
for he has torn us, that he may heal us;
he has struck us down, and he will bind us up.

Matt 4:23-24

And he went throughout all Galilee, teaching in their synagogues and proclaiming the gospel of the kingdom and healing every disease and every affliction among the people. So his fame spread throughout all Syria, and they brought him all the sick, those afflicted with various diseases and pains, those oppressed by demons, epileptics, and paralytics, and he healed them.

Luke 9:1-2

And he called the twelve together and gave them power and authority over all demons and to cure diseases, and he sent them out to proclaim the kingdom of God and to heal.

John 12:40

He has blinded their eyes
and hardened their heart,
lest they see with their eyes,
and understand with their heart, and turn,
and I would heal them.

1 Pet 2:24

He himself bore our sins in his body on the tree, that we might die to sin and live to righteousness. By his wounds you have been healed.

Life (46)

1 Sam 2:6; 1 Kings 17:21-22; Job 10:12, 12:10, 33:4; Ps 21:4, 80:18, 119:25, 119:40, 119:50, 119:88, 119:93, 119:107, 119:149, 119:149, 119:154, 119:156, 119:159; John 5:21, 5:26, 6:27, 6:33, 6:35, 6:48, 6:51, 6:54, 6:63, 10:10, 10:28, 11:25, 14:6, 17:2-3, 20:31; Acts 3:15, 17:25; Rom 2:7; 4:17, 6:23, 8:2, 8:10-11; 2 Cor 3:6; Gal 6:8; 1 Tim 6:13; 1 John 5:11-12, 5:16; Rev 11:11

1 Sam 2:6

The Lord kills and brings to life;

he brings down to Sheol and raises up.

Job 12:10

In his hand is the life of every living thing
and the breath of all mankind.

Job 33:4

The Spirit of God has made me,
and the breath of the Almighty gives me life.

John 5:21

For as the Father raises the dead and gives them life, so also the Son gives life to whom he will.

John 10:28

I give them eternal life, and they will never perish, and no one will snatch them out of my hand.

John 14:6

Jesus said to him, "I am the way, and the truth, and the life. No one comes to the Father except through me.

Acts 3:14-15

But you denied the Holy and Righteous One, and asked for a murderer to be granted to you, and you killed the Author of life, whom God raised from the dead. To this we are witnesses.

Acts 17:24-25

The God who made the world and everything in it, being Lord of heaven and earth, does not live in temples made by man, nor is he served by human hands, as though he needed anything, since he himself gives to all mankind life and breath and everything.

Rom 4:17

...as it is written, "I have made you the father of many nations"—in the presence of the God in whom he believed, who gives life to the dead and calls into existence the things that do not exist.

Orderer (2)

2 Sam 23:5; Jer 33:25

2 Sam 23:5

For does not my house stand so with God?
For he has made with me an everlasting covenant,
ordered in all things and secure.
For will he not cause to prosper
all my help and my desire?

Jer 33:35

Thus says the Lord: If I have not established my covenant with day and night and the fixed order of heaven and earth,

Organizer (0)

Physician (3)
Matt 9:12; Mark 2:17; Luke 5:31

Mark 2:17
And when Jesus heard it, he said to them, "Those who are well have no need of a physician, but those who are sick. I came not to call the righteous, but sinners."

Word (3)
John 1:1, 1:14; Rev 19:13

John 1:1
In the beginning was the Word, and the Word was with God, and the Word was God. He was in the beginning with God. All things were made through him, and without him was not any thing made that was made. In him was life, and the life was the light of men. The light shines in the darkness, and the darkness has not overcome it.

John 1:14
And the Word became flesh and dwelt among us, and we have seen his glory, glory as of the only Son from the Father, full of grace and truth.

Rev 19:13
He is clothed in a robe dipped in blood, and the name by which he is called is The Word of God.

Master (31)
(several parable passages are individual entries)
Jer 3:14; Mal 1:6; Matt 6:24, 10:24-25, 13:24-30, 15:27, 18:23-35, 20:1-16, 21:33-41, 24:45-51, 25:14-30; Mark 13:35; Luke 5:5, 8:24, 8:45, 9:33, 9:49, 12:35-48, 13:25, 14:12-24, 16:13, 17:13; John 13:16, 15:15, 15:20; Rom 14:4; Eph 6:9; Col 4:1; 2 Tim 2:21; 2 Pet 2:1; Jude 4

Matt 6:24
No one can serve two masters, for either he will hate the one and love the other, or he will be devoted to the one and despise the other. You cannot serve God and money.

Matt 15:27
She said, "Yes, Lord, yet even the dogs eat the crumbs that fall from their masters' table."

Matt 25:19-21
Now after a long time the master of those servants came and settled accounts with them. And he who had received the five talents came forward, bringing five talents more, saying, 'Master, you delivered to me five talents; here I have made five talents more.' His master said to him, 'Well done, good and faithful servant. You have been faithful over a little; I will set you over much. Enter into the joy of your master.'

Luke 8:24

And they went and woke him, saying, "Master, Master, we are perishing!" And he awoke and rebuked the wind and the raging waves, and they ceased, and there was a calm.

Col 4:1

Masters, treat your bondservants justly and fairly, knowing that you also have a Master in heaven.

2 Tim 2:21

Therefore, if anyone cleanses himself from what is dishonorable, he will be a vessel for honorable use, set apart as holy, useful to the master of the house, ready for every good work.

Counselor (14)

Job 12:13; Ps 16:7, 33:11, 73:24, 106:13, 107:11; Isa 5:19, 9:6, 11:2, 28:29, 46:10-11; Jer 32:18-19; Acts 20:27; Eph 1:11

Ps 33:11

The counsel of the Lord stands forever,
the plans of his heart to all generations.

Isa 9:6

For to us a child is born,
to us a son is given;
and the government shall be upon his shoulder,
and his name shall be called
Wonderful Counselor, Mighty God,
Everlasting Father, Prince of Peace.

Isa 11:2

And the Spirit of the Lord shall rest upon him,
the Spirit of wisdom and understanding,
the Spirit of counsel and might,
the Spirit of knowledge and the fear of the Lord.

Guide (13)

Exod 15:13; Deut 32:12; Ps 31:3, 48:14, 67:4, 73:24, 78:52, 78:72; Isa 42:16, 49:10, 58:11; John 16:13; Rev 7:17

Isa 42:16

And I will lead the blind
in a way that they do not know,
in paths that they have not known
I will guide them.
I will turn the darkness before them into light,
the rough places into level ground.

These are the things I do,
and I do not forsake them.

Isa 58:11
And the Lord will guide you continually
and satisfy your desire in scorched places
and make your bones strong;
and you shall be like a watered garden,
like a spring of water,
whose waters do not fail.

Rev 7:17
For the Lamb in the midst of the throne will be their shepherd,
and he will guide them to springs of living water,
and God will wipe away every tear from their eyes."

Instructor (17)

Exod 24:12; Neh 9:20; Job 22:22, 36:10; Ps 25:8, 25:12; Prov 15:33; Isa 28:26, 30:9; Jer 32:33, 35:13; Matt 10:5, 11:1, 23:10; Eph 6:4; 1 Thess 4:2; Heb 8:5

Neh 9:20
You gave your good Spirit to instruct them and did not withhold your manna from their mouth and gave them water for their thirst.

Matt 23:10
Neither be called instructors, for you have one instructor, the Christ.

Eph 6:4
Fathers, do not provoke your children to anger, but bring them up in the discipline and instruction of the Lord.

Lord (6,468)
- "lord" (3)

Matt 12:8; Mark 2:28; Luke 6:5

Gen 26:24
And the Lord appeared to him the same night and said, "I am the God of Abraham your father. Fear not, for I am with you and will bless you and multiply your offspring for my servant Abraham's sake."

Exod 6:2-3
God spoke to Moses and said to him, "I am the Lord. I appeared to Abraham, to Isaac, and to Jacob, as God Almighty, but by my name the Lord I did not make myself known to them.

Exod 6:6-7
Say therefore to the people of Israel, 'I am the Lord, and I will bring you out from under the burdens of the Egyptians, and I will deliver you from slavery to them, and I will redeem you with an outstretched arm and with great acts of

judgment. I will take you to be my people, and I will be your God, and you shall know that I am the Lord your God, who has brought you out from under the burdens of the Egyptians.'

Exod 15:1-3

Then Moses and the people of Israel sang this song to the Lord, saying,
"I will sing to the Lord, for he has triumphed gloriously;
the horse and his rider he has thrown into the sea.
The Lord is my strength and my song,
and he has become my salvation;
this is my God, and I will praise him,
my father's God, and I will exalt him.
The Lord is a man of war;
the Lord is his name."

Manager (0)

Owner (5)

- from a single parable

Matt 20:8, 21:40; Mark 12:9; Luke 20:13, 20:15

Luke 20:13

Then the owner of the vineyard said, 'What shall I do? I will send my beloved son; perhaps they will respect him.'

Teacher (116)

Exod 4:12, 4:15; 1 Kings 8.36, 2 Chron 6:27; Job 36:22; Ps 25:4-5, 25:9, 27:11, 51:6, 86:11, 90:12, 94:10, 94:12, 119:12, 119:26, 119:29, 119:33, 119:64, 119:66, 119:68, 119:108, 119:124, 119:135, 119:171, 132:12, 143:10; Isa 1:10, 2:3, 28:26, 30:20, 48:17; Micah 4:2; Matt 4:23, 7:28-29, 8:19, 9:11, 9:35, 10:24-25, 11:1, 12:38, 17:24, 19:16, 21:23, 22:16, 22:24, 22:33, 22:36, 23:8, 26:18, 26:55, 28:20; Mark 1:21-22, 2:13, 4:1-2, 4:38, 5:35, 6:2, 6:6, 6:34, 8:31, 9:17, 9:31, 9:38, 10:17, 10:20, 10:35, 11:17-18, 12:14, 12:19, 12:32, 12:38, 13:1, 14:14, 14:49; Luke 2:46, 3:12, 4:31-32, 5:17, 6:6, 6:40, 7:40, 8:49, 9:38, 10:25, 10:39, 11:1, 11:45, 12:12, 12:13, 13:10, 13:22, 18:18, 19:39, 19:47, 20:1, 20:21, 20:28, 20:39, 21:7, 21:37, 22:11, 23:5; John 1:38, 3:2, 3:10, 7:14, 7:16-17, 7:35, 8:4, 9:34, 11:28, 13:13-14, 14:26, 18:19, 20:16; 2 John 9

Job 36:22

Behold, God is exalted in his power;
who is a teacher like him?

Ps 51:6

Behold, you delight in truth in the inward being,
and you teach me wisdom in the secret heart.

Ps 86:11

Teach me your way, O Lord,
that I may walk in your truth;
unite my heart to fear your name.

Ps 119:29

Put false ways far from me
and graciously teach me your law!

Matt 7:28-29

And when Jesus finished these sayings, the crowds were astonished at his teaching, for he was teaching them as one who had authority, and not as their scribes.

John 7:16-18

So Jesus answered them, "My teaching is not mine, but his who sent me. If anyone's will is to do God's will, he will know whether the teaching is from God or whether I am speaking on my own authority. The one who speaks on his own authority seeks his own glory; but the one who seeks the glory of him who sent him is true, and in him there is no falsehood."

Judge (175)

Gen 15:14, 16:5, 18:25, 30:6; Exod 5:21, 6:6, 7:4, 12:12; Num 33:4; Deut 1:17, 32:41; Judg 11:27; 1 Sam 2:10, 24:12, 24:15; 1 Kings 8:32; 1 Chron 16:12, 16:14, 16:33; 2 Chron 6:23, 19:6, 20:12; Job 21:22, 22:12-13, 23:7, 24:1, 34:23, 36:17, 36:31; Ps 7:6, 7:8, 7:11, 9:4, 9:8, 9:16, 9:19, 10:5, 36:6, 48:11, 50:4, 50:6, 51:4, 58:11, 67:4, 75:2, 75:7, 76:8-9, 82:1-2, 82:8, 94:2, 96:10, 96:13, 97:8, 98:9, 105:5, 105:7, 110:6, 119:66, 119:120, 143:2, 149:9; Eccles 3:17, 11:9, 12:14; Isa 2:4, 3:13-14, 4:4, 11:3-4, 16:5, 26:8-9, 33:22, 34:5, 51:5, 58:2, 66:16; Jer 1:16, 2:35, 4:12, 11:20, 25:31, 48:21-25, 48:47, 51:52; Lam 3:59; Ezek 5:8, 5:10, 5:15, 7:3, 7:8, 7:27, 11:9, 11:9-11, 14:21, 16:38, 16:41, 17:20, 18:30, 20:4, 20:35-36, 21:27, 21:30, 22:2, 23:24, 23:36, 24:14, 25:11, 28:22, 28:26, 30:19, 33:20, 34:17, 34:20, 34:22, 35:11, 36:19, 38:22, 39:21, 44:24; Dan 7:22; Hos 6:5; Joel 3:2, 3:12; Amos 7:4; Micah 4:3, 7:9; Hab 1:12; Zeph 3:15; Mal 3:5; John 5:22, 5:24, 5:27, 5:30, 8:15-16, 8:26, 8:50, 9:39, 12:47-48, 16:8-11; Acts 7:7, 10:42, 17:30-31; Rom 2:2-3, 2:5, 2:16, 3:6, 11:33, 13:2, 14:10; 1 Cor 4:5, 5:13, 11:32; 2 Cor 5:10; 2 Thess 1:5; 1 Tim 1:12; 2 Tim 4:1, 4:8; Heb 10:30, 12:23, 13:4; James 4:12, 5:9; 1 Pet 1:17, 2:23, 4:5-6; 2 Pet 2:9; Jude 6, 9; Rev 6:10, 11:18, 14:7, 16:5, 16:7, 18:8, 18:20, 20:11-13

Ps 98:9

before the Lord, for he comes
to judge the earth.
He will judge the world with righteousness,
and the peoples with equity.

Isa 33:22

For the Lord is our judge; the Lord is our lawgiver;
the Lord is our king; he will save us.

Isa 66:16

For by fire will the Lord enter into judgment,
and by his sword, with all flesh;
and those slain by the Lord shall be many.

Ezek 20:35
And I will bring you into the wilderness of the peoples, and there I will enter into judgment with you face to face.

Micah 7:9
I will bear the indignation of the Lord
because I have sinned against him,
until he pleads my cause
and executes judgment for me.
He will bring me out to the light;
I shall look upon his vindication.

John 5:22
The Father judges no one, but has given all judgment to the Son,

John 5:30
I can do nothing on my own. As I hear, I judge, and my judgment is just, because I seek not my own will but the will of him who sent me.

John 9:39
Jesus said, "For judgment I came into this world, that those who do not see may see, and those who see may become blind."

Acts 17:30-31
The times of ignorance God overlooked, but now he commands all people everywhere to repent, because he has fixed a day on which he will judge the world in righteousness by a man whom he has appointed; and of this he has given assurance to all by raising him from the dead."

Heb 12:22-24
But you have come to Mount Zion and to the city of the living God, the heavenly Jerusalem, and to innumerable angels in festal gathering, and to the assembly of the firstborn who are enrolled in heaven, and to God, the judge of all, and to the spirits of the righteous made perfect, and to Jesus, the mediator of a new covenant, and to the sprinkled blood that speaks a better word than the blood of Abel.

Rev 20:11-12
Then I saw a great white throne and him who was seated on it. From his presence earth and sky fled away, and no place was found for them. And I saw the dead, great and small, standing before the throne, and books were opened. Then another book was opened, which is the book of life. And the dead were judged by what was written in the books, according to what they had done.

Evaluating (0)

Impartial (1)
1 Pet 1:17

Appendix 4

1 Pet 1:17

And if you call on him as Father who judges impartially according to each one's deeds, conduct yourselves with fear throughout the time of your exile,

Just (84)

Gen 18:25; Deut 10:17-18, 32:4, 33:21; 1 Kings 3:28; Ezra 9:15; Job 34:12, 37:23; Ps 9:4, 9:7, 10:18, 33:5, 37:6, 37:28, 72:1-2, 82:3, 89:14, 94:15, 97:2, 99:4, 101:1, 103:6, 111:7, 119:149, 140:12, 146:7; Prov 11:1, 16:11, 21:3, 29:26; Isa 1:27, 5:7, 5:16, 9:7, 16:5, 28:6, 28:17, 30:18, 32:1, 33:5, 40:14, 42:1, 42:3-4, 51:4, 56:1, 59:15, 61:8; Jer 5:4-5, 9:24, 10:24, 21:12, 22:3, 23:5, 30:11, 33:15, 46:28; Ezek 18:25, 18:29, 33:17, 33:20, 34:16; Dan 4:37; Hos 2:19, 12:6; Micah 3:8, 6:8; Zeph 2:3, 3:5; Mal 2:17; Matt 12:18-21, 23:23; Luke 7:29, 11:42, 18:7-8; John 5:30; Rom 3:8, 3:26; Heb 2:2; 1 Pet 2:23; 1 John 1:9; Rev 15:3, 16:5, 16:7, 19:2

Deut 32:4

The Rock, his work is perfect,
for all his ways are justice.
A God of faithfulness and without iniquity,
just and upright is he.

Jer 9:24

...but let him who boasts boast in this, that he understands and knows me, that I am the Lord who practices steadfast love, justice, and righteousness in the earth. For in these things I delight, declares the Lord.

Jer 10:24

Correct me, O Lord, but in justice;
not in your anger, lest you bring me to nothing.

Hos 2:19-20

And I will betroth you to me forever. I will betroth you to me in righteousness and in justice, in steadfast love and in mercy. I will betroth you to me in faithfulness. And you shall know the Lord.

Micah 6:8

He has told you, O man, what is good;
and what does the Lord require of you
but to do justice, and to love kindness,
and to walk humbly with your God?

Zeph 3:5

The Lord within her is righteous;
he does no injustice;
every morning he shows forth his justice;
each dawn he does not fail;
but the unjust knows no shame.

Rom 3:26

It was to show his righteousness at the present time, so that he might be just and the justifier of the one who has faith in Jesus.

1 Pet 2:23

When he was reviled, he did not revile in return; when he suffered, he did not threaten, but continued entrusting himself to him who judges justly.

1 John 1:9

If we confess our sins, he is faithful and just to forgive us our sins and to cleanse us from all unrighteousness.

Purifying (8)

Zeph 3:9; Zech 3:4; Mal 3:3; Phil 1:9-11; Titus 2:14; Heb 9:14, 10:22; 1 John 3:3

Titus 2:13-14

...waiting for our blessed hope, the appearing of the glory of our great God and Savior Jesus Christ, who gave himself for us to redeem us from all lawlessness and to purify for himself a people for his own possession who are zealous for good works.

Heb 9:14

...how much more will the blood of Christ, who through the eternal Spirit offered himself without blemish to God, purify our conscience from dead works to serve the living God.

Heb 10:22

...let us draw near with a true heart in full assurance of faith, with our hearts sprinkled clean from an evil conscience and our bodies washed with pure water.

Rewarder (39)

Gen 15:1; Num 18:28; Ruth 2:12; 1 Sam 24:19, 26:23; 2 Sam 22:21, 22:25; 1 Kings 8:32; 2 Chron 6:23, 15:7; Ps 18:20, 18:24, 19:11, 28:4, 58:11, 109:20, 127:3; Prov 13:13, 22:4, 25:21-22; Isa 40:10, 62:11; Jer 31:16, 32:18-19; Matt 5:12, 6:1-4, 6:6, 6:18, 10:41-42; Mark 9:41; Luke 6:23, 6:35; 1 Cor 3:14; Col 3:24; Heb 10:35-36, 11:6, 11:26; 2 John 8; Rev 11:18

2 Sam 22:25

And the Lord has rewarded me according to my righteousness,
according to my cleanness in his sight.

Jer 32:18-19

You show steadfast love to thousands, but you repay the guilt of fathers to their children after them, O great and mighty God, whose name is the Lord of hosts, great in counsel and mighty in deed, whose eyes are open to all the ways of the children of man, rewarding each one according to his ways and according to the fruit of his deeds.

Matt 6:3-4

But when you give to the needy, do not let your left hand know what your right hand is doing, so that your giving may be in secret. And your Father who sees in secret will reward you.

Luke 6:35

But love your enemies, and do good, and lend, expecting nothing in return, and your reward will be great, and you will be sons of the Most High, for he is kind to the ungrateful and the evil.

Heb 11:26

He considered the reproach of Christ greater wealth than the treasures of Egypt, for he was looking to the reward.

Redeemer (78)

Gen 48:15-16; Exod 6:6, 15:13; Deut 7:8, 9:26, 13:5, 15:15, 21:8, 24:18; 2 Sam 4:9, 7:23; 1 Kings 1:29; 1 Chron 17:21; Neh 1:10; Job 5:20, 19:25, 33:28; Ps 19:14, 25:22, 26:11, 31:5, 34:22, 44:26, 55:18, 69:18, 71:23, 72:14, 74:2, 77:15, 78:35, 78:42, 103:4, 106:10, 107:2, 111:9, 119:134, 119:154, 130:7-8; Prov 23:11; Isa 1:27, 29:22, 41:14, 43:1, 43:14, 44:6, 44:22-24, 47:4, 48:17, 48:20, 49:7, 49:26, 50:2, 51:10, 52:3, 52:9, 54:5, 54:8, 59:20, 60:16, 62:12, 63:4, 63:9, 63:16; Jer 15:21, 31:11, 50:34; Lam 3:58, Hos 7:13, 13:14; Micah 4:10, 6:4; Zech 10:8; Luke 1:68, 2:38, 21:28, 24:21; Acts 7:35; Romans 3:24, 8:23; 1 Cor 1:30; Gal 3:13, 4:5; Eph 1:7, 4:30; Col 1:14; Titus 2:14; Heb 9:12, 9:15; Rev 14:3-4

Deut 7:7-8

It was not because you were more in number than any other people that the Lord set his love on you and chose you, for you were the fewest of all peoples, but it is because the Lord loves you and is keeping the oath that he swore to your fathers, that the Lord has brought you out with a mighty hand and redeemed you from the house of slavery, from the hand of Pharaoh king of Egypt.

Ps 130:7-8

O Israel, hope in the Lord!
For with the Lord there is steadfast love,
and with him is plentiful redemption.
And he will redeem Israel
from all his iniquities.

Rom 3:23-25

...for all have sinned and fall short of the glory of God, and are justified by his grace as a gift, through the redemption that is in Christ Jesus, whom God put forward as a propitiation by his blood, to be received by faith. This was to show God's righteousness, because in his divine forbearance he had passed over former sins.

1 Cor 1:30

And because of him you are in Christ Jesus, who became to us wisdom from God, righteousness and sanctification and redemption,

Gal 3:13-14

Christ redeemed us from the curse of the law by becoming a curse for us—for it is written, "Cursed is everyone who is hanged on a tree"— so that in Christ Jesus the blessing of Abraham might come to the Gentiles, so that we might receive the promised Spirit through faith.

Gal 4:4-5

But when the fullness of time had come, God sent forth his Son, born of woman, born under the law, to redeem those who were under the law, so that we might receive adoption as sons.

Eph 1:7-10

In him we have redemption through his blood, the forgiveness of our trespasses, according to the riches of his grace, which he lavished upon us, in all wisdom and insight making known to us the mystery of his will, according to his purpose, which he set forth in Christ as a plan for the fullness of time, to unite all things in him, things in heaven and things on earth.

Heb 9:12

...he entered once for all into the holy places, not by means of the blood of goats and calves but by means of his own blood, thus securing an eternal redemption.

Heb 9:15

Therefore he is the mediator of a new covenant, so that those who are called may receive the promised eternal inheritance, since a death has occurred that redeems them from the transgressions committed under the first covenant.

Forgiving (76)

Exod 34:7; Lev 4:20, 4:26, 4:31, 4:35, 5:10, 5:13, 5:16, 5:18, 6:7, 19:22; Num 14:18-19, 15:25-26, 15:28, 30:5, 30:8, 30:12; 1 Kings 8:30, 8:34, 8:36, 8:39, 8:50; 2 Chron 6:21, 6:25, 6:27, 6:30, 6:39, 7:14; Neh 9:17; Ps 32:1, 32:5, 85:2, 86:5, 99:8, 103:3-4; Isa 33:24; Jer 31:34, 33:8, 36:3; Dan 9:9; Matt 6:12-15, 9:2, 9:6, 12:31-32, 18:21-35, 26:28; Mark 2:5, 2:7, 2:10, 3:28-29, 4:12, 11:25; Luke 1:77, 5:20-24, 6:37, 7:47-49, 11:4, 12:10, 23:34; Acts 2:38, 5:31, 8:22, 10:43, 13:38, 26:18; Rom 4:7; Eph 1:7, 4:32; Col 1:14, 2:13, 3:13; Heb 9:22; 10:17-18; James 5:15; 1 John 1:9, 2:12

Num 14:18-19

"...'The Lord is slow to anger and abounding in steadfast love, forgiving iniquity and transgression, but he will by no means clear the guilty, visiting the iniquity of the fathers on the children, to the third and the fourth generation.' Please pardon the iniquity of this people, according to the greatness of your steadfast love, just as you have forgiven this people, from Egypt until now."

Neh 9:17

They refused to obey and were not mindful of the wonders that you performed among them, but they stiffened their neck and appointed a leader to return to their slavery in Egypt. But you are a God ready to forgive, gracious and merciful, slow to anger and abounding in steadfast love, and did not forsake them.

Ps 85:2

You forgave the iniquity of your people;
you covered all their sin. Selah

Matt 12:31-32

Therefore I tell you, every sin and blasphemy will be forgiven people, but the blasphemy against the Spirit will not be forgiven. And whoever speaks a word against the Son of Man will be forgiven, but whoever speaks against the Holy Spirit will not be forgiven, either in this age or in the age to come.

Matt 26:28

...for this is my blood of the covenant, which is poured out for many for the forgiveness of sins.

Heb 9:22

Indeed, under the law almost everything is purified with blood, and without the shedding of blood there is no forgiveness of sins.

Heb 10:17-18

...then he adds,
"I will remember their sins and their lawless deeds no more."
Where there is forgiveness of these, there is no longer any offering for sin.

Justifier (18)

Isa 45:25; Luke 18:14; Rom 2:13, 3:20, 3:23-30, 4:5, 5:1, 5:9, 8:30, 8:33, 10:10; 1 Cor 6:11; Gal 2:16-17, 3:8, 3:11, 3:24; Titus 3:7; James 2:20-26

Rom 3:23-30

...for all have sinned and fall short of the glory of God, and are justified by his grace as a gift, through the redemption that is in Christ Jesus, whom God put forward as a propitiation by his blood, to be received by faith. This was to show God's righteousness, because in his divine forbearance he had passed over former sins. It was to show his righteousness at the present time, so that he might be just and the justifier of the one who has faith in Jesus.

Then what becomes of our boasting? It is excluded. By what kind of law? By a law of works? No, but by the law of faith. For we hold that one is justified by faith apart from works of the law. Or is God the God of Jews only? Is he not the God of Gentiles also? Yes, of Gentiles also, since God is one—who will justify the circumcised by faith and the uncircumcised through faith.

Rom 4:5

And to the one who does not work but believes in him who justifies the ungodly, his faith is counted as righteousness,

Rom 8:30

And those whom he predestined he also called, and those whom he called he also justified, and those whom he justified he also glorified.

Gal 3:8

And the Scripture, foreseeing that God would justify the Gentiles by faith, preached the gospel beforehand to Abraham, saying, "In you shall all the nations be blessed."

Titus 3:5-7

...he saved us, not because of works done by us in righteousness, but according to his own mercy, by the washing of regeneration and renewal of the Holy Spirit, whom he poured out on us richly through Jesus Christ our Savior, so that being justified by his grace we might become heirs according to the hope of eternal life.

Peace (96)

Exod 18:23; Lev 26:6; Judg 6:23-24, 18:6; 1 Kings 2:33; 1 Chron 12:18, 22:9, 22:18; 2 Chron 14:6-7, 34:28; Job 25:2; Ps 4:8, 29:11, 85:8, 85:10, 119:165, 147:14; Isa 9:6-7, 26:3, 26:12, 32:17-18, 48:18, 48:22, 53:5, 54:10, 54:13, 55:12, 57:19, 57:21, 60:17, 66:12; Jer 16:5, 28:9, 34:5; Ezek 34:25, 37:26; Haggai 2:9; Mal 2:5-6; Matt 10:34; Mark 4:39, 5:34; Luke 1:79, 2:14, 2:29, 7:50, 8:48, 12:51, 19:38, 24:36; John 14:27, 16:33, 20:19, 20:21, 20:26; Acts 10:36; Rom 1:7, 2:10, 5:1, 8:6, 14:17, 15:13, 15:33, 16:20; 1 Cor 1:3, 7:15, 14:33; 2 Cor 1:2, 13:11; Gal 1:3, 5:22; Eph 1:2, 2:14-17, 4:3, 6:15, 6:23; Phil 1:2, 4:7, 4:9; Col 1:2, 1:20, 3:15; 1 Thess 1:1, 5:23; 2 Thess 1:2, 3:16; 1 Tim 1:2; 2 Tim 1:2; Titus 1:4, Philem 3; Heb 7:2, 12:10-11, 13:20; 1 Pet 1:2; 2 Pet 1:2; 2 John 3; Rev 1:4

Judg 6:23-24

But the Lord said to him, "Peace be to you. Do not fear; you shall not die." Then Gideon built an altar there to the Lord and called it, The Lord Is Peace. To this day it still stands at Ophrah, which belongs to the Abiezrites.

Isa 9:6

For to us a child is born,
to us a son is given;
and the government shall be upon his shoulder,
and his name shall be called
Wonderful Counselor, Mighty God,
Everlasting Father, Prince of Peace.

Isa 53:5

But he was pierced for our transgressions;
he was crushed for our iniquities;
upon him was the chastisement that brought us peace,
and with his wounds we are healed.

Isa 54:10

For the mountains may depart
and the hills be removed,
but my steadfast love shall not depart from you,
and my covenant of peace shall not be removed,"
says the Lord, who has compassion on you.

Rom 5:1

Therefore, since we have been justified by faith, we have peace with God through our Lord Jesus Christ.

Rom 8:6

For to set the mind on the flesh is death, but to set the mind on the Spirit is life and peace.

Phil 4:7

And the peace of God, which surpasses all understanding, will guard your hearts and your minds in Christ Jesus.

1 Thess 5:23

Now may the God of peace himself sanctify you completely, and may your whole spirit and soul and body be kept blameless at the coming of our Lord Jesus Christ.

Heb 12:10-11

For they disciplined us for a short time as it seemed best to them, but he disciplines us for our good, that we may share his holiness. For the moment all discipline seems painful rather than pleasant, but later it yields the peaceful fruit of righteousness to those who have been trained by it.

Precious (6)

Ps 36:7, 139:17; Isa 28:16, 1 Pet 1:19, 2:6; 2 Pet 1:4

Ps 36:7

How precious is your steadfast love, O God!
The children of mankind take refuge in the shadow of your wings.

Isa 28:16

Therefore thus says the Lord God,
"Behold, I am the one who has laid as a foundation in Zion,
a stone, a tested stone,
a precious cornerstone, of a sure foundation:
'Whoever believes will not be in haste.'

1 Pet 1:18-19

knowing that you were ransomed from the futile ways inherited from your forefathers, not with perishable things such as silver or gold, but with the precious blood of Christ, like that of a lamb without blemish or spot.

Reconciler (5)

Rom 5:10-11; 2 Cor 5:18-20; Eph 2:16; Col 1:20, 1:22

Rom 5:10

For if while we were enemies we were reconciled to God by the death of his Son, much more, now that we are reconciled, shall we be saved by his life.

Col 1:19-20

For in him all the fullness of God was pleased to dwell, and through him to reconcile to himself all things, whether on earth or in heaven, making peace by the blood of his cross.

Rescuer (31)

2 Sam 22:18-20; Ps 18:17, 18:19, 18:48, 22:5, 22:8, 22:21, 31:2, 31:15, 35:17, 71:2, 71:4, 82:4, 91:15, 136:24, 144:7, 144:10-11; Isa 31:5, 49:24-25; Ezek 34:10, 34:12, 34:22; Dan 3:29; Amos 3:12; Micah 4:10; Acts 7:9-10, 12:11; 2 Tim 3:11, 4:17-18; 2 Pet 2:7, 2:9

Isa 49:24-25

Can the prey be taken from the mighty,
or the captives of a tyrant be rescued?
For thus says the Lord:
"Even the captives of the mighty shall be taken,
and the prey of the tyrant be rescued,
for I will contend with those who contend with you,
and I will save your children.

Ezek 34:12-16

As a shepherd seeks out his flock when he is among his sheep that have been scattered, so will I seek out my sheep, and I will rescue them from all places where they have been scattered on a day of clouds and thick darkness. 13 And I will bring them out from the peoples and gather them from the countries, and will bring them into their own land. And I will feed them on the mountains of Israel, by the ravines, and in all the inhabited places of the country. I will feed them with good pasture, and on the mountain heights of Israel shall be their grazing land. There they shall lie down in good grazing land, and on rich pasture they shall feed on the mountains of Israel. I myself will be the shepherd of my sheep, and I myself will make them lie down, declares the Lord God. I will seek the lost, and I will bring back the strayed, and I will bind up the injured, and I will strengthen the weak, and the fat and the strong I will destroy. I will feed them in justice.

2 Tim 4:17-18

But the Lord stood by me and strengthened me, so that through me the message might be fully proclaimed and all the Gentiles might hear it. So I was rescued from the lion's mouth. The Lord will rescue me from every evil deed and bring me safely into his heavenly kingdom. To him be the glory forever and ever. Amen.

Sanctifier (26)

Exod 29:43, 31:13; Lev 10:3, 20:8, 21:8, 21:15, 21:23, 22:9, 2:16, 22:32; Ezek 20:12, 37:28; John 17:17-19; Acts 20:32, 26:18; Rom 15:16; 1 Cor 1:2, 6:11; Eph 5:26; 1 Thess 5:23; Heb 2:11, 9:13-14, 10:10, 10:14, 10:29, 13:12

Acts 20:32

And now I commend you to God and to the word of his grace, which is able to build you up and to give you the inheritance among all those who are sanctified.

Acts 26:18

...to open their eyes, so that they may turn from darkness to light and from the power of Satan to God, that they may receive forgiveness of sins and a place among those who are sanctified by faith in me.

Eph 5:25-27

Husbands, love your wives, as Christ loved the church and gave himself up for her, that he might sanctify her, having cleansed her by the washing of water with the word, so that he might present the church to himself in splendor, without spot or wrinkle or any such thing, that she might be holy and without blemish.

1 Thess 5:23-24

Now may the God of peace himself sanctify you completely, and may your whole spirit and soul and body be kept blameless at the coming of our Lord Jesus Christ. He who calls you is faithful; he will surely do it.

Heb 9:13-14

For if the blood of goats and bulls, and the sprinkling of defiled persons with the ashes of a heifer, sanctify for the purification of the flesh, how much more will the blood of Christ, who through the eternal Spirit offered himself without blemish to God, purify our conscience from dead works to serve the living God.

Heb 10:14

For by a single offering he has perfected for all time those who are being sanctified.

Savior (35)

2 Sam 22:3; Ps 17:7, 106:21; Isa 43:3, 43:11, 45:15, 45:21, 49:26, 60:16, 63:8; Jer 14:8; Hos 13:4; Luke 1:47, 2:11; John 4:42; Acts 5:31, 13:23; Eph 5:23; Phil 3:20; 1 Tim 1:1, 2:3, 4:10; 2 Tim 1:10; Titus 1:3-4, 2:10, 2:13, 3:4, 3:6; 2 Pet 1:1, 1:11, 2:20, 3:2, 3:18; 1 John 4:14; Jude 25

2 Sam 22:2-3

He said,
"The Lord is my rock and my fortress and my deliverer,
my God, my rock, in whom I take refuge,
my shield, and the horn of my salvation,
my stronghold and my refuge,
my savior; you save me from violence.

Isa 43:11

I, I am the Lord,
and besides me there is no savior.

Isa 45:15

Truly, you are a God who hides himself,
O God of Israel, the Savior.

Acts 5:31

God exalted him at his right hand as Leader and Savior, to give repentance to Israel and forgiveness of sins.

2 Pet 1:11

For in this way there will be richly provided for you an entrance into the eternal kingdom of our Lord and Savior Jesus Christ.

Jude 24-25

Now to him who is able to keep you from stumbling and to present you blameless before the presence of his glory with great joy, to the only God, our Savior, through Jesus Christ our Lord, be glory, majesty, dominion, and authority, before all time and now and forever. Amen.

Searching (15)

1 Chron 28:9; Job 10:6, 13:9, 28:27; Ps 139:1-3, 139:23; Jer 17:10; Ezek 20:6, 34:11; Amos 9:3; Zeph 1:12; Matt 18:12-14; Rom 8:27; 1 Cor 2:10; Rev 2:23

1 Chron 28:9

And you, Solomon my son, know the God of your father and serve him with a whole heart and with a willing mind, for the Lord searches all hearts and understands every plan and thought. If you seek him, he will be found by you, but if you forsake him, he will cast you off forever.

Ps 139:1-4

O Lord, you have searched me and known me!
You know when I sit down and when I rise up;
you discern my thoughts from afar.
You search out my path and my lying down
and are acquainted with all my ways.
Even before a word is on my tongue,
behold, O Lord, you know it altogether.

Matt 18:12-14

What do you think? If a man has a hundred sheep, and one of them has gone astray, does he not leave the ninety-nine on the mountains and go in search of the one that went astray? And if he finds it, truly, I say to you, he rejoices over it more than over the ninety-nine that never went astray. So it is not the will of my Father who is in heaven that one of these little ones should perish.

1 Cor 2:10

...these things God has revealed to us through the Spirit. For the Spirit searches everything, even the depths of God.

Shepherd (26)

Gen 48:15, 49:24; Ps 23:1, 28:9, 80:1; Eccles 12:11; Isa 40:10-11; Jer 31:10; Ezek 34:12-16, 37:24; Micah 5:4, 7:14; Zech 10:2-3, 13:7; Matt 2:6, 9:36, 25:32, 26:21; Mark 6:34, 14:27; John 10:11, 10:14-16; Heb 13:20; 1 Pet 2:25, 5:4; Rev 7:17

Ps 23:1-4

The Lord is my shepherd; I shall not want.
He makes me lie down in green pastures.

He leads me beside still waters.
He restores my soul.
He leads me in paths of righteousness
for his name's sake.
Even though I walk through the valley of the shadow of death,
I will fear no evil,
for you are with me,
your rod and your staff,
they comfort me.

Ezek 34:15-16

I myself will be the shepherd of my sheep, and I myself will make them lie down, declares the Lord God. I will seek the lost, and I will bring back the strayed, and I will bind up the injured, and I will strengthen the weak, and the fat and the strong I will destroy. I will feed them in justice.

John 10:14-16

I am the good shepherd. I know my own and my own know me, just as the Father knows me and I know the Father; and I lay down my life for the sheep. And I have other sheep that are not of this fold. I must bring them also, and they will listen to my voice. So there will be one flock, one shepherd.

1 Pet 2:21

For you were straying like sheep, but have now returned to the Shepherd and Overseer of your souls.

Father (232)

Deut 32:6; Ps 68:5, 89:26; Isa 9:6, 63:16, 64:8; Jer 3:19; Ezek 22:7; Mal 2:10; Matt 5:16, 5:45, 5:48, 6:1, 6:4, 6:6, 6:8. 6:9, 6:14, 6:15, 6:18, 6:26, 6:32, 7:11, 7:21, 10:20, 10:29, 10:32, 10:33, 11:25, 11:26, 11:27, 12:50, 13:43, 15:13, 16:17, 16:27, 18:10, 18:14, 18:19, 18:35, 20:23, 23:9, 24:36, 25:34, 26:39, 26:42, 26:53, 28:19; Mark 8:38, 11:25, 13:32, 14:36; Luke 6:36, 9:26, 10:21, 10:22, 11:2, 11:13, 12:30, 15:12, 15:18, 15:21, 16:24, 22:29, 22:42, 23:34, 23:46, 24:49; John 1:14, 3:35, 4:21, 4:23, 5:17, 5:18, 5:19, 5:20, 5:21, 5:22, 5:23, 5:26, 5:36, 5:37, 5:45, 6:27, 6:32, 6:37, 6:40, 6:44, 6:45, 6:46, 6:57, 6:65, 8:16, 8:18, 8:19, 8:27, 8:28, 8:38, 8:41, 8:42, 8:49, 8:54, 10:15, 10:17, 10:18, 10:29, 10:30, 10:32, 10:36, 10:37, 10:38, 11:41, 12:26, 12:27, 12:28, 12:49, 12:50, 13:1, 13:3, 14:6, 14:7, 14:8, 14:9, 14:10, 14:11, 14:12, 14:13, 14:16, 14:20, 14:21, 14:23, 14:26, 14:28, 14:31, 15:1, 15:8, 15:9, 15:15, 15:16, 15:23, 15:24, 15:26, 15:27, 15:28, 15:32, 17:1, 17:5, 17:11, 17:21, 17:24, 17:25, 18:11, 20:17, 20:21; Acts 1:4, 1:7, 2:33; Rom 1:7, 6:4, 8:15, 15:6; 1 Cor 1:3, 8:6, 15:24; 2 Cor 1:2, 1:3, 11:31; Gal 1:1, 1:3, 1:4, 4:6; Eph 1:2, 1:3, 1:4, 4:6; Eph 1:2, 1:3, 1:17, 2:18, 3:14, 4:6, 5:20, 6:23; Phil 1:2, 2:11, 4:20; Col 1:2, 1:3, 1:12, 3:17; 1 Thess 1:1, 1:3, 3:11, 3:13; 2 Thess 1:1, 1:2, 2:16, 1 Tim 1:2; 2 Tim 1:2; Titus 1:4; Philem 3; Heb 12:9; James 1:17, 1:27, 3:9; 1 Pet 1:2, 1:3, 1:17; 2 Pet 1:17; 1 John 1:2, 1:3, 2:1, 2:13, 2:15, 2:16, 2:22, 2:23, 2:24, 3:1, 4:14, 5:1; 2 John 3, 4, 9; Jude 1; Rev 1:6, 2:27, 3:5, 3:21

Mal 2:10

Have we not all one Father? Has not one God created us? Why then are we faithless to one another, profaning the covenant of our fathers?

Matt 11:25-27

At that time Jesus declared, "I thank you, Father, Lord of heaven and earth, that you have hidden these things from the wise and understanding and revealed them to little children; yes, Father, for such was your gracious will. All things have been handed over to me by my Father, and no one knows the Son except the Father, and no one knows the Father except the Son and anyone to whom the Son chooses to reveal him.

1 Cor 8:6

...yet for us there is one God, the Father, from whom are all things and for whom we exist, and one Lord, Jesus Christ, through whom are all things and through whom we exist.

Eph 1:3

Blessed be the God and Father of our Lord Jesus Christ, who has blessed us in Christ with every spiritual blessing in the heavenly places,

Phil 2:9-11

Therefore God has highly exalted him and bestowed on him the name that is above every name, so that at the name of Jesus every knee should bow, in heaven and on earth and under the earth, and every tongue confess that Jesus Christ is Lord, to the glory of God the Father.

James 1:17-18

Every good gift and every perfect gift is from above, coming down from the Father of lights with whom there is no variation or shadow due to change. Of his own will he brought us forth by the word of truth, that we should be a kind of firstfruits of his creatures.

1 Pet 1:3-5

Blessed be the God and Father of our Lord Jesus Christ! According to his great mercy, he has caused us to be born again to a living hope through the resurrection of Jesus Christ from the dead, to an inheritance that is imperishable, undefiled, and unfading, kept in heaven for you, who by God's power are being guarded through faith for a salvation ready to be revealed in the last time.

Chastener (0)

Counselor (19)

Josh 9:14; Ezra 10:3; Job 12:13, 26:3; Ps 16:7, 32:8, 33:11, 73:24, 106:13, 107:11, 119:24; Isa 5:19, 9:6, 28:29, 46:10; Jer 32:19; Acts 20:27; Eph 1:11; Rev 3:18

Ps 33:11

The counsel of the Lord stands forever,
the plans of his heart to all generations.

Isa 9:6

For to us a child is born,
to us a son is given;
and the government shall be upon his shoulder,
and his name shall be called
Wonderful Counselor, Mighty God,
Everlasting Father, Prince of Peace.

Eph 1:11

In him we have obtained an inheritance, having been predestined according to the purpose of him who works all things according to the counsel of his will, so that we who were the first to hope in Christ might be to the praise of his glory.

Nurturing (0)

Protector (12)

Ezra 9:9; Ps 5:11, 20:1, 41:2, 59:1, 68:5, 91:14; Isa 27:5, 31:5; Zech 9:15, 12:8; 1 John 5:18

Ps 5:11-12

But let all who take refuge in you rejoice;
let them ever sing for joy,
and spread your protection over them,
that those who love your name may exult in you.
For you bless the righteous, O Lord;
you cover him with favor as with a shield.

Ps 68:5

Father of the fatherless and protector of widows
is God in his holy habitation.

Zech 12:8-9

On that day the Lord will protect the inhabitants of Jerusalem, so that the feeblest among them on that day shall be like David, and the house of David shall be like God, like the angel of the Lord, going before them. And on that day I will seek to destroy all the nations that come against Jerusalem.

Provider (17)

Gen 22:8, 22:14; Josh 1:13; 1 Sam 16:1; 2 Chron 29:36, 32:22; Job 38:41; Ps 65:9, 68:10, 78:20, 111:5; Jer 33:9, Ezek 34:29; 1 Cor 10:13; 1 Tim 6:17; Heb 11:40; 2 Pet 1:11

Gen 22:8

Abraham said, "God will provide for himself the lamb for a burnt offering, my son." So they went both of them together.

1 Cor 10:13

No temptation has overtaken you that is not common to man. God is faithful, and he will not let you be tempted beyond your ability, but with the temptation he will also provide the way of escape, that you may be able to endure it.

1 Tim 6:17

As for the rich in this present age, charge them not to be haughty, nor to set their hopes on the uncertainty of riches, but on God, who richly provides us with everything to enjoy.

Responsive (3)

2 Sam 21:14, 24:25; Luke 14:3

2 Sam 21:14

And they buried the bones of Saul and his son Jonathan in the land of Benjamin in Zela, in the tomb of Kish his father. And they did all that the king commanded. And after that God responded to the plea for the land.

Singer (1)

Zeph 3:17

Zeph 3:17

The Lord your God is in your midst,
a mighty one who will save;
he will rejoice over you with gladness;
he will quiet you by his love;
he will exult over you with loud singing.

Tester (41)

Gen 22:1; Exod 15:25, 16:4, 20:20; Deut 8:2, 8:16, 13:3; Judg 2:22, 3:1, 3:4, 7:4; 1 Chron 29:17; 2 Chron 32:31; Job 7:17-18; Ps 7:9, 11:4-5, 17:3, 26:2, 66:10, 81:7, 105:19; Prov 17:3; Eccles 3:18; Isa 28:16; Jer 9:7, 11:20, 12:3, 17:10, 20:12; Zech 13:9; Luke 8:13; 1 Cor 3:13; 2 Cor 8:1-2; 1 Thess 2:4; Heb 3:8, 11:17; James 1:3, 1:12; 1 Pet 1:7, 4:12; Rev 2:10

1 Chron 29:17

I know, my God, that you test the heart and have pleasure in uprightness. In the uprightness of my heart I have freely offered all these things, and now I have seen your people, who are present here, offering freely and joyously to you.

Eccles 3:18

I said in my heart with regard to the children of man that God is testing them that they may see that they themselves are but beasts.

Zech 13:9

And I will put this third into the fire,
and refine them as one refines silver,
and test them as gold is tested.
They will call upon my name,
and I will answer them.
I will say, 'They are my people';
and they will say, 'The Lord is my God.'

Luke 8:13

And the ones on the rock are those who, when they hear the word, receive it with joy. But these have no root; they believe for a while, and in time of testing fall away.

James 1:2-4

Count it all joy, my brothers, when you meet trials of various kinds, for you know that the testing of your faith produces steadfastness. And let steadfastness have its full effect, that you may be perfect and complete, lacking in nothing.

1 Pet 1:6-7

In this you rejoice, though now for a little while, if necessary, you have been grieved by various trials, so that the tested genuineness of your faith—more precious than gold that perishes though it is tested by fire—may be found to result in praise and glory and honor at the revelation of Jesus Christ.

Rev 2:10

Do not fear what you are about to suffer. Behold, the devil is about to throw some of you into prison, that you may be tested, and for ten days you will have tribulation. Be faithful unto death, and I will give you the crown of life.

IV. God's Glory

Chapter 11

Glory (286)

Exod 14:4, 14:17, 14:18, 15:1, 15:6, 15:11, 15:21, 16:7, 16:10, 24:16, 24:17, 29:43, 33:18, 33:22, 40:34, 40:35; Lev 9:6, 9:23, 10:3; Num 14:10, 14:21, 14:22, 16:19, 16:42, 20:6; Deut 5:24, 28:58; Josh 7:19; Judg 4:9; 1 Sam 6:5, 15:29; 1 Kings 8:11; 2 Kings 14:10; 1 Chron 16:10, 16:24, 16:28, 16:29, 16:35, 29:11, 29:13; 2 Chron 5:14, 7:1, 7:2, 7:3; Neh 9:5; Ps 8:1, 19:1, 22:23, 24:7, 24:8, 24:9, 24:10, 26:8, 29:1, 29:2, 29:3, 29:9, 50:15, 50:23, 57:5, 57:11, 63:2, 66:2, 71:8, 72:19, 76:4, 78:4, 79:9, 86:9, 86:12, 90:16, 96:3, 96:7, 96:8, 97:6, 102:15, 102:16, 104:31, 105:3, 106:20, 106:47, 108:5, 113:4, 115:1 138:5, 145:5; Prov 25:2; Isa 3:8, 4:2, 4:5, 6:3, 12:5, 24:15, 24:16, 24:23, 25:3, 26:15, 28:5, 35:2, 40:5, 42:8, 42:12, 42:21, 43:7, 44:23, 46:13, 48:11, 49:3, 58:8, 59:19, 60:1, 60:2, 60:21, 61:3, 63:12, 63:14, 66:18, 66:19; Jer 13:16; Ezek 1:28, 3:12, 3:23, 8:4, 9:3, 10:4, 10:18, 10:19, 11:22, 11:23, 24:25, 28:22, 39:13, 39:21, 43:2, 43:4, 43:5, 44:4; Dan 7:14; Hab 2:14; Haggai 1:8; Zech 2:5, 2:8; Matt 5:16, 9:8, 15:31, 16:27, 24:30, 25:31; Mark 2:12, 8:38, 10:37, 13:26; Luke 2:9, 2:14, 2:20, 4:15, 5:25, 5:26, 7:16, 9:26, 9:31, 9:32, 13:13, 13:17, 18:43, 19:38, 21:27, 24:26; John 1:14, 2:11, 7:18, 8:50, 8:54, 11:4, 11:40, 12:16, 12:23, 12:28, 12:41, 13:31, 13:32, 14:13, 15:8, 16:14, 17:1, 17:4, 17:5, 17:10, 17:22, 17:24, 21:19; Acts 3:13, 7:2, 7:55, 11:18, 21:20; Rom 1:23, 3:7, 3:23, 4:20, 5:2, 6:4, 8:18, 9:23, 11:36, 15:6, 15:7, 15:9, 16:27; 1 Cor 2:8, 6:20, 10:31, 11:7; 2 Cor 1:20, 3:18, 4:4, 4:6, 4:15, 8:19, 8:23, 9:13; Gal 1:5, 2:4; Eph 1:6, 1:12, 1:14, 1:17, 1:18, 3:16, 3:21; Phil 1:11, 2:11, 3:21, 4:19, 4:20; Col 1:11, 1:27, 3:4; 2 Thess 1:9, 1:10, 1:12, 2:14; 1 Tim 1:11, 1:17, 3:16; 2 Tim 2:10, 4:18; Titus 2:13; Heb 1:3, 2:7, 2:9, 2:10, 3:3, 13:21; James 2:1; 1 Pet 1:11, 1:21, 2:12, 4:11, 4:13, 4:14, 4:16, 5:1, 5:10; 2 Pet 1:3, 1:17, 2:10, 3:18; Jude 8, 24, 25; Rev 1:6, 4:9, 4:11, 5:12, 5:13, 7:12, 11:13, 14:7, 15:4, 15:8, 16:9, 19:1, 19:7, 21:11, 21:23

Exod 15:11

Who is like you, O Lord, among the gods?
Who is like you, majestic in holiness,
awesome in glorious deeds, doing wonders?

FOR I AM THE LORD YOUR GOD

Exod 24:17

Now the appearance of the glory of the Lord was like a devouring fire on the top of the mountain in the sight of the people of Israel.

Ps 102:16

For the Lord builds up Zion;
he appears in his glory;

Isa 24:23

Then the moon will be confounded
and the sun ashamed,
for the Lord of hosts reigns
on Mount Zion and in Jerusalem,
and his glory will be before his elders.

Isa 40:5

And the glory of the Lord shall be revealed,
and all flesh shall see it together,
for the mouth of the Lord has spoken.

Isa 42:8

I am the Lord; that is my name;
my glory I give to no other,
nor my praise to carved idols.

Ezek 1:28

Like the appearance of the bow that is in the cloud on the day of rain, so was the appearance of the brightness all around. Such was the appearance of the likeness of the glory of the Lord. And when I saw it, I fell on my face, and I heard the voice of one speaking.

John 1:14

And the Word became flesh and dwelt among us, and we have seen his glory, glory as of the only Son from the Father, full of grace and truth.

John 2:11

This, the first of his signs, Jesus did at Cana in Galilee, and manifested his glory. And his disciples believed in him.

John 12:27-28

"Now is my soul troubled. And what shall I say? 'Father, save me from this hour'? But for this purpose I have come to this hour. Father, glorify your name." Then a voice came from heaven: "I have glorified it, and I will glorify it again."

Acts 7:55

But he, full of the Holy Spirit, gazed into heaven and saw the glory of God, and Jesus standing at the right hand of God.

Appendix 4

Rom 6:4

We were buried therefore with him by baptism into death, in order that, just as Christ was raised from the dead by the glory of the Father, we too might walk in newness of life.

2 Cor 4:6

For God, who said, "Let light shine out of darkness," has shone in our hearts to give the light of the knowledge of the glory of God in the face of Jesus Christ.

Heb 1:3-4

He is the radiance of the glory of God and the exact imprint of his nature, and he upholds the universe by the word of his power. After making purification for sins, he sat down at the right hand of the Majesty on high, having become as much superior to angels as the name he has inherited is more excellent than theirs.

2 Pet 1 17-18

For when he received honor and glory from God the Father, and the voice was borne to him by the Majestic Glory, "This is my beloved Son, with whom I am well pleased," we ourselves heard this very voice borne from heaven, for we were with him on the holy mountain.

Jude 24-25

Now to him who is able to keep you from stumbling and to present you blameless before the presence of his glory with great joy, to the only God, our Savior, through Jesus Christ our Lord, be glory, majesty, dominion, and authority, before all time and now and forever. Amen.

Rev 21:10-11

And he carried me away in the Spirit to a great, high mountain, and showed me the holy city Jerusalem coming down out of heaven from God, having the glory of God, its radiance like a most rare jewel, like a jasper, clear as crystal.

Rev 21:23

And the city has no need of sun or moon to shine on it, for the glory of God gives it light, and its lamp is the Lamb.

Made in the USA
San Bernardino, CA
06 May 2017